RADICAL PERSPECTIVES ON SOCIAL PROBLEMS
READINGS IN CRITICAL SOCIOLOGY
THIRD EDITION

RADICAL PERSPECTIVES
ON SOCIAL PROBLEMS
READINGS IN CRITICAL SOCIOLOGY
THIRD EDITION

Frank Lindenfeld

Cheyney University of Pennsylvania

GENERAL HALL, INC.
Publishers
5 Talon Way
Dix Hills, New York 11746

RADICAL PERSPECTIVES ON SOCIAL PROBLEMS
Readings in Critical Sociology
Third Edition

GENERAL HALL, INC.
5 Talon Way
Dix Hills, New York 11746

Publisher: Ravi Mehra
Editor: Eileen Ostermann
Composition: *Graphics Division,* General Hall, Inc.

LIBRARY OF CONGRESS CATALOG CARD NUMBER: 86-080123

ISBN: 0-930390-73-3 [paper]
0-930390-74-1 [cloth]

Manufactured in the United States of America

To the memory of my parents, Rudolph and Marianne

Contents

13 Strategies for Change   368

Index   399

Preface

My main purpose in compiling this anthology is to make available a set of texts that reflect a critical, engaged viewpoint in sociology. The readings are designed for generalists, not specialists, in the hope that they will be useful to students and citizens in their attempts to understand, cope with, and change the world around them.

Much of the work of sociologists has tended to be "ideological" in the sense that *its underlying assumptions* have reflected support of existing social institutions. This anthology is intended to be a utopian antidote, an interpretation of the social world dedicated to the possibility and the desirability of radical change. My aim is to help cultivate the utopian sensibility: the ability to look at social patterns and to see them not only as they are and as they have been but as they might be, if. . . .

Human self-consciousness makes possible the deliberate transformation of social institutions. It is not necessary that we put up with the social world as we find it. If history is not predetermined and inevitable, then one of our tasks should be to help change it in the direction that we want.

The utopian outlook leads to the general question of what varieties of social arrangements would maximize the possibilities for human fulfillment and the ability of men and women to control the conditions that affect their lives.

Regarding work and the economy: How can we maximize people's control over, and pride in their work? How can we provide enough jobs for all? Can we reap the advantages of industrialization and automation without becoming victims of their disadvantages? What are the alternatives to bureaucratic organization? Can a democratically controlled cooperative economy eventually replace the existing capitalist system?

What kinds of educational arrangements best promote the conditions under which individuals can attain freedom and fulfillment? How can we eliminate racism and sexism? How should we deal with crime? Under what conditions could we have a society without prisons?

Regarding politics: Under what conditions might warfare be eliminated? How necessary is a strong, central government? What are the best strategies for promoting political changes? Is nonviolent revolution possible? Can we, and should we, build a third, "people's party"?

I do not pretend to have the answers, nor is there necessarily any one best answer to such questions. Some of the questions raised will be touched on by the selections in this book. Others remain to be dealt with. But this anthology should at least help sensitize readers to the possibilities of social invention and to some of the obstacles in the way.

I did not intend this to be a "balanced" book. Because the book was designed largely to help American students deal with their environment, most of the articles refer to the United States. The social prescriptions represented in the selections run along the spectrum from piecemeal reform to wholesale radical changes and revolution. In making choices I purposely selected writings that I felt constituted radical critiques of the established social order.

In this edition I have included articles from the first and second editions that have withstood the test of time and have added materials relevant to the 1980s, as well as new sections on strategies for change and economic alternatives. The student movement, the civil rights movement, protests against the Vietnam war, and the New Left of the late 1960s and early 1970s are now history. The outward mood of the country has become more conservative, but the structural problems remain. I hope that this volume will contribute to a resurgence of radical thought and action that may yet lead us away from the brink of nuclear war and toward a participatory socialist society based on freedom and equality.

Thanks to all my friends who contributed suggestions, and to Kathryn M. Lindenfeld for her patient editorial help. Because of limited space, I have had to omit a number of excellent articles I would have liked to include and to abridge others. Omissions are indicated by three centered asterisks when one or more paragraphs were omitted or by ellipsis points when the omission was minor. In a few cases I have left out or abridged lengthy footnotes.

-- F.L.

Part I   Introduction

1 | Social Science and Human Values

Psychologism and the myth of value neutrality are two major obstacles to understanding social problems. Psychologism is the explanation of social phenomena in terms of the attitudes and behavior of individuals rather than the structure of society. It is the attribution of structural characteristics to a mere sum of individual attitudes or milieux. The myth of value neutrality is simply that social scientists can be objective, when in fact they cannot. Although these are two separate obstacles, believers in value neutrality tend to prefer psychologistic to structural theories of social problems.

Sociology is necessarily value directed. Our very choice of problems and our phrasing of them are determined by what we take for granted. If we take for granted the existing social structure, we will focus on reforms of the system or on the failure of individuals to adjust to it, but we will not search for structural alternatives. Take poverty, for example. Supporters of the prevailing system might ask such questions as "What social reforms might reduce the extent of poverty?" or "How can we reeducate the poor so that they can better participate in the economy?" Critics, however, might begin by asking whether the cause of poverty is not to be found in the capitalist system itself.

Sociological theories are necessarily based on certain assumptions. According to John Horton, all theories about social problems are normative. They are based either on the assumption that the existing social order ought to be maintained or that it ought to be changed. The former he calls order theories, the latter conflict theories. Order theories define social problems in terms of individual failure to adjust to prevailing mores. Conflict theories define problems as struggles between competing groups. They are based on dissatisfaction with the prevailing system.

3

Horton shows how order and conflict theorists conceptualize the relationship of blacks to whites. Order theorists assume consensus among blacks and whites on the American creed; they see the problem as one of incomplete assimilation and unequal opportunity of sharing in the rewards of the great society. Conflict theorists define the problem as a struggle for black liberation.

One variety of order theory is "blaming the victim." According to this position, poverty is caused by characteristics of the poor, unemployment by the lazy nature of the unemployed, rape by the provocative actions of women, and so on. As William Ryan points out, victim blaming is an ideological process. Pinpointing the blame for social problems on their victims serves the interests of those who hold power and benefit most from society as it is. The alternative is conflict theory, which looks for structural causes of such problems. The selection from C. Wright Mills shows why conflict theory is more relevant and useful than order theory in empowering the dispossessed to deal with the problems that afflict them.

Mills distinguishes between personal troubles and public issues. Troubles affect individuals and their immediate social milieux; their statement and resolution lie within the scope of the individual and his or her relations with family and friends. Issues transcend the local troubles felt by individuals; they are experienced by many persons at the same time and often reflect a "crisis in institutional arrangements." Often, problems such as unemployment, racism, and sexism may be *thought* by those who suffer from them to be merely personal misfortunes, but they also can be seen as social issues that affect many others "in the same boat."

The distinction between troubles and issues shows why psychologism is inadequate to explain social problems. Psychologism views contradictions within political or economic institutions as though they were merely a sum of individual problems, and directs us to solve them by helping individuals. A social problem can be coped with on a personal basis by a few who are smart, aggressive, or rich, but it cannot be solved for everybody except by changing the social structure.

Applying Mills's conception, we see racism as a system of institutionalized segregation and discrimination, instead of merely the prejudiced attitudes of individuals. The cure for racism is not the education of whites to see blacks as equal but the provision of jobs or income for unemployed blacks and greater power for them as a social group. Similarly, we see the causes of unemployment in capitalism and the use of automation rather than in individual laziness or lack of skills. No matter how qualified a person may be, he or she will not find a job in a capitalist system when the work can be done more cheaply by machines. For the causes of war, we look to the existence of sovereign states with their arms races and military conscription, rather than to the aggressiveness of individual soldiers or statesmen. Belligerent political leaders may precipitate wars, but they cannot do so without armies and organized military production.

To say that psychologism does not adequately explain social phenomena is not to criticize psychology or psychiatry per se. These disciplines can be a source of personal growth and liberation. But they become potential instruments of repression when they hold that poverty or alienation, which are the faults of an exploitative system, can be ameliorated through personal effort or psychotherapy. Often such remedies only help individuals to adjust to a sick social order when, instead, they should join with other people to change it.

Answers to social inquiry are largely determined by the nature of our questions. Social phenomena can best be understood by asking questions about the social structure rather than about individuals within it. Furthermore, because objectivity is impossible in the study of human affairs, the only practical alternative is to recognize and explicate our assumptions and values.

The Promise

C. Wright Mills

Nowadays men often feel that their private lives are a series of traps. They sense that within their everyday worlds, they cannot overcome their troubles, and in this feeling, they are often quite correct: What ordinary men are directly aware of and what they try to do are bounded by the private orbits in which they live; their visions and their powers are limited to the close-up scenes of job, family, neighborhood; in other milieux, they move vicariously and remain spectors. And the more aware they become, however vaguely, of ambitions and of threats which transcend their immediate locales, the more trapped they seem to feel.

Underlying this sense of being trapped are seemingly impersonal changes in the very structure of continent-wide societies. The facts of contemporary history are also facts about the success and the failure of individual men and women. When a society is industrialized, a peasant becomes a worker; a feudal lord is liquidated or becomes a businessman. When classes rise or fall, a man is employed or unemployed; when the rate of investment goes up or down, a man takes new heart or goes broke. When wars happen, an insurance salesman becomes a rocket launcher; a store clerk, a radar man; a wife lives alone; a child grows up without a father. Neither the life of an individual nor the history of a society can be understood without understanding both.

Yet men do not usually define the troubles they endure in terms of historical change and institutional contradiction. The well-being they enjoy they do not usually impute to the big ups and downs of the societies in which they live. Seldom aware of the intricate connection between the patterns of their lives and the course of world history, ordinary men do not usually know what this connection means for the kinds of men they are becoming and for the kinds of history-making in which they might take part. They do not possess the quality of mind essential to grasp the interplay of man and society, of biography and history, of self and world. They cannot cope with their personal troubles in such ways as to control the structural transformations that usually lie behind them.

Surely it is no wonder. In what period have so many men been so totally exposed at so fast a pace to such earthquakes of change? That Americans have not known such catastrophic changes as have the men and women of other societies is due to historical facts that are now quickly becoming "merely history." The history that now affects every man is world history. Within this scene and this period, in the course of a single generation, one sixth of mankind is transformed from all that is feudal and backward into all that is modern, advanced, and fearful. Political colonies are freed; new and less visible forms of imperialism installed. Revolutions occur; men feel the intimate grip of new kinds of authority. Totalitarian societies rise, and are smashed to bits—or succeed fabulously. After two centuries of ascendancy, capitalism is shown up as only one way to make society into an industrial apparatus. After two centuries of hope, even formal democracy is restricted to a quite small portion of mankind. Everywhere in the underdeveloped world, ancient ways of life are broken up and vague expectations become urgent demands. Everywhere in the overdeveloped world, the means of authority and of violence become total in scope and bureaucratic in form. Humanity itself now lies before us, the super-nation at either pole concentrating its most coordinated and massive efforts upon the preparation of World War III.

The very shaping of history now outpaces the ability of men to orient themselves in accordance with cherished values. And which values? Even when they do not panic, men often sense that older ways of feeling and thinking have collapsed and that newer beginnings are ambiguous to the point of moral statis. Is it any wonder that ordinary men feel they cannot cope with the larger worlds with which they are so suddenly confronted? That they cannot understand the meaning of their epoch for their own lives? That—in defense of selfhood—they become morally insensible, trying to remain altogether private men? Is it any wonder that they come to be possessed by a sense of the trap?

It is not only information that they need—in this Age of Fact, information often dominates their attention and overwhelms their capacities to assimilate it. It is not only the skills of reason that they need—although their struggles to acquire these often exhaust their limited moral energy.

What they need, and what they feel they need, is a quality of mind that will help them to use information and to develop reason in order to achieve lucid summations of what is going on in the world and of what may be happening within themselves. It is this quality, I am going to contend, that journalists and scholars, artists and publics, scientists and editors are coming to expect of what may be called the sociological imagination.

1

The sociological imagination enables its possessor to understand the larger historical scene in terms of its meaning for the inner life and the external career of a variety of individuals. It enables him to take into account how individuals, in the welter of their daily experience, often become falsely conscious of their social positions. Within that welter, the framework of modern society is sought, and within that framework the psychologies of a variety of men and women are formulated. By such means the personal uneasiness of individuals is focused upon explicit troubles and the indifference of publics is transformed into involvement with public issues.

The first fruit of this imagination—and the first lesson of the social science that embodies it—is the idea that the individual can understand his own experience and gauge his own fate only by locating himself within his period, that he can know his own chances in life only by becoming aware of those of all individuals in his circumstances. In many ways it is a terrible lesson; in many ways a magnificent one. We do not know the limits of man's capacities for supreme effort or willing degradation, for agony or glee, for pleasurable brutality or the sweetness of reason. But in our time we have come to know that the limits of "human nature" are frighteningly broad. We have come to know that every individual lives, from one generation to the next, in some society; that he lives out a biography, and that he lives it out within some historical sequence. By the fact of his living he contributes, however minutely, to the shaping of this society and to the course of its history, even as he is made by society and by its historical push and shove.

The sociological imagination enables us to grasp history and biography and the relations between the two within society. That is its task and its promise. To recognize this task and this promise is the mark of the classic social analyst. It is characteristic of Herbert Spencer — turgid, polysyllabic, comprehensive; of E. A. Ross — graceful, muckraking, upright; of Auguste Comte and Emile Durkheim; of the intricate and subtle Karl Mannheim. It is the quality of all that is intellectually excellent in Karl Marx; it is the clue to Thorstein Veblen's brilliant and ironic insight, to Joseph Schumpeter's many-sided constructions of reality; it is the basis of the psychological sweep of W. E. H. Lecky no less than of the profundity and clarity of Max Weber. And it is the signal of what is best in contemporary studies of man and society.

No social study that does not come back to the problems of biography, of history, and of their intersections within a society has completed its intellectual journey. Whatever the specific problems of the classic social analysts, however limited or however broad the features of social reality they have examined, those who have been imaginatively aware of the promise of their work have consistently asked three sorts of questions:

1. What is the structure of this particular society as a whole? What are its essential components, and how are they related to one another? How does it differ from other varieties of social order? Within it, what is the meaning of any particular feature for its continuance and for its change?
2. Where does this society stand in human history? What are the mechanics by which it is changing? What is its place within and its meaning for the development of humanity as a whole? How does any particular feature we are examining

affect, and how is it affected by, the historical period in which it moves? And this period—what are its essential features? How does it differ from other periods? What are its characteristic ways of history-making?

3. What varieties of men and women now prevail in this society and in this period? And what varieties are coming to prevail? In what ways are they selected and formed, liberated and repressed, made sensitive and blunted? What kinds of "human nature" are revealed in the conduct and character we observe in this society in this period? And what is the meaning for "human nature" of each and every feature of the society we are examining?

Whether the point of interest is a great power state or a minor literary mood, a family, a prison, a creed—these are the kinds of questions the best social analysts have asked. They are the intellectual pivots of classic studies of man in society—and they are the questions inevitably raised by any mind possessing the sociological imagination. For that imagination is the capacity to shift from one perspective to another—from the political to the psychological; from examination of a single family to comparative assessment of the national budgets of the world; from the theological school to the military establishment; from considerations of an oil industry to studies of contemporary poetry. It is the capacity to range from the most impersonal and remote transformations to the most intimate features of the human self—and to see the relations between the two. Back of its use there is always the urge to know the social and historical meaning of the individual in the society and in the period in which he has his quality and his being.

That, in brief, is why it is by means of the sociological imagination that men now hope to grasp what is going on in the world, and to understand what is happening in themselves as minute points of the intersections of biography and history within society. In large part, contemporary man's self-conscious view of himself as at least an outsider, if not a permanent stranger, rests upon an absorbed realization of social relativity and of the transformative powers of history. The sociological imagination is the most fruitful form of this self-consciousness. By its use men whose mentalities have swept only a series of limited orbits often come to feel as if suddenly awakened in a house with which they had only supposed themselves to be familiar. Correctly or incorrectly, they often come to feel that they can now provide themselves with adequate summations, cohesive assessments, comprehensive orientations. Older decisions that once appeared sound now seem to them products of a mind unaccountably dense. Their capacity for astonishment is made lively again. They acquire a new way of thinking, they experience a transvaluation of values; in a word, by their reflection and by their sensibility, they realize the cultural meaning of the social sciences.

2

Perhaps the most fruitful distinction with which the sociological imagination works is between "the personal troubles of milieu" and "the public issues of social structure." This distinction is an essential tool of the sociological imagination and a feature of all classic work in social science.

Troubles occur within the character of the individual and within the range of his immediate relations with others; they have to do with his self and with those limited areas of social life of which he is directly and personally aware. Accordingly, the statement and the resolution of troubles properly lie within the individual as a biographical entity and within the scope of his immediate milieu — the social setting that is directly open to his personal experience and to some extent his willful activity. A trouble is a private matter: values cherished by an individual are felt by him to be threatened.

Issues have to do with matters that transcend these local environments of the individual and the range of his inner life. They have to do with the organization of many such milieux into the institutions of a historical society as a whole, with the ways in which various milieux overlap and interpenetrate to form the larger structure of social and historical life. An issue is a public matter: some value cherished by publics is felt to be threatened. Often there is a debate about what that value really is and about what it is that really threatens it. This debate is often without focus if only because it is the very nature of an issue, unlike even widespread trouble, that it cannot very well be defined in terms of the immediate and everyday environments of ordinary men. An issue, in fact, often involves a crisis in institutional arrangements, and often too it involves what Marxists call "contradictions" or "antagonisms."

In these terms, consider unemployment. When, in a city of 100,000, only one man is unemployed, that is his personal trouble, and for its relief we properly look to the character of the man, his skills, and his immediate opportunities. But when in a nation of 50 million employees, 15 million men are unemployed, that is an issue, and we may not hope to find its solution within the range of opportunities open to any one individual. The very structure of opportunities has collapsed. Both the correct statement of the problem and the range of possible solutions require us to consider the economic and political institutions of the society, and not merely the personal situation and character of a scatter of individuals.

Consider war. The personal problem of war, when it occurs, may be how to survive it or how to die in it with honor; how to make money out of it; how to climb into the higher safety of the military apparatus; or how to contribute to the war's termination. In short, according to one's values, to find a set of milieux and within it to survive the war or make one's death in it meaningful. But the structural issues of war have to do with its causes; with what types of men it throws up into command; with its effects upon economic and political, family and religious institutions, with the unorganized irresponsibility of a world of nation-states.

Consider marriage. Inside a marriage a man and a woman may experience personal troubles, but when the divorce rate during the first four years of marriage is 250 out of every 1000 attempts, this is an indication of a structural issue having to do with the institutions of marriage and the family and other institutions that bear upon them.

Or consider the metropolis—the horrible, beautiful, ugly, magnificent sprawl of the great city. For many upper-class people, the personal solution to "the problem of the city" is to have an apartment with private garage under it in the heart of the city, and 40 miles out, a house by Henry Hill, garden by Garrett Eckbo, on a hundred acres of private land. In these two controlled environments—with a small staff at each end and a private helicopter connection—most people could solve many of the problems of personal milieux caused by the facts of the city. But all this, however splendid, does not solve the public issues that the structural fact of the city poses. What should be done with this wonderful monstrosity? Break it all up into scattered units, combining residence and work? Refurbish it as it stands? Or, after evacuation, dynamite it and build new cities according to new plans in new places? What should those plans be? And who is to decide and to accomplish whatever choice is made? These are structural issues; to confront them and to solve them requires us to consider political and economic issues that affect innumerable milieux.

Insofar as an economy is so arranged that slumps occur, the problem of unemployment becomes incapable of personal solution. Insofar as war is inherent in the nation-state system and in the uneven industrialization of the

world, the ordinary individual in his restricted milieu will be powerless — with or without psychiatric aid — to solve the troubles this system or
lack of system imposes upon him. Insofar as the family as an institution
turns women into darling little slaves and men into their chief providers and
unweaned dependents, the problem of a satisfactory marriage remains incapable of purely private solution. Insofar as the overdeveloped
megalopolis and the overdeveloped automobile are built-in features of the
overdeveloped society, the issues of urban living will not be solved by personal ingenuity and private wealth.

What we experience in various and specific milieux, I have noted, is
often caused by structural changes. Accordingly, to understand the changes
of many personal milieux we are required to look beyond them. And the
number and variety of such structural changes increase as the institutions
within which we live become more embracing and more intricately connected
with one another. To be aware of the idea of social structure and to use it with
sensibility is to be capable of tracing such linkages among a great variety of
milieux. To be able to do that is to possess the sociological imagination.

3

What are the major issues for publics and the key troubles of private
individuals in our time? To formulate issues and troubles, we must ask
what values are cherished yet threatened, and what values are cherished and
supported, by the characterizing trends of our period. In the case both of
threat and of support we must ask what salient contradictions of structure
may be involved.

When people cherish some set of values and do not feel any threat to
them, they experience *well-being.* When they cherish values but *do* feel
them to be threatened, they experience a crisis — either as a personal trouble
or as a public issue. And if all their values seem involved, they feel the total
threat of panic.

But suppose people are neither aware of any cherished values nor experience any threat? That is the experience of *indifference,* which, if it
seems to involve all their values, becomes apathy. Suppose, finally, they are
unaware of any cherished values, but still are very much aware of a threat?
That is the experience of *uneasiness,* of anxiety, which, if it is total enough,
becomes a deadly unspecified malaise.

Ours is a time of uneasiness and indifference — not yet formulated in
such ways as to permit the work of reason and the play of sensibility. Instead

of troubles—defined in terms of values and threats—there is often the misery of vague uneasiness; instead of explicit issues there is often merely the beat feeling that all is somehow not right. Neither the values threatened nor whatever threatens them has been stated; in short, they have not been carried to the point of decision. Much less have they been formulated as problems of social science.

In the 1930s there was little doubt—except among certain deluded business circles—that there was an economic issue which was also a pack of personal troubles. In these arguments about "the crisis of capitalism," the formulations of Marx and the many unacknowledged re-formulations of his work probably set the leading terms of the issue, and some men came to understand their personal troubles in these terms. The values threatened were plain to see and cherished by all; the structural contradictions that threatened them also seemed plain. Both were widely and deeply experienced. It was a political age.

But the values threatened in the era after World War II are often neither widely acknowledged as values nor widely felt to be threatened. Much private uneasiness goes unformulated; much public malaise and many decisions of enormous structural relevance never become public issues. For those who accept such inherited values as reason and freedom, it is the uneasiness itself that is the trouble; it is the indifference itself that is the issue. And it is this condition, of uneasiness and indifference, that is the signal feature of our period.

All this is so striking that it is often interpreted by observers as a shift in the very kinds of problems that need now to be formulated. We are frequently told that the problems of our decade, or even the crises of our period, have shifted from the external realm of economics and now have to do with the quality of individual life—in fact with the question of whether there is soon going to be anything that can properly be called individual life. Not child labor but comic books, not poverty but mass leisure, are at the center of concern. Many great public issues as well as many private troubles are described in terms of "the psychiatric"—often, it seems, in a pathetic attempt to avoid the large issues and problems of modern society. Often this statement seems to rest upon a provincial narrowing of interest to the Western societies, or even to the United States—thus ignoring two-thirds of mankind; often, too, it arbitrarily divorces the individual life from the larger institutions within which that life is enacted, and which on occasion bear upon it more grievously than do the intimate environments of childhood.

Problems of leisure, for example, cannot even be stated without considering problems of work. Family troubles over comic books cannot be formulated as problems without considering the plight of the contemporary family in its new relations with the newer institutions of the social structure. Neither leisure nor its debilitating uses can be understood as problems without recognition of the extent to which malaise and indifference now form the social and personal climate of contemporary American society. In this climate, no problems of "the private life" can be stated and solved without recognition of the crisis of ambition that is part of the very career of men at work in the incorporated economy.

It is true, as psychoanalysts continually point out, that people do often have "the increasing sense of being moved by obscure forces within themselves which they are unable to define." But it is *not* true, as Ernest Jones asserted, that "man's chief enemy and danger is his own unruly nature and the dark forces pent up within him." On the contrary: "Man's chief danger" today lies in the unruly forces of contemporary society itself, with its alienating methods of production, its enveloping techniques of political domination, its international anarchy — in a word, its pervasive transformations of the very "nature" of man and the conditions and aims of his life.

It is now the social scientist's foremost political and intellectual task — for here the two coincide — to make clear the elements of contemporary uneasiness and indifference. It is the central demand made upon him by other cultural workmen — by physical scientists and artists, by the intellectual community in general. It is because of this task and these demands, I believe, that the social sciences are becoming the common denominator of our cultural period, and the sociological imagination our most needed quality of mind.

Order and Conflict Theories of Social Problems

John Horton

A . . . best seller, *The One Hundred Dollar Misunderstanding,*[1] should be required reading for every student of social problems and deviant behavior.

FROM *American Journal of Sociology,* May 1966, pp. 701–713, reprinted with permission of The University of Chicago Press.

The novel makes clear what is often dimly understood and rarely applied in sociology—the fundamentally social and symbolic character of existing theories of behavior. In the novel a square, white college boy and a Lolitaesque Negro prostitute recount their shared weekend experience. But what they have shared in action, they do not share in words. Each tells a different story. Their clashing tales express different vocabularies and different experiences. Gover stereotypically dramatizes a now hackneyed theme in the modern theater and novel—the misunderstandings generated by a conflict of viewpoints, a conflict between subjective representatives of "objective" reality.

Paradoxically, this familiar literary insight has escaped many social scientists. The escape is most baffling and least legitimate for the sociologists of deviant behavior and social problems. Social values define their phenomena; their social values color their interpretations. Whatever the possibilities of developing empirical theory in the social sciences, only normative theory is appropriate in the sociology of social problems. I would accept Don Martindale's definitions of empirical and normative theory:

> The ultimate materials of empirical theory are facts; the ultimate materials of normative theory are value-imperatives . . . empirical theory is formed out of a system of law. Normative theory converts facts and laws into requisite means and conditions and is unique in being addressed to a system of objectives desired by the formulator or by those in whose service he stands.[2]

The problem for the sociologist is not that normative theories contain values, but that these values may go unnoticed so that normative theories pass for empirical theories. When his own values are unnoticed, the sociologist who studies the situation of the American Negro, for example, is a little like the middle class white boy in Gover's novel, except that only one story is told, and it is represented as *the* story. The result could be a rather costly misunderstanding: the Negro may not recognize himself in the sociological story; worse, he may not even learn to accept it.

One of the tasks of the sociologist is to recognize his own perspective and to locate this and competing perspectives in time and social structure. In this he can use Weber, Mills, and the sociology of knowledge as guides. Following Weber's work, he might argue that insofar as we are able to theorize about the social world, we must use the vocabularies of explanation actually current in social life.[3] This insight has been expanded by C. W. Mills and applied to theorizing in general and to the character of American theorizing in particular. The key words in Mills's approach to theorizing are "situated actions" and "vocabularies of motive." His position is that theories of social behavior can be understood sociologically as typical symbolic explanations associated with historically situated actions.[4] Thus, Mills argues that the Freudian terminology of motives is that of an upper-bourgeois patriarchal group with a strong sexual and individualistic orientation. Likewise, explanations current in American sociology reflect the social experiences and social motives of the American sociologist. Mills contends that for a period before 1940, a single vocabulary of explanation was current in the American sociologist's analysis of social problems and that these motives expressed a small-town (and essentially rural) bias.[5] He interpreted the contemporary sociological vocabulary as a symbolic expression of a bureaucratic and administrative experience in life and work.[6]

Continuing in the tradition of Weber and Mills, I attempt to do the following: (1) propose a method of classifying current normative theories of deviant behavior and social problems; (2) discuss liberal and sociological approaches to the race question as an example of one of these theories; and (3) point out the implications of the normative character of theory for sociology. My general discussion of competing theories will be an elaboration of several assumptions:

1. All definitions and theories of deviation and social problems are normative. They define and explain behavior from socially situated value positions.
2. Existing normative theories can be classified into a limited number of typical vocabularies of explanation. Contemporary sociological theories of deviation are adaptations of two fundamental models of analysis rooted in nineteenth-century history and social thought. These are *order* and *conflict* models of society. Order models imply an *anomy* theory of societal discontent and an *adjustment* definition of social deviation. Conflict models imply an *alienation* theory of discontent and a *growth* definition of deviation.
3. In general, a liberalized version of order theory pervades the American sociological approach to racial conflict, juvenile delinquency, and other social problems. I use the term "liberal" because the sociological and the politically

liberal vocabularies are essentially the same. Both employ an order model of society; both are conservative in their commitment to the existing social order.

4. Alternatives to the liberal order approach exist both within the context of sociological theory and in the contemporary social and political fabric of American society. More radical versions of order models have been used by European sociologists such as Emile Durkheim; radical versions of order models are presently being used in American society by political rightists. The conflict vocabulary has been most clearly identified with Karl Marx and continues today in the social analysis of socialists and communists, while an anarchistic version of conflict theory pervades the politics of the so-called new left.

5. Current vocabularies for the explanation of social problems can be located within the social organization of sociology and the broader society. As a generalization, groups or individuals committed to the maintenance of the social status quo employ order models of society and equate deviation with non-conformity to institutionalized norms. Dissident groups, striving to institutionalize new claims, favor a conflict analysis of society and an alienation theory of their own discontents. For example, this social basis of preference for one model is clear in even the most superficial analysis of stands taken on civil rights demonstrations by civil rights activists and members of the Southern establishment. For Governor Wallace of Alabama, the 1965 Selma–Montgomery march was a negative expression of anomy; for Martin Luther King it was a positive and legitimate response to alienation. King argues that the Southern system is maladaptive to certain human demands; Wallace that the demands of the demonstrators are dysfunctional to the South. However, if one considers their perspectives in relationship to the more powerful Northern establishment, King and not Wallace is the order theorist.

In sociology, order analysis of society is most often expressed by the professional establishment and its organs of publication. Alienation analysis is associated with the "humanitarian" and "political" mavericks outside of, opposed to, or in some way marginal to the established profession of sociology.

Order and Conflict Theories: Anomy and Alienation
Analysis of Social Problems as Ideal Types

The terms "alienation" and "anomy"* current in the analysis of social problems derive historically from two opposing models of society — order and conflict models.[7] A comparison of the works of Marx and Mills (classical and contemporary conflict models) and Durkheim and Merton or Parsons (classical and contemporary order models) highlights the differences between the two social vocabularies. These competing vocabularies can be abstracted into ideal types of explanation, that is, exaggerated and ideologically consistent models which are only approximated in social reality.

The Order Vocabulary

Order theories have in common an image of society as a system of action unified at the most general level by shared culture, by agreement on values (or at least on modes) of communication and political organization. System analysis is synonymous with structural-functional analysis. System analysis consists of *statics* — the classification of structural regularities in social relations (dominant role and status clusters, institutions, etc.) — and *dynamics* — the study of the intrasystem processes: strategies of goal definition, socialization, and other functions which maintain system balance. A key concept in the analysis of system problems (social problems, deviation, conflict) is anomy. Social problems both result from and promote anomy. Anomy means system imbalance or social disorganization — a lack of or breakdown in social organization reflected in weakened social control, inadequate institutionalization of goals, inadequate means to achieve system goals, inadequate socialization, etc. At a social-psychological level of analysis, anomy results in the failure of individuals to meet the maintenance needs of the social system.

Order theories imply consensual and adjustment definitions of social health and pathology, of conformity and deviation. The standards for defining health are the legitimate values of the social system and its requisites for goal attainment and maintenance. Deviation is the opposite of social conformity and means the failure of individuals to perform their legitimate social roles; deviants are out of adjustment.

---

*As used here, *alienation* refers to beliefs held by members of a group in *opposition* to values and norms held by those in power. *Anomy* refers to a *lack* of belief among members of a group in the prevailing societal values and norms. —*ed.*

A contemporary example of an order approach to society and an adjustment interpretation of health and pathology has been clearly stated in Talcott Parsons's definition of mental health and pathology:

> Health may be defined as the state of optimum *capacity* of an individual for the effective performance of the roles and tasks for which he has been socialized. It is thus defined with reference to the individual's participation in the social system. It is also defined as *relative* to his "status" in the society, i.e., to differentiated type of role and corresponding task structure, e.g., by sex or age, and by level of education which he has attained and the like.[8]

The Conflict Vocabulary

Conflict theorists are alike in their rejection of the order model of contemporary society. They interpret order analysis as the strategy of a ruling group, a reification of their values and motivations, a rationalization for more effective social control. Society is a natural system for the order analyst; for the conflict theorist it is a continually contested political struggle between groups with opposing goals and world views. As an anarchist, the conflict theorist may oppose any notion of stable order and authority. As a committed Marxist, he may project the notion of order into the future. Order is won, not through the extension of social control, but through the radical reorganization of social life; order follows from the condition of social organization and not from the state of cultural integration.

Conflict analysis is synonymous with historical analysis: the interpretation of intersystem processes bringing about the transformation of social relations. A key concept in the analysis of historical and social change (as new behavior rather than deviant behavior) is alienation—separation, not from the social system as defined by dominant groups, but separation from man's universal nature or a desired state of affairs. Change is the progressive response to alienation; concepts of disorganization and deviation have no real meaning within the conflict vocabulary; they are properly part of the vocabulary of order theory where they have negative connotations as the opposites of the supreme values of order and stability. Within the conflict framework, the question of normality and health is ultimately a practical one resolved in the struggle to overcome alienation.

Conflict theory, nevertheless, implies a particular definition of health, but the values underlying this definition refer to what is required to grow and change, rather than to adjust to existing practices and hypothesized requirements for the maintenance of the social system. Health and pathology are defined in terms of postulated requirements for individual or social growth and adaptation. Social problems and social change arise from the exploitive and alienating practices of dominant groups; they are responses to the discrepancy between what is and what is in the process of becoming. Social problems, therefore, reflect, not the administrative problems of the social system, nor the failure of individuals to perform their system roles as in the order explanation, but the adaptive failure of society to meet changing individual needs.

A growth definition of health based on a conflict interpretation of society is implicit in Paul Goodman's appraisal of the causes of delinquency in American society. Unlike Parsons, he does not define pathology as that which does not conform to system values; he argues that delinquency is not the reaction to exclusion from these values, nor is it a problem of faulty socialization. Existing values and practices are absurd standards because they do not provide youth with what they need to grow and mature.

As was predictable, most of the authorities and all of the public spokesmen explain it (delinquency) by saying there has been a failure of socialization. They say that background conditions have interrupted socialization and must be improved. And, not enough effort has been made to guarantee belonging, there must be better bait or punishment.

But perhaps there has *not* been a failure of communication. Perhaps the social message has been communicated clearly to the young men and is unacceptable.

In this book I shall, therefore, take the opposite tack and ask, "Socialization to what? to what dominant society and available culture?" And if this question is asked, we must at once ask the other question, "Is the harmonious organization to which the young are inadequately socialized, perhaps against human nature, or not worthy of human nature, and *therefore* there is difficulty in growing up?"[9]

The conflict theorist invariably questions the legitimacy of existing practices and values; the order theorist accepts them as the standard of health.

Paradigm for the Analysis of Conflict and Approaches to Social Problems

In order more sharply to compare order and conflict models in terms of their implications for explanations of deviation and social problems, essential differences can be summarized along a number of parallel dimensions. These dimensions are dichotomized into order and conflict categories. The resulting paradigm can be used as a preliminary guide for the content analysis of contemporary as well as classical studies of social problems.

ORDER PERSPECTIVE	CONFLICT PERSPECTIVE

1. UNDERLYING SOCIAL PERSPECTIVE AND VALUE POSITIONS (IDEAL)

a. *Image of man and society*

Society as a natural boundary-maintaining system of action	Society as a contested struggle between groups with opposed aims and perspectives
Transcendent nature of society, an entity *sui generis,* greater than and different from the sum of its parts; lack of transcendence as lack of social control means anomy	Immanent conception of society and the social relationship; men are society; society is the extension of man, the indwelling of man; the transcendence of society is tantamount to the alienation of man from his own social nature
Positive attitude toward the maintenance of social institutions	Positive attitude toward change

b. *Human nature*

Homo duplex, man half egoistic (self-nature), half altruistic (socialized nature), ever in need of restraints for the collective good	*Homo laborans,* existential man, the active creator of himself and society through practical and autonomous social action

or

Tabula rasa, man equated with the socialization process

or

Homo damnatus, the division into morally superior and morally inferior men

c. *Values*

The social good: balance, stability, authority, order, quantitative growth ("moving equilibrium")	Freedom as autonomy, change, action, qualitative growth

ORDER PERSPECTIVE	CONFLICT PERSPECTIVE

2. MODES OF "SCIENTIFIC" ANALYSIS

Natural science model: quest for general and universal laws and repeated patterns gleaned through empirical research Structural–functional analysis	Historical model: quest for understanding (*Verstehen*) through historical analysis of unique and changing events; possible use of ideal type of generalization based on historically specific patterns.
Multiple causality; theory characterized by high level of abstraction, but empirical studies marked by low level of generalization (separation of theory from application)	Unicausality; high or low level of theoretical generalization; union of theory and practice in social research and social action
Conditions of objectivity: accurate correspondence of concepts to facts; rigid separation of observer and facts observed — passive, receptive theory of knowledge	Utility in terms of observer's interests; objectivity discussed in the context of subjectivity — activistic theory of knowledge
Analysis begins with culture as major determinant of order and structure and proceeds to personality and social organization	Analysis begins with organization of social activities or with growth and maintenance needs of man and proceeds to culture
Dominant concepts: ahistorical; high level of generality; holistic supra-individual concepts; ultimate referent for concepts — system needs considered universally (i.e., the functional prerequisites of any social system) or relativistically (i.e., present maintenance requirements of a particular social system)	Historical, dynamic; low level of generality and high level of historical specificity; ultimate referent for concepts — human needs considered universally (i.e., man's species nature) or relativistically (demands of particular contenders for power); referent often the future or an unrealized state of affairs.

ORDER PERSPECTIVE	CONFLICT PERSPECTIVE

3. ORDER AND CONFLICT THEORIES OF SOCIAL PROBLEMS AND DEVIATION

a. Standards for the definition of health and pathology

Health equated with existing values of a postulated society (or a dominant group in the society), ideological definition	Health equated with unrealized standards (the aspirations of) subordinate but rising groups), utopian definition

b. Evaluation of deviant behavior

Pathological to the functioning of the social system	Possibly progressive to the necessary transformation of existing relationships

c. Explanation of deviation or a social problem

A problem of anomy, inadequate control over competing groups in the social system; disequilibrium in the existing society	A problem of self-alienation, being thwarted in the realization of individual and group goals; a problem of illegitimate social control and exploitation

d. Implied ameliorative action

Extensive of social control (further and more efficient institutionalization of social system values); adjustment of individuals to system needs; working within the system; the administrative solution	Rupture of social control; radical transformation of existing patterns of interaction; revolutionary change of the social system

4. ORDER AND CONFLICT THEORIES AS SOCIALLY SITUATED VOCABULARIES

Dominant groups: the establishment and administrators of the establishment	Subordinate groups aspiring for greater power
Contemporary representatives: Parsonian and Mertonian approach to social problems as a liberal variant of order models; politically conservative approaches	C. W. Mills, new left (SNCC, SDS, etc.) approaches and old left (socialistic and communistic)

The order and conflict models as outlined represent polar ideal types which are not consistently found in the inconsistent ideologies of actual social research and political practice. If the models have any utility to social scientists, it will be in making more explicit and systematic the usually implicit value assumptions which underlie their categories of thinking. In this paper, as an exercise in the use of conflict-order models, I examine some of the normative assumptions which can be found in the approach of the sociologist and the political liberal to the Negro question. My thinking is intentionally speculative. I am not trying to summarize the vast literature on race relations, but merely showing the existence of an order pattern.

Liberals and Sociologists on the American Negro:
A Contemporary Adaptation of Order Theory

Contemporary liberalism has been popularly associated with a conflict model of society; actually it is a variant of conservative order theory. Within the model, conflict is translated to mean institutionalized (reconciled) conflict or competition for similar goals within the same system. Conflict as confrontation of opposed groups and values, conflict as a movement toward basic change of goals and social structures is anathema.

The liberal tendency of American sociology and the essentially conservative character of contemporary liberalism are particularly marked in the sociological analysis of the Negro question. In the field of race relations, an order model can be detected in (1) consensual assumptions about man and society: the "over-socialized" man and the plural society; (2) a selective pattern of interpretation which follows from these assumptions: (*a*) the explanation of the problem as a moral dilemma and its solution as one requiring adjustment through socialization and social control; (*b*) the explanation of the minority group as a reaction formation to exclusion from middle-class life; (*c*) an emphasis on concepts useful in the explanation of order (shared values as opposed to economic and political differences); an emphasis on concepts useful in the explanation of disorder or anomy within an accepted order (status competition rather than class conflict, problems of inadequate means rather than conflicting goals).

The Liberal View of Man:
Egalitarian Within an Elitist, Consensual Framework;
All Men Are Socializable to the American Creed

No one can see an ideological assumption as clearly as a political opponent. Rightist and leftist alike have attacked the liberal concept of man implicit in the analysis of the Negro question: conservatives because it is egalitarian, radicals because it is elitist and equated with a dominant ideology. The rightist believes in natural inequality; the leftist in positive, historical differences between men; the liberal believes in the power of socialization and conversion.

A certain egalitarianism is indeed implied in at least two liberal asserta- tions: (1) Negroes along with other men share a common human nature socializable to the conditions of society; (2) their low position and general inability to compete reflect unequal opportunity and inadequate socializa- tion to whatever is required to succeed within the American system. These assertations are, in a sense, basically opposed to the elitist-conservative argument that the Negro has failed to compete because he is naturally dif- ferent or has voluntarily failed to take full advantage of existing oppor- tunities.[10]

The conservative, however, exaggerates liberal egalitarianism; it is tempered with elitism. Equality is won by conformity to a dominant set of values and behavior. Equality means equal opportunity to achieve the same American values; in other words, equality is gained by losing one identity and conforming at some level to another demanded by a dominant group. As a leftist, J. P. Sartre has summarized this liberal view of man, both egalitarian and elitist. What he has termed the "democratic" attitude toward the Jew applies well to the American "liberal" view of the Negro:

> The Democrat, like the scientist, fails to see the particular case; to him the individual is only an ensemble of universal traits. It follows that his defense of the Jew saves the latter as a man and annihilates him as a Jew . . . he fears that the Jew will acquire a consciousness of Jewish collectivity. . . . "There are no Jews," he says, "there is no Jewish question." This means that he wants to separate the Jew from his religion, from his family, from his ethnic community, in order to plunge him into the democratic crucible whence he will emerge naked and alone, an individual and solitary particle like all other particles.[11]

The conservative would preserve a Negro identity by pronouncing the Negro different (inferior), the radical by proclaiming him part of the superior vanguard of the future society; but the liberal would transform him altogether by turning him into another American, another individual competing in an orderly fashion for cars, television sets, and identification with the American Creed. In their attack on the liberal definition of man, the conservative and leftist agree on one thing: the liberal seems to deny basic differences between groups. At least differences are reconcilable within a consensual society.

The Liberal Society: Structural Pluralism within a Consensual Framework

Thus, the liberal fate of minorities, including Negroes, is basically containment through socialization to dominant values. Supposedly this occurs in a plural society where some differences are maintained. But liberal pluralism like liberal egalitarianism allows differences only within a consensual framework. This applies both to the liberal ideal and the sociological description: the plural-democratic society *is* the present society.

This consensual pluralism should be carefully distinguished from the conflict variety. J. S. Furnivall has called the once colonially dominated societies of tropical Asia plural in the latter sense:

> In Burma, as in Java, probably the first thing that strikes the visitor is the medley of peoples — European, Chinese, Indian, native. It is in the strictest sense a medley, for they mix but do not combine. Each group holds to its own religion, its own culture and language, its own ideas and ways. As individuals they meet, but only in the marketplace, in buying and selling. There is a plural society, with different sections of the community living side by side, but separately, within the same political unit. Even in the economic sphere there is a division along racial lines.[12]

For Furnivall, a plural society has no common will, no common culture. Order rests on political force and economic expediency. For liberals and sociologists, American society has a common social will (the American Creed). Order rests on legitimate authority and consensus. The whole analysis of the Negro question has generally been predicated on this belief that American society, however plural, is united by consensus on certain values. Gunnar Myrdal's influential interpretation of the Negro question has epitomized the social will thesis:

> Americans of all national origins, classes, regions, creeds, and colors, have something in common: a social ethos, a political creed. . . . When the American Creed is once detected the ca-

cophony becomes a melody . . . as principles which ought to rule, the Creed has been made conscious to everyone in American society. . . . America is continuously struggling for its soul. The cultural unity of the nation is sharing of both the consciousness of sin and the devotion to high ideals.[13]

In what sense can a consensual society be plural? It cannot tolerate the existence of separate cultural segments. Robin M. Williams in a recent book on race relations writes: "The United States is a plural society which cannot settle for a mosaic of separate cultural segments, nor for a caste system."[14] Norman Podhoretz, a political liberal who has written often on the Negro question, has stated the issue more bluntly. In his review of Ralph Ellison's *Shadow and Act,* a series of essays which poses a threat of conflict pluralism by asserting the positive and different "cultural" characteristics of Negroes, Podhoretz states his consensual realism:

> The vision of a world in which many different groups live together on a footing of legal and social equality, each partaking of a broad general culture and yet maintaining its own distinctive identity: this is one of the noble dreams of the liberal tradition. Yet the hard truth is that very little evidence exists to suggest that such a pluralistic order is possible. Most societies throughout history have simply been unable to suffer the presence of distinctive minority groups among them; and the fate of minorities has generally been to disappear, either through being assimilated into the majority, or through being expelled, or through being murdered.[15]

The liberal and the sociologist operating with an order ideology positively fear the conflict type of pluralism. As Sartre rightly observed, the liberal who is himself identified with the establishment, although avowedly the friend of the minority, suspects any sign of militant minority consciousness. He wants the minority to share in American human nature and compete like an individual along with other individuals for the same values.

As Podhoretz has observed, pluralism never really meant coexistence of quite different groups:

> For the traditional liberal mentality conceives of society as being made up not of competing economic classes and ethnic groups,

but rather of competing *individuals* who confront a neutral body of law and a neutral institutional complex.[16]

How then can ethnic groups be discussed within the plural but consensual framework? They must be seen as separate but assimilated (contained) social structures. Among sociologists, Milton Gordon has been most precise about this pluralism as a description of ethnic groups in American society.

> Behavioral assimilation or acculturation has taken place in America to a considerable degree. . . . Structural assimilation, then, has turned out to be the rock on which the ships of Anglo-conformity and the melting pot have foundered. To understand that behavioral assimilation (or acculturation) without massive structural intermingling in primary relationships has been the dominant motif in the American experience of creating and developing a nation out of diverse peoples is to comprehend the most essential sociological fact of that experience. It is against the background of "structural pluralism" that strategies of strengthening intergroup harmony, reducing ethnic discrimination and prejudice, and maintaining the rights of both those who stay within and those who venture beyond their ethnic boundaries must be thoughtfully devised.[17]

Clearly then the liberal vocabulary of race relations is predicated on consensual assumptions about the nature of man and society. The order explanation of the Negro problem and its solution may be summarized as follows:

1. *An order or consensual model of society* — American society is interpreted as a social system unified at its most general level by acceptance of certain central political, social, and economic values. Thus, the Negro population is said to have been acculturated to a somewhat vaguely defined American tradition; at the most, Negro society is a variant or a reaction to that primary tradition.
2. *Social problems as moral problems of anomy or social disorganization within the American system* — Social problems and deviant behavior arise from an imbalance between goals

and means. The problems of the Negro are created by un-
ethical exclusion from equal competition for American
goals.

3. *The response to anomy: social amelioration as adjustment
   and extension of social control*—Liberal solutions imply
   further institutionalization of the American Creed in the
   opportunity structure of society and, therefore, the adjustment of the deviant to legitimate social roles.

The Race Question as a Moral Dilemma

A familiar expression of liberal-consensualism is Gunnar Myrdal's interpretation of the American race question as a moral dilemma. According
to this thesis, racial discrimination and its varied effects on the Negro—the
development of plural social structures, high rates of social deviation,
etc.—reflect a kind of anomy in the relationship between the American
Creed and social structure. Anomy means a moral crisis arising from an in-
congruity between legitimate and ethical social goals (for example, success
and equality of opportunity) and socially available opportunities to achieve
these goals. American society is good and ethical, but anomic because the
American Creed of equality has not been fully institutionalized; the ethic is
widely accepted in theory but not in practice.

Sidney Hook as a political liberal has likewise insisted that American
society is essentially ethical and that the Negro problems should be discussed
in these ethical terms:

> Of course, no society has historically been organized on the
> basis of ethical principles, but I don't think we can understand
> how any society functions without observing the operation of
> the ethical principles within it. And if we examine the develop-
> ment of American society, we certainly can say that we have
> made *some* progress, to be sure, but progress nevertheless—by
> virtue of the extension of our ethical principles to institutional
> life. If we want to explain the progress that has been made in the
> last twenty years by minority groups in this country—not only
> the Negroes, but other groups as well—I believe we have to take
> into account the effect of our commitment to democracy, im-
> perfect though it may be.[18]

The Solution: Working within the System

The liberal solution to the racial question follows from the American-dilemma thesis: the belief in the ethical nature and basic legitimacy of American institutions. Amelioration, therefore, becomes exclusively a question of adjustment within the system; it calls for administrative action: how to attack anomy as the imbalance of goals and means. The administrator accepts the goals of his organization and treats all problems as errors in administration, errors which can be rectified without changing the basic framework of the organization. Karl Mannheim has aptly characterized the bureaucratic and administrative approach to social problems. What he says about the perspective of the Prussian bureaucrat applies only too well to his counterpart in American society:

> The attempt to hide all problems of politics under the cover of administration may be explained by the fact that the sphere of activity of the official exists only within the limits of law already formulated. Hence the genesis or the development of law falls outside the scope of his activity. As a result of his socially limited horizon, the functionary fails to see that behind every law that has been made there lie the socially fashioned interests and the *Weltanschauungen* of a specific social group. He takes it for granted that the specific order prescribed by the concrete law is equivalent in order in general. He does not understand that every rationalized order is only one of many forms in which socially conflicting irrational forces are reconciled.[19]

The liberal administrator's solution to the Negro question entails the expansion of opportunities for mobility within the society and socialization of the deviant (the Negro and the anti-Negro) to expanding opportunities. Hence the importance of education and job training; they are prime means to success and higher status. Given the assumption that the American Creed is formally embodied in the political structure, the liberal also looks to legislation as an important and perhaps sole means of reenforcing the Creed by legitimizing changes in the American opportunity structure.

Negro Life as a Reaction Formation

Another important deduction has followed from the assumption of the political and cultural assimilation of the American Negro: whatever is different or distinct in his life style represents a kind of negative reaction to exclusion from the white society. The Negro is the creation of the white. Like the criminal he is a pathology, a reaction-formation to the problem of inadequate opportunities to achieve and to compete in the American system.

Myrdal states:

> The Negro's entire life, and consequently, also his opinions on the Negro problem are, in the main, to be considered as secondary reactions to more primary pressures from the side of the dominant white majority.[20]

More recently Leonard Broom has echoed the same opinion:

> Negro life was dominated by the need to adjust to white men and to take them into account at every turn . . . Taken as a whole, the two cultures have more common than distinctive elements. Over the long run, their convergence would seem inevitable. . . . Because Negro life is so much affected by poverty and subservience, it is hard to find distinctive characteristics that can be positively evaluated. In the stereotype, whatever is admirable in Negro life is assumed to have been adopted from the white man, while whatever is reprehensible is assumed to be inherently Negro.[21]

Conflict Theorist Looks at Order Theorist Looking at the Negro

A liberal order model—consensual pluralism, with its corollary approach to the race question as moral dilemma and reaction-formation—colors the sociological analysis of the race question. It is interesting that the fundamental assumption about consensus on the American Creed has rarely been subjected to adequate empirical test.[22] Lacking any convincing evidence for the order thesis, I can only wonder who the sociologist is speaking for. He may be speaking for himself in that his paradigm answers the question of how to solve the Negro problem without changing basic economic and political institutions. He probably speaks least of all for the Negro. The liberal sociologists will have some difficulty describing the world from the viewpoint of Negro "rioters" in Los Angeles and other cities. In any case, he will not agree with anyone who believes (in fact or in ideology) that the Negro may have a separate and self-determining identity. Such a view suggests conflict and would throw doubt on the fixations of consensus, anomy, and reaction-formation.

Conflict interpretations are minority interpretations by definition. They are rarely expressed either by sociologists or by ethnic minorities. However, a few such interpretations can be mentioned to imply that the end of ideology and, therefore, the agreement on total ideology has not yet arrived.

Ralph Ellison, speaking from a conflict and nationalistic perspective, has made several salient criticisms of the liberal American dilemma thesis. He has argued that Myrdal's long discussion of American values and conclusion of multiple causality have conveniently avoided the inconvenient question of power and control in American society.

> All this, of course, avoids the question of power *and* the question of who manipulates that power. Which to us seems more of a stylistic maneuver than a scientific judgment. . . . Myrdal's stylistic method is admirable. In presenting his findings he uses the American ethos brilliantly to disarm all American social groupings, by appealing to their stake in the American Creed, and to locate the psychological barriers between them. But he also uses it to deny the existence of an American class struggle, and with facile economy it allows him to avoid admitting that actually there exist two American moralities, kept in balance by social science.[23]

Doubting the thesis of consensus, Ellison is also in a position to attack Myrdal's interpretation of the American Negro as a reaction-formation, and assimilation to the superior white society as his only solution.

> But can a people (its faith in an idealized American Creed notwithstanding) live and develop for over three hundred years simply by reacting? Are American Negroes simply the creation of white men, or have they at least helped to create themselves out of what they found around them? Men have made a way of life in caves and upon cliffs, why cannot Negroes have made a life upon the horns of the white men's dilemma?
>
> Myrdal sees Negro culture and personality simply as the product of a "social pathology." Thus he assumes that "it is to

the advantage of American Negroes as individuals and as a group to become assimilated into American culture, to acquire the traits held in esteem by the dominant white American." This, he admits, contains the value premise that "here in America, American culture is 'highest' in the pragmatic sense. . . ." Which aside from implying that Negro culture is not also American, assumes that Negroes should desire nothing better than what whites consider highest. But in the "pragmatic" sense lynching and Hollywood, faddism and radio advertising are products of "higher" culture, and the Negro might ask, "Why, if my culture is pathological, must I exchange it for these?" . . . What is needed for our country is not an exchange of pathologies, but a change of the basis of society.[24]

Conclusion

The hostile action of Negro masses destroying white property is perhaps a more convincing demonstration of conflict theory than the hopes of Negro intellectuals. But as a sociologist I am not really interested in raising the question of whether a conflict definition of the race question is more correct than the more familiar order model. Each view is correct in a normative and practical sense insofar as it confirms to a viable political and social experience. What indeed is a correct interpretation of the Negro problem or any social problem? The answer has as much to do with consensus as with correspondence to the facts. Normative theories are not necessarily affected by empirical evidence because they seek to change or to maintain the world, not describe it.

Whenever there is genuine conflict between groups and interpretations, correctness clearly becomes a practical matter of power and political persuasion. This seems to be the situation today, and one can expect more heated debate. If conflict continues to increase between whites and Negroes in the United States, the liberal sociologist studying the "Negro problem" had better arm himself with more than his questionnaire. A militant Negro respondent may take him for the social problem, the sociologist as an agent of white society and the scientific purveyor of order theory and containment policy.

This clash of perspectives would be an illustration of my general argument: explanations of the Negro question or any other social problem invariably involve normative theory, values, ideologies, or whatever one may care to call the subjective categories of our thinking about society. Concepts of deviation and social problems can be discussed only in the context of some social (and therefore contestable) standard of health, conformity, and the good society. Terms like "moral dilemma," "pluralism," "assimilation," "integration" describe motives for desirable action: they are definitions placed on human action, not the action itself independent of social values.

The error of the sociologist is not what he thinks politically and liberally about his society, but that he is not aware of it. Awareness may help him avoid some of the gross errors of myopia: (1) mistaking his own normative categories for "objective" fact; thus, the liberal sociologist may mistake his belief in the consensual society for actual consensus; (2) projecting a normative theory appropriate to the experience of one group onto another group; this is what Ellison means when he says that the liberal sociologist is not necessarily speaking for the Negro. Indeed, the errors of myopia are perhaps greatest whenever the middle-class sociologist presumes to describe the world and motivation of persons in lower status. Seeing the lower-class Negro within a white liberal vocabulary may be very realistic politics, but it is not very accurate sociology.

Once the sociologist is involved in the study of anything that matters, he has the unavoidable obligation of at least distinguishing his vocabulary from that of the groups he is supposedly observing rather than converting. As a scientist, he must find out what perspectives are being employed, where they are operating in the society, and with what effect. Perhaps this awareness of competing perspective occurs only in the actual process of conflict and debate. Unfortunately, this is not always the situation within an increasingly professionalized sociology. The more professionalized the field, the more standardized the thinking of sociologists and the greater the danger of internal myopia passing for objectivity. But outside sociology debate is far from closed; conflict and order perspectives are simultaneously active on every controversial social issue. The liberal order model may not long enjoy uncontested supremacy.

Notes

1. Robert Gover, *The One Hundred Dollar Misunderstanding* (New York: Ballantine Books, 1961).
2. Don Martindale, "Social Disorganization: The Conflict of Normative and Empirical Approaches," in Howard Becker and Alvin Boskoff, eds., *Modern Sociological Theory* (New York: Dryden Press, 1959), p. 341.

3. For Weber's discussion of explanation in the social sciences, see *Max Weber: The Theory of Social and Economic Organizations,* trans. A. M. Henderson and Talcott Parsons (Glencoe, Ill.: Free Press, 1947), pp. 87–114.

4. C. Wright Mills, "Situated Actions and Vocabularies of Motive," *American Sociological Review,* V (December, 1940), 904–913.

5. C. Wright Mills, "The Professional Ideology of the Social Pathologists," *American Journal of Sociology,* XLIX (September, 1942), 165–180.

6. C. Wright Mills, *The Sociological Imagination* (New York: Oxford University Press, 1959).

7. In contemporary sociology, the concepts of alienation and anomy are often used synonymously. In practice, this usually means that alienation, a key term in conflict analysis, has been translated into a more conservative-order vocabulary; for a discussion of differences between past and present uses of these concepts see John Horton, "The Dehumanization of Anomie and Alienation," *British Journal of Sociology* 15 (December 1964): 283–300.

8. Talcott Parsons, "Definitions of Health and Illness in the Light of American Values and Social Structure," in E. Gartley Jaco, ed., *Patients, Physicians and Illness* (Glencoe, Ill.: Free Press, 1963), p. 176.

9. Paul Goodman, *Growing Up Absurd* (New York: Random House, 1960), p. 11.

10. For a conservative argument, see, among many others, Carleton Putman, *Race and Reason* (Washington, D.C.: Public Affairs Press, 1961).

11. Jean-Paul Sartre, *Anti-Semite and Jew,* trans. George J. Becker (New York: Grove Press, 1962), pp. 56–57.

12. J. S. Furnivall, *Colonial Policy and Practice* (London: Cambridge University Press, 1948), p. 304.

13. Gunnar Myrdal, *An American Dilemma* (New York: Harper & Bros., 1944), pp. 3–4.

14. Robin M. Williams, Jr., *Strangers Next Door* (Englewood Cliffs, N.J.: Prentice-Hall, 1964), p. 386.

15. Norman Podhoretz, "The Melting-Pot Blues," *Washington Post,* October 5, 1964.

16. Normal Podhoretz, as quoted in "Liberalism and the American Negro – a Round-Table Discussion" with James Baldwin, Nathan Glazer, Sidney Hook, Gunnar Myrdal, and Normal Podhoretz (moderator), *Commentary* 37 (March 1964): 25–26.

17. Milton Gordon, "Assimilation in America: Theory and Reality," *Daedalus* 90 (Spring 1961): 280, 283.

18. Hook, "Liberalism and the American Negro—a Round-Table Discussion," p. 31.

19. Karl Mannheim, *Ideology and Utopia* (New York: Harcourt, Brace & World, 1936), p. 118

20. Gunnar Myrdal, as quoted by Ralph Ellison, "An American Dilemma: A Review," in *Shadow and Act* (New York: Random House, 1964), p. 315.

21. Leonard Broom, *The Transformation of the American Negro* (New York: Harper & Row, 1965), pp. 22–23.

22. For a recent attempt to test the American dilemma thesis, see Frank R. Westie, "The American Dilemma: An Empirical Test," *American Sociological Review* 30 (August 1965): 527–538.

23. Ellison, *Shadow and Act,* p. 315.

24. *Ibid.,* pp. 316–317.

How to Blame the Victim

William Ryan

The generic process of Blaming the Victim is applied to almost every American problem. The miserable health care of the poor is explained away on the grounds that the victim has poor motivation and lacks health information. The problems of slum housing are traced to the characteristics of tenants who are labeled as "Southern rural migrants" not yet "acculturated" to life in the big city. The "multiproblem" poor, it is claimed, suffer the psychological effects of impoverishment, the "culture of poverty," and the deviant value system of the lower classes; consequently, though unwittingly, they cause their own troubles. From such a viewpoint, the obvious fact that poverty is primarily an absence of money is easily overlooked or set aside.

The growing number of families receiving welfare are fallaciously linked together with the increased number of illegitimate children as twin results of promiscuity and sexual abandon among members of the lower orders. Every important social problem—crime, mental illness, civil disorder, unemployment—has been analyzed within the framework of the victim-blaming ideology.

* * *

Blaming the Victim is, of course, quite different from old-fashioned conservative ideologies. The latter simply dismissed victims as inferior, genetically defective, or morally unfit; the emphasis is on the intrinsic, even hereditary, defect. The former shifts its emphasis to the environmental causation. The old-fashioned conservative could hold firmly to the belief that the oppressed and the victimized were born that way—"That way" being defective or inadequate in character or ability. The new ideology attributes defect and inadequacy to the malignant nature of poverty, injustice, slum life, and racial difficulties. The stigma that marks the victim and accounts for his victimization is an acquired stigma, a stigma of social, rather than genetic, origin. But the stigma, the defect, the fatal difference—though

FROM William Ryan, *Blaming the Victim* (New York: Vintage, 1971).

derived in the past from environmental forces — is still located *within* the victim, inside his skin. With such an elegant formulation, the humanitarian can have it both ways. He can, all at the same time, concentrate his charitable interest on the defects of the victim, condemn the vague social and environmental stresses that produced the defect (some time ago), and ignore the continuing effect of victimizing social forces (right now). It is a brilliant ideology for justifying a perverse form of social action designed to change, not society, as one might expect, but rather society's victim.

As a result, there is a terrifying sameness in the programs that arise from this kind of analysis. In education, we have programs of "compensatory education" to build up the skills and attitudes of the ghetto child, rather than structural changes in the schools. In race relations, we have social engineers who think up ways of "strengthening" the Negro family, rather than methods of eradicating racism. In health care, we develop new programs to provide health information (to correct the supposed ignorance of the poor) and to reach out and discover cases of untreated illness and disability (to compensate for their supposed unwillingness to seek treatment). Meanwhile, the gross inequities of our medical care delivery systems are left completely unchanged. As we might expect, the logical outcome of analyzing social problems in terms of the deficiencies of the victim is the development of programs aimed at correcting those deficiencies. The formula for action becomes extraordinarily simple: change the victim.

All of this happens so smoothly that it seems downright rational. First, identify a social problem. Second, study those affected by the problem and discover in what ways they are different from the rest of us as a consequence of deprivation and injustice. Third, define the differences as the cause of the social problem itself. Finally, of course, assign a government bureaucrat to invent a humanitarian action program to correct the differences.

* * *

The second step in applying this explanation is to look sympathetically at those who "have" the problem in question, to separate them out and define them in some way as a special group, a group that is *different* from the population in general. This is a crucial and essential step in the process, for that difference is in itself hampering and maladaptive. The Different Ones are seen as less competent, less skilled, less knowing — in short, less human. The ancient Greeks deduced from a single characteristic, a difference in language, that the barbarians — that is, the "babblers" who spoke a strange tongue — were wild, uncivilized, dangerous, rapacious, uneducated, lawless, and, indeed, scarcely more than animals. Automatically labeling strangers as savages, weird and inhuman creatures (thus explaining differences by exaggerating difference) not infrequently justifies mistreatment, enslavement, or even extermination of the Different Ones.

Blaming the Victim depends on a very similar process of identification (carried out, to be sure, in the most kindly, philanthropic, and intellectual manner) whereby the victim of social problems is identified as strange, different — in other words, as a barbarian, a savage. Discovering savages, then, is an essential component of, and prerequisite to, Blaming the Victim, and the art of Savage Discovery is a core skill that must be acquired by all aspiring Victim Blamers. They must learn how to demonstrate that the poor, the black, the ill, the jobless, the slum tenants, are different and strange.

* * *

Victim Blaming as Ideology

Blaming the Victim is an ideological process, which is to say that it is a set of ideas and concepts deriving from systematically motivated, but *unintended*, distortions of reality. In the sense that Karl Mannheim[1] used the term, an ideology develops from the "collective unconscious" of a group or class and is rooted in a class-based interest in maintaining the *status quo* (as contrasted with what he calls a *utopia*, a set of ideas rooted in a class-based interest in *changing the status quo*). An ideology, then, has several components: First, there is the belief system itself, the way of looking at the world, the set of ideas and concepts. Second, there is the systematic distortion of reality reflected in those ideas. Third is the condition that the distortion must not be a conscious, intentional process. Finally, though they are not intentional, the ideas must serve a specific function: maintaining the *status quo* in the interest of a specific group. Blaming the Victim fits this definition on all counts, as I will attempt to show. . . .

Most particularly, it is important to realize that Blaming the Victim is not a process of *intentional* distortion although it does serve the class interests of those who practice it. And it has a rich ancestry in American thought about social problems and how to deal with them.

Thinking about social problems is especially susceptible to ideological influences since, as John Seeley has pointed out,[2] defining a social problem is not so simple. "What is a social problem?" may seem an ingenuous question until one turns to confront its opposite: "What human problem is *not* a social problem?" Since any problem in which people are involved is social, why do we reserve the label for some problems in which people are involved and withhold it from others? To use Seeley's example, why is crime called a social problem when university administration is not?

* * *

We must particularly ask, "To whom are social problems a problem?" And usually, if truth were to be told, we would have to admit that we mean they are a problem to those of us who are outside the boundaries of what we have defined as the problem. Negroes are a problem to racist whites, welfare is a problem to stingy taxpayers, delinquency is a problem to nervous property owners.

Now, if this is the quality of our assumptions about social problems, we are led unerringly to certain beliefs about the causes of these problems. We cannot comfortably believe that *we* are the cause of that which is problematic to us; therefore, we are almost compelled to believe that *they* — the problematic ones — are the cause and this immediately prompts us to search for deviance. Identification of the deviance as the cause of the problem is a simple step that ordinarily does not even require evidence.

C. Wright Mills analyzed the ideology of those who write about social problems and demonstrated the relationship of their texts to class interest and to the preservation of the existent social order.[3] In sifting the material in 31 widely used textbooks in "social problems," "social pathology," and "social disorganization," Mills found a pervasive, coherent ideology with a number of common characteristics.

First, the textbooks present material about these problems, he says, in simple, descriptive terms, with each problem unrelated to the others and none related in any meaningful way to other aspects of the social environment. Second, the problems are selected and described largely according to predetermined norms. Poverty is a problem in that it deviates from the standard of economic self-sufficiency; divorce is a problem because the family is supposed to remain intact; crime and delinquency are problematic insofar as they depart from the accepted moral and legal standards of the community. The norms themselves are taken as givens, and no effort is made to examine them. Nor is there any thought given to the manner in which norms might themselves contribute to the development of the problems. (In a society in which everyone is assumed and expected to be economically self-sufficient, as an example, doesn't economic dependency almost automatically mean poverty? No attention is given to such issues.)

Within such a framework, then, deviation from norms and standards comes to be defined as failed or incomplete socialization — failure to learn the rules or the inability to learn how to keep to them. Those with social problems are then viewed as unable or unwilling to adjust to society's standards, which are narrowly conceived by what Mills calls "independent middle class persons verbally living out Protestant ideas in small town America." This, obviously, is a precise description of the social origins and status of almost every one of the authors.

In defining social problems in this way, the social pathologists are, of course, ignoring a whole set of factors that ordinarily might be considered relevant — for instance, unequal distribution of income, social stratification, political struggle, ethnic and racial group conflict, and inequality of power. Their ideology concentrates almost exclusively on the failure of the deviant. To the extent that society plays any part in social problems, it is said to have somehow failed to socialize the individual, to teach him how to adjust to circumstances, which, though far from perfect, are gradually changing for the better. Mills's essay provides a solid foundation for understanding the concept of Blaming the Victim.

This way of thinking on the part of "social pathologists," which Mills identified as the predominant tool used in *analyzing* social problems, also saturates the majority of programs that have been developed to *solve* social problems in America. These programs are based on the assumption that *individuals* "have" social problems as a result of some kind of unusual circumstances — accident, illness, personal defect or handicap, character flaw or maladjustment — that exclude them from using the ordinary mechanisms for maintaining and advancing themselves. For example, the prevalent belief in America is that, under normal circumstances, everyone can obtain sufficient income for the necessities of life. Those who are unable to do so are special deviant cases, persons who for one reason or another are not able to adapt themselves to the generally satisfactory income-producing system. In times gone by these persons were further classified into the worthy poor — the lame, the blind, the young mother whose husband died in an accident, the aged man no longer able to work — and the unworthy poor — the lazy, the unwed mother and her illegitimate children, the malingerer. All were seen, however, as individuals who, for good reasons or bad, were personal failures, unable to adapt themselves to the system.

In America health care, too, has been predominantly a matter of particular remedial attention provided individually to the more or less random group of persons who have become ill, whose bodily functioning has become deviant and abnormal. In the field of mental health, the same approach has been, and continues to be, dominant. The social problem of mental disease has been viewed as a collection of individual cases of deviance, persons who — through unusual hereditary taint, or exceptional distortion of character — have become unfit for normal activities. The solution to these problems was to segregate the deviants, to protect them, to give them *asylum* from the life of the community for which they were no longer competent.

This has been the dominant style in American social welfare and health activities, then: to treat what we call social problems, such as poverty, disease, and mental illness, in terms of the individual deviance of the special, unusual groups of persons who had those problems. There has also been a competing style, however — much less common, not at all congruent with the prevalent ideology, but continually developing parallel to the dominant style.

Adherents of this approach tended to search for defects in the community and the environment rather than in the individual; to emphasize predictability and usualness rather than random deviance; they tried to think about preventing rather than merely repairing or treating — to see social problems, in a word, as social. In the field of disease, this approach was termed public health, and its practitioners sought the cause of disease in such things as the water supply, the sewage system, the density and quality of housing conditions. They set out to prevent disease, not in individuals, but in the total population, through improved sanitation, inoculation against communicable disease, and the policing of housing conditions. In the field of income maintenance, this secondary style of solving social problems focused on poverty as a predictable event, on the regularities of income deficiency. And it concentrated on the development of standard, generalized programs affecting total groups. Rather than trying to fit the aged worker ending his career into some kind of category of special cases, it assumed all 65-year-old men should expect to retire from the world of work and have the security of an old age pension, to be arranged through public social activity. Unemployment insurance was developed as a method whereby all workers could be protected against the effects of the normal ups and downs of the business cycle. A man out of work could then count on an unemployment check rather than endure the agony of pauperizing himself, selling his tools or his car, and finding himself in the special category of those deserving of charity.

These two approaches to the solution of social problems have existed side by side, the former always dominant, but the latter gradually expanding, slowly becoming more and more prevalent.

Elsewhere[4] I have proposed the dimension of *exceptionalism–universalism* as the ideological underpinning for these two contrasting approaches to the analsis and solution of social problems. The *exceptionalist* viewpoint is reflected in arrangements that are private, voluntary, remedial, special, local, and exclusive. Such arrangements imply that problems occur to specially defined categories of persons in an unpredictable manner. The problems are unusual, even unique, they are exceptions to the rule, they occur as a result of individual defect, accident, or unfortunate circumstance and must be remedied by means that are particular and, as it were, tailored to the individual case.

The universalistic viewpoint, on the other hand, is reflected in arrangements that are public, legislated, promotive or preventive, general, national, and inclusive. Inherent in such a viewpoint is the idea that social problems are a function of the social arrangements of the community or the society and that, since these social arrangements are quite imperfect and inequitable, such problems are both predictable and, more important, preventable through public action. They are not unique to the individual, and the fact that they encompass individual persons does not imply that those persons are themselves defective or abnormal.

Consider these two contrasting approaches as they are applied to the problem of smallpox. The medical care approach is exceptionalistic; it is designed to provide remedial treatment to the special category of persons who are afflicted with the disease through a private, voluntary arrangement with a local doctor. The universalistic public health approach is designed to provide preventive inoculation to the total population, ordered by legislation and available through public means if no private arrangements can be made.

* * *

Misleading Exceptionalism

A major pharmaceutical manufacturer, as an act of humanitarian concern, has distributed copies of a large poster warning "LEAD PAINT CAN KILL!" The poster, featuring a photograph of the face of a charming little girl, goes on to explain that if children *eat* lead paint, it can poison them, they can develop serious symptoms, suffer permanent brain damage, even die. The health department of a major American city has put out a coloring book that provides the same information. While the poster urges parents to prevent their children from eating paint, the coloring book is more vivid. It labels as neglectful and thoughtless the mother who does not keep her infant under constant surveillance to keep it from eating paint chips.

Now, no one would argue against the idea that it is important to spread knowledge about the danger of eating paint in order that parents might act to forestall their children from doing so. But to campaign against lead paint *only* in these terms is destructive and misleading and, in a sense, an effective way to support and agree with slum landlords — who define the problem of lead poisoning in precisely these terms.

This is an example of applying an exceptionalistic solution to a universalistic problem. It is not accurate to say that lead poisoning results from the actions of individual neglectful mothers. Rather, lead poisoning is a social phenomenon supported by a number of social mechanisms, one of the most tragic by-products of the systematic toleration of slum housing. In New Haven, which has the highest reported rate of lead poisoning in the country, several small children have died and many others have incurred irreparable brain damage as a result of eating peeling paint. In several cases, when the landlord failed to make repairs, poisonings have occurred time and again through a succession of tenancies. And the major reason for the landlord's neglect of this problem was that the city agency responsible for enforcing the housing code did nothing to make him correct this dangerous condition.

The cause of the poisoning is the lead in the paint on the walls of the apartment in which the children live. The presence of the lead is illegal. To use lead paint in a residence is illegal; to permit lead paint to be exposed in a residence is illegal. It is not only illegal, it is potentially criminal since the housing code does provide for criminal penalties. The general problem of lead poisoning, then, is more accurately analyzed as the result of a systematic program of lawbreaking by one interest group in the community, with the toleration and encouragement of the public authority charged with enforcing that law. To ignore these continued and repeated law violations, to ignore the fact that the supposed law enforcer actually cooperates in lawbreaking, and then to load a burden of guilt on the mother of a dead or dangerously ill child is an egregious distortion of reality. And to do so under the guise of public-spirited and humanitarian service to the community is intolerable.

But this is how Blaming the Victim works. The righteous humanitarian concern displayed by the drug company, with its poster, and the health department, with its coloring book, is a genuine concern, and this is a typical feature of Blaming the Victim. Also typical is the swerving away from the central target that requires systematic change and, instead, focusing in on the individual affected. The ultimate effect is always to distract attention from the basic causes and to leave the primary social injustice untouched. And, most telling, the proposed remedy for the problem is, of course, to work on the victim himself. Prescriptions for cure, as written by the Savage Discovery set, are invariably conceived to revamp and revise the victim, never to change the surrounding circumstances. They want to change his attitudes, alter his values, fill up his cultural deficits, energize his apathetic soul, cure his character defects, train him and polish him and woo him from his savage ways.

Isn't all of this more subtle and sophisticated than such old-fashioned ideologies as Social Darwinism? Doesn't the change from brutal ideas about survival of the fit (and the expiration of the unfit) to kindly concern about characterological defects (brought about by stigmas of social origin) seem like a substantial step forward? Hardly. It is only a substitution of terms. The old, reactionary exceptionalistic formulations are replaced by new progressive, humanitarian exceptionalistic formulations. In education, the outmoded and unacceptable concept of racial or class differences in basic inherited intellectual ability simply gives way to the new notion of cultural deprivation: there is very little functional difference between these two ideas. In taking a look at the phenomenon of poverty, the old concept of unfitness or idleness or laziness is replaced by the newfangled theory of the culture of poverty. In race relations, plain Negro inferiority — which was good enough for old-fashioned conservatives — is pushed aside by fancy conceits about the crumbling Negro family. With regard to illegitimacy, we are not so crass as to concern ourselves with immorality and vice, as in the old days; we settle benignly on the explanation of the "lower-class pattern of sexual behavior," which no one condemns as evil, but which is, in fact, simply a variation of the old explanatory idea. Mental illness is no longer defined as the result of hereditary taint or congenital character flaw; now we have new causal hypotheses regarding the ego-damaging emotional experiences that are supposed to be the inevitable consequence of the deplorable child-rearing practices of the poor.

In each case, of course, we are persuaded to ignore the obvious: the continued blatant discrimination against the Negro, the gross deprivation of contraceptive and adoption services to the poor, the heavy stresses endemic in the life of the poor. And almost all our make-believe liberal programs aimed at correcting our urban problems are off target; they are designed either to change the poor man or to cool him out.

Why Blame the Victim?

We come finally to the question, Why? It is much easier to understand the process of Blaming the Victim as a way of thinking than it is to understand the motivation for it. Why do Victim Blamers, who are usually good people, blame the victim? The development and application of this ideology, and of all the mythologies associated with Savage Discovery, are readily exposed by careful analysis as hostile acts — one is almost tempted to say acts of war — directed against the disadvantaged, the distressed, the disinherited. It is class warfare in reverse. Yet those who are most fascinated and enchanted by this ideology tend to be progressive, humanitarian, and, in the best sense of the word, charitable persons. They would usually define themselves as moderates or liberals. Why do they pursue this dreadful war against the poor and the oppressed?

Put briefly, the answer can be formulated best in psychological terms — or, at least, I, as a psychologist, am more comfortable with such a formulation. The highly charged psychological problem confronting this hypothetical progressive, charitable person I am talking about is that of reconciling his own self-interest with the promptings of his humanitarian impulses. This psychological process of reconciliation is not worked out in a logical, rational, conscious way; it is a process that takes place far below the level of sharp consciousness, and the solution — Blaming the Victim — is arrived at subconsciously as a compromise that apparently satisfies both his self-interest and his charitable concerns. Let me elaborate.

First, the question of self-interest or, more accurately, class interest. The typical Victim Blamer is a middle-class person who is doing reasonably well in a material way; he has a good job, a good income, a good house, a good car. Basically, he likes the social system pretty much the way it is, at least in broad outline. He likes the two-party political system, though he may be highly skilled in finding a thousand minor flaws in its functioning. He heartily approves of the profit motive as the propelling engine of the economic system despite his awareness that there are abuses of that system, negative side effects, and substantial residual inequalities.

On the other hand, he is acutely aware of poverty, racial discrimination, exploitation, and deprivation, and, moreover, he wants to do something concrete to ameliorate the condition of the poor, the black, and the disadvantaged. This is not an extraneous concern; it is central to his value system to insist on the worth of the individual, the equality of men, and the importance of justice.

What is to be done, then? What intellectual position can he take, and what line of action can he follow that will satisfy both of these important motivations? He quickly and self-consciously rejects two obvious alternatives, which he defines as "extremes." He cannot side with an openly reactionary, repressive position that accepts continued oppression and exploitation as the price of a privileged position for his own class. This is incompatible with his own morality and his basic political principles. He finds the extreme conservative position repugnant.

He is, if anything, more allergic to radicals, however, than he is to reactionaries. He rejects the "extreme" solution of radical social change, and this makes sense since such radical social change threatens his own well-being. A more equitable distribution of income might mean that he would have less — a smaller or older house, with fewer yews or no rhododendrons in the yard, a less enjoyable job, or, at the least, a somewhat smaller salary. If black children and poor children were, in fact, reasonably educated and began to get high SAT scores, they would be competing with *his* children for the scarce places in the entering classes of Harvard, Columbia, Bennington, and Antioch.

So our potential Victim Blamers are in a dilemma. In the words of an old Yiddish proverb, they are trying to dance at two weddings. They are old friends of both brides and fond of both kinds of dancing, and they want to accept both invitations. They cannot bring themselves to attack the system that has been so good to them, but they want so badly to be helpful to the victims of racism and economic injustice.

Their solution is a brilliant compromise. They turn their attention to the victim in his post-victimized state. They want to bind up wounds, inject penicillin, administer morphine, and evacuate the wounded for rehabilitation. They explain what's wrong with the victim in terms of social experiences *in the past*, experiences that have left wounds, defects, paralysis, and disability. And they take the cure of these wounds and the reduction of these disabilities as the first order of business. They want to make the victims less vulnerable, send them back into battle with better weapons, thicker armor, a higher level of morale.

In order to do so effectively, of course, they must analyze the victims carefully, dispassionately, objectively, scientifically, empathetically, mathematically, and hardheadedly, to see what made them so vulnerable in the first place.

What weapons, now, might they have lacked when they went into battle? Job skills? Education?

What armor was lacking that might have warded off their wounds? Better values? Habits of thrift and foresight?

And what might have ravaged their morale? Apathy? Ignorance? Deviant lower-class cultural patterns?

This is the solution of the dilemma, the solution of Blaming the Victim. And those who buy this solution with a sigh of relief are inevitably blinding themselves to the basic causes of the problems being addressed. They are, most crucially, rejecting the possibility of blaming, not the victims, but themselves. They are all unconsciously passing judgments on themselves and bringing in a unanimous verdict of Not Guilty.

If one comes to believe that the culture of poverty produces persons *fated* to be poor, who can find any fault with our corporation-dominated economy? And if the Negro family produces young men *incapable* of achieving equality, let's deal with that first before we go on to the task of changing the pervasive racism that informs and shapes and distorts our every social institution. And if unsatisfactory resolution of one's Oedipus complex accounts for all emotional distress and mental disorder, then by all means let us attend to that and postpone worrying about the pounding day-to-day stresses of life on the bottom rungs that drive so many to drink, dope, and madness.

That is the ideology of Blaming the Victim, the cunning Art of Savage Discovery. The tragic, frightening truth is that it is a mythology that is winning over the best people of our time, the very people who must resist this ideological temptation if we are to achieve nonviolent change in America.

Notes

1. Karl Mannheim, *Ideology and Utopia,* trans. Louis Wirth and Edward Shils (New York: Harcourt, Brace & World, 1936). First published in German in 1929.
2. John Seeley, "The Problem of Social Problems," *Indian Sociological Bulletin, 2,* no. 3 (April 1965). Reprinted as Chapter 10 in *The Americanization of the Unconscious* (New York: International Science Press, 1967), pp. 142–128.
3. C. Wright Mills, "The Professional Ideology of Social Pathologists," *American Journal of Sociology* 49, no. 2 (September 1943): 165–181.
4. William Ryan, "Community Care in Historical Perspective: Implications for Mental Health Services and Professionals," *Canada's Mental Health,* supplement no. 60, March–April 1969. This formulation draws on, and is developed from, the *residual–institutional* dimension outlined in H. L. Wilensky and C. N. Lebeaux, *Industrial Society and Social Welfare* (paperback ed.: New York: Free Press, 1965). Originally published by Russell Sage Foundation, 1958.

Part II

Some Problems of Advanced Industrial Societies

2

Education for What?

The main functions of education are to transmit cultural patterns and values to the younger generation and to help perpetuate the existing social structure. The American educational system performs these functions well. From preschool through graduate school, the central values of the capitalist system are perpetuated through the curriculum and through the very structure of the educational institutions themselves. Liberal critics, pointing to the "underachievement" of inner-city high school graduates, say the system is not working well and needs reform. Radical critics, such as those represented in the two articles in this chapter, maintain that the system works only too well to perpetuate existing social and economic inequalities.

The implicit functions of education are more important than any explicit curriculum. The vital subjects in the schools are not spelling, arithmetic, or social studies but the ways of the capitalist-dominated culture and the perpetuation of the social order. The very origin of the term *curriculum* — from the Latin, meaning "race track" — indicates what schooling is really about in America. Students are taught to compete. They learn that one person can succeed only at the cost of another, and that life is a race where those who do well in school will be rewarded by being allowed to move into the more privileged positions in the society.

Educational institutions in America, according to Samuel Bowles, Herbert Gintis, and Peter Meyer, prepare youth to take their places in a bureaucratic system of alienated work with highly specialized and fragmented jobs, hierarchical authority, and inequalities of pay. The schools instill in the young a belief in the validity of the hierarchical division of labor and of meritocratic job assignment according to how well they perform on "objective" tests.

50

Thus, education perpetuates economic inequality and prepares the young for future job roles in the capitalist system. It does so by "legitimizing the allocation of individuals to economic positions on the basis of ostensibly objective merit." In fact, as these authors show, the intergenerational transmission of social and economic status has little relationship to the kind of cognitive merit rewarded by the educational system. When the effects of parents' social class are held constant, intelligence quotient (IQ) has little relationship with their children's economic success.

Illich likewise questions the validity of the technocratic–meritocratic ethos of the existing educational system. He looks forward to a classless society, based on participatory politics, in which technical knowledge is widely shared. This can happen, he says, only through a radical "deschooling" of society, since schools are based on false assumptions. Illich points to a "hidden curriculum"—the assumptions that the young can be prepared for adulthood in society only by going to schools and consuming knowledge as a commodity under the authority of certified teachers, that learning about the world is better than learning from the world, that what is not taught in school is of little importance. This hidden curriculum helps maintain the existing social system by instilling in the young the values and attitudes necessary for them to fit into the society as it is currently constituted.

One alternative to traditional schooling is the free school, where there are no grades or compulsory classes, and where children and adults treat one another as equals. At their best, such schools are communities where young children acquire learning naturally, in a protected environment that allows them to grow at their own pace. Even free schools, Illich warns, may incorporate much of what they profess to reject. Teachers who have grown up in an unfree society find it difficult to break away from its hidden assumptions and often unconsciously perpetuate the old system in a new guise.

Illich envisages a decentralized, postindustrial society where knowledge is communicated from adults to children and between one another in everyday activities instead of in schools. He says we must deprofessionalize education and rid ourselves of the superstition that only those with the proper credentials can teach. Further, we must extend the same principle to other fields so that all men and women learn a variety of trades and skills formerly the exclusive possession of specialists and technicians. We must build simple tools and machines so that ordinary persons can repair them. We must share medical knowledge so that we can keep our bodies healthy without having to rely on doctors. Illich does not, however, discuss the problem of how to bring about such a society. This topic is dealt with in later sections of the present anthology.

The Alternative to Schooling

Ivan Illich

For generations we have tried to make the world a better place by providing more and more schooling, but so far the endeavor has failed. What we have learned instead is that forcing all children to climb an open-ended education ladder cannot enhance equality but must favor the individual who starts out earlier, healthier, or better prepared; that enforced instruction deadens for most people the will for independent learning; and that knowledge treated as a commodity, delivered in packages, and accepted as private property once it is acquired, must always be scarce.

In response, critics of the educational system are now proposing strong and unorthodox remedies that range from the voucher plan, which would enable each person to buy the education of his choice on an open market, to shifting the responsibility for education from the school to the media and to apprenticeship on the job. Some individuals foresee that the school will have to be disestablished just as the church was disestablished all over the world during the last two centuries. Other reformers propose to replace the universal school with various new systems that would, they claim, better prepare everybody for life in modern society. These proposals for new educational institutions fall into three broad categories: the reformation of the classroom within the school system; the dispersal of free schools throughout society; and the transformation of all society into one huge classroom. But these three approaches — the reformed classroom, the free school, and the worldwide classroom — represent three stages in a proposed escalation of education in which each step threatens more subtle and more pervasive school control than the one it replaces.

I believe that the disestablishment of the school has become inevitable and that this end of an illusion should fill us with hope. But I also believe that the end of the "age of schooling" could usher in the epoch of the global

FROM *Saturday Review* (June 19, 1971), © 1971 Saturday Review, Inc. Reprinted by permission.

schoolhouse that would be distinguishable only in name from a global madhouse or global prison in which education, correction, and adjustment become synonymous. I therefore believe that the breakdown of the school forces us to look beyond its imminent demise and to face fundamental alternatives in education. Either we can work for fearsome and potent new educational devices that teach about a world which progressively becomes more opaque and forbidding for man, or we can set the conditions for a new era in which technology would be used to make society more simple and transparent, so that all men can once again know the facts and use the tools that shape their lives. In short, we can disestablish schools or we can deschool culture.

In order to see clearly the alternatives we face, we must first distinguish education from schooling, which means separating the humanistic intent of the teacher from the impact of the invariant structure of the school. This hidden structure constitutes a course of instruction that stays forever beyond the control of the teacher or of his school board. It conveys indelibly the message that only through schooling can an individual prepare himself for adulthood in society, that what is not taught in school is of little value, and that what is learned outside of school is not worth knowing. I call it the hidden curriculum of schooling, because it constitutes the unalterable framework of the system, within which all changes in the curriculum are made.

The hidden curriculum is always the same regardless of school or place. It requires all children of a certain age to assemble in groups of about 30, under the authority of a certified teacher, for some 500 to 1000 or more hours each year. It doesn't matter whether the curriculum is designed to teach the principles of fascism, liberalism, Catholicism, or socialism; or whether the purpose of the school is to produce Soviet or United States citizens, mechanics, or doctors. It makes no difference whether the teacher is authoritarian or permissive, whether he imposes his own creed or teaches students to think for themselves. What is important is that students learn that education is valuable when it is acquired in the school through a graded process of consumption; that the degree of success the individual will enjoy in society depends on the amount of learning he consumes; and that learning *about* the world is more valuable from learning *from* the world.

It must be clearly understood that the hidden curriculum translates learning from an activity into a commodity — for which the school monopolizes the market. In all countries knowledge is regarded as the first necessity for survival, but also as a form of currency more liquid than rubles or dollars.

We have become accustomed, through Karl Marx's writings, to speak about the alienation of the worker from his work in a class society. We must now recognize the estrangement of man from his learning when it becomes the product of a service profession and he becomes the consumer.

The more learning an individual consumes, the more "knowledge stock" he acquires. The hidden curriculum therefore defines a new class structure for society within which the large consumers of knowledge — those who have acquired large quantities of knowledge stock — enjoy special privileges, high income, and access to the more powerful tools of production. This kind of knowledge-capitalism has been accepted in all industrialized societies and establishes a rationale for the distribution of jobs and income. (This point is especially important in the light of the lack of correspondence between schooling and occupational competence established in studies such as Ivar Berg's *Education and Jobs: The Great Training Robbery.*)

The endeavor to put all men through successive stages of enlightenment is rooted deeply in alchemy, the Great Art of the waning Middle Ages. John Amos Comenius, a Moravian bishop, self-styled Pansophist, and pedagogue, is rightly considered one of the founders of the modern schools. He was among the first to propose 7 or 12 grades of compulsory learning. In his *Magna Didactica,* he described schools as devices to "teach everybody everything" and outlined a blueprint for the assembly-line production of knowledge, which according to his method would make education cheaper and better and make growth into full humanity possible for all. But Comenius was not only an early efficiency expert, he was an alchemist who adopted the technical language of his craft to describe the art of rearing children. The alchemist sought to refine base elements by leading their distilled spirits through 12 stages of successive enlightenment, so that for their own and all the world's benefit they might be transmuted into gold. Of course, alchemists failed no matter how often they tried, but each time their "science" yielded new reasons for their failure, and they tried again.

Pedagogy opened a new chapter in the history of Ars Magna. Education became the search for an alchemic process that would bring forth a new type of man, who would fit into an environment created by scientific magic. But, no matter how much each generation spent on its schools, it always turned out that the majority of people were unfit for enlightenment by this process and had to be discarded as unprepared for life in a man-made world.

Educational reformers who accept the idea that schools have failed fall into three groups. The most respectable are certainly the great masters of alchemy who promise better schools. The most seductive are popular magicians, who promise to make every kitchen into an alchemic lab. The most sinister are the new Masons of the Universe, who want to transform the entire world into one huge temple of learning. Notable among today's masters of alchemy are certain research directors employed or sponsored by the large foundations who believe that schools, if they could somehow be improved, could also become economically more feasible than those that are now in trouble, and simultaneously could sell a larger package of services. Those who are concerned primarily with the curriculum claim that it is outdated or irrelevant. So the curriculum is filled with new packaged courses on African Culture, North American Imperalism, Women's Lib, Pollution, or the Consumer Society. Passive learning is wrong—it is indeed—so we graciously allow students to decide what and how they want to be taught. Schools are prison houses. Therefore, principals are authorized to approve teach-outs, moving the school desks to a roped-off Harlem street. Sensitivity training becomes fashionable. So, we import group therapy into the classroom. School, which was supposed to teach everybody everything, now becomes all things to all children.

Other critics emphasize that schools make inefficient use of modern science. Some would administer drugs to make it easier for the instructor to change the child's behavior. Others would transform school into a stadium for educational gaming. Still others would electrify the classroom. If they are simplistic disciples of McLuhan, they replace blackboards and textbooks with multimedia happenings; if they follow Skinner, they claim to be able to modify behavior more efficiently than old-fashioned classroom practitioners can.

Most of these changes have, of course, some good effects. The experimental schools have fewer truants. Parents do have a greater feeling of participation in a decentralized district. Pupils, assigned by their teacher to an apprenticeship, do often turn out more competent than those who stay in the classroom. Some children do improve their knowledge of Spanish in the language lab because they prefer playing with the knobs of a tape recorder to conversations with their Puerto Rican peers. Yet all these improvements operate within predictably narrow limits, since they leave the hidden curriculum of school intact.

Some reformers would like to shake loose from the hidden curriculum, but they rarely succeed. Free schools that lead to further free schools produce a mirage of freedom, even though the chain of attendance is frequently interrupted by long stretches of loafing. Attendance through seduction inculcates the need for educational treatment more persuasively than the reluctant attendance enforced by a truant officer. Permissive teachers in a padded classroom can easily render their pupils impotent to survive once they leave.

Learning in these schools often remains nothing more than the acquisition of socially valued skills defined, in this instance, by the consensus of a commune rather than by the decree of a school board. New presbyter is but old priest writ large.

Free schools, to be truly free, must meet two conditions: First, they must be run in a way to prevent the reintroduction of the hidden curriculum of graded attendance and certified students studying at the feet of certified teachers. And, more importantly, they must provide a framework in which all participants—staff and pupils—can free themselves from the hidden foundations of a schooled society. The first condition is frequently incorporated in the stated aims of a free school. The second condition is only rarely recognized, and is difficult to state as the goal of a free school.

It is useful to distinguish between the hidden curriculum, which I have described, and the occult foundations of schooling. The hidden curriculum is a ritual that can be considered the official initiation into modern society, institutionally established through the school. It is the purpose of this ritual to hide from its participants the contradictions between the myth of an egalitarian society and the class-conscious reality it certifies. Once they are recognized as such, rituals lose their power, and this is what is now beginning to happen to schooling. But there are certain fundamental assumptions about growing up—the occult foundations—which now find their expression in the ceremonial of schooling, and which could easily be reinforced by what free schools do.

Among these assumptions is what Peter Schrag calls the "immigration syndrome," which impels us to treat all people as if they were newcomers who must go through a naturalization process. Only certified consumers of knowledge are admitted to citizenship. Men are not born equal, but are made equal through gestation by Alma Mater.

The rhetoric of all schools states that they form a man for the future, but they do not release him for his task before he has developed a high level of tolerance to the ways of his elders: education *for* life rather than *in* everyday life. Few free schools can avoid doing precisely this. Nevertheless they are among the most important centers from which a new lifestyle radiates, not because of the effect their graduates will have but, rather, because elders who choose to bring up their children without the benefit of properly ordained teachers frequently belong to a radical minority and because their preoccupation with the rearing of their children sustains them in their new style.

The most dangerous category of educational reformer is one who argues that knowledge can be produced and sold much more effectively on an open market than on one controlled by school. These people argue that most skills can be easily acquired from skill-models if the learner is truly interested in their acquisition; that individual entitlements can provide a more equal purchasing power for education. They demand a careful separation of the process by which knowledge is acquired from the process by which it is measured and certified. These seem to me obvious statements. But it would be a fallacy to believe that the establishment of a free market for knowledge would constitute a radical alternative in education.

The establishment of a free market could indeed abolish what I have previously called the hidden curriculum of present schooling—its age-specific attendance at a graded curriculum. Equally, a free market would at first give the appearance of counteracting what I have called the occult foundations of a schooled society: the "immigration syndrome," the institutional monopoly of teaching, and the ritual of linear initiation. But at the same time a free market in education would provide the alchemist with innumerable hidden hands to fit each man into the multiple, tight little niches a more complex technocracy can provide.

Many decades of reliance on schooling have turned knowledge into a commodity, a marketable staple of a special kind. Knowledge is now regarded simultaneously as a first necessity and also as society's most precious currency. (The transformation of knowledge into a commodity is reflected in a corresponding transformation of language. Words that formerly functioned as verbs are becoming nouns that designate possessions. Until recently dwelling and learning and even healing designated activities. They are now usually conceived as commodities or services to be delivered. We talk about the manufacture of housing or the delivery of medical care. Men are no longer regarded fit to house or heal themselves. In such a society people come to believe that professional services are more valuable than personal care. Instead of learning how to nurse grandmother, the teenager learns to picket the hospital that does not admit her.) This attitude could easily survive the disestablishment of school, just as affiliation with a church remained a condition for office long after the adoption of the First Amendment. It is even more evident that test batteries measuring complex knowledge-packages could easily survive the disestablishment of school—and with this would go the compulsion to obligate everybody to acquire a minimum package in the knowledge stock. The scientific measurement of each man's worth and the alchemic dream of each man's "educability to his full humanity" would finally coincide. Under the appearance of a "free" market, the global village would turn into an environmental womb where pedagogic therapists control the complex navel by which each man is nourished.

At present schools limit the teacher's competence to the classroom. They prevent him from claiming man's whole life as his domain. The demise of school will remove this restriction and give a semblance of legitimacy to the life-long pedagogical invasion of everybody's privacy. It will open the way for a scramble for "knowledge" on a free market, which would lead us toward the paradox of a vulgar, albeit seemingly egalitarian, meritocracy. Unless the concept of knowledge is transformed, the disestablishment of school will lead to a wedding between a growing meritocratic system that separates learning from certification and a society committed to provide therapy for each man until he is ripe for the gilded age.

For those who subscribe to the technocratic ethos, whatever is technically possible must be made available at least to a few whether they want it or not. Neither the privation nor the frustration of the majority counts. If cobalt treatment is possible, then the city of Tegucigalpa needs one apparatus in each of its two major hospitals, at a cost that would free an important part of the population of Honduras from parasites. If supersonic speeds are possible, then it must speed the travel of some. If the flight to Mars can be conceived, then a rationale must be found to make it appear a necessity. In the technocratic ethos poverty is modernized: Not only are old alternatives closed off by new monopolies, but the lack of necessities is also compounded by a growing spread between those services that are technologically feasible and those that are in fact available to the majority.

A teacher turns "educator" when he adopts this technocratic ethos. He then acts as if education were a technological enterprise designed to make man fit into whatever environment the "progress" of science creates. He seems blind to the evidence that constant obsolescence of all commodities comes at a high price: the mounting cost of training people to know about them. He seems to forget that the rising cost of tools is purchased at a high price in education: They decrease the labor intensity of the economy, make learning on the job impossible or, at best, a privilege for a few. All over the world the cost of educating men for society rises faster than the productivity of the entire economy, and fewer people have a sense of intelligent participation in the commonweal.

A revolution against those forms of privilege and power which are based on claims to professional knowledge must start with a transformation of consciousness about the nature of learning. This means, above all, a shift of responsibility for teaching and learning. Knowledge can be defined as a commodity only as long as it is viewed as the result of institutional enterprise or as the fulfillment of institutional objectives. Only when a man recovers the sense of personal responsibility for what he learns and teaches can this spell be broken and the alienation of learning from living be overcome.

The recovery of the power to learn or to teach means that the teacher who takes the risk of interfering in somebody else's private affairs also assumes responsibility for the results. Similarly, the student who exposes himself to the influence of a teacher must take responsibility for his own education. For such purposes educational institutions—if they are at all needed—ideally take the form of facility centers where one can get a roof of the right size over his head, access to a piano or a kiln, and to records, books, or slides. Schools, TV stations, theaters, and the like are designed primarily for use by professionals. Deschooling society means above all the denial of professional status for the second-oldest profession, namely teaching. The certification of teachers now constitutes an undue restriction of the right to free speech: the corporate structure and professional pretensions of journalism an undue restriction on the right to a free press. Compulsory attendance rules interfere with free assembly. The deschooling of society is nothing less than a cultural mutation by which a people recovers the effective use of its constitutional freedoms: learning and teaching by men who know that they are born free rather than treated to freedom. Most people learn most of the time when they do whatever they enjoy; most people are curious and want to give meaning to whatever they come in contact with; and most people are capable of personal intimate intercourse with others unless they are stupefied by inhuman work or turned off by schooling.

The fact that people in rich countries do not learn much on their own constitutes no proof to the contrary. Rather it is a consequence of life in an environment from which, paradoxically, they cannot learn much, precisely because it is so highly programed. They are constantly frustrated by the structure of contemporary society in which the facts on which decisions can be made have become elusive. They live in an environment in which tools that can be used for creative purposes have become luxuries, an environment in which channels of communication serve a few to talk to many.

A modern myth would make us believe that the sense of impotence with which most men live today is a consequence of technology that cannot but create huge systems. But it is not technology that makes systems huge, tools immensely powerful, channels of communication one-directional. Quite the contrary: Properly controlled, technology could provide each man with the ability to understand his environment better, to shape it powerfully with his own hands, and to permit him full intercommunication to a degree never before possible. Such an alternative use of technology constitutes the central alternative in education.

If a person is to grow up he needs, first of all, access to things, to places and to processes, to events and to records. He needs to see, to touch, to tinker with, to grasp whatever there is in a meaningful setting. This access is now largely denied. When knowledge became a commodity, it acquired the protections of private property, and thus a principle designed to guard personal intimacy became a rationale for declaring facts off limits for people without the proper credentials. In schools teachers keep knowledge to themselves unless it fits into the day's program. The media inform, but exclude those things they regard as unfit to print. Information is locked into special languages, and specialized teachers live off its retranslation. Patents are protected by corporations, secrets are guarded by bureaucracies, and the power to keep others out of private preserves — be they cockpits, law offices, junkyards, or clinics — is jealously guarded by professions, institutions, and nations. Neither the political nor the professional structure of our societies, East and West, could withstand the elimination of the power to keep entire classes of people from facts that could serve them. The access to facts that I advocate goes far beyond truth in labeling. Access must be built into reality, while all we ask from advertising is a guarantee that it does not mislead. Access to reality constitutes a fundamental alternative in education to a system that only purports to teach *about* it.

Abolishing the right to corporate secrecy — even when professional opinion holds that this secrecy serves the common good — is, as shall presently appear, a much more radical political goal than the traditional demand for public ownership or control of the tools of production. The socialization of tools without the effective socialization of know-how in their use tends to put the knowledge-capitalist into the position formerly held by the financier. The technocrat's only claim to power is the stock he holds in some class of scarce and secret knowledge, and the best means to protect its value is a large and capital-intensive organization that renders access to know-how formidable and forbidding.

It does not take much time for the interested learner to acquire almost any skill that he wants to use. We tend to forget this in a society where professional teachers monopolize entrance into all fields, and thereby stamp teaching by uncertified individuals as quackery. There are few mechanical skills used in industry or research that are as demanding, complex, and dangerous as driving cars, a skill that most people quickly acquire from a peer. Not all people are suited for advanced logic, yet those who are make rapid progress if they are challenged to play mathematical games at an early age. One out of 20 kids in Cuernavaca can beat me at Wiff 'n' Proof after a couple of weeks' training. In four months all but a small percentage of motivated adults at our CIDOC center learn Spanish well enough to conduct academic business in the new language.

A first step toward opening up access to skills would be to provide various incentives for skilled individuals to share their knowledge. Inevitably, this would run counter to the interest of guilds and professions and unions. Yet, multiple apprenticeship is attractive. It provides everybody with an opportunity to learn something about almost anything. There is no reason why a person should not combine the ability to drive a car, repair telephones and toilets, act as a midwife, and function as an architectural draftsman. Special-interest groups and their disciplined consumers would, of course, claim that the public needs the protection of a professional guarantee. But this argument is now steadily being challenged by consumer protection associations. We have to take much more seriously the objection that economists raise to the radical socialization of skills: that "progress" will be impeded if knowledge—patents, skills, and all the rest—is democratized. Their argument can be faced only if we demonstrate to them the growth rate of futile diseconomies generated by any existing educational system.

Access to people willing to share their skills is no guarantee of learning. Such access is restricted not only by the monopoly of educational programs over learning and of unions over licensing but also by a technology of scarcity. The skills that count today are know-how in the use of highly specialized tools that were designed to be scarce. These tools produce goods or render services that everybody wants but only a few can enjoy, and which only a limited number of people know how to use. Only a few privileged individuals out of the total number of people who have a given disease ever benefit from the results of sophisticated medical technology, and even fewer doctors develop the skill to use it.

The same results of medical research have, however, also been employed to create a basic tool kit that permits Army and Navy medics, with only a few months of training, to obtain results, under battlefield conditions, that would have been beyond the expectations of full-fledged doctors during World War II. On an even simpler level any peasant girl could learn how to diagnose and treat most infections if medical scientists prepared dosages and instructions specifically for a given geographic area.

All these examples illustrate the fact that educational considerations alone suffice to demand a radical reduction of the professional structure that now impedes the mutual relationship between the scientist and the majority of people who want access to science. If this demand were heeded, all men could learn to use yesterday's tools, rendered more effective and durable by modern science, to create tomorrow's world.

Unfortunately, precisely the contrary trend prevails at present. I know a coastal area in South America where most people support themselves by fishing from small boats. The outboard motor is certainly the tool that has changed most dramatically the lives of these coastal fishermen. But in the area I have surveyed, half of all outboard motors that were purchased between 1945 and 1950 are still kept running by constant tinkering, while half the motors purchased in 1965 no longer run because they were not built to be repaired. Technological progress provides the majority of people with gadgets they cannot afford and deprives them of the simpler tools they need.

Metals, plastics, and ferro cement used in buildings have greatly improved since the 1940s and ought to provide more people the opportunity to create their own homes. But while in the United States, in 1948, more than 30 percent of all one-family homes were owner-built, by the end of the 1960s the percentage of those who acted as their own contractors had dropped to less than 20 percent.

The lowering of the skill level through so-called economic development becomes even more visible in Latin America. Here most people still build their own homes from floor to roof. Often they use mud, in the form of adobe, and thatchwork of unsurpassed utility in the moist, hot, and windy climate. In other places they make their dwellings out of cardboard, oildrums, and other industrial refuse. Instead of providing people with simple tools and highly standardized, durable, and easily repaired components, all governments have gone in for the mass production of low-cost buildings.

It is clear that not one single country can afford to provide satisfactory modern dwelling units for the majority of its people. Yet, everywhere this policy makes it progressively more difficult for the majority to acquire the knowledge and skills they need to build better houses for themselves.

Educational considerations permit us to formulate a second fundamental characteristic that any post-industrial society must possess: a basic tool kit that by its very nature counteracts technocratic control. For educational reasons we must work toward a society in which scientific knowledge is incorporated in tools and components that can be used meaningfully in units small enough to be within the reach of all. Only such tools can socialize access to skills. Only such tools favor temporary associations among those who want to use them for a specific occasion. Only such tools allow specific goals to emerge in the process of their use, as any tinkerer knows. Only the combination of guaranteed access to facts and of limited power in most tools renders it possible to envisage a subsistence economy capable of incorporating the fruits of modern science.

The development of such a scientific subsistence economy is unquestionably to the advantage of the overwhelming majority of all people in poor countries. It is also the only alternative to progressive pollution, exploitation, and opaqueness in rich countries. But, as we have seen, the dethroning of the GNP cannot be achieved without simultaneously subverting GNE (Gross National Education—usually conceived of as manpower capitalization). An egalitarian economy cannot exist in a society in which the right to produce is conferred by schools.

The feasibility of a modern subsistence economy does not depend on new scientific inventions. In depends primarily on the ability of a society to agree on fundamental, self-chosen anti-bureaucratic and anti-technocratic restraints.

These restraints can take many forms, but they will not work unless they touch the basic dimensions of life. (The decision of Congress against development of the supersonic transport plane is one of the most encouraging steps in the right direction.) The substance of these voluntary social restraints would be very simple matters that can be fully understood and judged by any prudent man.

* * *

All such restraints would be chosen to promote stable and equal enjoyment of scientific know-how. The French say that it takes a thousand years to educate a peasant to deal with a cow. It would not take two generations to help all people in Latin America or Africa to use and repair outboard motors, simple cars, pumps, medicine kits, and ferro cement machines if their design does not change every few years. And since a joyful life is one of constant meaningful intercourse with others in a meaningful environment, equal enjoyment does translate into equal education.

At present a consensus on austerity is difficult to imagine. The reason usually given for the impotence of the majority is stated in terms of political or economic class. What is not usually understood is that the new class structure of a schooled society is even more powerfully controlled by vested interests. No doubt an imperialist and capitalist organization of society provides the social structure within which a minority can have disproportionate influence over the effective opinion of the majority. But in a technocratic society the power of a minority of knowledge capitalists can prevent the formation of true public opinion through control of scientific know-how and the media of communication. Constitutional guarantees of free speech, free press, and free assembly were meant to ensure government by the people. Modern electronics, photo-offset presses, time-sharing computers, and telephones have in principle provided the hardware that could give an entirely new meaning to these freedoms. Unfortunately, these things are used in modern media to increase the power of knowledge-bankers to funnel their program-packages through international chains to more people, instead of being used to increase true networks that provide equal opportunity for encounter among the members of the majority.

Deschooling the culture and social structure requires the use of technology to make participatory politics possible. Only on the basis of a majority coalition can limits to secrecy and growing power be determined without dictatorship. We need a new environment in which growing up can be classless, or we will get a brave new world in which Big Brother educates us all.

Education, IQ, and the Legitimation of the Social Division of Labor

*Samuel Bowles, Herbert Gintis,
and Peter Meyer*

I. Education, Meritocracy, and the Legitimation of Inequality

Throughout history, patterns of privilege have been justified by elaborate ideological superstructures. Dominant classes desirous of a stable social order have consistently nurtured these ideologies, blocking the emergence of alternatives insofar as their power permitted. In U.S. capitalism, this ideology has been intimately bound with the twin concepts of technocracy and meritocracy.

Several related aspects of the social relations of production are legitimized in parts by the technocratic ideology. To begin, there are the overall characteristics of work in advanced U.S. capitalism: bureaucratic organization, hierarchical lines of authority, job fragmentation, and unequal pay. It is essential that the individual accept, and indeed come to see as natural, these undemocratic and unequal realities of the workaday world. Moreover, the staffing of these positions must appear egalitarian in process and just in outcome, in accordance with the formal principle of "equality for all before the law" in a liberal democracy.

While these twin concepts refer to the legitimation of capitalism as a social system, they have their counterpart in the individual's personal life. Not only must individuals come to accept the overall social relations of production, but must also respect the authority and competence of their own "supervisors," and justify their own authority over others. That workers be resigned to their position in production is imperative, that they be reconciled is preferable.

The hallmark of the technocratic perspective is its reduction of a complex web of social relations in production to a few rules of technological efficacy. In this view the hierarchical division of labor arises from its superior capacity to coordinate collective activity and nurture expertise.

FROM *Berkeley Journal of Sociology* 20 (1975–1976): 236–264. This paper is adapted from Bowles and Gintis, *Schooling in Capitalist America: Educational Reform and the Contradictions of Economic Life* (Basic Books, 1975). The authors would like to acknowledge the Ford Foundation for the financial support in conducting the research on which this is based.

To motivate the most able individuals to undertake the necessary training and preparation for high level occupational roles, salaries and status must be closely associated with level in the work hierarchy. Thus Davis and Moore, in their highly influential "functional theory of stratification," locate the "determinants of differential reward" in "differential functional importance" and "differential scarcity of personnel." "Social inequality," they conclude, "is thus an unconsciously evolved device by which societies insure that the most important positions are conscientiously filled by the most qualified persons."[1]

The technocratic–meritocratic ideology not only fails to explain the logic of capitalism, but is in direct conflict with a significant body of empirical data. Nevertheless, it has remained a constant theme of mainstream social science since the rise of the factory system in the United States. In 1919, Henry Goddard, eminent contributor to the "new science of mental levels" could assuage the conscience of his Princeton University audience by noting:

> . . . the fact is, [a] workman may have a ten year intelligence while you have a twenty. To demand of him such a home as you enjoy is as absurd as to insist that every laborer should receive a graduate fellowship. How can there be such a thing as social equality with this wide range of mental capacity?[2]

More than 50 years later, Richard Herrnstein can still satisfy his *Atlantic Monthly* audience with a simple variation on the theme:

> If virtually anyone is smart enough to be a ditch digger, and only half the people are smart enough to be engineers, then society is, in effect, husbanding its intellectual resources by holding engineers in greater esteem and paying them more.[3]

The robustness of this perspective (even those who reject it have nagging doubts) is due in no small part to its incorporation in major social institutions — factories, offices, government bureaus and schools. For this technocratic justification of the hierarchical division of labor leads smoothly to a meritocratic view of the process of matching individuals to jobs. An efficient and impersonal bureaucracy assesses the individual purely in terms of his or her expected contribution to production. The main determinants of job fitness are seen as those cognitive and psycho-motor capacities relevant to the worker's technical ability to do the job. The technocratic view of production and the meritocratic view of job assignment yield an important corollary which, while widely accepted, is empirically incorrect: namely that there is always a strong tendency of a capitalist economy to abjure caste, class, sex, color and ethnic origins in occupational placement.

* * *

The relation between U.S. education and the meritocratic ideology is intimate. First, the distribution of rewards by the school is seen as being primarily oriented toward the cognitive achievement, and is therefore fair.[4] Second, schools are seen as being primarily oriented toward the development of cognitive skills. Third, higher levels of schooling are seen as perhaps the strongest determinant of economic success. It is concluded that cognitive skills, which are seen as a major determinant of success, are developed in fair and open competition in school. Given the organization and stated objectives of schools it is easy to see how people would come to accept this. We shall show that it is largely without empirical support.

The linking of technical skills to economic success indirectly via the educational system strengthens the legitimation process. First, the day-to-day contact of parents and children with the competitive, cognitively oriented school environment buttresses in a very immediate and systematic way the technocratic perspective on economic organization. Second, by rendering the outcome (educational attainment) dependent not only on ability but also on motivation, drive to achieve, perseverance, and sacrifice, the status allocation mechanism acquires heightened legitimacy. Furthermore, personal attributes are tested and developed over a long period of time, enhancing the apparent objectivity and achievement orientation of the stratification system. Third, by gradually "cooling out" individuals at different educational levels, the student's aspirations are relatively painlessly brought into line with his probable career opportunities. By the time most students terminate schooling they have validated for themselves their inability or unwillingness to be a success at the next highest level. Through competition, success, and defeat in the classroom, students are reconciled to their social positions.

The "objective" educational system has etched the meritocratic perspective deeply into both popular culture and social science "methodology." In no case is this more clear than in the recent controversy over "open admissions" in colleges and universities. Open enrollment has been called on by militant minority groups to counteract the impediments of discrimination and poor secondary education.[5] Commentators have almost uniformly deemed the admissions of students to higher education irrespective to IQ, test scores, or grades as counter to efficiency and economic rationality.[6] Should not the most "able" be granted the right to further educational resources, since they will be the most capable of benefiting themselves and society? So goes the argument. But if social efficiency is the objective, the justification for a "meritocratic" admissions policy must rest on the assertion that "smart" people *benefit more* from college than those with lower test scores or grades. Stated more technically, the return to higher education, namely its impact on the individual's cognitive capacities, or productivity, must be positively related to prior test scores: the higher the test score the greater the expected return.

In a study exploring the cognitive "value added" in higher education, Alexander Astin, Director of the American Council on Education, found that there is no evidence that "smart" high school seniors learn "more" in college despite the fact that they tend to go to "better" institutions.[7] But the more important question for our purposes is the way in which test scores affect the economic productivity of education, and particularly of the predominant contemporary "sorting mechanism," higher education. The fact that throughout U.S. history people have simply assumed the economic rationality of sorting by IQ and test scores in education speaks highly for the persuasiveness of the meritocratic ideology. Yet available evidence by no means substantiates this view. For instance, we turn to the excellent study of Daniel C. Rogers,[8] who investigated the lifetime earnings of 1827 males who were in the eighth or ninth grades in 1935, in various cities of Connecticut and Massachusetts, and who took an IQ test in that year. Rogers found that the economic return to a year of schooling is the same *at all levels of IQ*. Thus at least from an economic point of view, higher education benefits all "ability levels" fairly equally, so the usual justification for selective enrollment is quite dubious.

We do not propose to justify open admissions on grounds of pure economics or social efficiency. Rather, we wish to emphasize that the "meritocratic orientation" of higher education, far from serving "economic rationality," is actually a facade facilitating the stratification of the labor force. Open admissions threatens this legitimation mechanism by rendering school success a relatively weaker factor in the opportunity to obtain higher education.

Experience with open enrollment also seems to support our assertion that the ostensible meritocratic and objective nature of selective admissions serves mainly the reproduction of the labor force through stratification. The City College of New York, which began an extensive program of open enrollment in 1970, asked Alexander W. Astin and his associates at the American Council on Education to evaluate its first year of operation. They found that regular and open enrollment students improved their test scores at the same rate, and there was no evidence that academic standards were lower in the first year. Of course, the test scores of open enrollment students were initially lower than those of regulars (by the end of the freshman year the test scores of open enrollment students had attained the level of entering regular students). Nonetheless, while 50 percent of the open enrollment students progressed at the normal rate, the proportion of regular students who did so were only slightly higher than 60 percent. In their interim report, Astin and Rossman conclude:

> Whether a student was regularly admitted or was an open-admissions student proved relatively unimportant in predicting his or her success in the first year. Although the two groups did indeed differ in many ways, it is clear that open-admissions students brought a number of personal characteristics besides past achievements that proved to be important for college.[9]

In sum, we are confident in our assertion that the ostensibly objective and meritocratic selection and reward system of U.S. education serves not some abstract notion of efficiency, rationality, and equity, but to the legitimization of economic inequality and the smooth staffing of hierarchically ordered work roles. All societies reward individual excellences. Which ones they reward, to what extent, and through what social process, however, is intimately tied to the social relations of economic life. When these social relations are autocratic, hierarchical and alienated, this fact cannot but be reflected in the oppressive and inegalitarian reward system — whence the record of U.S. education. Egalitarian and cooperative education is thus consistent only with a transformation of the economic system itself.

II. Education, Income, and Cognitive Attainment

Why does education increase people's income? The traditional explanation — which we have labeled the technocratic–meritocratic perspective

—presents a simple and compelling picture. Earnings reflect economic productivity. In a technologically advanced society, an individual's economic productivity depends partly on the level of cognitive skills he or she has attained. Each year of education increases cognitive skill levels, thus indirectly leading to higher income.

Were this view correct, our heavy emphasis on the legitimating role of education would be more than a little misleading. For in this case the competitive educational system would be a meritocratic "game" in which the stakes (economic success) were directly related to the criteria of winning or losing (cognitive attainment) in a very rational and even technological way.[10] Again, were this view correct, education could be as egalitarian as people's innate biological capacities allowed—which would be quite far if our argument in Section III is widely generalizable. Moreover, were the technocratic–meritocratic perspective correct, the persistence of repressive education—in the face of alternatives which appear to offer both a more democratic environment and a more effective vehicle for the transmission of cognitive skills—would merely reflect an irrational institutional inertia on the part of the school system. If schools could be made more humane *and* more efficient producers of intellectual skills, why haven't all parties concerned—educators, students, employers, parents, workers, school boards, everybody—celebrated the opportunity? The answer, we believe, lies in a simple but frequently overlooked fact: the role of schools in promoting cognitive growth by no means exhausts their social functions. The traditional "cognitive" perspective on education is erroneous. While skills are developed in schools and a skilled labor force is necessary in a technologically advanced society, a cognitive approach to the educational system cannot provide the basis for understanding the relation between schools and the economy.

In particular, we shall demonstrate that although higher levels of schooling and economic success tend to go together, the intellectual abilities developed or certified in school make little causal contribution to getting ahead economically. Only a minor portion of the substantial statistical association between schooling and economic success can be accounted for by the school's role in developing cognitive skills. The predominant economic function of schools is thus not the development or identification of intellectual skills. Elsewhere we have suggested that the economic importance of schooling rests on the accreditation of individuals, as well as the production and selection of non-cognitive personality traits and other personal attributes related to submission to the hierarchical order of the capitalist enterprise.[11] Thus an educational system truly "meritocratic" in terms of the individual traits *actually needed* by the capitalist economy would be a transparent totalitarian monstrosity. A more humane school system, producing a more intellectually adept graduate, could fail miserably in its most elemental function: the preparation of children for economic life.

* * *

While our more general claim — that the primary economic function of schooling is not the production or selection of intellectual skills — can be verified through a wide variety of data sources,[12] our major illustration will be drawn from an extensive sample which we have subjected to close statistical analysis.[13]

The data, most of which was collected by the U.S. Census Current Population Survey in 1962, refer to "non-Negro" males, aged 24–65, from non-farm background, and whose work history is in the experienced labor force. The data relating to childhood IQ and adult cognitive attainment are from a 1966 survey by the National Opinion Research Center and the California Guidance Study.[14] The quality of the data precludes any claims to precision in our estimation. Yet our main propositions remain supported even making allowance for substantive degrees of error. We must emphasize, however, that the validity of our basic propositions does not depend on our particular data set. While we believe our data base to be the most representative and carefully constructed from available sources, we have checked our results against several other data bases. When corrections are made for measurement error and restriction of range statistical analysis of each of these data bases strongly supports all of our major propositions.[15] Nor do our results depend on the choice of income as the measure of economic success. . . .

We must first choose a convenient way to represent the statistical association between level of educational attainment in years and earnings in dollars. While our results are clearly independent of any particular statistical representation, some representations are more easily interpretable than others. We have chosen the top-quintile-by-decile method, illustrated in Figure 1.[16] We first order all individuals from lowest to highest in terms of level of education attainment in years, and divide them into 10 equal parts ("deciles"). We then determine the percentage of individuals in

FIGURE 1

Differences in Cognitive Test Scores Do Not Explain the Association between Education and Income

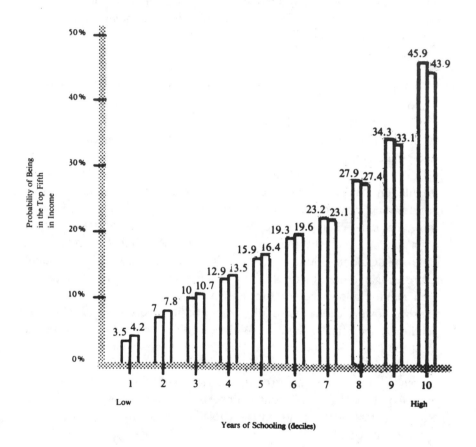

The left hand bar of each pair shows the estimated probability that a man is in the top fifth of the income distribution if he is in the given decile of education. the right hand bar of each pair shows the estimated probability that a man is in the top fifth of the income distribution if he has an average adult cognitive test score and is in the given decile of education.

Note that the bars of any given pair are very close, showing that the income-education relationship is almost the same for individuals with the identical cognitive attainments as for all individuals.

Figure 1 is calculated from data presented in Samuel Bowles and Valerie Nelson, "The 'Inheritance of IQ' and the Intergenerational Reproduction of Economic Inequality", *Review of Economics and Statistics,* 61, 1 (February 1974).

each decile who are in the top fifth of the sample (the "top quintile") in income. We thus find the *probability* that an individual with a given level of education has of attaining the top 20 percent of the income distribution.

These results are illustrated by the left of the paired bars in Figure 1. This figure, for instance, illustrates that an individual in the top tenth of education has a 45.9 percent chance of attaining the top fifth in income, while an individual in the bottom decile in education has only a 3.5 percent chance. Thus, Figure 1 illustrates the well-known importance of education in achieving economic success.

Just as the technocratic–meritocratic theory asserts, education is also closely associated with cognitive attainments: the correlation between the armed forces qualification test scores and years of schooling is .62 in our sample. Thus, a person in the top decile in education has a 57.7 percent chance of falling in the top fifth in cognitive scores, while a person in the bottom decile in education has less than a 1 percent chance.[17]

But is the higher average cognitive attainment of the more highly educated the *cause* of their greater likelihood of achieving economic success? This, of course, is the crucial question. If the "cognitive" theory is correct, two individuals with the *same* test scores but *different* levels of education should have, on the average, exactly the same expected incomes. Thus, if we restrict our observation to individuals with the same test scores, at whatever level, the association illustrated by the left-hand bars in Figure 1 should disappear—i.e., they should describe a horizontal straight line.

The results of "holding constant" test scores at their average level is exhibited in the right-hand bars of Figure 1. Far from showing no relation ship, the right-hand bars show that holding cognitive attainments constant barely changes the education–income relationship. For instance, the chance of falling in the top fifth in income only drops from 45.9 percent to 43.9 percent for the top decile in education, while rising from 3.5 percent to only 4.2 percent for the lowest educational decile. Hardly comforting for the traditional theory![18]

Since the association between level of economic success and years of schooling is reduced only slightly when we look at individuals with the same level of adult cognitive skills, the association of schooling and economic success is largely unrelated to the differences in cognitive skills observed between workers with differing levels of education. Numerous other studies support these conclusions.[19] It is clear that if the association of schooling and economic success derives primarily from the in-school generation or identification of cognitive abilities, then there should be little economic advantage to additional schooling for individuals of the same cognitive abilities. But, the above discussion reveals that the economic advantage associated with more years of schooling remains substantial when cognitive test scores are held constant.

The reader may find our argument, despite its wide statistical support, not only counter-intuitive, but actually incredible. For the figures seem to refute the manifest observation that the economy could not operate without the cognitive skills of workers, and that these skills are acquired in school. This observation is correct, and by no means contradicted by our data. What our argument suggests is merely that the educational system produces skills in such profusion, and the possibilities for acquiring additional skills on the job are sufficiently great, that skill differences among individuals who are acceptable for a given job on the basis of other criteria (which include race, sex, personality and credentials) are of little economic import.

If the cognitive skills learned in school do not mediate the association of education and economic success, what does? We believe it is precisely the social relations of the educational encounter which prepare individuals for economic life, rather than the academic outcomes themselves. The school is a bureaucratic order with hierarchical authority, rule-orientation, stratification by "ability" (tracking), as well as by age, role differentiation by sex, and a system of external incentives much like pay and status in the sphere of work. Thus schools tend to reproduce forms of consciousness corresponding to the structure of class relations in the dominant economic sphere.

* * *

III. IQism: Or, If You're So Smart Why Aren't You Rich?

If the role of IQ in the system of social and economic privilege does not arise naturally from technical requirements of work in the advanced economy, how did IQ and related tests become established as a means of allocating individuals to educational and occupational slots? We believe the present relationship between schooling, IQ, and economic stratification grew out of a more or less coordinated attempt in the early years of this century to produce a disciplined and fragmented labor force and to lend a veneer of objectivity and technological rationality to the finely articulated hierarchical division of labor which characterizes the social relations of production of corporate capitalism.

The argument that differences in genetic endowments are of central and increasing importance in the stratification systems of highly technological societies has been advanced, in similar forms, by a number of contemporary researchers.[20] At the heart of this argument lies the venerable thesis that IQ as measured by tests such as the Stanford–Binet, is largely inherited via genetic transmission, rather than molded through environmental influences.[21]

Environmentalists, while correctly emphasizing the paucity and unrepresentativeness of the data underlying the genetic interpretation, have presented rather weak evidence for their own position and have made little dent in the genetic position.[22] Unable to controvert convincingly the central proposition of the genetic school, environmentalists have emphasized that it bears no important social implications. They have claimed that, although raised in the context of the economic and educational deprivation of blacks in the United States, the genetic theory says nothing about the "necessary" degree of racial inequality, or the limits of compensatory education. First, environmentalists deny that there is any evidence that the average IQ difference between blacks and whites (amounting to about 15 points) is genetic in origin,[23] and second, they deny that any estimate of heritability tells us much about the capacity of "enriched environments" to lessen IQ differentials, either within or between racial groups.[24]

But the environmentalists' defense has been costly. First, plausible, if not logical, inference now lies on the side of the genetic school, and it's up to environmentalists to "put up or shut up" as to feasible environmental enrichment programs. Second, in their egalitarian zeal vis-à-vis racial differences, the environmentalists have sacrificed the modern liberal interpretation of social stratification. The modern liberal approach is to attribute social class differences to "unequal opportunity." That is, while the criteria for economic success are objective and achievement-oriented, the failures and successes of parents are passed onto their children via distinct learning and cultural environments. Thus the achievement of a more equal society merely requires that all youth be afforded the educational and other social conditions of the best and most successful.[25] They have not successfully challenged the proposition that IQ differences among whites of differing social class backgrounds *are* rooted in differences in genetic endowments. Indeed, the genetic school's data comes precisely from observed differences in the IQ of whites across socioeconomic levels! The liberal failure to question the causal role of IQ in getting ahead economically completes the rout. The fundamental tenet of modern liberal social policy—that "progressive social welfare measures" can gradually reduce and eliminate social class difference, cultures of poverty and affluence, and inequalities of opportunity—

seems to be undercut. Thus the proposition, adhered to by present day conservatives and liberals of past generations, that social classes sort themselves out on the basis of innate individual capacity to cope successfully in the social environment, and hence tend to reproduce themselves from generation to generation, is restored.[26]

The vigor of reaction to Jensen's argument reflects the liberals' agreement that IQ is a basic determinant (at least ideally) of occupational status and intergenerational mobility. Indeed, the conceptual framework of the testers themselves would appear to insure this result. The originator of the IQ test, Alfred Binet, derived his concept of "intelligence" from the requisites of social and economic success:

> An individual is normal when he is able to conduct himself in life without need of the guardianship of another, and is able to perform work sufficiently remunerative to supply his personal needs, and finally when his intelligence does not exclude him from the social rank of his parents. As a result of this, an attorney's son who is reduced by his intelligence to the condition of a menial employee is a moron; likewise the son of a master mason, who remains a servant at thirty years is a moron; likewise a peasant, normal in ordinary surroundings of the fields, may be considered a moron in the city.[24]

The relationship of IQ and occupational success was even more confidently asserted by Lewis Terman, himself a New Deal liberal and perhaps the most influential of the early twentieth century advocates of IQ testing in the United States.

> At every step in the child's progress the school should take account of his vocational possibilities. Preliminary investigations indicate that an IQ below 70 rarely permits anything better than unskilled labor; that the range from 70 to 80 is pre-eminently that of semi-skilled labor; from 80 to 100 that of the skilled or ordinary clerical labor, from 100 to 110 or 115 that of the semi-professional pursuits, and that above these are the grades of intelligence which permit one to enter the professions or the larger fields of business. Intelligence tests can tell us whether a child's native brightness corresponds more nearly to the median of (1) the professional classes, (2) those in the semi-professional pursuits,

(3) ordinary skilled workers, (4) semi-skilled workers, or (5) unskilled laborers. This information will be of great value in planning the education of a particular child and also in planning the differentiated curriculum here recommended.[28]

Jensen is thus merely stating what the testers had taken for granted: "psychologists' concept of the 'intelligence demands' of an occupation . . . is very much like the general public's concept of the prestige or 'social standing' of an occupation, and both are closely related to an independent measure of . . . occupational status."[29] Jensen continues, quoting the sociologist O. D. Duncan:[30] . . . 'intelligence' . . . is not essentially different from that of achievement or status in the occupational sphere . . . what we now *mean* by intelligence is something like the probability of acceptable performance (given the opportunity) in occupations varying in social status."

* * *

Few will be surprised that such statements are made by the "conservative" genetic school. But why, amidst a spirited liberal counterattack in which the minutest details of the genetic hypothesis are contested and scathingly criticized, is the validity of the genetic school's description of the social function of intelligence so blandly accepted? The widespread agreement among participants in the debate, that IQ is an important determinant of economic success, can hardly be explained by compelling empirical evidence adduced in support of the position. Quite the contrary.

The most immediate support for the IQ theory of social stratification—which we will call IQism—flows from the correlation between IQ and income, ranging from .27 to .29 in our sample and the correlation between socioeconomic background and childhood IQ ranging from .40 to .43.[31] The latter relationship is indeed substantial. Having a parent in the top decile in socioeconomic status (assuming a bivariate normal distribution) gives a child a 42 percent chance of being in the top fifth in IQ, while having a parent in the bottom socioeconomic status decile gives a child only a 4.9 percent chance.

Thus, the proponent of IQism argues that higher social class (or race) is associated with a higher IQ, which in turn leads to a greater chance of economic success. We shall show, however, that this inference is simply erroneous. Specifically, we will demonstrate the truth of the following proposition:

the fact that economic success tends to run in the family arises almost completely independently from any inheritance of IQ; genetic or environmental. Thus, while one's economic status tends to resemble that of one's parents, only a minor portion of this association can be attributed to social class differences in childhood IQ, and a virtually negligible portion to social class differences in genetic endowments, even if one were to accept the Jensen estimates of heritability. Thus, a perfect (obviously hypothetical) equalization of IQ's among individuals of differing social backgrounds would reduce the intergenerational transmission of economic status by a negligible amount.

We conclude that a family's position in the class structure is reproduced primarily by mechanisms operating independently of the inheritance, production, and certification of intellectual skills.

Our statistical technique for the demonstration of these propositions will again be that of linear regression analysis. This technique allows us to derive numerical estimates of the independent contribution of each of the separate but correlated influences (socioeconomic background, childhood IQ, years of schooling, adult cognitive attainment) on economic success, by answering the question: what is the magnitude of the association between any one of these influences among individuals who are equal on some or all the others? Equivalently, it answers the question: what are the probabilities of attaining particular levels of economic success among individuals who are in the same decile in some or all of the above influences but one, and in varying deciles in this one variable alone?

We begin with the statistical association between socioeconomic background and adult income, illustrated by the left-hand bars in Figure 2. The correct way of posing the question of the role of IQ in the transmission of economic status across generations is the following: to what extent is this very substantial statistical association between socioeconomic background and economic success attenuated when childhood IQ is held constant? If the proponents of IQism are correct, the attenuation should be substantial. Yet, a comparison of the left-hand and right-hand bars of Figure 2 shows that the statistical association between family background and income is hardly affected by holding childhood IQ constant.[32]

The lack of importance of the specifically genetic mechanism operating via IQ in the intergenerational reproduction of economic inequality is even more striking. Figure 3 exhibits the degree of association between socioeconomic background and income which can be attributed to the genetic inheritance of IQ alone. This figure assumes that all direct influences

FIGURE 2

**The Transmission of Parents' Economic Status
Cannot Be Explained by IQ Difference**

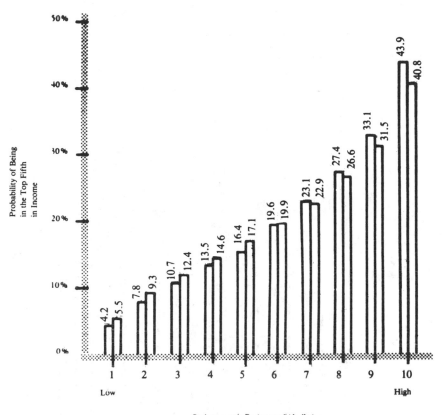

Socioeconomic Background (deciles)

The left-hand bar of each pair shows the estimated probability that a man is in the top fifth of the income distribution if he is in the given decile of socioeconomic background (an average measure of his father's education, father's occupational status, and parents' income). The right hand bar shows the estimated probability that a man is in the top fifth of the income distribution if he has the average childhood IQ and is in the given decile of socioeconomic background.

Note that the bars of any given pair are very nearly the same height, showing that the income-socioeconomic background relationship is almost the same for individuals with identical IQ's as for all individuals.

Figure 2 is calculated from data reported in Bowles and Nelson "The 'Inheritance of IQ'" (1974). . . .

FIGURE 3

**Hypothetical Relationship between Socioeconomic Background and Income
Attributable to the Genetic Inheritance of IQ**

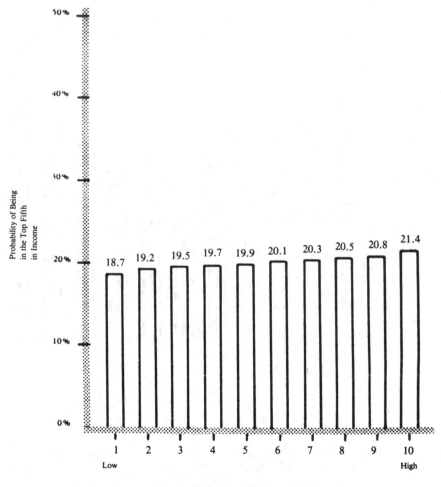

Socioeconomic Background (deciles)

Figure 3 is calculated from data reported in Bowles and Nelson "The 'Inheritance of IQ'"
(1974), Table 3. It is based on a partial correlation of .02 between income and socioeconomic
background, calculated via IQ paths alone, calculated by the use of path analysis.

of socioeconomic background upon income have been eliminated, and that the non-cognitive components of schooling's contribution to economic success are eliminated as well (the perfect meritocracy based on intellectual ability). On the other hand, it assumes Jensen's estimate for the degree of heritability of IQ. A glance at Figure 3 shows that the resulting level of intergenerational inequality in this highly hypothetical example would be negligible.

Our proposition is thus supported: the intergenerational transmission of social and economic status operates primarily via non-cognitive mechanisms, despite the fact that the school system rewards higher IQ — an attribute significantly associated with higher socio-economic background.

The lack of importance of IQ in explaining the relation between socioeconomic background and economic success, together with the fact that most of the association between IQ and income can be accounted for by the common association of these variables with education and socioeconomic background, support our major assertion: IQ is not an important criterion for economic success.

* * *

Differences in IQ, even if genetically inherited, cannot explain the historical pattern of economic and educational inequalities. The persistence of poverty, the intractability of inequality of incomes and inequality of economic and social opportunity cannot be attributed to genetically inherited differences in IQ. The disappointing results of the War on Poverty cannot be blamed on the genes of the poor.

The power and privilege of the capitalist class are often inherited, but not through superior genes. Try asking David Rockefeller to hand over his capital in return for 30 or more IQ points! Chances are, he would agree with Karl Marx:

> One thing is clear — nature does not produce on the one side owners of money or commodities, and on the other, men possessing nothing but their own labor power. This relation has no natural basis, neither is its social basis one that is common to all historical periods. It is clearly the result of past historical development, the product of many economical revolutions, of the extinction of a whole series of older forms of social production.[33]

IV. Conclusion

In this paper we have suggested that education plays an important part in the reproduction of the social division of labor by legitimating the allocation of individuals to economic positions on the basis of ostensibly objective merit. However, the basis for assessing merit — competitive academic performance — is only weakly associated with the personal attributes which contribute to individual success in economic life. Thus, the legitimation process in education assumes a largely symbolic form.

The legitimation process, moreover, is fraught with its own contradictions; for the technocratic-meritocratic ideology, when manifested in civil rights and fair employment legislation, progressively undermines the overt forms of discrimination which divide the workforce into racially, sexually, and ethnically distinct segments. Ironically, the partial success of the meritocratic ideology has helped to create a political basis for working class unity. With the irrationality of these forms of discrimination increasingly exposed, the justification of inequality must increasingly rely on educational inequalities and IQism. Yet, workers, minorities, and others have fought hard and to some extent successfully to reduce educational inequality, with little effect on economic inequality itself. This has tended to increase conflicts within education, and to cast further doubts on the fairness of the income distribution process. Thus, even the symbolism of meritocracy is threatened.

Yet, as we have suggested, the contribution of education to social reproduction goes far beyond symbolic legitimation. In addition, the educational system plays a central role in preparing individuals for the world of alienated work and class domination. Such a class analysis of education is necessary, we believe, to understand the dynamics of educational change and also the structural relations among social class, education, and economic success — relations which we have seen in this paper to be inexplicable in terms of cognitive variables and the "technical relations of production."

Notes

1. Kingsley Davis and Wilbert E. Moore, in Reinhard Bendix and Seymour Lipset, eds., *Class, Status and Power* (New York: Free Press, 1966).
2. Quoted in Leon Kamin, *The Science and Politics of IQ*, (Potomac, Md: Erlbaum Associates, 1974).

3. Richard Herrnstein, "IQ," *Atlantic Monthly,* (September 1971).
4. Recent studies indeed indicate a lack of social class or racial bias in school grades; given a student's cognitive attainment, his or her grades seem not to be affected by class or racial origins, at least on the high school level. See Robert Hauser, "Schools and the Stratification Process," *American Journal of Sociology* 74 (May 1969)) 587–611; Barbara Heyns, "Curriculum Assignment and Tracking Policies in 48 Urban Public High Schools" (Ph.D. dissertation for the University of Chicago, 1971); and Christopher Jencks, *Inequality: A Reassessment of the Effects of Family and Schooling in America* (New York: Basic Books, 1972). On the other hand, school grades are by no means based on cognitive achievement alone. An array of behavior and personality traits are rewarded as well—particularly those relevant to the student's future participation in the production system. See Chapters 2 and 4 of Bowles and Gintis *Schooling in Capitalist America: Educational Reform and the Contradictions of Life Economic* (New York: Basic Books, 1975).
5. For an extended treatment see Jerome Karabel, "Community Colleges and Social Stratification" *Harvard Educational Review* 424, no. 42 (November 1972).
6. See Daniel Bell, *The Coming of Post-Industrial Society* (New York: Basic Books, 1973), part 3.
7. Alexander W. Astin, "Undergraduate Achievement and Institutional 'Excellence,'" *Science* 161 (August 1968).
8. Daniel C. Rogers, "Private Rates of Return to Education in the U.S., A Case Study," *Yale Economic Essays,* (Spring 1969).
9. Alexander W. Astin and Jack E. Rossman, "The Case for Open Admissions: A Status Report," *Change* 5, no. 6 (Summer 1973).
10. Of course, as Noam Chomsky has brilliantly argued, even in this case the institutional arrangements would not satisfy the elementary dictates of justice and equity. See Noam Chomsky, "Psychology and Ideology," *Cognition: International Journal of International Psychology* 1, no. 1 (1972).
11. Samuel Bowles and Herbert Gintis, "IQ in the U.S. Class Structure", *Social Policy* 3, nos. 4 and 5 (November/December 1972; January/February 1973).
12. See Herbert Gintis, "Education, Technology and the Characteristics of Worker Productivity" *American Economic Review,* May 1971, and Ivar Berg, *Education and Jobs: The Great Training Robbery* (Boston: Beacon Press, 1971).
13. Much of the discussion in this section has been adapted from Samuel Bowles and Valerie Nelson, "The 'Inheritance of IQ' and the Intergenerational Reproduction of Economic Inequality," *Review of Economics and Statistics* 61, no. 1 (February 1974); and Bowles and Gintis, "IQ in U.S. Class Structure."
14. Peter Blau and Otis D. Duncan, *The American Occupational Structure* (New York: John Wiley, 1967); O. D. Duncan, "Achievement and Ability," *Eugenics Quarterly,* March 1968; and Samuel Bowles, "Schooling and Inequality from Generation to Generation" *Journal of Political Economy* 80, no. 3, part II (May/June 1972). Similar calculations for other age groups yield results consistent with our three propositions.
15. Bowles "Schooling and Inequality from Generation to Generation", and Jencks, *Inequality.*
16. Most popular discussions of the relation of IQ and economic success—e.g., Arthur R. Jensen, "Estimation of the Limits of Heritability of Traits by Comparison of Monozygotic and Dizygotic Twins," *Proceedings of the National Academy of Science,* (1967); Herrnstein, "IQ"; and Jencks, *Inequality*—present statistical material in terms of "correlation coefficients" and "contribution to expanded variance." We believe that these technical expressions convey little information. The top-quintile-by-decile method and later tables, we feel, is operationally more accessible to the reader, and reveals the patterns of mobility and causality only implicit in summary statistics of the correlation variety. . . .

17. "Cognitive Test Scores" are measured by a form of the Armed Forces Qualification Test, which is strongly affected both by childhood IQ and years of schooling, and hence can be considered a measure of adult cognitive achievement.
18. The method of linear regression analysis assumes that the level at which cognitive scores are held constant is irrelevant, as all effects are linear and additive. We have set this level at the average for the sample to render the education-income associations, before and after holding cognitive skills constant, closely comparable. Changing the level of cognitive scores merely moves this curve up or down. The assumption of linearity is, moreover, a good approximation to reality. See Christopher Jencks, "The Effects of Worker Characteristics on Economic Success: An Inquiry into Non-Linear Ties, Interactions, and Unmeasured Variables Using the NORC Veterans Sample" (Cambridge, MA.: Center for Educational Policy Research, July 1973), and Rogers, "Private Rates of Return to Education in the U.S."
19. See Gintis "Education, Technology and the Characteristics".
20. Carl Bereiter, "The Future of Individual Differences," *Harvard Educational Review,* Reprint Series, no. 2 (1969); Arthur R. Jensen, "How Can We Boost IQ and Scholastic Achievement?" *Harvard Educational Review* 39, no. 1 (1969); Herrnstein, "IQ"; and J. Eysenck, *The IQ Argument* (New York: Library Press, 1971).
21. By IQ we mean those cognitive capacities which are measured by IQ tests. We have avoided the use of the word "intelligence" as in its common usage it ordinarily connotes a broader range of capacities.
22. Jerome S. Kagan, "Inadequate Evidence and Illogical Conclusions," *Harvard Educational Review,* Reprint Series, no. 2 (1969); and J. McV. Hunt, "Has Compensatory Education Failed?" *Harvard Educational Review.* Reprint Series, no 2 (1969). But see the devastating critique of Kamin, *The Science and Politics of IQ,* which casts considerable doubt on the genetic position.
23. Does the fact that a large component of the differences in IQ among whites is genetic mean that a similar component of the differences in IQ between blacks and whites is determined by the former's inferior gene pool? Clearly not. First of all, the degree of heritability is an *average,* even among whites. For any two individuals, and *a fortiori,* any two groups of individuals, observed IQ differences may be due to any proportion of genes and environment—it is required only that they average properly over the entire population. For instance, *all* of the difference in IQ between identical twins is environmental, and presumably a great deal of the difference between adopted brothers is genetic. Similarly, we cannot say whether the average difference in IQ between Irish and Puerto Ricans is genetic or environmental. In the case of blacks, however, the genetic school's inference is even more tenuous. [Light and Smith have shown that even accepting Jensen's estimates of the heritability of IQ, the black-white IQ difference could easily be explained by the average environmental differences between the races. . . . See Richard J. Light and Paul V. Smith, "Accumulating Evidence: Procedures for Resolving Contradictions Among Different Research Studies," *Harvard Educational Review* 41, no. 4 (November 1971)].
24. Most environmentalists do not dispute Jensen's assertion that existing large-scale compensatory programs have produced dismal results. But this does not bear on the genetic hypothesis. As Jensen himself notes, the degree of genetic transmission of any trait depends on the various alternative environments which individuals experience. Jensen's estimates of heritability rest *squarely* on the existing array of educational processes and technologies. Any introduction of new social processes of mental development will change the average unstandardized level of IQ, as well as its degree of heritability. . . .
25. James S. Coleman *et al., Equality of Educational Opportunity* (Washington, D.C.: U.S. Government Printing Office, 1966).

26. E.g. Edward A. Ross, *Social Control* (New York: Macmillan, 1906); Lewis M. Terman, *Intelligence Tests and School Reorganization* (New York: World Books, 1923); and Joseph Schumpeter, *Imperialism and Social Classes* (New York: Kelley, 1951). This is not to imply that all liberal social theorists hold the IQ ideology. McClelland and Lewis, among others, explicitly reject IQ as an important determinant of social stratification. See Oscar Lewis, "The Culture of Poverty," *Scientific American* 215 (October 1966); and David McClelland, *Achieving Society* (New York: Free Press, 1967).
27. Alfred Binet and T.H. Smith, *The Development of Intelligence in Children* (Baltimore: Williams and Wilkins, 1916), p. 266, quoted in Clarence J. Karier, "Ideology and Evaluation: In Quest of Meritocracy" (unpublished paper for the University of Illinois, Champaigne, 1973), p. 11.
28. Terman, *Intelligence Tests,* pp. 27–28, quoted in Karier, "Ideology and Evaluation,' p. 11.
29. Jensen, p. 14.
30. Otis D. Duncan, "Properties and Characteristics of the Socio-economic Index" and "A Socio-economic Index for All Occupations" in Albert J. Reiss, ed. *Occupations and Social Status* (New York: The Free Press, 1961), pp. 90–91.
31. These data are from Bowles and Nelson "The 'Inheritance of IQ'". Socioeconomic background is measured here by a weighted sum of parents' income, father's occupational status, and father's education. Childhood IQ is measured by the Stanford–Binet or its equivalent. The estimated zero correlation coefficient betwen socioeconomic background and early childhood IQ is .399, as reported in Bowles and Nelson "The 'Inheritance of IQ'", 1974. The relationship is slightly stronger for men of other age groups than ages 35–44 years used in the figure: .410 for ages 25–34, .410 for ages 45–54, and .426 for ages 55–64.
32. This figure is based on the correlation betwen socioeconomic background and income via the genetic inheritance of IQ alone. The correlation was computed by the path model presented in Bowles and Nelson "The 'Inheritance of IQ'", 1974. . . .
33. Karl Marx, *Capital,* vol. 1 (New York: International Publishers, 1967), p. 169.

3 Issues in Ecology

Ecology provides a holistic perspective of relationships between our species and nature. Based on the premise that human communities must live in a lasting balance with the natural environment, ecology focuses on the interconnections between phenomena usually treated separately by specialists. It provides us with a critical light with which to examine present-day society and illuminate workable alternatives. Ecology questions many of the assumptions of our social order, among them:

1. Growth (of cities, of production, and so on) is good.
2. Humans should have dominion over nature.
3. Production and consumption should be separate; cities and regions (as well as countries) should specialize in production, exporting what they do best and importing the rest.

These assumptions are false. Bigger is not necessarily better. Often the most efficient producers are not the largest but those of medium size. The best quality of life is seldom found in the largest cities; medium-size cities and towns have lower crime rates, less congestion, more open space and parkland, and fewer traffic problems. The concentration of factories and people in huge metropolitan areas leads to complex logistic problems and requires inordinate amounts of energy. According to Murray Bookchin, ecological principles suggest decentralization into balanced communities that use local materials and energy. Smaller regional economies can use a combination of sun, wind, water, and geothermal power instead of fossil fuels and atomic reactors. Smaller cities need fewer cars, trucks, and freeways because people live closer to their work and materials do not have to be carried as far. Even a small degree of decentralization would alleviate some of our more pressing problems because the difference between tolerable and intolerable crowding in schools, hospitals, and on streets is often a matter of only a few percentage points.

The ecological perspective allows us to see the waste inherent in a system in which food is shipped 3000 miles to be consumed in an area capable of growing its own food, and where machines are designed so that when they break down, they must be thrown away instead of repaired. We need smaller, self-reliant communities and regions that can produce most of what they consume, and technology that will allow consumers to repair or recycle many of the products they use instead of discarding them.

The topsy-turvy growth of cities and suburbs has polluted the environment and destroyed our natural resources. This destruction of the environment reflects a Western assumption that humans can and should dominate nature. An alternative assumption, the ecological one, is that humans should come to terms with the environment, that they should live *with* nature instead of *against* it. There are simply not enough resources on earth for us to continue exploiting them at the present rate. For example, we will probably run out of oil before the middle of the next century. According to Bookchin, nothing short of adopting the ecological view will prevent us from destroying the environment and eventually the human species itself.

Urban transportation systems in America are a good example of how a private-profit economy and a disregard for the natural environment have combined to produce air pollution, waste, avoidable deaths and accidents, and long hours spent commuting to and from work. Instead of taking it for granted that a new freeway must be built to accommodate auto traffic, ecologists ask, Why do so many people have to travel so far? They examine the decentralization of urban facilities and places of work as an alternative to road building. They ask whether greater use of trolleys, trains, and bicycles might not reduce our dependence on motor vehicles — and at the same time reduce air pollution, oil consumption, and traffic accidents.

These problems are of considerable magnitude. As Michael McFadden points out, automobiles kill 50,000 Americans a year; cars produce an estimated 60 percent of all air pollution; motor vehicles account for almost half of domestic oil consumption. Because of the inadequacy of public transit, many of the poor must devote a quarter of their income to maintaining an automobile. To reduce dependence on the auto, McFadden suggests improving public transit and redesigning cities to facilitate the use of bicycles and encourage pedestrian traffic. Instead of using our tax dollars to pay for the construction of nuclear missile systems and space vehicles to transport people to the moon, it is high time we redirected public resources to build, reconstruct, and maintain a network of comfortable, convenient, and free transit systems and bicycle paths in and around our major cities.

The "ecology" campaigns that have recently become popular in this country have neutralized the critical and reconstructive aspects of ecology by dramatizing chiefly the less important issues. It is good that we have begun to install anti-smog devices in automobiles and to recycle the paper, metal, and glass that used to be thrown away. But these things only make business more profitable by lowering the costs of raw materials and providing markets for new products. They do not confront more basic problems, such as automania, the overconcentration of people and industries in metropolitan areas, and the environmental pollution still caused by automobiles and by business in obtaining raw materials and getting rid of wastes. Emphasizing the peripheral aspects of ecology makes us feel we have "done something" and thus blinds us to the need to reconstruct the society and create a truly livable environment.

Ecology and Revolutionary Thought

Murray Bookchin

There is one science . . . that may yet restore and even transcend the liberatory estate of the traditional sciences and philosophies. It passes rather loosely under the name "ecology"—a term coined by Haeckel a century ago to denote "the investigation of the total relations of the animal both to its inorganic and to its organic environment."[1] At first glance, Haeckel's definition is innocuous enough; and ecology narrowly conceived of as one of the biological sciences, is often reduced to a variety of biometrics in which field workers focus on food chains and statistical studies of animal populations. There is an ecology of health that would hardly offend the sensibilities of the American Medical Association and a

FROM *Post Scarcity Anarchism* by Murray Bookchin. Ramparts Press, Palo Alto, CA 94303. Copyright © 1971 by Murray Bookchin. Reprinted with permission.

concept of social ecology that would conform to the most well-engineered notions of the New York City Planning Commission.

Broadly conceived of, however, ecology deals with the balance of nature. Inasmuch as nature includes man, the science basically deals with the harmonization of nature and man. The explosive implications of an ecological approach arise not only because ecology is intrinsically a critical science — critical on a scale that the most radical systems of political economy have failed to attain — but also because it is an integrative and reconstructive science. This integrative, reconstructive aspect of ecology, carried through to all its implications, leads directly into anarchic areas of social thought. For, in the final analysis, it is impossible to achieve a harmonization of man and nature without creating a human community that lives in a lasting balance with its natural environment.

The Critical Nature of Ecology

The critical edge of ecology, a unique feature of the science in a period of general scientific docility, derives from its subject matter — from its very domain. The issues with which ecology deals are imperishable in the sense that they cannot be ignored without bringing into question the survival of man and the survival of the planet itself. The critical edge of ecology is due not so much to the power of human reason — a power which science hallowed during its most revolutionary periods — but to a still higher power, the sovereignty of nature. It may be that man is manipulable, as the owners of the mass media argue, or that elements of nature are manipulable, as the engineers demonstrate, but ecology clearly shows that the totality of the natural world — nature viewed in all its aspects, cycles and interrelationships — cancels out all human pretensions to mastery over the planet. The great wastelands of the Mediterranean basin, once areas of a thriving agriculture or a rich natural flora, are historic evidence of nature's revenge against human parasitism.

No historic examples compare in weight and scope with the effects of man's despoliation — and nature's revenge — since the days of the Industrial Revolution, and especially since the end of World War II. Ancient examples of human parasitism were essentially local in scope; they were precisely *examples* of man's potential for destruction, and nothing more. Often, they were compensated by remarkable improvements in the natural ecology of a region, such as the European peasantry's superb reworking of the soil during centuries of cultivation and the achievements of Inca agriculturists in terracing the Andes Mountains during the pre-Columbian times.

Modern man's despoliation of the environment, like his imperialisms, is global in scope. It is even extraterrestrial, as witness the disturbances of the Van Allen Belt a few years ago. Today human parasitism disrupts more than the atmosphere, climate, water resources, soil, flora and fauna of a region: it upsets virtually all the basic cycles of nature and threatens to undermine the stability of the environment on a worldwide scale.

As an example of the scope of modern man's disruptive role, it has been estimated that the burning of fossil fuels (coal and oil) adds 600 million tons of carbon dioxide to the air annually, about .03 percent of the total atmospheric mass — this, I may add, aside from an incalculable quantity of toxicants. Since the Industrial Revolution, the overall atmospheric mass of carbon dioxide has increased by 25 percent over earlier, more stable, levels. It can be argued on very sound theoretical grounds that this growing blanket of carbon dioxide, by intercepting heat radiated from the earth, will lead to more destructive storm patterns and eventually to melting of the polar ice caps, rising sea levels, and the inundation of vast land areas. Far removed as such a deluge may be, the changing proportion of carbon dioxide to other atmospheric gases is a warning about the impact man is having on the balance of nature.

A more immediate ecological issue is man's extensive pollution of the earth's waterways. What counts here is not the fact that man befouls a given stream, river, or lake — a thing he has done for ages — but rather the magnitude water pollution has reached in the past two generations. Nearly all the surface waters of the United States are now polluted. Many American waterways are open cesspools that properly qualify as extensions of urban sewage systems. It is a euphemism to describe them as rivers or lakes. More significantly, large amounts of ground water are sufficiently polluted to be undrinkable, and a number of local hepatitis epidemics have been traced to polluted wells in suburban areas. In contrast to surface-water pollution, the pollution of ground or subsurface water is immensely difficult to eliminate and tends to linger on for decades after the sources of pollution have been removed.

An article in a mass-circulation magazine appropriately describes the polluted waterways of the United States as "Our Dying Waters." This despairing, apocalyptic description of the water pollution problem in the United States really applies to the world at large. The waters of the earth are literally dying. Massive pollution is destroying the rivers and lakes of Africa,

Asia, and Latin America, as well as the long-abused waterways of highly industrialized continents, as media of life. (I speak here not only of radioactive pollutants from nuclear bomb tests and power reactors, which apparently reach all the flora and fauna of the sea; the oil spills and the
discharge of diesel oil have also become massive pollution problems, claiming marine life in enormous quantities every year.)

Accounts of this kind can be repeated for virtually every part of the
biosphere. Pages could be written on the immense losses of productive soil
that occur annually in almost every continent of the earth; on lethal air
pollution episodes in major urban areas; on the worldwide distribution of
toxic agents, such as radioactive isotopes and lead; on the chemicalization
of man's immediate environment — one might say his very dinner table —
with pesticide residues and food additives. Pieced together like bits of a
jigsaw puzzle, these affronts to the environment form a pattern of destruction that has no precedent in man's long history on earth.

Obviously, man could be described as a highly destructive parasite
who threatens to destroy his host — the natural world — and eventually
himself. In ecology, however, the word "parasite" is not an answer to a
question, but raises a question itself. Ecologists know that a destructive
parasitism of this kind usually reflects the disruption of an ecological situation; indeed, many species that seem highly destructive under one set of
conditions are eminently useful under another set of conditions. What im-
parts a profoundly critical function to ecology is the question raised by
man's destructive abilities: What is the disruption that has turned man into
a destructive parasite? What produces a form of parasitism that results not
only in vast natural imbalances but also threatens the existence of humanity
itself?

Man has produced imbalances not only in nature, but, more fundamentally, in his relations with his fellow man and in the very structure of
his society. The imbalances man has produced in the natural world are
caused by the imbalances he has produced in the social world. A century
ago it would have been possible to regard air pollution and water contamination as the result of the self-seeking activities of industrial barons
and bureaucrats. Today, this moral explanation would be a gross oversimplification. It is doubtless true that most bourgeois enterprises are still
guided by a public-be-damned attitude, as witness the reactions of power
utilities, automobile concerns and steel corporations to pollution problems.
But a more serious problem than the attitude of the owners is the size of the
firms themselves — their enormous proportions, their location in a par-

ticular region, their density with respect to a community or waterway, their requirements for raw materials and water, and their role in the national division of labor.

What we are seeing today is a crisis in social ecology. Modern society, especially as we know it in the United States and Europe, is being organized around immense urban belts, a highly industrialized agriculture, and, capping both, a swollen, bureaucratized, anonymous state apparatus. If we put all moral considerations aside for the moment and examine the physical structure of this society, what must necessarily impress us is the incredible logistical problems it is obliged to solve — problems of transportation, of density, of supply (of raw materials, manufactured commodities and foodstuffs), of economic and political organization, of industrial location, and so forth. The burden this type of urbanized and centralized society places on any continental area is enormous.

Diversity and Simplicity

The problem runs even deeper. The notion that man must dominate nature emerges directly from the domination of man by man. The patriarchal family planted the seed of domination in the nuclear relations of humanity; the classical split in the ancient world between spirit and reality — indeed, between mind and labor — nourished it; the antinaturalist bias of Christianity tended to its growth. But it was not until organic community relations, feudal or peasant in form, dissolved into market relationships that the planet itself was reduced to a resource for exploitation. This centuries-long tendency finds its most exacerbating development in modern capitalism. Owing to its inherently competitive nature, bourgeois society not only pits humans against each other, it also pits the mass of humanity against the natural world. Just as men are converted into commodities, so every aspect of nature is converted into a commodity, a resource to be manufactured and merchandised wantonly. The liberal euphemisms for the process involved are "growth," "industrial society," and "urban blight." By whatever language they are described, the phenomena have their roots in the domination of man by man.

The phrase "consumer society" complements the description of the present social order as an "industrial society." Needs are tailored by the mass media to create a public demand for utterly useless commodities, each carefully engineered to deteriorate after a predetermined period of time. The plundering of the human spirit by the marketplace is paralleled by the plundering of the earth by capital. (The liberal identification is a metaphor that neutralizes the social thrust of the ecological crisis.)

Despite the current clamor about population growth, the strategic ratios in the ecological crisis are not the population growth rates of India but the production rates of the United States, a country that produces more than half of the world's goods. Here, too, liberal euphemisms like "affluence" conceal the critical thrust of a blunt word like "waste." With a ninth of its industrial capacity committed to war production, the United States is literally trampling upon the earth and shredding ecological links that are vital to human survival. If current industrial projections prove to be accurate, the remaining 30 years of the century will witness a fivefold increase in electric power production, based mostly on nuclear fuels and coal. The colossal burden in radioactive wastes and other effluents that this increase will place on the natural ecology of the earth hardly needs description.

In shorter perspective, the problem is no less disquieting. Within the next five years, lumber production may increase an overall 20 percent; the output of paper, 5 percent annually; folding boxes, 3 percent annually; plastics (which currently form 1 to 2 percent of municipal wastes), 7 percent annually. Collectively, these industries account for the most serious pollutants in the environment. The utterly senseless nature of modern industrial activity is perhaps best illustrated by the decline in returnable (and reusable) beer bottles from 54 billion bottles in 1960 to 26 billion [10 years later]. Their place has been taken over by "one-way" bottles (a rise from 8 to 21 billion in the same period) and cans (an increase from 38 to 53 billion). The "one-way" bottles and the cans, of course, pose tremendous problems in solid waste disposal.

The planet, conceived of as a lump of minerals, can support these mindless increases in the output of trash. The earth, conceived of as a complex web of life, certainly cannot. The only question is whether the earth can survive its looting long enough for man to replace the current destructive social system with a humanistic, ecologically oriented society.

Ecologists are often asked, rather tauntingly, to locate with scientific exactness the ecological breaking point of nature—the point at which the natural world will cave in on man. This is equivalent to asking a psychiatrist for the precise moment when a neurotic will become a nonfunctional psychotic. No such answer is ever likely to be available. But the ecologist can supply a strategic insight into the directions man seems to be following as a result of his split with the natural world.

From the standpoint of ecology, man is dangerously oversimplifying his environment. The modern city represents a regressive encroachment of the synthetic on the natural, of the inorganic (concrete, metals, and glass) on the organic, of crude, elemental stimuli on variegated, wide-ranging ones. The vast urban belts now developing in industrialized areas of the world are not only grossly offensive to the eye and the ear, they are chronically smog-ridden, noisy, and virtually immobilized by congestion.

The process of simplifying man's environment and rendering it increasingly elemental and crude has a cultural as well as a physical dimension. The need to manipulate immense urban populations—to transport, feed, employ, educate, and somehow entertain millions of densely concentrated people—leads to a crucial decline in civic and social standards. A mass concept of human relations—totalitarian, centralistic, and regimented in orientation—tends to dominate the more individuated concepts of the past. Bureaucratic techniques of social management tend to replace humanistic approaches. All that is spontaneous, creative, and individuated is circumscribed by the standardized, the regulated, and the massified. The space of the individual is steadily narrowed by restrictions imposed upon him by a faceless, impersonal social apparatus. Any recognition of unique personal qualities is increasingly surrendered to the manipulation of the lowest common denominator of the mass. A quantitative, statistical approach, a beehive manner of dealing with man, tends to triumph over the precious individualized and qualitative approach which places the strongest emphasis on personal uniqueness, free expression, and cultural complexity.

The same regressive simplification of the environment occurs in modern agriculture.[2] The manipulated people in modern cities must be fed, and to feed them involves an extension of industrial farming. Food plants must be cultivated in a manner that allows for a high degree of mechanization—not to reduce human toil but to increase productivity and efficiency, to maximize investments, and to exploit the biosphere. Accordingly, the terrain must be reduced to a flat plain—to a factory floor, if you will—and natural variations in topography must be diminished as much as possible. Plant growth must be closely regulated to meet the tight schedules of food-processing factories. Plowing, soil fertilization, sowing, and harvesting must be handled on a mass scale, often in total disregard of the natural ecology of an area. Large areas of the land must be used to cultivate a single crop—a form of plantation agriculture that not only lends itself to mechanization but also to pest infestation. A single crop is the ideal environment for the proliferation of pest species. Finally, chemical agents must be used lavishly to deal with the problems created by insects, weeds, and plant diseases, to regulate crop production, and to maximize soil exploitation. The real symbol of modern agriculture is not the sickle (or, for that matter, the tractor) but the airplane. The modern food cultivator is represented not by the peasant, the yeoman, or even the agronomist — men who could be expected to have an intimate relationship with the unique qualities of the land on which they grow crops — but the pilot or chemist, for whom soil is a mere resource, an inorganic raw material.

The simplification process is carried still further by an exaggerated regional (indeed, national) division of labor. Immense areas of the planet are increasingly reserved for specific industrial tasks or reduced to depots for raw materials. Others are turned into centers of urban population, largely occupied with commerce and trade. Cities and regions (in fact, countries and continents) are specifically identified with special products — Pittsburgh, Cleveland, and Youngstown with steel, New York with finance, Bolivia with tin, Arabia with oil, Europe and the United States with industrial goods, and the rest of the world with raw materials of one kind or another. The complex ecosystems which make up the regions of a continent are submerged by an organization of entire nations into economically rationalized entities, each a way station in a vast industrial belt system, global in its dimensions. It is only a matter of time before the most attractive areas of the countryside succumb to the concrete mixer, just as most of the Eastern seashore areas of the United States have already succumbed to subdivisions and bungalows. What will remain in the way of natural beauty will be debased by trailer lots, canvas slums, "scenic" highways, motels, food stalls, and the oil slicks of motor boats.

The point is that man is undoing the work of organic evolution. By creating vast agglomerations of concrete, metal, and glass, by overriding and undermining the complex, subtly organized ecosystems that constitute local differences in the natural world — in short, by replacing a highly complex, organic environment with a simplified, inorganic one — man is disassembling the biotic pyramid that supported humanity for countless millennia. In the course of replacing the complex ecological relationships, on which all advanced living things depend, for more elementary relationships, man is steadily restoring the biosphere to a stage which will be able to support only simpler forms of life. If this great reversal of the evolutionary process continues, it is by no means fanciful to suppose that the preconditions for higher forms of life will be irreparably destroyed and the earth will become incapable of supporting man himself.

Ecology derives its critical edge not only from the fact that it alone, among all the sciences, presents this awesome message to humanity, but also because it presents this message in a new social dimension. From an ecological viewpoint, the reversal of organic evolution is the result of appalling contradictions between town and country, state and community, industry and husbandry, mass manufacture and craftsmanship, centralism and regionalism, the bureaucratic scale and the human scale.

The Reconstructive Nature of Ecology

Until recently, attempts to resolve the contradictions created by urbanization, centralization, bureaucratic growth, and stratification were viewed as a vain counterdrift to "progress" — a counterdrift that could be dismissed as chimerical and reactionary. The anarchist was regarded as a forlorn visionary, a social outcast, filled with nostalgia for the peasant village or the medieval commune. His yearning for a decentralized society and for a humanistic community at one with nature and the needs of the individual — the spontaneous individual, unfettered by authority — were viewed as the reactions of a romantic, of a declassed craftsman or an intellectual "misfit." His protest against centralization and stratification seemed all the less persuasive because it was supported primarily by ethical considerations — by utopian, ostensibly "unrealistic," notions of what man could be, not by what he was. In response to this protest, opponents of anarchist thought — liberals, rightists, and authoritarian "leftists" — argued that they were the voices of historic reality, that their statist and centralist notions were rooted in the objective, practical world.

Time is not very kind to the conflict of ideas. Whatever may have been the validity of libertarian and non-libertarian views a few years ago, historical development has rendered virtually all objections to anarchist thought meaningless today. The modern city and state, the massive coal–steel technology of the Industrial Revolution, the later, more rationalized, systems of mass production and assembly-line systems of labor organization, the centralized nation, the state and its bureaucratic apparatus — all have reached their limits. Whatever progressive or liberatory role they may have possessed, they have now become entirely regressive and oppressive. They are regressive not only because they erode the human spirit and drain the community of all its cohesiveness, solidarity and ethico-cultural standards; they are regressive from an objective standpoint, from an ecological standpoint. For they undermine not only the human spirit and the human community but also the viability of the planet and all living things on it.

It cannot be emphasized too strongly that the anarchist concepts of a balanced community, a face-to-face democracy, a humanistic technology, and a decentralized society—these rich libertarian concepts—are not only desirable, they are also necessary. They belong not only to the great visions of man's future, they now constitute the preconditions for human survival. The process of social development has carried them out of the ethical, subjective dimensions into a practical, objective dimension. What was once regarded as impractical and visionary has become eminently practical. And what was once regarded as practical and objective has become eminently impractical and irrelevant in terms of man's development toward a fuller, unfettered existence. If we conceive of demands for community, face-to-face democracy, a humanistic liberatory technology, and decentralization merely as reactions to the prevailing state of affairs—a vigorous "nay" to the "yea" of what exists today—a compelling, objective case can now be made for the practicality of an anarchist society.

A rejection of the prevailing state of affairs accounts, I think, for the explosive growth of intuitive anarchism among young people today. Their love of nature is a reaction against the highly synthetic qualities of our urban environment and its shabby products. Their informality of dress and manners is a reaction against the formalized, standardized nature of modern institutionalized living. Their predisposition for direct action is a reaction against the bureaucratization and centralization of society. Their tendency to drop out, to avoid toil and the rat race, reflects a growing anger towards the mindless routine bred by modern mass manufacture in the factory, the office or the university. Their intense individualism is, in its own elemental way, a *de facto* decentralization of social life— a personal withdrawal from mass society.

What is most significant about ecology is its ability to convert this often nihilistic rejection of the status quo into an emphatic affirmation of life—indeed, into a reconstructive credo for a humanistic society. The essence of ecology's reconstructive message can be summed up in the word "diversity." From an ecological viewpoint, balance and harmony in nature, in society and, by inference, in behavior, are achieved not by mechanical standardization but by its opposite, organic differentiation. This message can be understood clearly only by examining its practical meaning.

Let us consider the ecological principle of diversity—what Charles Elton calls the "conservation of variety"—as it applies to biology, specifically to agriculture. A number of studies—Lotka's and Volterra's mathematical models, Bause's experiments with protozoa and mites in controlled environments, and extensive field research—clearly demonstrate that fluctuations in animal and plant populations, ranging from mild to pestlike proportions, depend heavily upon the number of species in an ecosystem and on the degree of variety in the environment. The greater the variety of prey and predators, the more stable the population; the more diversified the environment in terms of flora and fauna, the less likely there is to be ecological instability. Stability is a function of variety and diversity: if the environment is simplified and the variety of animal and plant species is reduced, fluctuations in population become marked and tend to get out of control. They tend to reach pest proportions.

In the case of pest control, many ecologists now conclude that we can avoid the repetitive use of toxic chemicals such as insecticides and herbicides by allowing for a greater interplay between living things. We must leave more room for natural spontaneity, for the diverse biological forces that make up an ecological situation. "European entomologists now speak of managing the entire plant–insect community," observes Robert L. Rudd. "It is called manipulation of the biocenose.[3] The biocenetic environment is varied, complex and dynamic. Although numbers of individuals will constantly change, no one species will normally reach pest proportions. The special conditions which allow high populations of a single species in a complex ecosystem are rare events. Management of the biocenose or ecosystem should become our goal, challenging as it is."[4]

The "manipulation" of the biocenose in a meaningful way, however, presupposes a far-reaching decentralization of agriculture. Wherever feasible, industrial agriculture must give way to soil and agricultural husbandry; the factory floor must yield to gardening and horticulture. I do not wish to imply that we must surrender the gains acquired by large-scale agriculture and mechanization. What I *do* contend, however, is that the land must be cultivated as though it were a garden; its flora must be diversified and carefully tended, balanced by fauna and tree shelter appropriate to the region. Decentralization is important, moreover, for the development of the agriculturist as well as for the development of agriculture. Food cultivation, practiced in a truly ecological sense, presupposes that the agriculturist is familiar with all the features and subtleties of the terrain on which the crops are grown. He must have a thorough knowledge of the physiography of the land, its variegated soils—crop land, forest land, pasture land—its mineral and organic content and its micro-climate, and he must be engaged in a continuing study of the effects produced by new flora and fauna. He must develop his sensitivity to the land's possibilities and needs while he becomes an organic part of the agricultural situation. We can hardly hope to achieve this high degree of sensitivity and integration in the food cultivator without reducing agriculture to a human scale, without bringing agriculture within the scope of the individual. To meet the demands of an ecological approach to food cultivation, agriculture must be rescaled from huge industrial farms to moderate-sized units.

The same reasoning applies to a rational development of energy resources. The Industrial Revolution increased the *quantity* of energy used by man. Although it is certainly true that preindustrial societies relied primarily on animal power and human muscles, complex energy patterns developed in many regions of Europe, involving a subtle integration of resources such as wind and water power, and a variety of fuels (wood, peat, coal, vegetable starches, and animal fats).

The Industrial Revolution overwhelmed and largely destroyed these regional energy patterns, replacing them first by a single energy system (coal) and later by a dual system (coal and petroleum). Regions disappeared as models of integrated energy patterns—indeed, the very concept of *integration through diversity* was obliterated. As I indicated earlier, many regions became predominantly mining areas, devoted to the extraction of a single resource, while others were turned into immense industrial areas, often devoted to the production of a few commodities. We need not review the role this breakdown in true regionalism has played in producing air and water pollution, the damage it has inflicted on large areas of the countryside, and the prospect we face in the depletion of our precious hydrocarbon fuels.

We can, of course, turn to nuclear fuels, but it is chilling to think of the lethal radioactive wastes that would require disposal if power reactors were our sole energy source. Eventually, an energy system based on radioactive materials would lead to the widespread contamination of the environment—at first in a subtle form, but later on a massive and palpably destructive scale. Or we could apply ecological principles to the solution of our energy problems. We could try to re-establish earlier regional energy patterns, using a combined system of energy provided by wind, water, and solar power. We would be aided by devices more sophisticated than any known in the past.

Solar devices, wind turbines, and hydro-electric resources, taken singly, do not provide a solution for our energy problems and the ecological disruption created by conventional fuels. Pieced together as a mosaic, as an organic energy pattern developed from the potentialities of a region, they could amply meet the needs of a decentralized society. In sunny latitudes, we could rely more heavily on solar energy than on combustible fuels. In areas marked by atmospheric turbulence, we could rely more heavily on wind devices; and in suitable coastal areas or inland regions with a good network of rivers, the greater part of our energy would come from hydro-electric installations. In all cases, we would use a *mosaic* of non-combustible, combustible, and nuclear fuels. The point I wish to make is that by diversifying our use of energy resources, by organizing them into an ecologically balanced pattern, we could combine wind, solar, and water power in a given region to meet the industrial and domestic needs of a given community with only a minimum use of harmful fuels. And, eventually, we might sophisticate our non-combustion energy devices to a point where all harmful sources of energy could be eliminated.

As in the case of agriculture, however, the application of ecological principles to energy resources presupposes a far-reaching decentralization of society and a truly regional concept of social organization. To maintain a large city requires immense quantities of coal and petroleum. By contrast, solar, wind, and tidal energy reach us mainly in small packets; except for spectacular tidal dams, the new devices seldom provide more than a few thousand kilowatt-hours of electricity. It is difficult to believe that we will ever be able to design solar collectors that can furnish us with the immense blocks of electric power produced by a giant steam plant; it is equally difficult to conceive of a battery of wind turbines that will provide us with enough electricity to illuminate Manhattan Island. If homes and factories are heavily concentrated, devices for using clean sources of energy will probably remain mere playthings; but if urban communities are reduced in size and widely dispersed over the land, there is no reason why these devices cannot be combined to provide us with all the amenities of an industrialized civilization. To use solar, wind, and tidal power effectively, the megalopolis must be decentralized. A new type of community, carefully tailored to the characteristics and resources of a region, must replace the sprawling urban belts that are emerging today.

To be sure, an objective case for decentralization does not end with a discussion of agriculture and the problems created by combustible energy resources. The validity of the decentralist case can be demonstrated for nearly all the "logistical" problems of our time. Let me cite an example from the problematical area of transportation. A great deal has been written about the harmful effects of gasoline-driven motor vehicles—their wastefulness, their role in urban air pollution, the noise they contribute to the city environment, the enormous death toll they claim annually in the large cities of the world and on highways. In a highly urbanized civilization it would be useless to replace these noxious vehicles by clean, efficient, virtually noiseless, and certainly safer battery-powered vehicles. The best of our electric cars must be recharged about every hundred miles—a feature which limits their usefulness for transportation in large cities. In a small, decentralized community, however, it would be feasible to use these electric vehicles for urban or regional transportation and establish monorail networks for long-distance transportation.

It is fairly well known that gasoline-powered vehicles contribute enormously to urban air pollution, and there is a strong sentiment to "engineer" the more noxious features of the automobile into oblivion. Our age characteristically tries to solve all its irrationalities with a gimmick—afterburners for toxic gasoline fumes, antibiotics for ill health, tranquilizers for psychic disturbances. But the problem of urban air pollution is too intractable for gimmicks; perhaps it is more intractable than we care to believe. Basically, air pollution is caused by high population densities—by an excessive concentration of people in a small area. Millions of people, densely concentrated in a large city, necessarily produce serious *local* air pollution merely by their day-to-day activities. They must burn fuels for domestic and industrial reasons; they must construct or tear down buildings (the aerial debris produced by these activities is a major source of urban air pollution); they must dispose of immense quantities of rubbish; they must travel on roads with rubber tires (the particles produced by the erosion of tires and roadway materials add significantly to air pollution). Whatever pollution-control devices will produce in the quality of urban air will be more than canceled out by future megalopolitan growth.

There is more to anarchism than decentralized communities. If I have examined this possibility in some detail, it has been to demonstrate that an anarchist society, far from being a remote ideal, has become a precondition for the practice of ecological principles. To sum up the critical message of ecology: if we diminish variety in the natural world, we debase its unity and wholeness; we destroy the forces making for natural harmony and for a lasting equilibrium; and, what is even more significant, we introduce an absolute retrogression in the development of the natural world which may eventually render the environment unfit for advanced forms of life. To sum up the reconstructive message of ecology: if we wish to advance the unity and stability of the natural world, if we wish to harmonize it, we must conserve and promote variety. To be sure, mere variety for its own sake is a vacuous goal. In nature, variety emerges spontaneously. The capacities of a new species are tested by the rigors of climate, by its ability to deal with predators and by its capacity to establish and enlarge its niche. *Yet the species that succeeds in enlarging its niche in the environment also enlarges the ecological situation as a whole.* To borrow E. A. Gutkind's phrase, it "expands the environment,"[5] both for itself and for the species with which it enters into a balanced relationship.

How do these concepts apply to social theory? To many readers, I suppose, it should suffice to say that, inasmuch as man is part of nature, an expanding natural environment enlarges the basis for social development. But the answers to the question go much deeper than many ecologists and libertarians suspect. Again, allow me to return to the ecological principle of wholeness and balance as a product of diversity. Keeping this principle in mind, the first step towards an answer is provided by a passage in Herbert Read's "The Philosophy of Anarchism." In presenting his "measure of progress," Read observes: "Progress is measured by the degree of differentiation within a society. If the individual is a unit in a corporate mass, his life will be limited, dull, and mechanical. If the individual is a unit of his own, with space and potentiality for separate action, then he may be more subject to accident or chance, but at least he can expand and express himself. He can develop — develop in the only real meaning of the word — develop in consciousness of strength, vitality, and joy."

Read's thought, unfortunately, is not fully developed, but it provides an interesting point of departure. What first strikes us is that both the ecologist and the anarchist place a strong emphasis on spontaneity. The ecologist, insofar as he is more than a technician, tends to reject the notion of "power over nature." He speaks, instead of "steering" his way through an ecological situation, of *managing* rather than *recreating* an ecosystem. The anarchist, in turn, speaks in terms of social spontaneity, of releasing the potentialities of society and humanity, of giving free and unfettered rein to the creativity of people. Both, in their own way, regard authority as inhibitory, as a weight limiting the creative potential of a natural and social situation. Their object is not to *rule* a domain, but to *release* it. They regard insight, reason, and knowledge as a means for fulfilling the potentialities of a situation, as facilitating the working out of the logic of a situation, not as replacing its potentialities with preconceived notions or distorting their development with dogmas.

Turning to Read's words, what strikes us is that both the ecologist and the anarchist view differentiation as a measure of progress. The ecologist uses the term "biotic pyramid" in speaking of biological advances; the anarchist, the word "individuation" to denote social advances. If we go beyond Read we will observe that, to both the ecologist and the anarchist, an ever-increasing unity is achieved by growing differentiation. *An expanding whole is created by the diversification and enrichment of its parts.*

Just as the ecologist seeks to expand the range of an ecosystem and promote a free interplay between species, so the anarchist seeks to expand the range of social experience and remove all fetters to its development. Anarchism is not only a stateless society but also a harmonized society which exposes man to the stimuli provided by both agrarian and urban life, to physical activity and mental activity, to unrepressed sensuality and self-directed spirituality, to command solidarity and individual development, to regional uniqueness and worldwide brotherhood, to spontaneity and self-discipline, to the elimination of toil and the promotion of craftsmanship. In our schizoid society, these goals are regarded as mutually exclusive, indeed as sharply opposed. They appear as dualities because of the very logistics of present-day society — the separation of town and country, the specialization of labor, the atomization of man — and it would be preposterous to believe that these dualities could be resolved without a general idea of the *physical* structure of an anarchist society. We can gain some idea of what such a society would be like by reading William Morris's *News From Nowhere* and the writings of Peter Kropotkin. But these works provide us with mere glimpses. They do not take into account the post–World War II developments of technology and the contributions made by the development of ecology. This is not the place to embark on "utopian writing," but certain guidelines can be presented even in a general discussion. And in presenting these guidelines, I am eager to emphasize not only the more obvious ecological premises that support them but also the humanistic ones.

An anarchist society should be a decentralized society, not only to establish a lasting basis for the harmonization of man and nature *but also to add new dimensions to the harmonization of man and earth.* The Greeks, we are often reminded, would have been horrified by a city whose size and population precluded a face-to-face, often familiar, relationship between citizens. There is plainly a need to reduce the dimensions of the human community — partly to solve our pollution and transportation problems, partly also to create *real* communities. In a sense, we must *humanize* humanity. Electronic devices such as telephones, telegraphs, radios, and television receivers should be used as little as possible to mediate the relations between people. In making collective decisions — the ancient Athenian ecclesia was, in some ways, a model for making social decisions — all members of the community should have an opportunity to acquire in full the measure of anyone who addresses the assembly. They should be in a position to absorb his attitudes, study his expressions, and weigh his motives as well as his ideas in a direct personal encounter and through face-to-face discussion.

Our small communities should be economically balanced and well rounded, partly so that they can make full use of local raw materials and energy resources, partly also to enlarge the agricultural and industrial stimuli to which individuals are exposed. The member of a community who has a predilection for engineering, for instance, should be encouraged to steep his hands in humus; the man of ideas should be encouraged to employ his musculature; the "inborn" farmer should gain a familiarity with the workings of a rolling mill. To separate the engineer from the soil, the thinker from the spade, and the farmer from the industrial plant promotes a degree of vocational overspecialization that leads to a dangerous measure of social control by specialists. What is equally important, professional and vocational specialization prevents society from achieving a vital goal: the humanization of nature by the technician and the naturalization of society by the biologist.

I submit that an anarchist community would approximate a clearly definable ecosystem; it would be diversified, balanced, and harmonious. It is arguable whether such an ecosystem would acquire the configuration of an urban entity with a distinct center, such as we find in the Greek *polis* or the medieval commune, or whether, as Gutkind proposes, society would consist of widely dispersed communities without a distinct center. In any case, the ecological scale for any of these communities would be determined by the smallest ecosystem capable of supporting a population of moderate size.

A relatively self-sufficient community, visibly dependent on its environment for the means of life, would gain a new respect for the organic interrelationships that sustain it. In the long run, the attempt to approximate self-sufficiency would, I think, prove more efficient than the exaggerated national division of labor that prevails today. Although there would doubtless be many duplications of small industrial facilities from community to community, the familiarity of each group with its local environment and its ecological roots would make for a more intelligent and more loving use of its environment. I submit that, far from producing provincialism, relative self-sufficiency would create a new matrix for individual and communal development — a oneness with the surroundings that would vitalize the community.

The rotation of civic, vocational, and professional responsibilities would stimulate the senses in the being of the individual, creating and rounding our new dimensions in self-development. In a complete society we could hope to create complete men; in a rounded society, rounded men. In the Western world, the Athenians, for all their shortcomings and limitations, were the first to give us a notion of this completeness. "The *polis* was made for the amateur," H. D. F. Kitto tells us. "Its ideal was that every citizen (more or less, according as the *polis* was democratic or oligarchic) should play his part in all of its many activities — an ideal that is recognizably descended from the generous Homeric conception of *arete* as an all-round excellence and an all-round activity. It implies a respect for the wholeness or the oneness of life, and a consequent dislike of specialization. It implies a contempt for efficiency — or rather a much higher ideal of efficiency; and efficiency which exists not in one department of life, but in life itself."[6] An anarchist society, although it would surely aspire to more, could hardly hope to achieve less than this state of mind.

If the ecological community is ever achieved in practice, social life will yield a sensitive development of human and natural diversity, falling together into a well balanced, harmonious whole. Ranging from community through region to entire continents, we will see a colorful differentiation of human groups and ecosystems, each developing its unique potentialities and exposing members of the community to a wide spectrum of economic, cultural, and behavioral stimuli. Falling within our purview will be an exciting, often dramatic, variety of communal forms — here marked by architectural and industrial adaptations to semi-arid ecosystems, there to grasslands, elsewhere by adaptation to forested areas. We will witness a creative interplay between individual and group, community and environment, humanity and nature. The cast of mind that today organizes differences among humans and other life-forms along hierarchical lines, defining the external in terms of its "superiority" or "inferiority," will give way to an outlook that deals with diversity in an ecological manner. Differences among people will be respected, indeed fostered, as elements that enrich the unity of experience and phenomena. The traditional relationship which pits subject against object will be altered qualitatively; the "external," the "different," the "other" will be conceived of as individual parts of a whole all the richer because of its complexity. This new sense of unity will reflect the harmonization of interests between individuals and between society and nature. Freed from an oppressive routine, from paralyzing repressions and insecurities, from the burdens of toil and false needs, from the trammels of authority and irrational compulsion, individuals will finally, for the first time in history, be in a position to realize their potentialities as members of the human community and the natural world.

Notes

1. Quoted in Angus M. Woodbury, *Principles of General Ecology* (New York: Blackiston, 1954), p. 4.
2. For insight into this problem the reader may consult *The Ecology of Invasions* by Charles S. Elton (New York: Wiley, 1958), *Soil and Civilization* by Edward Hyams (London: Thames and Hudson, 1952), *Our Synthetic Environment* by Murray Bookchin [pseud. Lewis Herber] (New York: Knopf, 1962), and *Silent Spring* by Rachel Carson (Boston: Houghton Mifflin, 1962). The last should be read not as a diatribe against pesticides but as a plea for ecological diversification.
3. Rudd's use of the word "manipulation" is likely to create the erroneous impression that an ecological situation can be described by simple mechanical terms. Lest this impression arise, I would like to emphasize that our knowledge of an ecological situation and the practical use of this knowledge are matters of insight rather than power. Charles Elton states the case for the management of an ecological situation when he writes: "The world's future has to be managed, but this management would not be like a game of chess . . . [but] more like steering a boat."
4. Robert L. Rudd, "Pesticides: The *Real* Peril," *The Nation* 189, (1959): p.401.
5. E. A. Gutkind, *The Twilight of the Cities* (New York: Free Press of Glencoe, 1962), pp. 55–144.
6. H. D. F. Kitto, *The Greeks* (Chicago: Aldine, 1951), p. 16.

Free People's Transit

Michael J. McFadden

Why when our world is at the mercy of over 50,000 nuclear warheads, when our cities are strangled by poverty, corruption, and pollution, when thousands of people are dying of starvation every day, should we want to spend any of our energy promoting bicycles? . . .

FROM WIN August 17, 1978. Reprinted by permission of the author.

The Problem

Most of us realize in a peripheral sort of way that the automobile is the villain of the American transit scene. The following list of a dozen dirty facts and statistics proves how true that is. An analysis of societal myths and secrets a la Max Weber and Bill Moyers explores in more depth some of the misconceptions people commonly have about American transportation.

1. The average recent year has seen 25 million auto accidents killing 50,000 people and injuring five million more. U.S. government estimates indicate that up to 40 percent of the cars currently produced will cause someone injury or death.

2. In just the last 50 years, more than *three times as many* Americans have been directly killed by the auto than have died in all the battles of all the wars we have *ever* fought.

3. The automotive transit system accounts for 60 percent of the nation's air pollution (over 80 percent in some urban areas) and 91 percent of the carbon monoxide.

4. General Motors, through its holding company National City Lines, ripped up 88 percent of our electric streetcar systems during the period 1935–1955.

5. While only 2 or 3 percent of the land area of our cities is given to parks, many cities devote half or more of the land to the automobile and its services. In Los Angeles, the figure is an incredible 62 percent!

6. The typical American car owner spends *one of every four* waking hours supporting and using his or her car, and travels about 8000 miles in it. That is only five miles per hour—the speed of a fast walk!

7. In-city traffic often averages below 10 mph while creating over 80 percent of our urban noise pollution.

8. The automotive transport system is a major cause of our energy crisis and "need" for nuclear power: it accounts for one-fifth of our energy consumption and almost one-half of our oil consumption while consuming almost *10 times* the energy produced by all U.S. nuclear plants.

9. Automotive advertising expenditures approach $1 billion per year, traffic jam cost is estimated at $5 billion, economic losses

from accidents are $40 billion, and projected costs just for maintenance of our road network through 1990 hit $329 billion. In addition to this, one-sixth of American business enterprise and employment is auto-related, while 11 of our 22 biggest corporations are heavily or entirely dependent on the auto industry.

11. The AAA reported 365 million animal deaths from motor vehicles in 1968.

12. In 1975, 130 million American drivers drove a total of 133 trillion miles, with 8 of every 10 workers driving to their job.

Secrets

The automobile is a killer. Again and again in the above "dirty dozen" it is clear that the automobile is dangerous and even murderous. However, the auto industry has been fighting desperately against safety features that would cut profits or make the consumer think twice about how dangerous the car really is. On some levels, people are aware of the direct hazards of the automobile—parents in particular have constant worries about their children playing in the street. On other levels, the danger of the auto is seemingly erased as people happily hop into their cars at every opportunity and in every state of consciousnes or lack thereof.

The automobile wastes unthinkable amounts of our precious energy. Our automotive transport system consumes over 100 billion gallons of fuel each year, one-half of our oil and one-fifth of our energy. This has led not only to people freezing to death in fuelless homes during winter but also to the brink of war during the Middle East oil embargo. The fuel-hungry auto may even have been behind the Vietnam war as oil companies greedily sought claims off that country's coast.

This massive fuel consumption has also enabled power industries to call an energy crunch and thereby push the "necessity" of nuclear power as a "short-term solution" to our problems. The U.S. automotive transit system uses 15 quadrillion (15,000,000,000,000,000) BTUs of energy a year. All our present nuclear power plants combined only produce 1.8 quadrillion BTUs. A sizable cut in auto transit would free up so much fuel that any claim of a "critical need" for nuclear power would look downright silly.

Cars impoverish people. Much of working-class America is what we might call car-poor. One-third of American families have incomes under

$10,000, and 92 percent of these are buying, feeding, fixing, and insuring a car (for 15 percent it's two cars) at an annual cost approaching or exceeding a quarter of their income (1978 data). To say the children go to bed hungry while the gas tank is full is not exaggeration in our autocentric society. True, the car-poor family may have made a "free choice" to buy the car (though with the power of advertising and societal pressures this could well be disputed), but we often find that for many low-income families there has been no choice due to car ownership job requirements (unbelievably common) or complete lack of decent mass transportation.

General Motors destroyed our country's electric mass transit base. According to a 1973 U.S. Senate subcommittee report, in 1936, GM, Firestone, and Standard Oil created National City Lines, which immediately began to buy and destroy the nation's electric mass transit systems. By 1955, 88 percent of our streetcar network was eliminated and replaced by inefficient GM buses. Of course, to GM's great surprise, the buses often did not work as well as planned and so many commuters bought GM cars. Poor GM. On top of the failure of its buses to adequately replace the hundred-odd electric railway lines it had torn up in 45 cities, GM had to face the indignity of going to court where it was slapped with a monumental fine of $5,000. Its treasurer, H. C. Grossman, a key actor in the "motorization" campaigns, was clobbered with a $1 fine. Poor Mr. Grossman.

There is also evidence that GM has made deliberate efforts to keep our buses inefficient and substandard so people will buy cars.

Myths

Cars are the fastest, most efficient means of ground transit and they cut "distance." It has been said that George Washington made better time galloping around Philadelphia in 1776 than he could today if he drove. Given the speed of in-city traffic, that is probably true. A bicycle might well beat out both horse and car with ease. In urban commuter races, the bicycle almost always beats the car hands down.

Over longer inter-city distances either bicycle or horse would undoubtedly lose to the car (unless our modern-day Washington ran into a traffic jam, or out of gas, or jammed his transmission, etc.), but the car couldn't hope to compete with rail transit in either speed or efficiency. An individual going from New York to Washington, D.C. by Metroliner would arrive in three hours as opposed to at least four if he or she drove. If the United States had rail transit approaching the quality of that in Japan or some other countries, the trip could take well under two hours.

As for efficiency, a half-full train would be 12 times as efficient as the car both in fuel usage and passengers per hour transported along a given corridor, while producing only $\frac{1}{400}$ the carbon monoxide per passenger mile.

Finally, people conceive of the car as lessening "distance." Actually, by developing what Ivan Illich calls a "radical monopoly" over transportation, cars have *increased* distance. We are literally forced to consume transportation in larger and larger quanta; our society is increasingly structured so that we have almost no choice but to perform that consumption through the automobile. No longer can you run to the corner store for milk if you live in suburbia — it is now a five- to ten-minute car ride away. No more walking to work 15 minutes away — four out of five commuting Americans now drive to work in trips that commonly consume a good part of an hour. The kids no longer run down the block to play with school-chums — they now need to be ferried across the cloverleaf. The dream of suburbia as simultaneously close to country and city has turned into a nightmare of successive rings of suburban developments — with the peacefulness of the country pushed ever further away.

The automobile gives power and freedom to the individual. In actuality, the auto both disempowers and enslaves. On the economic level it enslaves through the enormous amount of wage-earning work that must be performed to buy and maintain it. An "auto junkie" can spend several hundred hours a year just paying for his or her "habit." On other levels the enslavement comes through the disempowerment. Without the car, the individual's powers of transport, of controlling his or her destination (destiny), of winning the loved one, become nil. The carless individual, along with, heaven forbid, the individual *who doesn't drive*, is an aberration and an obstacle to the smooth flow of traffic in our society. The merely temporarily carless, those whose cars are snowed-in or being repaired, are comparatively lucky. In a few days when they (i.e., their cars) recover they can rejoin society, return to work, get food from the "local" store, and visit their friends again.

Of course even with a car, the power and freedom to crawl along in bumper-to-bumper traffic and choose between Exxon and Shell is of debatable value.

The auto's increasing demand for new roads must be met. This is the myth that the auto industry, city governments, and municipal engineers ram down the throats of citizens protesting new highways. They conjure up visions of greater and greater congestion on existing roads, mountains of pollution, and external traffic jams. But the fallacy is exposed by the experience of places where existing roads have been closed.

The classic example was New York City's plan to enlarge Fifth Avenue where it cuts through Washington Square Park. Irate citizens not only succeeded in opposing the plan but got the existing thoroughfare through the park shut down. Fuming traffic engineers predicted doom for the surrounding neighborhood in the form of an overwhelming crush of traffic seeking alternate routes. In reality the traffic just disappeared. With the loss of the Fifth Avenue artery a percentage of motorists simply decided to take other means of transportation or go a completely different route.

This phenomenon is called "attrition," i.e., the number of cars in an urban area rise and fall as the attractiveness of driving there changes. New roads or parking facilities, in making driving more attractive, will ultimately increase the number of traffic jams, deaths, dangerously polluted days, etc. Conversely, by reducing highway facilities, the number of cars will go down as more and more people decide to use mass transit, bicycle, or move closer to work.

The bicycle is a toy, not a serious mode of transportation. It is estimated that over 80 percent of personal vehicle miles traveled in China are traveled by bicycle. The first of England's "new towns," Stevenage, has a population of 72,000 and was designed with separate roads for bicycles and cars. In Tanzania there are plans to expand the capital city of Dodoma into a city of a half million by the year 2000 with 75 percent of vehicle transit to be by bicycle in that year.

For those who say that such use of the bicycle could never be accepted in America there is the example of Davis, California. Davis launched a program encouraging its citizens to bike rather than drive and through this and other measures has cut energy use in half. Other cities in the United States could easily emulate this with some success as most urban car trips are for distances under five miles with only one person—the driver—aboard.

Bicycling takes only one-fifth the energy of walking, and thus the bicycle is the most efficient moving vehicle (with the cyclist as the most efficient moving being) on earth. The bicycle, a classic example of intermediate and appropriate technology, is almost immune to planned obsolescence due to its simplicity and ease of manufacture, is easy to repair, can carry 10 times its own weight, affords faster urban transit than the car, and is pollution-free!

A Better Way

It's easy to say that our present transportation base is far from ideal. But what would be ideal? What would a world with truly free transit look like?

There would have to be vastly improved mass transit systems. Mass transit must be able to guarantee fast, quiet, comfortable, and uncrowded rides with never an excessive wait for the next vehicle. In addition, access to these systems must be within easy reach of all who want to use them. Such transit systems are available with today's technology and merely require commitment and funding to become reality.

Cars would not be totally eliminated, but their numbers would be a tiny percentage of what they are today, and many or all of those could be electric powered from solar charged generators or utilize other pollution-free technology.

The bicycle will not be quite the same as it is today either. Practical bicycles were only perfected in the late 1800s and bicycle technology was barely in its infancy when its development was aborted by the internal combustion engine. New and revived developments would include such things as reclining multi-person capability cycles, flat-proof tires, power-assisted cycles that store energy from downhill braking, and energy-producing shock absorbers, "automatic transmission" sliding gear bicycles, rail bikes, and arm-powered tricycles for the handicapped or infirm.

Most importantly, the bicycle–mass transit combination would afford the door-to-door convenience so highly prized (yet seldom achieved due to parking problems) by old-society motorists. Key-operated racks (such as are now on buses in San Diego) on the outside of mass transit vehicles would allow quick attaching and releasing of bicycles and would be the rule.

Try to picture New York or Philadelphia with only a few thousand autos instead of a few million. Sidewalks would be widened into promenades with trees, benches, fountains, and recreation areas. Children and pets could be allowed to run about freely with minimal supervision. The air would be clear, and a good bit of the oily soot that now coats the cities would disappear.

In many areas of the cities, cars would be banned altogether, and, as shown by the experience of car bannings around the world, roadside businesses would flourish. Gas stations and vast parking lots could be converted into playgrounds, gardens, and vest-pocket parks. Think what Los Angeles would be like if it reclaimed even half of that 62 percent of land for human use. Perhaps the 1930s orange groves would even return!

Transformation of the automotive transit base would help to bring about a lessening of Third World exploitation. Resource demand would be lowered significantly and a number of major multi-national corporations would be severely weakened by the loss of the motoring market and its accessories. Decreased energy demands would further undermine support for the nuclear powered monoliths.

Commuters no longer cut off from each other by 4000 pounds of Detroit nightmare fiercely competing for road and parking space would be able to see and know each other as human beings. Respect for the body and its health would increase as more people cycled or walked to their destinations.

Businesses would once again spring up within walking or cycling distance of homes. Personal empowerment would flow from anyone's being able to quickly learn almost all there is to know about bicycle maintenance. (No more staring helplessly down at a dead hulk with a streaming radiator!) Feminists will rejoice as millions of women at present "trapped" in their homes would now be able to hop independently on their own bicycles and go where they damn well please.

The world will indeed look different if people get around without cars. It will be cleaner, healthier, safer, less cluttered, quieter, less macho, less centralized, freer.

But looking around us today, it seems the auto has such a firm stranglehold on society that nothing could ever dislodge it. I don't believe that that is true. I believe that by using the right methods on a variety of levels, we can not only dislodge the car, we can dismember it.

Getting There

Changing our auto-centric transit base will be a gigantic task. Some of the most powerful corporate interests in the world will fight very hard if they feel that this lucrative piece of their profit pie is threatened.

Our first task is to change people's entrenched attitudes and beliefs that the car is a God-given postulate of modern society. We have a complex and deeply embedded web of myths to unwind and secrets to expose to a public that will often feel personally threatened or attacked by our message and will therefore do its best not to hear us. We have to speak in such a way that we can be heard and with statements and arguments convincing and stunning enough to break through that public wall of apathy and indifference.

One of the great beauties of nonviolent direct action is that it comprises techniques which allow a lot of communication about very threatening topics to take place while keeping the actual level of threat low. This prevents powerful defense mechanisms from coming into play and maximizes the actual amount of true communication. In confronting automotive society we are often going to be talking to people who already feel some level of guilt or insecurity stemming from passing acquaintance with facts like the "dirty dozen." To lay too much stress on the negative at the beginning of a campaign against "autocracy" is to invite hostility and closed ears and minds. People know their auto habit is destructive. Many longtime drivers have themselves hit people or pets or at least had unpleasant memories of near-misses. People feel trapped by inescapable circumstances: how else can they get around in any practical way except by car?

In the beginning we must stress the positive: show people the fun and freedom of traveling by bicycle; stage events such as commuter races that show that the bike and mass transit are a faster and cheaper way of traveling downtown. Agitate for changes to make bicycling and public transit more attractive: bike routes, secure bike parking, lower transit fares (or *no* fares!) and allowing bikes on trains as is already done on New York/New Jersey's PATH and California's BART. At your next neighborhood health fair stress the health aspects of cycling and walking and give "safe cycling" lessons.

To work on this level would be somewhat frustrating to the more dedicated anti-automobile activists, but there are some fairly satisfying intermediate steps that can be taken before launching into a full-fledged attack on motordom. An example would be to push for the creation of selective "safe" streets in your community and throughout residential neighborhoods. "Safe" streets have traffic limited to a maximum speed of 15 mph, enforced by synchronized stop lights. Large signs should be posted prominently on these streets stating that pedestrians, children, pets, and cyclists have the undisputed right of way. The safety emphasis will find ready listeners among parents and pet owners, while restraint from seeking total auto bans saves us from alienating car owners on these streets.

Each such "safe" street created serves multifold purposes. First, it makes it easier, safer, and more attractive to walk or cycle by providing routes where there will be only a few slow-moving cars. Second, it hinders car movement slightly, thereby contributing to auto attrition. Finally, having a few such streets scattered around will lead to people on nearby streets agitating for the same privilege. What at first seemed to be a minor reform with negligible effects or threat to hard-core motorists could easily spread to the point where driving around in residential areas becomes as difficult and slow as driving downtown. It is at this point that wide segments of the public will be ready to consider abandoning their cars and utilizing the alternatives of walking, cycling, and mass transit.

Beyond the "safe" streets are streets without cars. Europe and Canada have seen a number of demonstrations by cyclists, sometimes numbering in the thousands, who have demanded bans on urban auto use. The last year or so has seen many exciting activities and developments. In Amsterdam 9000 cyclists rallied to the slogan of "Amsterdam without cars" and blocked traffic throughout the city all afternoon. In Montreal 400 cyclists illegally took their bikes on the subway (and subsequently showed up in court waving front wheels high to protest the dozen arrests), while in New York 1000 stormed the Queensborough Bridge (No arrests: A permanent bike lane was instituted the next day!). Perhaps the most promising recent development has been the formation of an International Bicycle and Transit Activists Network with regular meetings, coordinated inter-city demonstrations, a clipping service, and a newsletter.

Valuable allies for bicycle activists can often be found among the urban mass transit commuters. They are all too aware of the short shrift given the carless in our society and may be ready to agitate for more transit funding. Information sharing and consciousness-raising are especially valuable in this area, as many of these commuters are unaware of the funding priorities that give mass transit barely a tenth of the funding of the Highway Trust Fund, and they may have never even considered the practicality of supplementing their mass transit use with bicycles.

It is important to realize that the bicycle is unlikely to ever stand alone as the primary transit base in this country. The same may well be true for even sophisticated systems of public transit. However, the two modes taken together do stand a realistic hope of moving the automobile to a secondary position in our transportation complex.

Conclusion

No one in the social change movement works in a vacuum: what each of us does individually affects us all collectively. A movement to change the transit base in our society will, if large enough, help and strengthen the efforts of anti-nuke organizers, anti-corporate and labor organizers, self-empowerment and environmental groups, and will in turn be helped by them.

Transportation is a gut issue — it affects everybody, everybody is concerned about it on a day-to-day level. In America, where living and working conditions are substandard for millions of people, where life is strangled by a gigantic military budget and threatened with the possibility of hundreds of nuclear power plants, the "transit movement" has understandably failed to attract mass support. Hopefully, however, presently apolitical commuters, cyclists, and fume-choked pedestrians will come together to break free from the stranglehold of automotive society. Working in concert with other branches of the movement, bicycle and public transit activists can help us all bring about a world in which people are more important than profits.

Bibliography

Ballantine, Richard, *Richard's Bicycle Book* (New York: Ballantine Books, 1972, revised ed.)
Breines, S. and W. Dean, *The Pedestrian Revolution* (New York: Vintage Books, 1975).
De Bell, Garrett, *The Environmental Handbook* (New York: Ballantine Books, 1975).
Illich, Ivan, *Energy and Equity* (New York: Harper and Row, 1974).
Illich, Ivan, *Tools for Conviviality* (New York: Harper and Row, 1973).
Italian Art and Landscape Foundation, *More Streets for People* (1973).
Leavitt, Helen, *Superhighway—Superhoax* (New York: Ballantine Books, 1970).
Love, Sam (ed.), *Earth Tool Kit* (New York: Pocket Books, 1971).
McCullagh, James, *Pedal Power* (Emmaus, Pa.: Rodale Press, 1977).
Schneider, Kenneth, *Autokind vs. Mankind* (New York: Schocken, 1971).
Snell, Bradford C., *American Ground Transport* (Senate Committee on the Judiciary, Subcommittee on Antitrust and Monopoly; Washington, D.C.: U.S. Government Printing Office, 1974).
Swatak, Paul, *The User's Guide to the Protection of the Environment* (New York: Ballantine Books/Friends of the Earth, 1977).
Wattenberg, Ben, *The U.S. Fact Book, The Statistical Abstract 1978* (New York: Grosset and Dunlap, 1978).

4

Crime
and
the Law

The chief purpose of law and law enforcement is to uphold the interests of the ruling groups in a society. The function of police on the domestic level, and the army on the international level, is to protect existing privileges. In capitalist nations like the United States the laws stress protection of private property because that is the chief concern of the ruling groups. In state socialist countries like Russia, though the laws may be different, their purpose is the same: to uphold the existing system of power and privilege.

There are laws to protect property, government, and persons. But none of these laws promote justice in any way, according to Peter Kropotkin, nor do they prevent crime. The best way to eliminate crime is to reconstruct society, not to pass laws. Eliminate private property[1] and economic inequality, and you won't need laws protecting property. Abolish the state and you won't need legislation about crimes against the state. Crimes against the person, such as murder, rape, and assault, are not deterred by the existence of laws. There will probably always be some "crimes of passion," but their incidence will be much reduced in a properly reconstructed society.

Richard Vogel shows that economic downturns in America are related to increases in the numbers of new prisoners. This does not "prove" that unemployment causes crime, yet it does point to some causal relationship between economic crises in capitalist society and the rate of incarceration. A disturbing statistic is that although blacks constitute about 11 percent of the total population, they account for half of all prisoners. Vogel says this reflects higher unemployment rates, especially among black males. Over and above economic factors, I would add, the high incarceration rate of

117

blacks and other minorities in this country is also a reflection of racism in the society as a whole.

The United States has the dubious distinction of being second only to the Soviet Union and South Africa in the proportion of its population behind bars. The purpose of correction, Dennis Sullivan points out, is to inflict the punishment deemed necessary by the state to control so-called deviants. During the twentieth century an entire correction industry has grown in this country, encompassing thousands of jails and prisons, juvenile detention centers, halfway houses, and so on, staffed by hundreds of thousands of correctional personnel who make a living this way. Most criminologists see crime as an individual attribute of criminals, caused by various factors in their personal background. They come up with countless schemes for resocialization, few of which ever really work. Given the existence of a society based on private property and class distinctions, and a state based on coercion, many of the dispossessed will continue to commit crimes. What is needed, Sullivan suggests, is the reconstruction of our commodity-based society into communities based on human brotherhood, love, and mutual aid.

If we really wanted to eliminate murder, we would abolish the state, because states maintain themselves by preparing for and waging wars. As Bourne put it, war is the health of the state.[2] The state commits more crimes than individuals do, but individuals are punished and states are not.[3] The punishment of soldiers for perpetrating "war crimes" only masks the criminality of their governments. The trial of American officers for ordering the massacre of Vietnamese civilians at My Lai diverted public attention from the much greater culpability of the government that sent them there in the first place.

Cooperation with and obedience to authority that is seen as legitimate is what makes repressive government possible. Well-intentioned people who do not question their government go about their everyday jobs and pay their taxes because they don't see how their actions contribute to harming others far away. (Because most people obey voluntarily, force can be used effectively against the few who refuse.) Evils like the Vietnam war are facilitated by a complex system for the most part comprised of millions of individuals who never see the actual violence. This system includes the engineers and machinists who make the weapons, the revenue agents who collect taxes so the army can buy them, the truck drivers who transport them, and soldiers who finally use them. For every soldier sent to the front, there are dozens of persons who carry out research, procure supplies, transmit messages, and so on. Once the entire war machine is set in motion, it takes relatively few individuals to do the actual dirty work of dropping bombs, burning villages, guarding concentration camps, and torturing or killing prisoners.

Notes

1. The so-called right of private property, Kropotkin says, is actually the right to appropriate the product of other people's labor. Industrialists do not build their factories with their own hands, but exploit the labor of others and reap the profits. Similarly, the wealthy live in houses that others have built, and that derive much of their value from the labor that others have put into making roads, building other houses, and planting parks.
2. Randolph S. Bourne, *War and the Intellectuals* (New York: Harper & Row, 1964).
3. See Alex Comfort, *Authority and Delinquency in the Modern State* (London: Routledge and Kegan Paul, 1950).

Law and Authority

Peter Kropotkin

In existing States a fresh law is looked upon as a remedy for evil. Instead of themselves altering what is bad, people begin by demanding a *law* to alter it. If the road between two villages is impassable, the peasant says: — "There should be a law about parish roads." If a park-keeper takes advantage of the want of spirit in those who follow him with servile observance and insults one of them, the insulted man says, "There should be a law to enjoin more politeness upon park-keepers." If there is stagnation in agriculture or commerce, the husbandman, cattle-breeder, or corn speculator argues, "It is protective legislation that we require." Down to the old clothes man there is not one who does not demand a law to protect his own little trade. If the employer lowers wages or increases the hours of labor, the politician in embryo exclaims, "We must have a law to put all that to rights." In short, a law everywhere and for everything! A law about fashions, a law about mad dogs, a law about virtue, a law to put a stop to all the vices and all the evils which result from human indolence and cowardice.

FROM *Kropotkin's Revolutionary Pamphlets,* edited by Roger N. Baldwin. (New York: Vanguard Press, 1927), pp. 196–206; 212–218.

We are so perverted by an education which from infancy seeks to kill in us the spirit of revolt, and to develop that of submission to authority; we are so perverted by this existence under the ferrule of a law which regulates every event in life—our birth, our education, our development, our love, our friendship—that, if this state of things continues, we shall lose all initiative, all habit of thinking for ourselves. Our society seems no longer able to understand that it is possible to exist otherwise than under the reign of law, elaborated by a representative government and administered by a handful of rulers. And even when it has gone so far as to emancipate itself from the thralldom, its first care has been to reconstitute it immediately. "The Year I of Liberty" has never lasted more than a day, for after proclaiming it men put themselves the very next morning under the yoke of law and authority.

Indeed, for some thousands of years, those who govern us have done nothing but ring the changes upon "Respect for law, obedience to authority." This is the moral atmosphere in which parents bring up their children, and school only serves to confirm the impression. Cleverly assorted scraps of spurious science are inculcated upon the children to prove necessity of law; obedience to the law is made a religion; moral goodness and the law of the masters are fused into one and the same divinity. The historical hero of the schoolroom is the man who obeys the law, and defends it against rebels.

Later when we enter upon public life, society and literature, impressing us day by day and hour by hour as the water-drop hollows the stone, continue to inculcate the same prejudice. Books of history, of political science, of social economy, are stuffed with this respect for law. Even the physical sciences have been pressed into the service by introducing artificial modes of expression, borrowed from theology and arbitrary power, into knowledge which is purely the result of observation. Thus our intelligence is successfully befogged, and always to maintain our respect for law. The same work is done by newspapers. They have not an article which does not preach respect for law, even where the third page proves every day the imbecility of that law, and shows how it is dragged through every variety of mud and filth by those charged with its administration. Servility before the law has become a virtue, and I doubt if there was ever even a revolutionist who did not begin in his youth as the defender of law against what are generally called "abuses," although these last are inevitable consequences of the law itself.

* * *

The critics analyze the sources of law, and find there either a god, product of the terrors of the savage, and stupid, paltry and malicious as the priests who vouch for its supernatural origin, or else, bloodshed, conquest by fire and sword. They study the characteristics of law, and instead of perpetual growth corresponding to that of the human race, they find its distinctive trait to be immobility, a tendency to crystalize what should be modified and developed day by day. They ask how law has been maintained, and in its service they see the atrocities of Byzantinism, the cruelties of the Inquisition, the tortures of the Middle Ages, living flesh torn by the lash of the executioner, chains, clubs, axes, the gloomy dungeons of prisons, agony, curses and tears. In our own days they see, as before, the axe, the cord, the rifle, the prison; on the one hand, the brutalized prisoner, reduced to the condition of a caged beast by the debasement of his whole moral being, and on the other, the judge, stripped of every feeling which does honor to human nature, living like a visionary in a world of legal fictions, revelling in the infliction of imprisonment and death, without even suspecting, in the cold malignity of his madness, the abyss of degradation into which he has himself fallen before the eyes of those whom he condemns.

They see a race of law-makers legislating without knowing what their laws are about; today voting a law on the sanitation of towns, without the faintest notion of hygiene, tomorrow making regulations for the armament of troops, without so much as understanding a gun; making laws about teaching and education without ever having given a lesson of any sort, or even an honest education to their own children; legislating at random in all directions, but never forgetting the penalties to be meted out to ragamuffins, the prison and the galleys, which are to be the portion of men a thousand times less immoral than these legislators themselves.

Finally, they see the jailer on the way to lose all human feelings, the detective trained as a blood-hound, the police spy despising himself; "informing," metamorphosed into a virtue; corruption, erected into a system; all the vices, all the evil qualities of mankind countenanced and cultivated to insure the triumph of law.

All this we see, and, therefore, instead of inanely repeating the old formula, "Respect the law," we say, "Despise law and all its attributes!" In place of the cowardly phrase, "Obey the law," our cry is "Revolt against all laws!"

Only compare the misdeeds accomplished in the name of each law with the good it has been able to effect, and weigh carefully both good and evil, and you will see if we are right.

Relatively speaking, law is a product of modern times. For ages and ages mankind lived without any written law, even that graved in symbols upon the entrance stones of a temple. During that period, human relations were simply regulated by customs, habits and usages, made sacred by constant repetition, and acquired by each person in childhood, exactly as he learned how to obtain his food by hunting, cattle-rearing, or agriculture.

All human societies have passed through this primitive phase, and to this day a large proportion of mankind have no written law. Every tribe has its own manners and customs; customary law, as the jurists say. It has social habits, and that suffices to maintain cordial relations between the inhabitants of the village, the members of the tribe or community. Even amongst ourselves — the "civilized" nations — when we leave large towns, and go into the country, we see that there the mutual relations of the inhabitants are still regulated according to ancient and generally accepted customs, and not according to the written law of the legislators. The peasants of Russia, Italy, and Spain, and even of a large part of France and England, have no conception of written law. It only meddles with their lives to regulate their relations with the State.* As to relations between themselves, though these are sometimes very complex, they are simply regulated according to ancient custom. Formerly, this was the case with mankind in general.

* * *

But as society became more and more divided into two hostile classes, one seeking to establish its domination, the other struggling to escape, the strife began. Now the conqueror was in a hurry to secure the results of his actions in a permanent form, he tried to place them beyond question, to make them holy and venerable by every means in his power. Law made its appearance under the sanction of the priest, and the warrior's club was placed at its service. Its office was to render immutable such customs as were to the advantage of the dominant minority. Military authority undertook to ensure obedience. This new function was a fresh guarantee to the power of the warrior; now he had not only mere brute force at his service; he was the defender of law.

If law, however, presented nothing but a collection of prescriptions serviceable to rulers, it would find some difficulty in insuring acceptance and obedience. Well, the legislators confounded in one code the two currents of custom of which we have just been speaking, the maxims which represent principles of morality and social union wrought out as a result of life in common, and the mandates which are meant to ensure external existence

*Kropotkin was writing about 19th century Europe — Ed.

to inequality. Customs, absolutely essential to the very being of society, are, in the code, cleverly intermingled with usages imposed by the ruling caste, and both claim equal respect from the crowd. "Do not kill," says the code, and hastens to add, "And pay tithes to the priest." "Do not steal," says the code, and immediately after, "He who refuses to pay taxes, shall have his hand struck off."

Such was law; and it has maintained its two-fold character to this day. Its origin is the desire of the ruling class to give permanence to customs imposed by themselves for their own advantage. Its character is the skillful commingling of customs useful to society, customs which have no need of law to insure respect, with other customs useful only to rulers, injurious to the mass of the people, and maintained only by the fear of punishment.

Like individual capital, which was born of fraud and violence, and developed under the auspices of authority, law has no title to the respect of men. Born of violence and superstition, and established in the interests of consumer, priest, and rich exploiter, it must be utterly destroyed on the day when the people desire to break their chains.

* * *

The millions of laws which exist for the regulation of humanity appear upon investigation to be divided into three principal categories: protection of property, protection of persons, protection of government. And by analyzing each of these three categories, we arrive at the same logical and necessary conclusion: *the uselessness and hurtfulness of law.*

Socialists know what is meant by protection of property. Laws on property are not made to guarantee either to the individual or to society the enjoyment of the produce of their own labor. On the contrary, they are made to rob the producer of a part of what he has created, and to secure to certain other people that portion of the produce which they have stolen either from the producer or from society as a whole. When, for example, the law establishes Mr. So-and-So's right to a house, it is not establishing his right to a cottage he has built for himself, or to a house he has erected with the help of some of his friends. In that case no one would have disputed his right. On the contrary, the law is establishing his right to a house which is *not* the product of his labor; first of all because he has it built for him by others to whom he has not paid the full value of their work, and next because that house represents a social value which he could not have produced for himself. The law is establishing his right to what belongs to everybody in general and to nobody in particular. The same house built in the midst of Siberia would not have the value it possesses in a large town, and, as we know, that value arises from the labor of something like fifty generations of men who have built the town, beautified it, supplied it with water and gas, fine promenades, colleges, theatres, shops, railways and roads leading in all directions. Thus, by recognizing the right of Mr. So-and-So to a particular house in Paris, London, or Rouen, the law is unjustly appropriating to him a certain portion of the produce of the labor of mankind in general. And it is precisely because this appropriation and all other forms of property bearing the same character are a crying injustice, that a whole arsenal of laws and a whole army of soldiers, policemen, and judges are needed to maintain it against the good sense and just feeling inherent in humanity.

Half our laws — the civil code in each country — serves no other purpose than to maintain this appropriation, this monopoly for the benefit of certain individuals against the whole of mankind. Three-fourths of the causes decided by the tribunals are nothing but quarrels between monopolists — two robbers disputing over their booty. And a great many of our criminal laws have the same object in view, their end being to keep the workman in a subordinate position towards his employer, and thus afford security for exploitation.

As for guaranteeing the product of his labor to the producer, there are no laws which even attempt such a thing. It is so simple and natural, so much a part of the manners and customs of mankind, that law has not given it so much as a thought. Open brigandage, sword in hand, is no feature of our age. Neither does one workman ever come and dispute the produce of his labor with another. If they have a misunderstanding they settle it by calling in a third person, without having recourse to law. The only person who exacts from another what the other has produced, is the proprietor, who comes in and deducts the lion's share. As for humanity in general, it everywhere respects the right of each to what he has created, without the interposition of any special laws.

As all the laws about property which make up thick volumes of codes and are the delight of our lawyers have no other object than to protect the unjust appropriation of human labor by certain monopolists, there is no reason for their existence, and on the day of the revolution, social revolutionists are thoroughly determined to put an end to them. Indeed, a bonfire might be made with perfect justice of all laws bearing upon the so-called rights of property, all title-deeds, all registers, in a word, of all that is in any way connected with an institution which will soon be looked upon as a blot in the history of humanity, as humiliating as the slavery and serfdom of past ages.

The remarks just made upon laws concerning property are quite as applicable to the second category of laws; those for the maintenance of government, i.e., constitutional law.

It again is a complete arsenal of laws, decrees, ordinances, orders in council, and what not, all serving to protect the diverse forms of representative government, delegated or usurped, beneath which humanity is writhing. We know very well — anarchists have often enough pointed out in their perpetual criticism of the various forms of government — that the mission of all governments, monarchical, constitutional, or republican, is to protect and maintain by force the privileges of the classes in possession, the aristocracy, clergy and traders. A good third of our laws — and each country possesses some tens of thousands of them — the fundamental laws on taxes, excise duties, the organization of ministerial departments and their offices, of the army, the police, the church, etc., have no other end than to maintain, patch up, and develop the administrative machine. And this machine in its turn serves almost entirely to protect the privileges of the possessing classes. Analyze all these laws, observe them in action day by day, and you will discover that not one is worth preserving.

About such laws there can be no two opinions. Not only anarchists, but more or less revolutionary radicals also are agreed that the only use to be made of laws concerning the organization of government is to fling them into the fire.

The third category of law still remains to be considered; that relating to the protection of the person and the detection and prevention of "crime." This is the most important because most prejudices attach to it; because, if law enjoys a certain amount of consideration, it is in consequence of the belief that this species of law is absolutely indispensable to the maintenance of security in our societies. These are laws developed from the nucleus of customs useful to human communities, which have been turned to account by rulers to sanctify their own domination. The authority of the chiefs of tribes, of rich families in towns, and of the king, depended upon their judicial functions, and even down to the present day, whenever the necessity of government is spoken of, its function as supreme judge is the thing implied. "Without a government men would tear one another to pieces," argues the village orator. "The ultimate end of all government is to secure twelve honest jurymen to every accused person," said Burke.

Well, in spite of all the prejudices existing on this subject, it is quite time that anarchists should boldly declare this category of laws as useless and injurious as the preceding ones.

First of all, as to so-called crimes — assaults upon persons — it is well known that two-thirds, and often as many as three-fourths, of such "crimes" are instigated by the desire to obtain possession of someone's wealth. This immense class of so-called crimes and misdemeanors will disappear on the day on which private property ceases to exist. "But," it will be said "there will always be brutes who will attempt the lives of their fellow citizens, who will lay their hands to a knife in every quarrel, and revenge the slightest offense by murder, if there are no laws to restrain and punishments to withhold them." This refrain is repeated every time the right of society to *punish* is called in question.

Yet there is one fact which at the present time is thoroughly established; the severity of punishment does not diminish the amount of crime.

* * *

We are continually being told of the benefits conferred by law, and the beneficial effect of penalties, but have the speakers ever attempted to strike a balance between the benefits attributed to laws and penalties, and the degrading effect of these penalties upon humanity? Only calculate all the evil passions awakened in mankind by the atrocious punishments formerly inflicted in our streets! Man is the cruelest animal upon earth. And who has pampered and developed the cruel instincts unknown, even among monkeys, if it is not the king, the judge, and the priests, armed with law, who caused flesh to be torn off in strips, boiling pitch to be poured into wounds, limbs to be dislocated, bones to be crushed, men to be sawn asunder to maintain their authority? Only estimate the torrent of depravity let loose in human society by the "informing" which is countenanced by judges, and paid in hard cash by governments, under pretext of assisting in the discovery of "crime." Only go into the jails and study what man becomes when he is deprived of freedom and shut up with other depraved beings, steeped in the vice and corruption which oozes from the very walls of our existing prisons. Only remember that the more these prisons are reformed, the more detestable they become. Our model modern penitentiaries are a hundred-fold more abominable than the dungeons of the Middle Ages. Finally, consider what corruption, what depravity of mind is kept up among men by the idea of obedience, the very essence of law; of chastisement; of authority having the right to punish, to judge irrespective of our conscience and the esteem of our friends; of the necessity for executioners, jailers, and informers — in a word, by all the attributes of law and authority. Consider all this, and you will assuredly agree with us in saying that a law inflicting penalties is an abomination which should cease to exist.

Peoples without political organization, and therefore less depraved than ourselves, have perfectly understood that the man who is called "criminal" is simply unfortunate; that the remedy is not to flog him, to chain him up, or to kill him on the scaffold or in prison, but to help him by the most brotherly care, by treatment based on equality, by the usages of life among honest men. In the next revolution we hope that this cry will go forth:

"Burn the guillotines; demolish the prisons; drive away the judges, policemen, and informers — the impurest race upon the face of the earth; treat as a brother the man who has been led by passion to do ill to his fellow; above all, take from the ignoble products of middle-class idleness the possibility of displaying their vices in attractive colors; and be sure that but few crimes will mar our society."

The main supports of crime are idleness, law, and authority; laws about property, laws about government, laws about penalties and misdemeanors; and authority, which takes upon itself to manufacture these laws and to apply them.

No more laws! No more judges! Liberty, equality, and practical human sympathy are the only effectual barriers we can oppose to the anti-social instincts of certain among us.

Capitalism and Incarceration

Richard D. Vogel

"There are no political prisoners in America," say the right-wing ideologists every time the question comes up. "The people are who are in prison deserve to be there." This pat answer, however, does not survive concrete analysis. To understand fully the function of the American prison system we need only analyze the historical trends of incarceration and discover how they are related to the economic conditions of the country at large.

FROM *Monthly Review*, March 1983, pp. 30–41. Copyright © 1983 by Monthly Review Inc. Reprinted by permission of Monthly Review Foundation.

The data for this analysis are readily available. Annual reports on the change in the number of prisoners and the total prisoner population in the nation are published by the U.S. Department of Justice in the *National Prisoner Statistics,*[1] and an analysis of the state of the national economy is maintained in the form of detailed employment trends by the U.S. Department of Labor and reported in the *Handbook of Labor Statistics.*[2] The present analysis relies primarily on data taken from these public records.

The relationship between capitalism and imprisonment during the last half century can be presented graphically.

Figure 1 shows the parallel trends of incarceration rates for all state institutions in the country (the solid line) and national unemployment rates (the broken line) for the 51 years 1927 through 1978. The data used are three-year averages, In this way minor year-to-year fluctuations are smoothed out, thus providing easier observation of the relationship over the long run. Incidentally, the period represented in Figure 1 corresponds to what the American Correctional Association calls the "modern era of penal progress."[3] Let's take a close look at this "progress."

The unemployment rates in Figure 1 (and throughout this analysis) relate to involuntary unemployment — the annual average proportion of the total labor force that is jobless but seeking employment.

The incarceration rates in Figure 1 are the number of persons per 100,000 estimated year-end civilian population who were committed to state prisons by the courts during the year. Because incarcerations are reported as rates (proportions of the total population) they allow meaningful comparisons over time.

The parallel trends in unemployment and imprisonment depicted in Figure 1 are striking and deserve careful analysis because this relationship is the key to understanding the prison problem under capitalism. The chart includes the worst economic crisis in U.S. history, the Great Depression of the 1930s, when the number of jobless workers in the nation rose to almost one out of every four (24.9 percent) in 1933. Unemployment dropped to its lowest level (1.2 percent in 1944) during the full economic mobilization of World War II. Immediately after the war, joblessness began to increase at a steady rate and then dropped slightly during the Korean war (1950–1952). After 1953 unemployment in the nation continued on a general upward trend through the recession of the late 1950s and early 1960s. The rate of jobless workers dropped sharply throughout the 1960s with the escalation of the Vietnam war, reaching a low of 3.5 percent in 1969.

The post-Vietnam period shows a rapid increase in unemployment that surpassed the highest rate of the post–World War II years. And though this

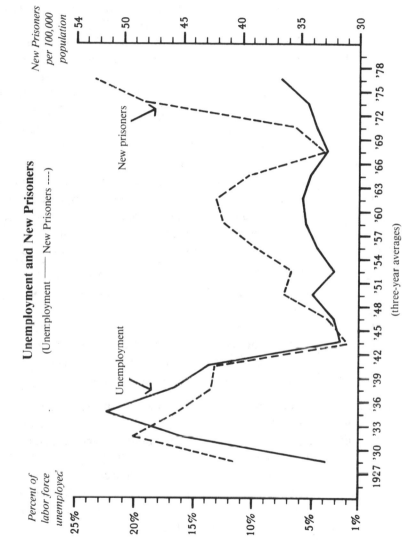

FIGURE 1

Unemployment and New Prisoners

(Unemployment ⸺ New Prisoners ----)

analysis stops at 1978, the latest unemployment rates exceed even those of the immediate pre–World War II period.

Figure 1 shows that fluctuations in the trend of committing people to prison are intimately connected to the movements of the national economy. The graph reveals an extremely high incarceration rate during the Great Depression when, in 1931, 52 persons per 100,000 civilian population were sent to prison. And corresponding to the lowest level of unemployment in American history, the lowest rate of imprisonment was during World War II (28.4 per 100,000 in 1944).

Immediately after the war, incarceration rates shot up and continued on an upward trend until 1961, with a minor break during the Korean war. The period of the Vietnam war displayed a drop in new incarcerations nearly as low as the years of World War II. Another dramatic increase in incarceration rates accompanied the military demobilization following the U.S. defeat in Vietnam and the subsequent economic crisis in this country.

It should be noted in passing that this relationship between war mobilization and prison populations has never been a secret. During World War II, Thorsten Sellin, then America's foremost authority on prisons, advised a convention of the American Prison Association about the postwar problems prison officials would have to face:

> As a result of the war our prison population has been falling. One reason is that the age group in which there has always been the most crime has been drafted. Many of the prospective customers are in the armed forces. *When the army is demobilized, if accompanied by considerable economic dislocations, our prisons will be full again.*[4] (Emphasis added.)

Sellin, staunch defender of the lofty principles of justice and punishment in America, was also a realist, advising the convention to increase the construction of facilities to accommodate the mass confinements that were sure to come in the war's wake.

His predictions, of course, came true. The same phenomenon accompanied the post-Vietnam demobilization; however, the rate of increase was much faster and has already gone much higher than any of the interwar years. The only significant break in the decade from 1968 to 1978 came in the year 1974. This temporary slackening in the rate of incarceration can be attributed to two interrelated factors.

The first was the fact that the American prison system had just been racked by a series of violent insurrections within the walls (e.g., the Attica uprising in New York), and prison officials, trying to cope with overcrowded and understaffed facilities, were refusing to accept new prisoners from the courts.

The second reason for the drop in new prisoners received in 1974 was the fact that the prison reform movement that had started in the late 1960s was at its zenith. Outside groups were exerting considerable pressure on state legislatures, and prisoner-initiated lawsuits challenging the abuses of the system had gotten as far as the federal courts. In a couple of states, suits charging that overcrowding constituted cruel and unusual punishment resulted in court orders to reduce prison populations.

However, the increased pressure from the recession of 1975 finally decided the issue, and the high level of imprisonment resumed for the remainder of the decade. In 1975 the incarceration rate hit the highest point of modern times (53 per 100,000), surpassing even the highest rate of the Great Depression.

The overall trends and year-by-year correspondence between economic conditions and imprisonment establish quite clearly the relationship between capitalism and incarceration—prisons under capitalism are, as Marx pointed out long ago, dumping grounds for the industrial reserve army. In very few respects are the social consequences of the un- and underemployment of people under capitalism as clear as they are in the fluctuations of the prison population.

The historical relationship between economic conditions and imprisonment under capitalism can be carried further. Figure 1 not only depicts the general history of incarceration but also indicates some important changes that have taken place in the system.

First, it should be noted that, given the overall relationship between unemployment and incarceration, one would have expected the incarceration rates of the period of the Great Depression to have gone much higher than they actually did. And, conversely, one would not have expected the incarceration rates to skyrocket in the immediate post-Vietnam period, given the comparatively moderate unemployment rates of that time.

The decade of the Great Depression deserves closer attention for two reasons. In addition to the fact that incarceration rates were below predictable levels, the 1930s witnessed the first attempt in American history to alleviate the problems caused by mass unemployment through direct economic relief programs. These two facts are closely interrelated.

Figure 2 shows the relationship between relief programs in millions of dollars (the broken line) and the rate of new prisoners received in state institutions from the courts (the solid line) for the years 1929 through 1940.

As can be seen, the incarceration rates increased sharply until 1931 and then began to drop off. From the year 1931 until the beginning of economic recovery (and the decline of relief programs in 1940), the relationship between economic relief and incarcerations was inverse—the more money that was spent on economic relief, the lower the rates of incarceration. This special relationship, like the overall relationship between unemployment and incarceration, underscores the economic basis of the prison question in America.

The post-Vietnam period in American penal history deserves equal attention. The fact that incarceration rates are much higher than would be predicted from prevailing unemployment rates after 1971 signals a change in the prison system that deserves careful consideration. This rapid acceleration in imprisonment indicates that the prison system has become even more sensitive to the booms and busts of monopoly capitalism than ever before. The ramification of this development should not be taken lightly—it signals a new height in the sophistication of repression in America.

Incarceration and the National Question

Another central issue in the analysis of the American prison system is the fact that over 60 percent of the inmate population of the nation consists of minority people, while these minorities compose less than 25 percent of the population at large. Advocates of prison reform are quick to lament racial discrimination in the criminal justice system but always steer clear of the basic structure of capitalism that accounts for the national disparity in the prison system.

The heavy concentration of minority people in prison should come as no surprise in view of this simple fact: the unemployment rate of black males is typically twice that of white males. This startling difference has held throughout the post–World War II period. The very consistency of the much higher black male unemployment rate represents a basic fact about the economic life of the national minorities as compared to the population at large. By commonly accepted bourgeois standards, white males have faced serious unemployment only in times of economic recession. In contrast, minority males have faced recession (and depression) levels of unemployment since the end of World War II, with exceptions only during the economic mobilization of the Korean and Vietnam wars.

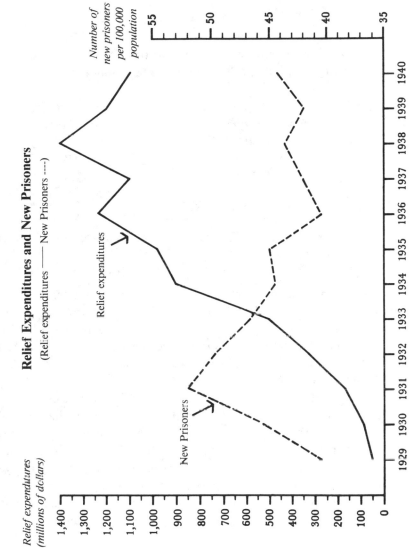

FIGURE 2

Relief Expenditures and New Prisoners

(Relief expenditures ——— New Prisoners ----)

The predictable result of this differential oppression is a disproportion of national minority people in America's prisons. Table 1 compares the black proportion of the national prisoner population to the black proportion of the national population at large from 1940 through 1974.

TABLE 1

A Comparison of the Black Prisoner Population with the Black Proportion of the National Population 1940–1974

Year	Black Proportion of the National Prisoner Population	Black Proportion of the National Population
1940	30.0%	10.4%
1950	35.3	10.7
1960	38.1	11.4
1970	43.0	11.1
1974	47.0	11.4

Source: Census Bureau, U.S. Department of Commerce and U.S. Department of Justice.

The data in Table 1 show that not only have black Americans always been over-represented in the prison system but the concentration of minority prisoners has been steadily increasing, from 30 percent in 1940 to 47 percent in 1974. The sensitivity of this issue has become such that 1974 was the last year that prisoner population by race was reported in public records by the U.S. Justice Department.

Further, it needs to be noted that the Justice Department, like the Labor Department, includes all Spanish-surnamed people in the "white" category and their reports do not, therefore, accurately reflect the true proportion of national minority people behind bars. Inspection of the detailed census data gathered on the institutionalized population every ten years discloses an average 16 percent for Spanish surnamed prisoners. When this number is added to the black proportion of the prisoner population, we get 63 percent as the average national minority prisoner population in America in 1974.

The increasing rate of oppression of national minorities in the American prison system is a direct consequence of the deepening crisis of monopoly capitalism and its differential impact on the national minorities.

The Politics of Imprisonment

The observation that oppression breeds resistance is nowhere better verified than inside the American prison system. There have been three major waves of prison disturbances in modern American penal history that we need to examine. The first of these waves was in 1929–1930, in which there were 11 major uprisings across the nation. The second wave started in 1952 and ended in 1955. During these four years, there were 47 major disturbances that resulted in property damage in excess of $10 million and considerable loss of life. The last wave was from 1968 through 1971, in which there were 40 major disturbances, including the revolt at Attica prison in upstate New York, which ended with the death of 10 hostages and 29 inmates and the wounding of 89 other people. Although these three waves of prison insurrections continue to puzzle bourgeois penologists, we need only put them into historical perspective to grasp their political significance.

The three waves of uprisings — 1929–1939, 1952–1955, and 1968–1971 — all took place during periods of economic recession and immediately after periods of relative prosperity when both the rate of new prisoners received and total prisoner populations were relatively low and stable. In all three periods the massive uprisings took place when the prisons of the nation were beginning to fill up again.

During these periods of rapid influx, the prisoner population undergoes significant changes. Masses of young people in the prime of life are being dumped into prison by the economic pressures of the stagnant economy, and they are more likely to react against the oppression.

During these initial periods of build-up, the prisons are least prepared to handle these people. After several years of functioning as custodians for reduced prisoner populations of older and more tractable inmates, neither the guards nor the prison administrators are equal to the task. At the beginning of the build-up the prisons do not have the facilities of human-power that they need for the job. During these critical periods the prison system must operate on the basis of a peculiar variation of the law of supply and demand by first accommodating the overload and then justifying their need for more funds, guards, buildings, etc., by pointing to the swollen populations. It has been during each of these critical periods, during the lag when the demand on the prison system surpasses the resources, that the widespread uprisings have taken place.

In short, economic crises in capitalist society at large lead to massive incarcerations, which in turn lead to penal crises. The crises in the prisons eventually lead to reactionary penal administration and intensified repression.

Where will it go from here? Between 1971 — and the end of the last series of prison uprisings — and 1981, the total prisoner population in America (including all state and federal institutions) increased from 197,838 to 369,009, an increase of more than 45 percent for the decade. In addition to this new all-time high, the last decade has also seen the highest rates and fastest increase in mass incarceration in the history of the country. These glaring facts, in conjunction with the current trends of the increasing concentration of national minority people in the prisons and the ever increasing sensitivity of the prison system to the demands of monopoly capitalism, insure that the prison problem in America can only get worse.

But, despite these new developments, the prison problem as a political issue has faded into the background. In the face of the current massive incarcerations, most liberals have abandoned efforts at prison reform, while conservatives, mouthing their slogans of law and order, are stuck with the dilemma of trying to accommodate the huge prison populations and, at the same time, hold down government spending on the prisons, as well as on various social services. In Texas, the largest and fastest growing state prison system in the nation, prisoners are living outside in tents, while the courts and state officials squabble about what to do with the overflow.

Is the American prison system a time bomb set to go off again? Probably not in the near future. The review of the history of mass insurrections in American prisons shows that the rebellions have always coincided with the initial stages of mass imprisonment, not during the periods of peak incarceration.

The current situation in the prisons bears this out. There have been sporadic outbreaks of violence since the last major wave of uprisings, but they have all been efficiently suppressed. The institutions are all overcrowded and the conditions inside are as bad as they have ever been. But the prison problem is currently being contained quite securely by tough administrations, armed not only with bars and guns, but also with the new prison technology of razor wire, taser guns, disabling gases, closed-circuit television and other monitoring devices, and, most of all, reactionary politics.

Reactionary politicians play on the fears and worries of the people about street and other crimes. Their proposals for still more repression, however, provide no solution. Longer prison sentences and harsher treatment of prisoners clearly have no bearing on the root cause of the growth of crime: unemployment and racism. What this study makes clear is that, at a minimum, only an effective job-creation program would help. Short of a major social transformation, militant struggle against racism and for a new WPA* (or its equivalent) is the only meaningful approach to the reduction of crime and the prison population.

*The reference is to the Works Progress Administration, founded in 1935 to provide work for the jobless on public-works projects. — Ed.

Notes

1. U.S. Department of Justice, *National Prisoner Statistics* (Washington, D.C.: U.S. Government Printing Office). These reports are published annually, but their circulation is limited. Summaries of these reports can be found in the annual *Statistical Abstract of the United States.*
2. U.S. Department of Labor, *Handbook of Labor Statistics* (Washington, D.C.: U.S. Government Printing Office). Annual.
3. American Correctional Association, *Manual of Correctional Standards* (Washington, D.C., 1966), p. 13.
4. *New York Times,* November 21, 1943, p. 29.

The Mask of Love

Dennis Sullivan

Corrections as Commodity

Twenty years ago, the word "corrections" as a term that contained meaning in itself was not a part of our language. The emergence of the word as a self-contained entity is highly significant to those concerned about issues of crime, punishment, and justice, for its presence requires a radically different framework for posing questions about these matters. The term does not reflect simply the enormous growth in personnel and hardware that is taking place in the American correctional system or the updating and broadening in scope of an antiquated, nineteenth-century penology, as most profesionals surmise. Rather, I believe that "corrections" is a term of despair and breakdown, stemming from a quantum leap into centralized existence. It reflects a new way we have come to relate to each other for our

FROM Dennis Sullivan, *The Mask of Love* (Port Washington, N.Y.: Kennikat Press, 1980). Reprinted by permission of Associated Faculty Press, Inc. Copyright 1980 by Kennikat Press.

safety. It reflects an economy of relationship that regards the processes, activities, feelings, and experiences that lead to community safety and social unity as a commodity that is defined, prepared, and delivered by a core of experts and consumed by a docile clientele.

This economy of relationship — whether in a capitalist or state socialist context — is based on the belief that outside the state–professional complex there is no salvation, no personal rehabilitation, healing, or growth, no community integration or safety. Those who believe that this situation constitutes a severe crisis for human beings are faced with an additional dilemma, since within the social conditions prescribed by this twentieth-century multinational existence, as Ivan Illich notes, "crisis has come to mean that moment when doctors, diplomats, bankers, and assorted social engineers take over and liberties are suspended" (1978:4), not when people huddle together to provide for each other through mutual aid.

* * *

The change that has occurred in corrections is not a singular phenomenon but can be understood in relation to all human services. The same commodity orientation can be found in medicine, education, work, and religion, where basic human needs and their satisfaction are treated as a commodity to be purchased as a service produced or performed by someone else — namely, the expert. A person purchases sanity from a therapist, earns an education from a teacher, regains health from a physician, alleviates fears of being hurt from a public safety specialist, and is reborn by receiving revelation from a mediary. These terms and concepts put human experience into a world of ownership, production, and consumption. They are part of the character of our present market-intensive society in which convivial or social means toward community are being replaced by what Illich refers to as "manipulative industrial ware" (1978:3).

For some people such a framework might be seen as an indirect incrimination of what they do, for it places the agencies and agents of justice as well as the total complex of human services squarely in the political-economic arena, a context in which those involved in help delivery have struggled not to see themselves. It is seen as an affront to the helping image. But it is precisely within this framework of need satisfaction as political economy that corrections has emerged and receives its meaning. Whether corrections is viewed as a means to correct crime, issue punishment, or generate safety in communities, it reflects a professionalized commodity orientation toward human experience. It is the opposite of mutual aid, a social, face-to-face process of which each of us is capable.

A necessary concomitant of this growing commodity orientation toward human experience has been the disappearance or growing inaccessibility, perhaps even the permanent loss, of the resources tools, or instincts of mutual aid — the instincts of sociality by which we foster a face-to-face existence. The concept and practice of mutual aid that once bonded people together as neighbors has been nearly totally displaced by professionalism, self-reliance by law, neighborliness by commodities and services, the sharing of gifts and hospitality by payment and insurance plans.

As our social relationships become increasingly those of strangers, unwilling or unable to provide safety or protection for each other freely by mutual aid, we find ourselves collectively coming full circle — that is, we find ourselves having to purchase mutual aid as a commodity individually. It should come as no surprise that there are increasing numbers of people, whom I refer to as "correctionalists," who make a living off the effects of these stranger relationships, of the forfeiture of mutual aid, in the same way that educators live on society's alienation from self, doctors prosper on the division between work and leisure that has destroyed health, and politicians thrive on the distribution of welfare which, in the first instance, was financed by those they are paid to assist. Illich has described how these institutions have become forms of appropriation and erode our sense of competency and autonomy (1978:4). While in the narrow sense the term "correctionalist" may refer to a criminologist, a criminal justice bureaucrat, a policymaker, a researcher, a planner, or any person who delivers or produces justice as a commodity, the term extends to anyone who teaches or heals or consoles another through the circuitous route of commodity and paid service.

Whereas once dependence on commodities or purchase for survival was a sign of bad times — the gravity of one's hardship assessed by how much a person had to purchase from another for survival — in our present culture consumption and purchase have become a sign of personal worth, something to be counted as a blessing and shown off. To *have* a therapist, a lawyer, a string of personal physician–specialists for every part of the body, or to have had a certified education is considered a sign of prosperity. The same applies to correcting our hurts or social harms. To *have* a well-managed, well-financed, professionally staffed, well-researched justice complex that produces safety is considered a sign of progress. This purchase orientation must be understood in a still larger social–economic context, that of having needs or being needy in our present society. To be without, to be needy, is among the greatest social disgraces. Ironically, it has become less a disgrace to purchase one's needs or necessities from a professional stranger — even if it entails becoming a captive to the supplier — than to admit one's dependence and seek support for it from one's neighbors. The result is that there always remain hidden away one's needs, frailty, emptiness, loneliness, those elements that give each of us personal definition (our uniqueness) and bring us together to support each other through mutual aid.

* * *

Rehabilitation: Never a Possibility

It is important to recognize when discussing the demise of rehabilitation — whether it is referred to as treatment, reintegration, or reformation — that as a process or means of healing or making whole, via the state, it was never a possibility. There are only certain kinds of perceptions and experiences that can exist within given economic structures — the extreme being that something cannot be its opposite at the same time. But this was precisely the problem with rehabilitation, namely, that as a form of state-directed aid its underlying and necessary principle of shared responsibility for health and growth had to be sacrificed for the monopolization of the process by the state and its privatizing professions. What rehabilitation stood for at its roots — both philosophically and structurally — is diametrically opposed to the ideology, structure, and function of the state. The underlying principle of rehabilitation is that there is no human justification for punishment ever in correcting relationship, whereas the state's very existence is based on the principle that punishment is a political — and therefore human — necessity. Let me explain.

Rehabilitation as a treatment modality had its roots in the principles and processes of psychiatry and psychoanalysis. The underlying concern of these methods is "to uncover the principle of union, or communion, buried beneath the surface separation, the surface declarations of independence, the surface signs of private property" (Brown, 1966:142) to bring about unity within a person and the unity of self with the whole, with what is other. Through the mutual exploration of dreams, the primitive, the unconscious by therapist and patient, a common humanity, a basic human goodness is confirmed, accompanied by the revelation that magic as well as madness are everywhere, are factors to be reckoned with by every person in his or her struggle to be human, throughout life, as well as by every civilization. We discover as well that sickness and health are not limited to certain age groups or to certain classes of people or to certain kinds of people biologically. Sickness is a continuing state of self, of every person struggling to be free from illusions and the meaninglessness of externally imposed boundaries. Similarly health is a continuing state of self, awareness that "the distinction between self and external world is not an immutable fact, but an artificial construction. It is a boundary line; like all boundaries not natural but conventional; like all boundaries, based on love and hate" (Brown, 1966:142). Sickness and health, like love and hate, power and cooperation are ever-present in each of us simultaneously. And if competition and power are believed to be at the core of the human essence, so also then are cooperation and mutual aid equally situated at that core (Rogers, 1961). It is the existing social–economic conditions — whether they are based on principles of competition and power or cooperation and mutual aid — that brings forth and reinforces the meaningfulness and authenticity of one or the other state of self: sickness or health. When social conditions are personally supportive, based on trust and cooperation there blossoms a wholesomeness of self, where previously there had been depression, neurosis, madness, under conditions of power (Jourard, 1968). The unity or rehabilitation of a person is as possible or impossible as the unity of the "corporation soul" about him.

Through the principles of psychoanalysis we discover that at the level of the unconscious we all share the same dream of being free, as well as the same persistent despair of ever reaching that goal. Personal problems along the way may be unique to specific persons at given times, but they are not the result of a fixed, determining force which reflects a flaw in the basic nature of the human organism. If this were the case — that is, if one organism were flawed by nature — so are we all. Rather, personal problems are universal because each of us is part of a finite human community, struggling to find meaning. They are also unique because each of us finds this meaning or completion in different ways, for our needs and struggles are unique.

Healing, rehabilitating, overcoming madness, are not some thing, or object therefore; they do not emerge in what is given to one person and consumed by another, but in people being present to and supportive of each other through their own words and gestures. Healing or rehabilitation is a deeply personal experience, but it is also shared in that people begin to unmask what they were hiding, begin to break down the surface separations that kept them apart. Healing comes in the experiencing and expression of our needs among others, for through our needs we begin to recognize that each is unique but also that the needs we have are universal, belong to others, that all suffer from the weakness, vulnerability, and ignorance of the human condition. Healing, as with sickness, is an equalizing process, for it asserts the primacy of human experience as connectedness with each other. It requires the dismantling of any political–economic system that maintains ownership, separateness, and disconnectedness. Such a system is by nature anti-human, for it destroys the very process of connectedness that gives us a true sense of our humanity. Our sense of humanity may be our frailness, but it is also our strength.

The very existence and continuation of the state, on the other hand, requires the maintenance of life based on private property, class distinctions, separateness, and surface declarations. The existence of the state presupposes that the means of production (to meet human needs) is not the shared work of humanity, but that each individual creates or produces an object entirely by him or herself, having the right to appropriate it. The same is true, therefore, of sickness and health. Sickness and health are not shared or universal phenomena but are person- or group-specific—namely, for those who do not produce and who do not appropriate for themselves what they produce. The state is based upon this privatized notion of production and health, reinforces the personal pathology theme of sickness, thereby creating a place for itself as rehabilitator. All are subject to rehabilitation who are excluded from what the state defines as the essence of health—producing, appropriating, adult, white, male. He or "it" is the standard of health, sanity, non-criminality.

State ideology asserts, therefore, under the cloak of scientific method, that Black, Indian, Hispanic, and Mexican Americans are prone to criminality, that women are prone to madness, that children are prone to delinquency and self-centeredness, and that their acts are the result of personal and group-specific pathologies, flaws they alone possess and which they alone should take responsibility for—that is, to be punished for. The schisms of age, race, sex, and class that are created and maintained by a competition-based capitalist economy are exploited by the state to justify its role as rehabilitator. Healing, providing competency, becomes the sole function of state-trained, state-licensed personnel who are willing to accept surface declarations, surface separations—that is, the political—as the fully real. Human responsibility is not responsibility to community but to consuming the state–professional concoctions of reality.

* * *

Punishment Facts

To justify the maintenance and continuing expansion of the state punishment complex, correctionalists have maintained an allegiance to science, shifting their justifications from the criminal act to the criminal, then back again to the criminal act. What correctionalists, who view life processes in a pendulum fashion, fail to recognize is that the problem with punishment is not what form the justifications take but that relationship leading to human experience requires justification at all. Moreover, they seem to omit the fact that no matter what justification is selected, hierarchical, power-based relationships are created and maintained which are essentially destructive to the human spirit. Nevertheless, the history of corrections and penology continues to be an endless parading of new punishment forms, exhibited before an impatient public, selected with the depth and feeling of winning bingo numbers.

As government and private funding agency monies have flowed into the pockets of correctionalists, into their agencies and universities through indirect costs, they have searched for the core of the criminal, that core place within a person where they might apply the doses of scientifically prepared and state-certified punishment. Correctionalists have descended upon the correctional client like a hawk, peering into his or her chromosomes, intelligence level, skull shape, tattoos, sexual habits, work habits, speech patterns, clothing design, and writing styles. They have scaled prisoner perception of time, of authority, of self, over time and under different authorities. The roles he or she assumed during imprisonment were charted, their relationships with all kinds of prison staff were studied methodically, with guards, fellow prisoners, cottage parents, therapists, counselors, teachers, lawyers, even the researchers themselves. There was no sign of human growth or personal wholeness from the punishment methods.

Various types of sentences were introduced. Longer sentences were tried, then shorter sentences; then longer sentences were reintroduced. Determinate sentences were changed to indeterminate sentences, then back again to determinate sentences. Fines were introduced, then fines with jail, probation plus a fine, probation plus jail, parole, then parole revocation. The result was the same — no sign of human growth or personal wholeness with punishment.

Prisoners were placed in halfway houses, in group homes, on parole or work release, off parole. They were persuaded to live according to the principles of token economies, aversive therapies, psychotherapy, psychodrama, psychosurgery, reality therapy. The effects were weighed and reweighed with the latest statistical tools, but to no avail when it came to human experience or competency to live cooperatively among others.

Prisoners have been put under varying degrees of supervision in special cottages, special tiers, given special food to eat, special books to read, special medicines. Collegefields, Essexfields, Highfields — all kinds of fields treatment have been given. Prisoners have been put into maximum, medium, minimum, maximum–maximum, and solitary confinement quarters. They have been forced to live under various degrees of deprivation of sound, touch, and light. Their behavior has been recorded microscopically, like bacteria on a laboratory slide. Deprivation upon deprivation has been imposed and its effects studied and analyzed. The data are subject to rigorous analyses by graduate students and stored in increasingly larger computers for dissertations on punishment. The name of the place of confinement is changed from "penitentiary" to "correctional institution," "facility," "center," even "home." The prisoner is given new titles as a way to increase self worth such as "inmate," "ward," "patient," "resident," "citizen," and "student." The effects of these changed conditions have been measured and remeasured but as far as human experience goes, to no avail. There is no sign of human growth, no sign of community among those on whom the state's endless benefits are bestowed.

The list is endless. New forms of status, new communication arrangements, new managerial styles, new forms of managed cooperation, new identities, new skills, new bodies, new minds, plans, programs, thoughts, contracts, privileges, tokens — and still the experience of the whole correctional system remains an inhuman experience, showing no signs of human growth or the growth of community based on warmth and caring.

If one examines the activities of the American correctional system from its inception, we see that the state has never had a positive influence in reducing hurtful behavior for, as I have emphasized throughout, it takes away the very aspects of persons that bring them closer together. Epidemics of crime have come and gone, without any demonstrable impact on the part of the state. From the colonial period on official wars have been waged with stocks, gallows, fines and whips, public and private shamings, prisons, therapies, beatings, killings, rifles, teargas, drugs, lethal injection, and psychosurgery. Computers, businesslike management strategies, college-educated personnel, have been introduced as supports for the ever-new technological hardware, yet there is no evidence or sign of human growth or community-based competency. In fact, the opposite is true, we witness daily a steady deterioration in community as the state increases its repertoire of illusions about its effectiveness. Even the new, freshly educated personnel introduced by state officials as organizational window dressing burn out at a quicker rate than ever. Crime and harm seem to ebb and flow according to changes in the economic conditions of society and to the extent to which people's needs are being met directly by themselves or are being turned into profit-inducing commodities (Rusche and Kirchheimer, 1968).

Finally, if anyone can speak of an organic way to live, correctional officialdom in every aspect contradicts this condition. In instances where human concerns have been shown by correctional personnel and received by their clients, they have had to disown their affiliation with the state-professional complex and involve themselves in the life of the community or those they help. The Catholic Worker Movement in America is a good example of this (Day, 1972). Those who work as part of the state are distrusted for the state's needs always take precedence. Those correctionalists who come with the hope that accompanies innovation are quickly disillusioned and cast into despair. Even the redone setting of an old red barn is to no avail to counteract the poisonous effects of the system, as Nagel notes:

> The institutions were new and shiny, yet in all their finery they still seemed to harden everyone in them. Warm people enter the system wanting desperately to change it, but the problems they find are so enormous and the tasks so insurmountable that these warm people turn cold. In time they can no longer allow themselves to feel, to love, to care. To survive, they must become callous. The prison experience is corrosive for those who guard and those who are guarded (1975:148).

It is not possible to claim one's humanity and consider oneself part of the human community if one finds meaning in punishment, as Pat McAnany has noted: "It is the struggle with the meaninglessness of punishment in our present context that pushes us toward justice beyond the law courts. It does make sense, though it might not be totally explainable, that a man 'pay' for his crime. *But it will only make sense when there is a moral universe within which we all operate.*" How can anyone continue to live by and support punishment-based acts, given the history of punishment, namely, that wherever it has reared its head, people and communities begin to disintegrate.

Punishment and Experience

It is possible to contradict these facts on punishment as most correctionalists seem to do or at least tend to avoid them, and argue that punishment as a means of correcting may not work, but that it is because of existing administrative conditions such as insufficient budget allowances, insufficient personnel, lack of public support, lack of educated or well-prepared personnel. This is in fact what the classic liberal has continued to assert throughout his or her lifetime, providing an endless procession of change agent roles for themselves, by which they can purify state agencies or state clientele through management. This is essentially the thinking of the superprofessional, namely, that punishment will work with the correct admixture of advanced management. As I did earlier with the more specific notion of rehabilitation, I would like to discuss the underlying philosophical foundations of punishment in relation to human experience and to show that punishment as a means to human experience, whether we call it learning or working or healing, is an impossibility, for it destroys the essence or means of experience, human presence.

Human experience, human growth, and deeply personal relationships cannot emerge without one's presence, without the present expression of one's being. As Martin Buber stated, "I become through my relation to the *Thou,* as I become I, I say *Thou*" (1958:11). And vice versa, as each "thou" is spoken, the conditions for me to become myself are created, so that I repeat my "thou" once again. Human relationship, at a minimum, suggests an exchange that moves toward the full engagement and expression of both parties. This does not mean that both parties must be or are equal in every respect, but there must be some foundation of equality, a common ground of experience from which both might express themselves, might experience together, and thus be present to each other. This common ground constitutes the human need, the well-being of each.

Therefore the quality of presence, of being present, as I am using the term here, means more than "I am here." It carries with it a deep sense of one's own personage as viable and sharing, containing an element of collectivity or universality. By being present to another, I am present to all and can affirm: "I am here, in this place, with these beings. I am part of history." It is through such an experience of self and others that I develop an awareness of self as creator of what is and what might be. I can begin to move beyond the immediacy of the here and now and take possession of my past and create a future of meaning for myself. Human presence allows a person to transcend what is presently binding and to find meaning in pursuing his or her dreams, for a person's dreams have their grounding in present relationship. The more genuine or real the relationship—the more each partner gives and receives freely—the more each partner can abandon absolutes, fixed points, and a priori abstractions as prerequisites for experiencing.

* * *

Punishment, in any form, destroys presence and any hope of human growth for it destroys vulnerability, the very possibility of interdependence. Punishment is a way of relating in the face of which the person being punished can never let up from holding on to the world as he or she has known it, can never prepare to relinquish the needs that once gave him or her insufficient definition (e.g., power) and become receptive to what exists presently. The punished is always forced to hide from the impact of the punishing agent, who also must live in a non-present, one-dimensional world for his or her own survival. One cannot punish and be present at the same time, for presence defies punishment. Each is forced, therefore, to become absent to each other.

The studies of relationship in prison and other social arrangements in which relationship is based on punishment demonstrate that wards and staff, supervisors and those supervised, helpers and their clientele, assume roles that enable them to abstract themselves from relationships of meaning and presence. Eugene Debs describes this process of self-abstraction in the prison:

> The guard and the inmate cease to be human beings when they meet in prison. The one becomes a domineering petty official and the other a cowering convict. The rules enforce this relation and absolutely forbid any intimacy with the human touch in it between them. The guard looks down upon the convict he now has at his mercy, who has ceased to be a man and is known only by his number, while, little as the guard may suspect it, the prisoner looks down upon him as being even lower than an inmate (1927:15, 25).

The same distancing imposition of self upon another that Debs describes can be found in the family of today, the school, the medical center and the workplace in which relationship is treated as commodity. People organize in ways that inhibit intimacy, that create and maintain distance from each other as well as from their inner selves. The core of self that spells collective consciousness, connectedness with all that is human and creative is excised from one's sense of reality. Punishment supports its own unique form of separation from present reality. Punishment promotes the very schizo-existence that justifies its continuation. Contrary to the often-repeated proverb, revenge is never sweet.

References

Brown, Norman O. *Love's Body.* (New York: Vintage, 1966).
Buber, Martin. *Paths in Utopia.* (Boston: Beacon, 1958).
Day, Dorothy. *The Long Loneliness.* (New York: Curtis, 1972).
Debs, Eugene. *Walls and Bars.* (Chicago: Socialist Party, 1927).
Illich, Ivan. *Toward a History of Needs.* (New York: Pantheon, 1978).
Jourard, Sidney. *Disclosing Man to Himself.* (New York: Van Nostrand, 1968).
McAnany, Pat, Dennis Sullivan, and E. Tromanhauser. "The ex-offender movement in Chicago." Paper presented at the annual meeting of the American Society of Criminology, Toronto, Canada, 1973.
Nagel, William C. *The New Red Barn: A Critical Look at the Modern American Prison.* (New York: Walker, 1973).
Rogers, Carl R. *On Becoming a Person.* (Boston: Houghton Mifflin, 1961).
Rusche, George, and Otto Kircheimer. *Punishment and Social Structure.* (New York: Russell and Russell, 1968).

5 || Work and Alienation

During the twentieth century, America has evolved into a postindustrial society in which most jobs are in service—government, insurance, transportation, and so on. The workplace itself has changed through the increasing use of computers and automation. In consequence, human labor is needed less and less frequently for the production of necessities; this creates the possibility of a considerable reduction in the average workweek. At the same time, however, millions are unemployed and many who do have jobs are alienated from their work, sustained mainly by the promise of their next paycheck.

Unemployment and alienated work result from a system in which a wealthy minority owns and controls the means of production; the division of labor is carried to an extreme; and workplaces are organized as hierarchic, bureaucratic systems. Specialization and rationalization alienate men and women from their work. The work itself is channeled into patterns predetermined by the managers; roles and functions of personnel are often defined without considering human needs and desires. The remedies for dealing with these problems fall into two basic categories: reform versus structural change.

Many reforms have been suggested, ranging from job enlargement, where workers learn to do a variety of tasks, to converting military production to peaceful uses, thus generating more employment. One of the more intriguing proposals is the guaranteed income. Providing unemployed persons with a guaranteed annual income could eliminate poverty, replace the welfare system, and free people to engage in work of their own choosing. This reform promises a "floor" below which no one in the society would be allowed to sink. It also would stabilize the economic system by protecting it from the upheavals that often accompany massive unemployment. Moreover, transnational corporations would continue to reap large profits from their operations in this country and abroad. Though desirable, the guaranteed income would not essentially alter the capitalist system or the power of the managerial class within it.

The alternative is socialism. As I point out, many people erroneously equate socialism with the state-socialist, centrally directed economy found in the Soviet Union. Such systems cope with unemployment at the cost of reducing human freedom, and they do not solve the problem of alienated work.

One positive socialist suggestion is to begin by establishing democratically organized workers' cooperatives, either as buyouts of plants shut down by their corporate owners or as new businesses.[1] The cumulative development of such cooperatives into networks aided by support and technical assistance groups marks a transition from reform to structural change. The goal would be to build an alternative to both capitalism and state socialism, a participatory socialist system based on a market economy, with a large cooperative sector and small private and state-owned sectors.

Only when workers control the workplace will most alienated labor disappear. Under workers' control, people will benefit from the fruits of their labor by sharing in profits and influencing the decisions that affect their work. There will continue to be managers and professionals, but managers will be responsible to directors elected by the workers, not appointed by wealthy stockholders, and professional knowledge will be shared widely instead of hoarded.

A utopian variant of socialism is a society in which each person works according to his or her ability and interests and receives what he or she needs. There would be free distribution of basic necessities to all, and wage labor would be abolished. This could be accomplished through a dual economy consisting of a necessity sector (in which all members of society would be obligated to work for a few years in exchange for receiving free necessities the rest of their lives).[2] According to Gorz, the use of microcomputers and automated production can lead us beyond capitalism and state socialism into a society that liberates humankind from toil, although, as he warns, it can also lead to a regimented technocratic elitist system:

> Confronted with a technological revolution which permits the
> production of a growing volume of commodities with diminishing

quantities of labour and capital, the aims and methods of economic management clearly *cannot* remain those of capitalism, any more than social relations can remain based on the sale of labor power, that is, on waged work. But neither can this management be socialist, since the principle "to each according to his labor" has become obsolete and the socialisation of the productive process (which, according to Marx, was to be completed by socialism) has already been accomplished. Automation, therefore, takes us *beyond capitalism and socialism*. And this is the central issue — what *kind* of "beyond"? There are two basic alternatives: fully *"programmed"* . . . technocratic societies, or a liberated society, which Marx called "communist," in which the necessary production of necessities occupies only a small part of everyone's time and where (waged) *work* ceases to be the main activity.[3]

Notes

1. For a further discussion of workers' cooperatives, see Chapter 13.
2. See Paul and Percival Goodman, in Chapter 11.
3. Andre Gorz, *Paths to Paradise: On the Liberation from Work* (Boston: South End Press, 1985), p. 32.

‖ ‖ # Unemployment, Alienation, and Industrial Society

‖ ‖ *Frank Lindenfeld*

In the "postindustrial"[1] economy of present-day capitalist America, many who want to work cannot find jobs, while most of those who are employed find that they have little control over their work. The productive capacity of this economy, augmented by the increasing use of computers and automation, makes possible a generous material abundance. Properly shared, such abundance could free all of us from the worries of subsistence living. The

This paper is a revision of "Work, Alienation and the Industrial Order," which appeared in Don H. Zimmerman *et al.*, eds., *Understanding Social Problems* (New York: Praeger, 1976).

use of automation promises to liberate workers from the drudgery and tedium of boring, repetitive labor and to enable them to use more of their creative talents in their work. Unfortunately, within our capitalist system, computers and automation have been used to displace workers and to centralize further the control of top management. I examine these and related problems in more detail below, and discuss possible solutions to them.

Problems

Unemployment

The most salient problem of work is that many who want jobs cannot find them. The official rate of unemployment jumped sharply from 3.8 percent of the labor force in 1967 to 9.6 percent by 1983. The 9 million jobless during 1985 represented an unemployment rate of about 8 percent. The problem of unemployment is especially severe among minority groups and the young. As Table 1 indicates, unemployment is twice as high among blacks and other minorities as among whites, and twice as high among teenagers as among those age 20 and over. The hardest hit, black teenagers, had an unemployment rate of close to 45 percent in 1983.

TABLE 1

U.S. Unemployment Rate, by Age, Sex, and Race among Those Sixteen Years and Older, 1983

Unemployment Rate by Age	White		Black and Other Minorities	
	Men	Women	Men	Women
20+ years	7.9	6.9	16.5	15.2
16–19 years	20.2	18.3	44.9	44.6
Total	8.8	7.9	18.5	17.0

Source: U.S. Bureau of Statistics.

Official data on unemployment tend to be underestimates. Many of those counted as not being in the labor force would be willing to work if jobs were available. Government definitions of the unemployed include only those who are looking for work, excluding those who are so discouraged that they have stopped searching for jobs. Counting not only the official and unofficial unemployed but also the underemployed and part-time workers seeking full employment, housewives and students who would work if they could find jobs, those between age 55 and 64 who are not working, and those in manpower training programs, the real rate of unemployment is closer to double the official figures (Gross and Moses, 1972).

Unemployment results in part from corporate decisions to close high-wage plants and transfer the production of goods or services to low-wage regions or countries. Another cause of unemployment is automation. Under capitalism, labor is replaced by machines whenever it is cheaper to do so, regardless of the social consequences. Automation has sharply reduced the number of workers needed in agriculture and mining, has made possible a continuing expansion of industrial output with a stable or declining number of production employees, and has begun to make deep inroads in the service industries. Thousands of bank workers, for example, have been replaced by machines that automatically sort checks. This process will accelerate in the coming years (Gorz, 1985).

One of the chief difficulties of job displacement caused by automation is that often those whose work is taken over by machines are relatively unskilled and uneducated. When they lose their jobs, they have difficulty finding other jobs. Even when they obtain employment after "retraining," they may find their new jobs eliminated by automation within a few years. The growth of service industries may take up some of the slack, but even here the trend is toward farming-out services to branch operations located in other countries *and* the replacement of service workers by automated machines. ·

Can our society provide enough jobs to go around? The simplest solution would be to share available work by reducing the average workweek. A reduction from 40 to 30 or even 20 hours would provide more free time from work for the majority while increasing the potential number of jobs. As a first step, those who have jobs might be asked to give up 10 percent of their total wages in return for a reduction of 10 hours (or 25 percent) in the average workweek and an *increase* of 20 percent in their hourly compensation. This would allow for the creation of additional 30-hour jobs that would spread the available work and income more equitably.[2]

Another way to provide more jobs would be through public policies designed to stimulate small businesses and workers' cooperatives, both of which have a better track record in providing new jobs than large corporations have. Birch (1979) has shown that two-thirds of all new jobs generated recently in this country have been provided by the birth or expansion of firms with fewer than 20 employees. The network of workers' cooperatives in the Basque region of Spain has been quite successful in creating jobs, and there is reason to hope that the same could happen in this country (see Gutierrez-Johnson in Chapter 12). We could also create jobs through an expansion in public investment for currently unmet needs such as low-income housing, mass transportation, nursing care, and other human services. At the same time, there would have to be major cuts in military spending.

Continuing to pour billions of dollars into arms production and war-related industry will not create enough jobs. Quite apart from the undesirable social consequences, which include the militarization of the society and the greater likelihood of engaging in wars, there are detrimental economic effects of such investment for military purposes, as Melman (1970) documents:

1. Producing more guns means we have less butter. More military production means less civilian production, as machinery, labor and talent, natural resources and energy that could have been used for creating civilian goods and services are preempted by the military.

2. The Vietnam war and continuing massive military expenditures during the 1970s and 1980s have been a major factor contributing to inflation in the United States. (The military expenditures projected by the Reagan administration for the fiscal year 1986 were $473 billion, or about 64 percent of the total government budget.)[3] The purchasing power of the dollar has gone down because of military consumption of energy, resources, goods and services.[4]

3. The economy has been depleted by an overconcentration on research and development, investment, and production into military channels. Only a minority of the engineers, scientists, and technicians engaged in research and development in this country are working on civilian projects.

4. A high level of military spending creates unemployment by providing fewer job opportunities than comparable spending on civilian uses because military production is capital intensive rather than labor intensive. Each $1 billion spent

on the military instead of the civilian sector has resulted in between 10,000 and 21,000 fewer jobs (Anderson, 1975).

5. Jobs usually have a "multiplier" effect of creating other jobs. For example, schools provide jobs not only for teachers but also for those working to produce textbooks, films, or calculators used in schools. The multiplier effect of military production in generating additional jobs is smaller than the effect of comparable civilian production.

Income Distribution

Not only are there not enough jobs, but income is very unequally distributed. If we divide the American population into fifths according to income, we find that the richest fifth receives about 42 percent of all income. The relative share of the bottom fifth is only 5 percent. Such inequality has persisted since the beginning of this century (see Table 2) and points to the continuing problem of poverty in our society.[5]

TABLE 2

Distribution of Before-Tax Income in the United States, by Fifths of the Population, 1910-1981 (in percent)

Date	Total	Richest Fifth	Middle Three Fifths	Poorest Fifth
1910	100	46	46	8
1929	100	51	43	5
1950	100	44	52	4
1968	100	44	52	4
1981	100	42	53	5

Source: Gabriel Kolko, *Wealth and Power in America* (New York: Praeger, 1962), p. 14.; Herman Miller, *Rich Man, Poor Man* (New York: Crowell, 1972), p. 50.; *Statistical Abstract of the U.S., 1982-1983,* p. 435.

The inequality of income distribution has remained basically unaltered by income taxes. On paper, the law provides for progressively higher taxes on higher income. But because of the many tax loopholes and special provisions that apply to the wealthy, income taxes reduce their relative share of income by one or two percentage points.[6]

The highest incomes in this country — six-figure salaries — go to a handful of top managers of corporate enterprises and to the capitalist class of which they are a part. This class, not usually included in standard comparisons of income from different occupations, derives most of its income from ownership of stocks and bonds, interest on bank deposits, rents from properties, or capital gains. Next in income are independent professionals, including doctors and dentists who work for themselves (see Table 3). Below them are professional, technical, managerial and administrative workers in corporate or government bureaucracies. Around the middle of the income range are sales and clerical workers, craftsmen and foremen, and semi-skilled operatives. The bottom of the income distribution includes service workers, laborers, farmers, and farm workers. As Table 3 indicates, women received less money than men in every category of unemployment. On the average, they are paid 60 cents for every dollar earned by men.

Job Satisfaction

National sample surveys have shown that most American workers are "satisfied" with their jobs.[7] One of the main variables associated with job satisfaction is occupational status: The higher the job status, the greater the proportion of workers who say they are satisfied. Studies of job attitudes show that the proportion of those who say they would choose the same kind of work if they were to begin their careers again is directly related to job status. Between 70 and 93 percent of professionals, 41 and 52 percent of white-collar and skilled blue-collar workers, and 16 to 31 percent of unskilled blue-collar workers would choose the same kind of work again (Blauner, 1966:477); Wilensky, 1966:134).

Part of the reason for the correlation between job status and job satisfaction is that many higher-status jobs pay more and are more interesting and challenging than lower-status jobs. A second reason is inherent in the status or prestige attached to certain occupations. One of the things that is "wrong" with many blue-collar jobs is that they are socially defined as "lower" than white-collar jobs, even at the same rate of pay. A third reason is that higher-status jobs are associated with having more control over working conditions, pace of work, and so on. Among jobs at the same status levels, the more control a worker feels she or he has, the greater the job satisfaction (Blauner, 1966). Other studies have shown that job satis-

TABLE 3

Income of Civilian Labor Force, by Occupational Category and Sex, 1980

Occupational Category	Median Income, full-time, year-round workers (in dollars)	
	Male	Female
Self-employed doctors and dentists	37,321	*
High-salaried employees		
Professional and technical	23,026	15,285
Managers and officials	23,558	12,936
Other White-Collar workers		
Sales	19,910	9,748
Clerical	18,247	10,997
Blue-Collar workers		
Craftsmen and foremen	18,671	11,701
Operatives	15,702	9,440
Laborers	12,157	9,747
Service workers		
All except private household	13,097	7,982
Private household	*	4,567
Farm income		
Farmers and managers	7,482	*
Farm laborers	8,402	*

* Base number less than 75,000

Source: U. S. Bureau of the Census, *Current Population Reports,* series P-60, no. 132. Data for self-employed, other than for doctors and dentists, are omitted.

faction is also positively linked with having a high degree of variety and autonomy at one's work.

The analysis of job satisfaction does not go deep enough. Is it possible that workers report that they are "satisfied" with their jobs yet feel estranged from them?

Alienation

In most contemporary work organizations, the trend is toward specialization, rationalization, and centralized managerial control. In offices and factories, major policies are determined by a few at the top; decisions made by those lower in the hierarchy generally concern only the means predetermined by others, and often even the means are rigidly prescribed. Employees are confined to a strictly limited sphere of competence in which they carry out orders to make some part of a larger product they may never see in completed form. Workers accept these alienating working conditions because of economic compulsion—they need jobs in order to live.

The modern division of labor is aptly described by sociologist Daniel Bell:

The logic of hierarchy . . . is thus not merely the sociological fact of increased supervision which every complex enterprise demands, but a peculiarly technological imperative. In a simple division of labor, for example, the worker had a large measure of control over his own working conditions, that is, the set-up and make-ready, the cleaning and repairing of machines, obtaining his own materials, and so on. Under a complex division of labor these tasks pass out of his control, and he must rely on management to see that they are properly done. This dependence extends along the entire proces of production. As a result, modern industry has had to devise an entirely new managerial superstructure which organizes and directs production. This superstructure draws all possible brain-work away from the shop; everything is centered in the planning and schedule and design departments. And in this new hierarchy there stands a figure known neither to the handicrafts nor to the industry in its infancy—the technical employee. With him, the separation of functions becomes complete. The worker at the bottom, attending only to a detail, is divorced from any decision or modification about the product he is working on (Bell, 1962:234–235).

The logic of the division of labor is that of efficiency. The cooperation of many, each engaged in producing a small part, is thought to provide a greater output than the same number separately producing the whole item. The skilled worker who assembles a whole radio is replaced by semiskilled operatives who put together various subassemblies, and eventually these are replaced by automatic machines that make human labor superfluous. The skilled carpenter who makes and fits doors, windows, and floors is replaced by a crew with less complex skills, those who specialize in installing prefabricated wall sections, for example. In medicine, the general practitioner gives way to specialists in particular diseases or parts of the body. In academia, the broad-ranging intellect is replaced by more narrowly trained experts who explore subsections of arbitrarily defined areas of knowledge.

The technically most efficient methods are not always the most satisfying to those engaged in the work. Often one has to choose between technical efficiency (concentration on *production*) and employee happiness (concentrations on the *producers*).[8]

What makes the postindustrial age unique is the possibility of consistently resolving conflicts between efficiency and happiness in favor of the latter. There is no need to dream of the efficiency of a full and rational "utilization" of human and technological resources when muscle power becomes superfluous and machines are readily available. We may consciously opt for *inefficiency*, for less "production" than is theoretically attainable, because we place other values first (Bell, 1962). Actually, decentralized organizations are often more efficient and less costly than centralized ones. But the important thing is that decentralization is a more desirable form of human organization because it promises to overcome the alienating conditions into which most employees are locked in industrial societies (Goodman, 1965).

What are these conditions? As Marx put it in 1844:

> What constitutes the alienation of labor? First, that the work is *external* to the worker, that it is not part of his nature; and that, consequently, he does not fulfill himself in his work but denies himself, has a feeling of misery rather than well being, does not develop freely his mental and physical energies but is physically exhausted and mentally debased. The worker therefore feels himself at home only during his leisure time, whereas at work he feels homeless. His work is not voluntary but imposed, *forced labor*. It is not the satisfaction of a need, but only a *means* for

satisfying other needs. Its alien character is clearly shown by the fact that as soon as there is no physical or other compulsion it is avoided like the plague (Marx, 1961:98–99).

Contemporaries, including Seeman (1959) and Blauner (1964), have clarified the concept of alienation by distinguishing five separate dimensions, but the basic idea remains close to that of Marx. The most important aspects of alienation are powerlessness, meaninglessness, and self-estrangement.

Employees are powerless in that their voice does not count for much, they cannot say what should be produced, how, at what price, and for whom.

Meaninglessness refers to the fact that the employee in a bureaucratic organization is engaged in one small, standardized task and rarely gets to see or understand the whole process or product. Only a few at the top know how all the highly subdivided jobs are interrelated. Self-estrangement may occur when work is not done for its own sake, or for the sake of what the work itself accomplishes, but primarily for the money. Self-estrangement means workers do not express themselves fully or utilize their talents in their work.

The opposite of alienated labor is work pursued for its intrinsic worth and meaning. This, according to C. Wright Mills, is the Renaissance view of work as craftsmanship:

> There is no ulterior motive in work other than the product being made and the process of its creation. The details of daily work are meaningful because they are not detached in the worker's mind from the product of the work. The worker is free to control his own working action. The craftsman is thus able to learn from his work; and to use and develop his capacities and skills in its prosecution. There is no split of work and play, or work and culture. The craftsman's way of livelihood determines and infuses his entire mode of living (Mills, 1951:220).

It is helpful at this point to distinguish between objective social conditions and the subjective perceptions and feelings that arise in response to them. Alienation refers to the *objective* relationship of the employee to his work. To distinguish the subjective awareness of that relationship, Blauner (1966:473) suggests the use of the term *estrangement*. Estrangement is the

subjective aspect of alienating working conditions. The condition of alienation may not necessarily be perceived or understood as such by the
alienated. Thus, I doubt whether any great numbers of American employees *feel* estranged from their work. They accept doing something they
may not entirely like in return for their paycheck.

But the fact is that they are being used.[9] With the exception of the self-
employed, the ends of work are not determined by the worker but by others
to whom he is subordinate. This is the typical condition of employees.
Modern industrialism uses employees as means to the ends of those in control of industrial or governmental hierarchies.

There are, of course, variations in working conditions, compensation,
and employment security. These factors influence the subjective perception
of workers, their satisfaction with their jobs, and the degree to which they
feel estranged. Subjective awareness of alienation varies greatly. Some of
those who are being used may be aware of the fact and resent it, in which
case we can say that they feel estranged. But many who are used are not particularly aware of this, or if they are, they are not resentful because they
receive high pay; are not closely supervised; can vary the pace of work; or
because they are genuinely unaware of the possibilities of alternatives.

Herein lies the paradox of the relative contentment of American
employees. If the work is dull, or even stupid and meaningless, at least the
pay is high, the hours are short, and there are attractive fringe benefits,
such as vacations, medical insurance, and pension systems. For meaning in
their lives, people do not look so much to production as to consumption (of
clothes, cars, television, homes), and they turn increasingly to do-it-
yourself projects, gardening, travel, and so on.

The growth of labor unions in the United States provided many employees with the power to resist being pushed around and treated in a way
that violated their dignity. Through collective bargaining, unions resisted
management pressures for speed-ups in production and arbitrary firing of
employees. In recent years, union membership has been declining; less than
one in five American workers belongs to a union now. And in the non-
unionized fields, especially in smaller and marginal enterprises, most
employees are still vulnerable to the whims of the boss or the foreman.

American trade unions have not helped to develop workers' consciousness of alienation. The role of the unions in the United States has
been to raise wages and improve working conditions and fringe benefits
through collective bargaining. The unions have rarely offered any serious
challenge to management's prerogative of setting basic goals and policies.

With the exception of groups such as the Industrial Workers of the World, unions have tended to accept the worker's powerlessness over broad policies in return for sharing with the managers a slightly larger slice of the bread.

Unions have acquired a vested interest in the smooth running of business enterprises and often perform the very important function for management of "stabilizing" the labor situation. Moreover, the unions themselves have become larger, bureaucratic structures over which the average worker has as little power as he has over management.

Recently, some unions have begun to move in new directions as locals have become involved in efforts to preserve jobs by helping workers to form cooperatives to buy plants threatened with shutdowns. This was the case of two supermarkets in Philadelphia, discussed in Chapter 12.

Toward Solutions

There are basically two types of solutions to the problems of work discussed above: reform and structural change. The remedies I discuss are basically reforms; they can be implemented without any structural alterations in the society. Adopted on a large scale, however, one of them — the principle of workers' control embodied in workers' cooperatives — would involve a deep structural transformation of the entire economy.

Job Enlargement

The purpose of job enlargement is to make employees feel more positive toward their work by making their tasks more varied. Progressive employers have successfully improved attitudes of employees through various paternalistically instituted job enlargement schemes. In enlarged jobs, workers participate in different phases of making a complex product, instead of engaging in only one repetitive task. Job enlargement typically provides more variety, more control over the pace of the work, and more flexible scheduling. In place of the extreme division of labor and hierarchical patterns characteristic of older-style industry, some modern managers set goals for "teams" of workers to fulfill. Thus products may be partly assembled by work teams instead of on assembly lines, and worker suggestions incorporated into the work process, without diminishing quantity production and with a definite increase in both quality and worker satisfaction.

Jenkins cites a number of examples of successful experiments in industrial democracy. One of the most far-reaching job-restructuring programs was carried out at one of the divisions of Procter & Gamble. At a highly automated plant in Lima, Ohio, 125 employees worked in three shifts. In this factory, there were no barriers between jobs; in fact, there were no job classifications. The workers were known as members of the plant "community," with responsibility for hiring and firing and a large degree of control over plant operations. There were no time clocks. Workers determined pay scales themselves, and all salaries were known openly (Jenkins, 1973).

In Sweden, both the Saab and Volvo companies have been moving away from assembly-line production of cars. In place of the conveyor-belt system, workers are divided into production groups, with each group responsible for assembling certain parts of the car. The teams of workers can vary the pace and divide the work among themselves as they choose (Jenkins, 1973).

To the extent that job-enlargement programs involve a genuine shift in power from management to employees, they are a step in the right direction. But the new patterns do not necessarily alter the powerless and subordinate position of employees.[10] This is illustrated by the results of a short-lived experiment in democracy at the innovative Polaroid Corporation. Because of a special rush job, 120 machine operators were put on a new schedule. In place of the usual eight hours at the machine, each one spent an hour in training and two hours doing coordinating work. The program was *too* successful, however, because it eliminated the need for managers. The managers did not want their workers *that* qualified, and so when the rush job was finished, they abolished the program (Jenkins, 1973).

Almost any change that gives employees more control over the pattern and pace of their work promises to increase job satisfaction. Job enlargement, therefore, should be seen as a desirable positive reform attainable within the existing capitalist system. Another reform, one that deals with the crisis of unemployment, is the guaranteed annual income.

The Guaranteed Income

The idea of the guaranteed income, originally proposed by economist Robert Theobold (1965), is to break the link between jobs and income by providing direct money payments to low-income persons, with no conditions attached. To make his proposal politically acceptable, Theobold added the idea that payments to jobless persons should be proportionate to the level of income they were used to receiving. Essentially a device to redistribute income, the guaranteed income would be paid for through the tax system.[11]

The guaranteed income is suggested as a solution to the interconnected problems of poverty, welfare, and unemployment. Its cost would be high. In its initial stages, such a program might cost $50 billion annually, over and above present welfare expenditures.[12] Like the welfare system, the guaranteed income would provide every family and every adult individual with an economic floor. This proposal avoids government make-work programs and would replace most of the present machinery of welfare assistance. It would probably reduce the degradation to which (poor) recipients of government subsidies are at present subjected. Unlike the present system, it would not penalize the poor for earning money or make their subsidy depend on the judgment of a social worker about their morals or spending habits.

The economic problem with which the guaranteed income deals is the imbalance between production and consumption in postindustrial capitalist society. As Theobold puts it:

> Today's socioeconomic system . . . assumes that the overwhelming proportion of those seeking jobs can find them and that the incomes received will allow the job-holder to live in dignity. Such a distribution mechanism requires that enough effective demand exist to take up all the goods and services that can be produced by all the capital and labor that can be effectively used (Theobold, 1973:136).

But this system is breaking down. Not only are many uneducated and unskilled persons out of work, but increasing numbers of middle-class persons with both skills and education are being displaced by machines and forced out of work.

A major effect of the guaranteed income would be to speed the elimination of low-paying and degrading jobs. It would help transform the relationship between employer and employee into one of voluntary cooperation instead of economic coercion. The competition of the guaranteed income would force employers to be fair. People would be able to resign from their job if they did not like their working conditions, without fear their families would starve. The guaranteed income would also enable more persons to work as artists and craftsmen, or to take advantage of opportunities for higher education.

This reform is radical in that it promises increasing freedom from toil, but it has conservative implications as well. It would stabilize the existing system by protecting it from the upheavals that accompany massive unemployment. The potentially discontented would be "bought off" by receiving the fringe benefits of being part of an affluent system. Contrary to Theobold's intentions, there might well be strings of political conformity attached to the guaranteed income — dissidents might face the threat of having their income cut off by the government. Further, the proposal eliminates poverty but not extreme wealth. Capitalists would continue to reap large profits from corporate operations in this country and abroad; because of their wealth, they would probably continue to have a disproportionately large influence on government domestic and foreign policies.

So far, I have discussed two reforms that deal with the problems of work — job enlargement and the guaranteed income. While such reforms may help, for more complete solutions we will have to transcend the capitalist political economy.

Beyond Reform: A Mixed Socialist Economy

Within a capitalist economy, the use of advanced technology leads to alienated work, unemployment and a continuing crisis of overproduction and underconsumption. Capitalist enterprises are run for the private profit of their owners and managers.

The wage gains of unionized workers have encouraged management to adopt automation at a faster rate: The higher the price of labor, the more attractive becomes its replacement by machines. But the more machines introduced to replace workers, the fewer jobs available in private industry, the higher the general level of unemployment. Unemployed workers do not have adequate purchasing power (in the absence of full unemployment benefits or a guaranteed annual income), and so inventories begin to pile up. This is a central contradiction inherent in a capitalist economy.

One answer to the problem of how best to remedy the problems of capitalism is to replace private ownership and control of industry with public ownership and control, and to institute some degree of public planning, for example through price controls. This is usually referred to as socialism.[13] Socialism is often erroneously equated with centralized state control of all industry, as in the Soviet Union. Socialist economies can (and should) be decentralized to a large degree. The mere substitution of state socialism for capitalism will not eliminate alienation in work. Powerlessness, economic compulsion, and subordination are just as likely to be the lot of the average employee under state socialism as under capitalism. Indeed, these conditions may be even more pronounced in socialist economies. It is doubtful whether knowing that industry is owned by the nation has given workers in the Soviet Union a sense of meaning and joy in their work. That feeling can come about only when work is freely chosen and when workers have a direct say in its organization.

There is little reason to expect that state socialist managers would be less likely than capitalist ones to treat employees as means to the ends of production. If anything, industrial discipline can be even tighter under state socialism because employees have no place else to go. Under state socialism, some of the excesses of capitalism would be avoided, but such socialism has its own pitfalls. These can be surmounted through decentralization of industry and economic control, and by combining it with a democratic system of workers' cooperatives. Instead of a monolithic state socialism, I would advocate a "mixed" market economy consisting of private, cooperative, and public sectors. The public, or nationalized, sector might include such natural monopolies as the postal and railroad systems. Capitalist firms would continue to function, but through tax or other policies, would be kept from expanding beyond a certain size. Public policy would encourage the formation of networks of workers' cooperatives, owned and controlled by their members. Pioneering work in the development of such an economy has been done in Yugoslavia, which includes the principle of democratic workers' management of industry in its constitution.[14]

The building blocks of such a cooperative sector within a mixed economy would be cooperatives based on the principle of workers' control. Such control must be distinguished from mere participation in management. The difference is a question of power. Participation means that workers are consulted, but that the final decision still rests with the boss. *Control* means that the final decision rests with the workers. Workers' control means that the workers themselves determine what products or services they will supply, how they will organize the work, and what they will do with the profits. Under workers' control, all who work in an organization help to determine production goals, wages, prices, and investments. All major decisions are shared. In small organizations, issues may be resolved by the group meeting as a whole. In larger organizations, policies may be set and managers appointed by a board of directors elected democratically by the workers.

Common to workers' cooperatives are certain principles (Lindenfeld and Rothschild-Whitt, 1982:6–7, based on Vanek, 1971):

> 1. Full worker participation in decision making exists at all levels of the organization. Enterprises are controlled by those

who work in them. In small organizations, decisions are generally made by the entire collective in frequent meetings. Larger organizations have some kind of management positions, but managers are selected by democratically chosen boards of directors and can be recalled by the members; the workforce as a whole retains ultimate authority.

2. All who work in an organization share in its net income and decide democratically how income and surplus should be distributed. The tendency is toward equality. Often, such systems include some provision for paying workers partly according to need (e.g., number of family members). The net effect is to flatten the stratification pyramid within the enterprise, region, or society, as the case may be.

3. The means of production (land, buildings, machinery) are socially owned and are kept in trust as community assets. They may be owned either directly by a firm's workers or by a trust controlled by them, or may be leased from community organizations or government.

4. The main purpose of each firm is not the maximization of profit but the maximization of community well-being. This includes fair income for those who work in the enterprise and workers' control of their own work, with jobs as personally rewarding as possible. Community well-being also includes providing goods or services that are socially useful, of high quality, and ecologically sound. Priority would be given to the conservation of energy and natural resources and to the growth of the organization to an appropriate, medium size. In times of trouble, workers are not laid off but share reduced hours or lower incomes.

5. Profit, or surplus after paying overhead and wages, belongs to all who worked to create it. It may be shared in the form of bonuses, or it may be used for social community purposes such as education, health clinics, or day-care centers. A vital use of the surplus is for reinvestment within the firm or in other worker-managed enterprises to create new jobs. Labor-managed systems may be able to create more employment than capitalist systems, as the economic growth of Yugoslavia and of the Mondragon network (see Gutierrez-Johnson in Chapter 12) seem to indicate.

The first faint steps toward the development of a cooperative sector within the United States have already been taken. By the mid-1980s there were thousands of small worker-owned, democratically managed businesses in this country, including restaurants, "new wave" food cooperatives, alternative schools, child-care centers (see Brown in Chapter 13), health clinics, and newspapers. There were hundreds of medium-size firms owned and controlled by their workers, including a number of cooperative plywood factories in the Pacific Northwest and the worker-owned tree-planting cooperatives in the same area (Gunn, 1984). Many, like the two supermarkets in Philadelphia, (see Lindenfeld in Chapter 12) were the result of employee takeovers of failing businesses. Some, like the Atlas chain, (see Panken in Chapter 12) have come about through the creative use of employee stock-ownership legislation.

Workers' cooperatives thrive best when they have the help of technical support groups and access to financing, and when they do not exist in isolation but as part of a network of similar organizations. In the Basque area of Spain, a successful network of a few hundred cooperative organizations provides employment for some 20,000 persons. This network includes producers' co-ops, educational organizations, consumer co-ops, and a bank that supplies technical help and loans (see Gutierrez-Johnson in Chapter 12). In this country there have been few linkages between the various cooperative enterprises. Some financial institutions, such as the National Co-op Bank, provide loans to cooperatives, and there are now technical support groups to aid workers' co-ops, such as ICA (Industrial Cooperative Association) in Boston and PACE (Philadelphia Association for Cooperative Enterprise). So far, however, most members of workers' cooperatives do not have a very highly developed political consciousness, and few see themselves as part of a wider movement for worker control.

Summary

The problems of work discussed herein derive primarily from our capitalist economy. The faults of capitalism stem from its principle of production for private profit instead of for social use. This creates unemployment for many and alienation among those who do have jobs; it also leads to injustice in distribution, to the perpetuation of class inequalities, and to the neglect of community needs. Reforms such as job enlargement, reduction of the workweek, and the guaranteed income could alleviate some of the problems. For a more complete solution, it would be desirable to develop a mixed economy with a large cooperative sector, where workers determine goals, working conditions, and distribution of profits and where the power of managers is subordinate to policies set by workers or their democratically elected delegates. Developing a large cooperative sector could be an intermediate step toward the creation of an egalitarian society where wage work will no longer exist and basic necessities will be free to all. Such a society, made possible by advances in computerized, automated mass production, would allow for the fullest development of craftsmanship, creative talents, and leisure arts. Achieving this is not merely a utopian dream but a practical possibility that can be achieved on a broad scale when enough people become conscious of its desirability and join together to bring it about.

Notes

1. Postindustrial means that only a small proportion of the workforce is still engaged in extracting raw materials or in manufacturing (Touraine, 1971; Bell, 1973); today, 7 out of every 10 American workers are employed in finance, trade, insurance, transportation services, or government.
2. In practice, a 10 percent wage cut might produce only 5 percent more jobs because many organizations would find that their workers can produce as much in 30 hours as they formerly did in 40, and because adding employees creates additional administrative costs.
3. This includes $310 billion for current military expenditures, and $163 billion to pay for past wars, including veterans' benefits and 80 percent of the interest on the national debt, most of which was incurred to pay for wars. Government statistics underplay the relative importance of military expenditures by including social security trust funds in the total on which percentages are calculated, and by burying past military expenses in non-military categories.
4. More civilian dollars chase fewer goods because so much production is consumed by the military. Hence, prices rise.
5. Definitions of poverty vary, of course, depending on one's political sympathies. According to the Census Bureau, about 29 million Americans were living below the poverty level in 1980. This includes many paid at or below the minimum wage, as well as the underemployed, the chronically unemployed, and many of those who depend on welfare, social security, or retirement pensions.
6. See data on before- and after-tax income, 1941–1957, in U.S. Bureau of the Census, 1960:163, 165. See also Miller, 1971, and Kolko, 1962.
7. Such data should be interpreted with caution because of the cultural norm (especially in the professions) that constrains us to say that we like our jobs. To be dissatisfied with one's work is to call into question a part of the very meaning of one's life, and that is not something most of us want to do. In addition, questions on job satisfaction do not go far enough. If the pay is high, the job secure, and the working conditions tolerable, many persons will report that they are "satisfied." What they *mean* is that, given the existing structure of opportunities, what they are doing compares favorably with other work that is available.

8. The Israeli *kibbutzim,* committed to a ideology of nonspecialization in work, have never-theless found that economic pressures make the attainment of this ideal difficult in prac-tice. Nonspecialization was found to be less efficient from the strict, short-run, technical point of view. When production values are given highest priority, being able to change jobs is likely to remain an unrealized ideal. See Vallier, 1962.
9. I was tempted to use the term "exploited" instead of "used." But "exploited" is perhaps too strong. The larger American business firms do not generally have a policy of conscious ex-ploitation of the domestic labor force. For on the contrary, many managers of modern in-dustrial bureaucracies pride themselves on their sense of public responsibility and believe in looking after the welfare of employees as "good business." Nor do most American employees feel exploited. Exploitation is a more approrpiate term for those with the lowest-paying jobs, such as auto-wash attendants or farm laborers in this country or for employees of American corporations in the Third World. In a similar context, Touraine (1971) speaks of "dependent participation."
10. The same is true of management-instituted "quality of work life" programs that involve employees in discussions of how to improve production.
11. One mechanism that has been proposed for implementing the guaranteed annual income is the "negative" income tax. Above a certain income, taxes would continue to be levied progressively. Poor persons, those below that income, would receive money from the government. Some negative income tax proposals incorporate a "work incentive" feature; others do not. Most present welfare systems do not have such a work-incentive mechanism; low-income people who find jobs have their welfare benefits reduced by the amount of their income, leaving them with little economic incentive to work.
12. The exact cost would depend on the socially and politically acceptable definition of what constitutes the poverty line. Assume that, on the average, each of 25 million poor persons receives a net subsidy of $4000. The total gross cost of the guaranteed income program would then be $100 billion annually. The *net* additional cost would probably be closer to $50 billion, however, because the guaranteed income would replace a variety of existing costly social welfare measures. While such a sum is staggering, it represents only a frac-tion of the current military budget. It could be financed by using funds currently allocated for military purposes without raising taxes a penny.
13. A variant of socialism is a dual economy with mass production of necessities coupled with a luxury market system. Such a dual economy would be based on the principle that a certain proportion of social production should be set aside to provide for the minimum subsistence needs of all. Production of necessities would require the labor of so few that it could even be done by volunteers. This presupposes a social consciousness different from the selfishness and individualism that we have been used to (see Goodman and Goodman in Chapter 11).
14. While Yugoslavia practices economic democracy, it has not yet embraced political democracy and remains a one-party state.

References

Anderson, Marion. "The empty pork barrel." WIN 11 (May 8, 1975): 4–8.
Bell, Daniel. "Work and its discontents." *The End of Ideology.* (New York: Collier, 1962).
Bell, Daniel. *The Coming of Post-Industrial Society.* (New York: Basic Books, 1973).
Birch, David. "Generating new jobs: Are government incentives effective?" *Commentary* July, 1979.
Blauner, Robert. *Alienation and Freedom.* (Chicago: University of Chicago Press, 1964).
Blauner, Robert. "Work satisfaction and industrial trends in modern society." In *Class, Status and Power,* edited by Reinhard Bendix and Seymour Lipset. (New York: Free Press, 1966).

Centers, Richard. *The Psychology of Social Classes*. (Princeton: Princeton University Press, 1949).

Goodman, Paul. *People or Personnel*. (New York: Random House, 1965).

Goodman, Paul, and Percival Goodman. *Communitas* (New York: Vintage, 1960).

Gorz, Andre. *Paths to Paradise: On the Liberation from Work*. (Boston: South End Press, 1985).

Gross, Bertram, and Stanley Moses. "Measuring the real work force: 25 million unemployed." *Social Policy* 1972, 3.

Gunn, Christopher E. *Workers' Self Management in the United States* (Ithaca: Cornell University Press, 1984).

Jenkins, David. *Job Power: Blue and White Collar Democracy*. (New York: Praeger, 1973).

Lindenfeld, Frank, and Joyce Rothschild-Whitt, eds. *Workplace Democracy and Social Change*. (Boston: Porter Sargent, 1982).

Marx, Karl. "Economic and philosophical manuscripts," translated by T. B. Bottomore. In Erich Fromm, *Marx's Concept of Man*. (New York: Unger, 1961).

Melman, Seymour. *Pentagon Capitalism*. (New York: McGraw Hill, 1970).

Miller, Herman. *Rich Man, Poor Man*. (New York: Crowell, 1971).

Mills, C. Wright. *White Collar*. (New York: Oxford University Press, 1951).

Morse, Nancy C., and Robert S. Weiss. "The function and meaning of work and the job." *American Sociological Review* (1955) 20.

Seeman, Melvin. "The meaning of alienation." *American Sociological Review* (1959) 24.

Statistical Abstract of the United States, 1982-1983.

Theobold, Robert. *Free Men and Free Markets*. (New York: Doubleday, 1965).

Theobold, Robert. "Guaranteed income tomorrow: Toward post-economic motivation." In *The Future of Work*, edited by Fred Best. (Englewood Cliffs, N.J.: Prentice-Hall, 1973).

Touraine, Alain. *The Post Industrial Society*. (New York: Random House, 1971).

U.S. Bureau of the Census. *Current Population Reports*, series P. 60, no. 132, 1981.

Vallier, Ivan. "Structural differentiation, production imperatives and communal norms: The kibbutz in crisis." *Social Forces* (1962) 40.

Vanck, Jaroslav. *The Participatory Economy: An Evolutionary Hypothesis and a Development Strategy*. (Ithaca: Cornell University Press, 1971).

Wilensky, Harold L. "Work as a social problem." In *Social Problems*, edited by Howard S. Becker. (New York: Wiley, 1966).

6 | Women, Men, and Sexism

The spread of Western-style industrialization throughout the world has resulted in the exploitation of women. Everywhere, women earn less money than men; economic development, as Ivan Illich points out, is accompanied almost universally by job discrimination (and by violence) against women. Sex discrimination exists in the reported, officially taxed economy, as well as in the unreported, black market economy. Women workers in industrial societies such as the United States are as far behind their male counterparts today as they were a century ago. Illich reminds us that "neither educational opportunities, nor legislative provisions, nor revolutionary rhetoric . . . have changed the magnitude by which women, in their earnings, stand below men."

A third economic sector underpins the reported and unreported economies and makes it possible for them to function. This sector is the netherworld that Illich terms "shadow work"—the time, trouble, and labor by which consumers turn purchased commodities into usable ones. Shadow work includes housework but is broader in its meaning. It includes, for example, the cost and effort expended in daily commuting by car to and from paid jobs in rush-hour traffic. The locus of shadow work is the family as consumer unit. Even if consumer goods were all produced by robots, Illich argues, there would continue to be a necessary complement of shadow work to be performed in connection with their consumption. In the realm of shadow work, women carry an even heavier burden of discrimination than they do in paid work.

In the United States, men are dominant over women in most realms. Monica Frölander-Ulf reminds us that men control the major corporations

172

and the political system; in these institutions, women have token representation but generally are relegated to the less important work. Women also take care of the home and the children, even when they hold paying jobs.

Certain occupations continue to be almost exclusively male, others predominantly female. According to the U.S. Bureau of Labor Statistics, in 1983 over 90 percent of the jobs in these occupations were held by men: engineers, dentists, pilots, firefighters, police, carpenters, bricklayers, electricians, plumbers, roofers, auto mechanics, and welders. At the same time, more than 90 percent of the workers in these occupations were women: preschool and kindergarten teachers, registered nurses, dental assistants, bank tellers, bookkeepers, secretaries, receptionists, typists, sewing machine operators, and domestic service workers. Combined with the fact that women earn considerably less than men in every job category, this occupational division by sex illustrates a pattern of continuing discrimination against women in the workplace.

Sexism may have originated with the patriarchal ideology that was part of the agricultural societies from which Western cultures evolved. Whatever its origins, sexism is maintained by a political economy with a division of labor in which men occupy positions of power while women are relegated to lesser positions and do much of the shadow work. Since lower wages for women mean more profits for business, sexism has become an integral part of the capitalist system.

The pattern of male dominance that is characteristic of American society is only one of several possible cultural patterns. In some other, so-called primitive cultures, there is a greater balance between women and men. To restore a balance between the sexes, says Frölander-Ulf, we need to build a society in which all forms of inequality have been eliminated. This implies a structural change so that power and control over productive resources rest in the hands of the great majority, the working people, instead of the capitalist or managerial class.

At the same time, I would add, it may be desirable to explore alternatives to the family system as we know it, which could reduce the burden of shadow work on women. Alternatives might include group foster care in whic professional parents or nurses care for children in boardinghouses; a family living style based on the Israeli *kibbutz,* which has managed to abolish wage labor and provide free goods and services for all its members;[1] and various communal arrangements by which a number of couples and their children could provide economic security for their members through sharing resources and income at the same time as they encouraged men to participate fully in child care and domestic activities, equalizing the share of men and women in shadow work.

Notes

1. The *kibbutz* has not yet managed to abolish the sexist division of labor, however. Most laundry and child care is still done by women.

Female and Male — A Balance*

Monica Frölander-Ulf

In the United States, for all of its diversity and complexity, we find some dominant patterns of thought about femaleness and maleness. Women and men are viewed as opposing forces that are in a permanent state of disequilibrium. Such a pattern of thought corresponds to a reality in which men are still dominant.

For example, in the economic realm, control of strategic resources is heavily concentrated in the hands of a few — mostly men. Only 2 percent of corporate board directors are women. The division of labor between women and men is still very marked: women shoulder the majority of childcare and household tasks, and most women employed in the wage-labor sector (over 50 percent of all women between 16 and 64 years of age) are heavily concentrated in typically "female jobs," or the pink-collar ghetto. A little over 11 percent of all women workers can be found in the female professions (e.g., elementary and secondary school teachers, nurses, social workers, librarians): 61 percent hold pink-collar jobs, such as clerical and service work, retail sales, and textile manufacturing and only 26 percent work in mixed and male occupations. "Women's work" is usually less well paid than "men's work." Lower pay means that an average women worker earns about 60 percent of what an average male worker earns. (The percentage has actually decreased since the 1950s when it was 64 percent.) Over half of all working-age women are employed outside the home; of these,

*Written especially for this volume. My thanks go to Dr. Beth Prinz for her useful comments and suggestions.

two-thirds work not necessarily because they want to, but because they are single, widowed, separated, or divorced, or because their husbands earn less than $15,000 a year (1983 figures). Many of these women thus work two jobs—one eight hours a day, five days a week, and the other (housework and childcare) conservatively estimated at four hours a day, seven days a week. One for low pay, the other for no pay.[1]

We also know that a rapidly increasing number of families with children are supported by women with no male partner to share the burden, and that these families have a great probability of being poor. In 1982, almost 30 percent of all white families headed by women were poor; about 57 percent of Hispanic and black female-headed households were living below the poverty level.[2]

In the realm of politics a few token appointments of women to high-level cabinet posts and some significant gains in the number of women in lower level elective offices do not hide the fact that in 1984 only about 5 percent of congressional representatives and 2 percent of senators were women. Or that 1 percent of top-management positions and 5.5 percent of middle-management positions were held by women. Or that, of the 96 AFL-CIO affiliated labor unions, only 2 had a female president in 1985. Or that only 3 percent of federal judges were women.[3]

This is not to imply that all women are economically dependent on men or that all women have less power than men. Class inequities cross-cut female–male inequalities, and it would be a mistake to assume that the female–male issue can be analyzed in isolation from two other major sources of inequality in the United States, namely class and race. Thus the economic dependence, deprivation, and powerlessness of an unemployed black or Native American (Indian) man may be infinitely greater than the disabilities suffered by a white female major stockholder of a large multinational company as a result of sexism. However, cross-cutting class, all women are affected by the ideology of female inferiority. This ideology still suggests that women because of their reproductive function as childbearers are, or should be, physically weaker than men, that women are easily victimized by men unless protected by a man (!), that motherhood (not fatherhood) is incompatible with public roles and employment, and that female fertility, as evidenced by menstruation, is something to hide or be ashamed of. In common speech, humanity is still referred to as "man," a person is called "he," and God is male, as is Jesus Christ and even the Devil!

All of this, we have been taught, is normal and natural and is rooted in women's genes and hormones. Women are the end product of a long, male-dominated evolutionary process.

We are served the popular image of the caveman dragging his newest wife by the hair into his cave, where she will spend the rest of her life having babies, cooking, and cleaning, jealous of other women, who may steal her man. Her husband is out with his buddies, bringing home the bacon (or mammoth meat). There is also the scientific version of this image, the man-the-hunter theory of evolution. This theory assumes that hunting activities (presumed to be always male) prompted the major advances in biological and socio-cultural evolution such as increased brain size, bipedalism, language, technology and social organization, leaving women completely outside the mainstream of human evolution. Or we may be taught that female and male roles are God-given and presented with quotations from the Bible as support for such a belief. None of these "explanations" give us any other alternative but to accept things as they are—a permanent disequilibrium where male outweighs female.

But American society is dynamic and full of contradictions. Rapidly changing technology and various forms of inequality create the conditions for conflict and social change. Thus, many of those who suffer from these inequalities have not been satisfied with their lot, but want change. The women's movement contains a multitude of expressions of dissatisfaction with the present imbalance and proposes an equally wide array of solutions ranging from the extreme of a complete separation of the sexes to the obliteration of the differences between female and male. Others champion the retention of a distinction between female and male ideal personalities while demanding the upgrading of women's status. The women's movement has also prompted many to reexamine the evidence of the causes of inequality between women and men. Let me comment briefly on the issue of causality and suggest what I believe should and could be done to create a society in which no one, women or man, would have to suffer from a lack of dignity or self-esteem.

Ideas that suggest that inequality between women and men is inevitable and natural are in fact just that—ideas. The function of these ideas is to compel us to accept things as they are and thus to allow the constant reproduction of the disequilibrium. The real source of inequality between women and men is to be found in the way society is organized and, most particularly, in the level of development of technology and the organization of the economy. No one denies that women and men are biologically different (although these differences form a continuum rather than two distinct categories. To do so would be absurd. But there is nothing natural or inevitable about translating these differences into inequality.

Societies very different from ours can teach us a number of important things. A serious study of the earliest form of human technological adaptation, gathering and hunting, leads to the following conclusions:

1. The caveman or "man the hunter" never did exist, except in our own minds. Equality between women and men, in spite of, or perhaps because of, the differences between them, has in fact been a reality.
2. Relatively recent human cultural evolution has brought increasing inequalities between women and men, as well as inequalities of class, race, ethnicity and others.

Many of us have been led to believe that capitalist industrialization has been a great boon to women (and is yet to save all those women living in Third World countries when they "catch up" with us). In reality, the improvements in women's status in the United States in the last hundred years have been improvements only over the short term, and are not relative to the earliest, or "primitive" societies.

The gathering and hunting societies also can provide us with clues to the causative variables that shape the lives of women and men. What were the gathering and hunting societies like? In the midst of much variation, we find some patterns.

The nomadic life typical of hunters and gatherers leads to little surplus production. People produce what they need; to produce more would quickly become a burden. Resources — the game and plants — are available to anyone who lives in an area; private ownership of these resources is unknown. Sharing excess food among everyone in the group is the norm, a custom that provides security for all and reduces the amount of time spent by an individual acquiring food. Some division of labor does exist, but with much overlap. Long-distance tracking is done mostly by men; gathering food tends to be more often carried out by women, as is infant care and food preparation. In many societies women also hunt, build the homes, and travel long distances carrying babies, heavy loads of food, and firewood. Women and men are their own bosses and make their own decisions concerning production. No work hours have to be kept; women and men can easily combine concern for their children and relatives with "work." In fact, no separation exists between domestic work and wage work, or between work and leisure.

The old and the wise and the talented are respected, but they have no material privileges. Decisions are made mostly by consensus, and disagreements are often settled through group pressure on those who are wrong, or simply by splitting up when no other solution can be found. Under traditional conditions physical violence and coercion is rare and is discouraged, since no individual or group has a monopoly of resources or positions of power. No class distinctions exist, nor is there dominance by either sex.[4]

In these societies, the ideology emphasizes equilibrium not only in human relationships but also between humans and other forms and realms of life. "Normal" women are strong, active, and sometimes aggressive (although aggression is discouraged for all). Women and men can show their emotions openly (men cry and show tenderness); the onset of menstruation is celebrated publicly as a joyful event for the whole community; motherhood is compatible with full involvement in community life. This does not mean that female and male are seen as identical, or androgynous. Far from it. In the ideological realm, male and female spheres are often clearly separated, but it is an opposition that simultaneously implies unity and balance. The supernatural all-encompassing force is androgynous, female and male. For example, the forest is for the BaMbuti of Zaire both father and mother. The supernatural force is also expressed as the sun, which is male, and the moon, which is female. Among the Beaver Indians of North America, the universe is depicted as a circle with a cross in the center describing the four cardinal points, each asociated with various natural and human characteristics: North is white, night, winter, dangerous, and male; south is yellow, day, summer, good, and female; east is red, spring, birth and birth blood, good, and male; west is red, fall, menstrual blood, dangerous, and female. Both halves of the circle (one-half is winter and fall, or north and west, the other half is summer and spring, or south and east) are made up of one male and one female season, which implies union and continuity. The male and female seasons are of unequal length. The cold half has a long male season (winter) and a short female season (fall); i.e., male outweighs female. The warm half has a long female season (summer) and a short male season (spring); i.e., female outweighs male. Thus both halves need the counterbalance of the opposite half. The center of the axis is the point at which all the attributes of the four directions meet: the warm and the cold, the good and the harmful, female and male. The center contains all worldly attributes and is also the point of transcendence into supernatural realms. Young women and men try to acquire visions in which they come to the center and are then reborn with supernatural power, bestowed by animal guardians, that will help and protect them. Here is a view of the whole world in equilibrium, in which female and male are different and opposed yet equal, and where, in the very essence of existence, the oppositions are merged into one.[5]

The idea of female inferiority and male superiority is neither natural, inevitable, nor with us since the origin of humanity; rather, it is a condition of specific forms of economic, political, and social organization. How, then, can we explain the present imbalance in the relationship between women and men? This is of course a complex issue, and others in this volume also have discussed it. Here I shall just outline some of the major factors that I think are important.

In an industrial economy, work and home are separated as most people have to sell their labor (to the owners of productive property) to make a living. The employers want to maximize their profits and thus keep tight control over the workforce by fixed, long, and continuous work hours. This is often incompatible with the needs of the household, especially child care. As a result, a division of labor emerged among the middle classes, who could afford it, with men becoming the main wage workers while women did unpaid work at home. Herein lies the main reason why men are supposed to be less caring and emotional than women: Men must love children and wives enough to support them materially, but not so much that work is disrupted or productivity lessened. Employment also often requires competition among one's peers and aggressive behavior to "get ahead." Household work is of less value in a market economy in which only money-generating work is considered "real work." Consequently, women's work has been undervalued, an estimation that carried over into the market in paying of low wages for "women's work." This of course is also useful to the executives who try to maximize their profits by keeping labor costs down. Women, are not only useful to the profit makers as low-cost labor, but as a labor reserve as well.[6] The divisions among the workers make organizing more difficult by pitting one group against the other in competition for well-paying jobs. Sexism (and racism) is good for business. Of course, many other factors have contributed to sexual inequities: a long history of patriarchal, agricultural societies with their supporting patriarchal ideologies that preceded the Western industrial societies and, in the United States, a tradition of physical violence and militarism. What is important to note is that "the enemy" is not women's genes — or boy friends, husbands, fathers, or brothers — but the economic and political organization of American society.

How do we re-create a balance? Of course we cannot all become hunters and gatherers again. There are no simple solutions. The ultimate answer lies in the creation of a society that eliminates all forms of inequality. I do not believe that we should strive only for women occupying half of all political offices, half of all "men's jobs," half of all positions of religious leadership, etc. Nor is it sufficient that men do half of all the housework and child care. If millions of people — women and men, blacks and whites and ethnic minorities — remain poor and powerless and degraded, we still have not solved the problem. We need to build a society where the economy is rationally planned so that resources can be used for the benefit of all people rather than for producing enormous wealth for a few. This requires a political system in which power is truly in the hands of the working people and requires control over productive resources by the workers themselves. While we are working toward these, admittedly utopian, goals, we can do smaller things as well. We can pressure the government and private corporations to be truly concerned and responsible for the well-being of families by offering them all the supports they need, e.g., minimum-wage levels and guaranteed income at levels which make it possible for families to remain together and adequately to feed, clothe, and shelter their members; flexible work hours to allow women and men to take care of family matters and care for sick children; parental leave with pay and adequate and available low-cost child care at work and at meetings so that parenthood (not just motherhood) will become compatible with public roles for women and men; the elimination of barriers enabling women to enter "male occupations"; the institution of comparable pay for comparable work. These issues are not "women's issues" but issues concerning the well-being of all of us, women and men.

We also need to create a balance on the level of ideology (although an ideology of equality will be commonly accepted only after the institution of an objective reality of equality) in the language we use, in a redefinition of feminine and masculine. Such an ideology would allow for a wider range of expression for both women and men and a reorganization of all our relationships so that we can see one another, not as dominant/subservient, active/passive, strong/weak, aggressive/nurturant, not as enemies, but as partners who share a common humanity and whose differences are mutually respected. We need to change our view of the world and of human relationships as a hierarchy, expressed in terms of superiority and inferiority, dominance and subservience. We view society as a triangle with power centralized in mostly male hands at the top. Perhaps we need to think, as many Native American societies did, in terms of a circle, where female and male are opposed and yet unified, where they are different and equal, and where, in the center, the worldly attributes lose their significance in the recognition of the unity of all life.

Notes

1. "Special Report: Women Workers." *Economic Notes* 50(2):1–8, (February 1982), "An Overview of Women in the Workforce." National Commission on Working Women, 2000 P St. N.W., Suite 508, Washington, DC 20036.
2. "An Overview of Minority Women in the Workforce." National Commission on Working Women, Washington, DC.
3. "Women and the Vote—1984." National Commission on Working Women, Washington, DC; "Special Report: Women Workers." *Op. cit.,* p 8.
4. Turnbull, Colin, "Mbuti Womanhood." In F. Dahlberg, ed., *Woman the Gatherer.* (New Haven: Yale University Press, 1981); Leacock, Eleanor, "Women in Egalitarian Society: Implications for Social Evolution." *Current Anthropology* 19(2):247–278, (1978).
5. Ridington, Robin and Tonia Ridington, "The Inner Eye of Shamanism and Totemism." In Tedlock, Dennis and Barbara Tedlock, eds., *Teachings of the American Earth.* (New York: Liveright, 1975).
6. Afro-Americans and other racial minorities have similarly been used as low cost labor and as labor reserves. Racist assumptions of inferior intelligence and abilities have served to justify the exclusion of minorities from well-paid occupations and the undervaluation of their work.

Sexism in the Economy

Ivan Illich

Proof of economic discrimination against women does not have to be established here. The evidence is already overwhelming. Fifteen years of feminist research has removed all doubts. However, two major tasks remain. First, we must learn to distinguish three separate arenas in all modern economies. In each of these arenas women are economically discriminated against, albeit in different ways. The three forms of discrimination were heretofore confused. Second, we must grow to understand the difference between this threefold *economic* discrimination against women and the patriarchal subordination of women in societies not yet penetrated by the

FROM Ivan Illich, *Gender* (New York: Pantheon Books, 1982), pp. 22–60. Reprinted by permission. *Footnotes omitted.*

cash nexus. Thus, sexist discrimination will serve as a speculum that mirrors what is called "economy" in advanced industrial societies. Any economy based on formal exchanges between the producer and the consumer of goods and/or services is first divided into a statistically reported and an unreported sector – the arenas of *reported* and *unreported discrimination* against women on the job. And then there always exists another economy, the shadow of the former, which is the third arena of *discrimination* against women: that found in the nether sector of *shadow work*.

The Reported Economy

Over the years, discrimination against women in paid, taxed, and officially reported jobs has not changed in severity but has grown in volume. At present, 51 percent of U.S. women are in the labor force; in 1880, only 5 percent were employed outside the home. Today, women comprise 42 percent of the U.S. labor force; in 1880, only 15 percent. Today, half of all married women have their own income from a job, while only 5 percent had outside, paying jobs a century ago. Today, the law keeps all curricula and careers open for women, but in 1880 many of both were closed to them. Today, women averagely spend 28 years in employment; in 1880, the average was 5. These all seem like significant steps toward economic equality, until you apply the one measuring stick that counts. The median yearly earnings of the average full-time employed woman still hovers around a magical ratio (3:5) of a man's average earnings: 59 percent, give or take 3 percent – the same percentage as 100 years ago. Neither educational opportunities nor legislative provisions nor revolutionary rhetoric – political, technological, or sexual – have changed the magnitude by which women, in their earnings, stand below men. What at first sight looks like so many steps toward equity is, in the perspective of the average woman, only a series of events by which more women have been quietly incorporated into the population that is economically discriminated against on grounds of sex. The current median lifetime income of a female college graduate, even if she has an advanced degree, is still only comparable to that of male high school dropouts.

When I was first faced with this evidence I could not believe it. I reacted as I had years earlier when confronted with other evidence – when I was studying the effectiveness of the medical establishment. I had been unable to believe that since 1880 the probable lifetime remaining to a middle-aged male in the U.S. had not appreciably changed. I also could not believe that a 25-fold increase in constant dollars for medical care, of which a disproportionate amount now went for the treatment and prevention of diseases affecting people in the fourth quarter of their lifespan, had resulted in no important increase in adult life expectancy. It took months for the significance of this information to sink in. It is true that the survival rate of infants has increased enormously; more people live to be 45. Bodies mangled in accidents can be reconstructed with plastic and aluminum; many infectious diseases have almost been wiped out. But the probable remaining lifespan of an adult man has not been significantly altered. And the increase or decrease that has occurred around the timeless threshold of death has little to do with medical efforts. Knowledge about the impotence of money, surgery, chemistry, and goodwill in the struggle against death is constantly repressed in our societies. It belongs to those facts that must seemingly be denied by ritual and myth.

Although totally different, economic discrimination against women as a group constitutes a reality that is equally unpalatable to most non-cynical contemporaries. As polio and diptheria have almost disappeared, so has the exclusion of girls from grammar and high schools. Just as we have seat belts to protect us against crashes, so we have TV monitors to protect against rape. Just as we have affirmative action for the health of the poor, so we have special scholarships to get women to the top.

It is hard to face the fact no program whatsoever has changed either average adult life expectancy or the wage differential between the sexes.

The unchanged wage differential between the sexes is just one aspect of the economic discrimination practiced against women on the job, just as the unchanged male adult life expectancy is only one aspect of modern medicine's failure to improve "health." It can also be argued that the enormous exertions of the modern health establishment *have* added significantly to adult life expectancy. Without these efforts, some argue, life expectancy in a world of smog and stress would be even further below that of adults in many poor countries. In the same way, it can be argued that the concerted struggles of legislators, unions, feminists, and idealists have prevented the wage differential from increasing in a progressively commodity-intensive and therefore sexist society. It can be argued that such a pessimistic view of industrial society is entirely appropriate. There is good evidence that the decline of life expectancy at all ages that has been observed over the last 20 years in the USSR is only the forerunner of a similar trend to be expected in most industrialized countries, and that the cancellation, due to the present job crisis, of many so-called advances toward equal opportunity is actually a movement that will not be reversed. However, whether you take the optimist's or the pessimist's stance, one thing seems empirically clear: The proportion of earnings withheld because of sex from half the total population seems a factor as fixed as the remaining lifespan of adult males; or, as others argue, as fixed as the incidence of cancer as a herd phenomenon in the human race.

During the 1960s, women's research dealt mostly with two themes: physical violence against women by rapists, husbands, or physicians; and working conditions for wage labor. The patterns discovered by both kinds of research are extremely uniform, and depressing. In every country, discrimination and violence spread at the same rate as economic development: the more money earned, the more women earn less — and experience rape. Seldom has such an injustice been ignored for so long and then, within 10 years, been so smugly acknowledged. Research on work during this first wave of women's studies at American universities dealt primarily with wage labor: low pay, limited opportunities, degrading roles, misrepresentation on union boards, and precarious job security. Worldwide, most women work in non-unionized urban jobs, and in only a few categories; when they do belong to a union, they are seldom taken into account in contracts. Even when the union is made up primarily of women, men are the key representatives for it during contract negotiations. However you look at it, new research on the fact that economic progress increases economic discrimination is pointless. Such research could only result in sterile redundance, more academic degrees for would-be careerists, and more smugness by those who would use it to bolster their hand-me-down explanatory theories.

Most of the early postwar feminist research was movement-borne and action-oriented. Some of its proponents followed liberal rhetoric calling for equal opportunity—cum—affirmative action; others busied themselves with holy writ, chewing on Marx, Freud, and Reich to get another establishment's approval. Reproduction was discovered. Women's rights and workers' rights then seemed compatible with industrial development and progress. In spite of its weakness and dullness, this research remains fundamental for our understanding of how industrial society works. It revealed a surprising homogeneity of discrimination against women at work in socialist and capitalist, rich and poor, Latin and Anglo, Catholic, Protestant, and Shinto societies; at equal levels of income, women in such different places as France and Japan got more or less the same kind of bad deal. The pattern of women's exclusion from privileged wages is more uniform than what is practiced against blacks, Koreans, Malasians, or Puerto Ricans and Turks. In addition, nowhere are women establishing a female regime; there is a Tanzania for Nyerere, an Israel for Begin, but no Amazonia in sight. The nation-state is invariably sexist.

The Unreported Economy

There are many kinds of economic activities on which governments and their economists cannot or do not report. In some cases, they cannot get the data; others they could not name or measure, even if they cared to record them. A plethora of names has been given to this accumulation of activities, which economists exclude from their usual statistics. Some call it the informal sector, others the D-sector, others the fourth sector, which they add to the primary "extraction," the secondary "manufacture," and the tertiary "service" sectors of the economy. Others speak about the household economy, the modern barter economy, the economy of "transfers in kind," or the non-monetary market. Still others speak about the area of self-service, self-help, and self-initiated activities. Marxists have no difficulty labeling this kind of work; they call it "social reproduction," and then they themselves divide into sects, each of which claims to know best what that means. To complete the confusion, among feminists during the mid-1970s it became fashionable to call all these activities "women's work," and to describe men who do it, in a fem-sexist epithet, as *male housewives.*

The volume of this unofficial economy is not easy to measure. It is made up of a hodgepodge of gainful activities for which no legally recognized salary is paid and for which no social security accrues, as well as of activities remunerated in kind. Much of it consists of unofficial trading, in the barter of favors or in cold cash, all of which elude the tax collector and the statistician. In Yugoslavia you must bring the government doctor a chicken if you want his attention, and in Poland eggs for the clerk are appropriate to obtain a marriage license. In Russia more than three-fourths of all eggs, milk, cheese, and fresh vegetables purchased by individual households come from the black market; books circulate on the sly or through self-publishing. In the United States, this market includes the marijuana grower from California who raises and markets a multi-billion-dollar cash crop, and the import agent of Afghan heroin, together with the policeman who is on his payroll. It also comprises the wetback who harvests the grapes, the lawyer for whom you cut the grass and who in exchange sees to it that your illegally constructed house passes county inspection, the mechanic who puts a new carburetor into the car of the accountant who, in turn, fills out the tax return for the gas station. All these clean-cut transactions, each a money-measured trade between contracting partners, are part of the unreported economy. Some of these activities actually use money as a medium of exchange; others barter; all are clearly economic transactions, and on none are statistics properly kept. Some of them are legal, others criminal. Some victimize the client more than professional services, others much less. For both parties, some are more monetarily advantageous than formal, bureaucratic proceedings, while others constitute outright exploitation. But all of them are explicit exchanges of services, products, or currency that fit a market model.

Some attempts have been made to measure the size of this underground economy, at least by comparing it to the gross national product. The British government assumes that it loses an amount equal to 7.5 percent of GNP (and not just of salaries!) through tax evasion. This is probably only a small fraction of the market it cannot record. The Internal Revenue Service in Washington, D.C., estimated that in 1976 activities generating $135 billion in personal or corporate income were not reported to federal agencies. This is from a report on tax evasion, not on legally ambiguous tax dodging via business expenses, fabricated loss, and the like, which might account for an equal amount of revenue. Recent estimates suggest that in the United States this forgotten economy is growing much faster than the formal economy, outdistancing even inflation. If the monetary (but statistically unreported) and the non-monetary markets of the United States are added together, their value certainly rivals the non-military economy on which economists base their overall indicators, predictions, and prescriptions. And, while in the formal, taxed, and statistically reported economy the labor force is to a large measure engaged in the artificial creation of pseudowork, producing useless articles, unwanted services, futile social controls, and costly economic intermediation, the real efficiency of the unreported economy is on the average much higher. The thriving black-market economy is the reason why countries like Italy have survived 10 years during each of which economists confidently predicted impending bankruptcy, and why the people's democracies of Eastern Europe have survived theoretically impossible levels of mismanagement.

Throughout, one thing is certain: Even if we carefully exclude from the unreported market all subsistence activities and all typically female housework (both of which, in their own ways, do not fit the market model), this formerly unobserved economy, growing proportionately faster than the reported GNP, contains a share of discrimination against women that has only occasionally been dealt with as an issue. Yet, in this sector of the market economy, where new jobs are created as reported unemployment rises, women might be getting an even worse deal than in the sector the economist's data dragnets can filter and measure. Here, no anti-discrimination or equal-opportunity laws apply. In contrast to male moonlighters, drug dealers, and bribe takers, whose pursuits are lucrative if sometimes unlawful, women are left with the shoddy consolation of pros-titution, puny extortions, and fencing. Women who attempt moonlighting typically wash dishes next door or do typing at work — or, more recently, cover the night shift on the text composer.

Most of the proponents of the Chicago-bred discipline that calls itself "new home economics" and most recent policy studies focusing on the unreported economy have at least one feature in common: They recognize that both black-market labor, which evades taxes, and unpaid housework (for which some demand payment out of tax funds) make a major contribu-tion to the GNP. But new studies on the hidden economy also have led to a new confusion between hitherto unreported market activities and unpaid female housework. The inability to draw a clear distinction between unreported and unpaid work constitutes the theoretical weakness of the new economic school and makes the "new home economics" treacherous for women. Women know that they are excluded from the desirable jobs in the growing arena of illegitimate work — even more so than from taxed wage labor — while their housework is a form of *bondage*. Drawing a for-mal distinction between "unreported" economic activities, from which women are unequally excluded and others, to which women are unequally bonded, is crucial. Taking housework as a paradigm of an "ideal type" of economic activity, it has two characteristics that distinguish it from black-market labor: Its value is imputed and its performance cannot be disinter-mediated. It is part of the modern nether economy that all contemporary money implies and that money therefore cannot measure.

Shadow Work

By the mid 1970s, the orientation of women's research on women's work and its economic analysis had changed. Studies began to struggle with insights that could not be properly expressed in the categories to which we had become accustomed in the fields of history, economics, ethnology, or anthropology. For their kind of research, the point was not women's smaller bite into the salary cake. Something quite different was of greater significance: how to explain that in every industrial society women are discriminated against in employment only to be forced, when off the job, to do a new kind of *economically* necessary work without any pay attached to it. It was obvious to all concerned that women regularly lose out when they apply for a job, when they seek advancement, when they try to hold on to a paying position. But outside of and along with wage labor, which had spread during the nineteenth century, a second kind of unprecedented economic activity had come into being. To a greater extent and in a different manner from men, women were drafted into the economy. They were — and are — deprived of equal access to wage labor only to be bound with even greater inequality to work that did not exist before wage labor came into being.

The best evidence of the existence of the new nether economy comes from historians of housework. Their writings made me understand that the difference between housework past and present cannot adequately be put into traditional language, nor satisfactorily expressed in the categories of class analysis or social-science jargon. What housework is now, women of old did not do. However, the modern woman finds it hard to believe that her ancestor did not have to work in a nether economy. Irrefutably, the new historians of housework describe the typical activity of the housewife as something unlike anything women have done outside industrial society, as something that cannot be suitably accounted for as just one more facet of the unreported economy, and as something the dogmatic categories of "social reproduction" simply cannot meaningfully signify.

Looking more closely at the phenomena anthropologists and historians of housework study, I began to see that the contemporary labor market, both reported and unreported, constitutes only the tip of an iceberg. True to this metaphor, most of the toil that supports the visible tip is below the waterline, work done in the nether economy. As employment in the various kinds of wage labor increases, the submerged drudgery must expand even faster. And modern housework is a typical, but not exclusive, part of that nether world's reality — work that is not only unreported but also impenetrable by the economic searchlight. And, since no commonly accepted nomenclature has yet been devised to make the distinction between housework and unreported market activities explicit, I shall contrast the spectrum of remunerated work done in the reported and unreported economy with a nether economy of shadow work, which forms its complement.

Unlike the production of goods and services, shadow work is performed by the consumer of commodities, specifically, the consuming household. I call shadow work any *labor* by which the consumer transforms a purchased commodity into a usable good. I designate as shadow work the time, toil, and effort that must be expended in order to add to any purchased commodity the value without which it is unfit for use. Therefore, shadow work names an activity in which people must engage to whatever degree they attempt to satisfy their needs by means of commodities. By introducing the term "shadow work," I distinguish the procedure for cooking eggs today from that followed in the past. When a modern housewife goes to the market, picks up the eggs, drives them home in her car, takes the elevator to the seventh floor, turns on the stove, takes butter from the refrigerator, and fries the eggs, she adds value to the commodity with each one of these steps. This is not what her grandmother did. The latter looked for eggs in the chicken coop, cut a piece from the lard she had rendered, lit some wood her kids had gathered on the commons, and added the salt she had bought. Although this example might sound romantic, it should make the economic difference clear. Both women prepare fried eggs, but only one uses a marketed commodity and highly capitalized production goods: car, elevator, electric appliances. The grandmother carries out woman's gender-specific tasks in creating subsistence; the new housewife must put up with the household burden of shadow work.

Changes in housework reach far below the surface. Rising standards of living have made it more capital-intensive by providing numerous machines and gadgets. The investment in the household equipment of a median Canadian family—and the same would be true in every other modern home—is now higher than the median plant investment per factory job in two-thirds of all nations. As a result, housework has become more sedentary, and the incidence of varicose veins has decreased. For a minority of women, this has meant an interesting, well-paid, part-time job and free time "to write their books or go fishing." But the "new" kind of housework most present-day women perform has also become more lonely, more dull, more impersonal, more time-polluting. Valium consumption and addiction to TV soap operas have often been regarded as indicators of this new, muffled stress. But, much more fundamentally, housework has become the paradigm for the new unpaid economic activity that in a computer-policed and microprocessor-equipped society is economically more fundamental than productive labor, whether this production is recorded by economists or not.

Shadow work could not have come into existence before the household was turned into an apartment set up for the economic function of upgrading value-deficient commodities. Shadow work could not become unmistakably women's work before men's work had moved out of the house to factory or office. Henceforth, the household had to be run on what the paycheck bought—one paycheck for the engineer and almost inevitably several to feed the hod carrier's family, whose wife took in piecework, while his last daughter hired out as a domestic. The unpaid upgrading of what wage labor produced now became women's work. Women were then defined in terms of the new use to which they were being put. Both kinds of work, wage labor and its shadow, proliferated with industrialization. The two new functions, that of the breadwinner and that of the dependent, began to divide society at large: He was identified with overalls and the factory, she with an apron and the kitchen. For the wage labor she was able to find as a sideline, she received sympathy and low pay.

While, during the nineteenth century, technological change revolutionized work outside the household, at first it had little impact on housework routine, except for tightening the enclosure into which each housewife was locked. Tap water put an end to her carrying the jugs to and fro, but also to her meeting friends at the well. While women's work was economically without precedent, technically it seemed to go on as always. Indoor plumbing and the new fuels, gas and electricity, which were to become nearly universal in U.S. urban areas by 1920 and in small towns by 1930, were for the great majority of people no more than technological possibilities at the turn of the century. Only as recently as the second quarter of this century did technology really change the material reality of housework; simultaneously, radio and TV began to act as substitutes for community conversation. Industry then started to produce machinery for *shadow work*. As industrial work became less labor-intensive, housework, without diminishing, became by several orders of magnitude more capital-intensive.

Economic progress is usually measured by the number of work places, meaning jobs, that are created. But it can with equal right be called the process by which more goods are offered on the market, each new commodity requiring a greater "input" of shadow work. Development conventionally means that production has become more capital-intensive; it can just as well be described as the course through which more and more capital-intensive shadow work is made necessary for the achievement of a minimum level of well-being. It is highly improbable that the volume of productive wage labor will ever again increase anywhere in the world, or that make-work, now called "service," will be paid for as extravagantly as has occurred up to now. Rather, I expect that automated production will decrease the overall volume of wage labor and lead to the marketing of commodities requiring more, not less, unpaid toil by the buyer/user. This shadow side of economic growth—a foreseeable increase in shadow work as wage labor decreases—will further accentuate a new kind of sexual discrimination, a discrimination *within* shadow work.

Shadow work is not women's exclusive domain. It is as clearly genderless as wage labor. Unpaid work to upgrade industrial production is done by males, too. The husband who crams for an exam on a subject he hates, solely to get a promotion; the man who commutes every day to the office—these men are engaged in shadow work. True, the typical "consumer" is "the household," and this is run by a woman—the expression being but a euphemism for her toil. But if women alone carried the burden of shadow work, it would be silly to say that, within the realm of shadow work, discrimination works against women. Yet this is precisely what happens. In shadow work much more intensely than in wage labor, women are discriminated against. They are tied to more of it, they must spend more time on it, they have less opportunity to avoid it, its volume does not diminish when they take outside employment, and they are penalized more cruelly when they refuse to do it. What women are cheated out of through discrimination in reported and unreported jobs is only a small fraction of the shadow price due them for their unpaid shadow work in the home.

* * *

Shadow work, however, cannot be measured in units of currency, although it is possible to transform a specific activity now exacted as shadow work into labor done for wages. This has been tried in the case of commuters. Some Austrian unions, following the lead of a Swedish union, obtained recognition by the employers that commuting was part of their employees' work. Commuting, they argued, is a burdensome task imposed on each worker. It becomes necessary because factories are located not where workers live, but where property is cheap, highways numerous, and sites for executive residential areas close. Commuting constitutes that shadow work by which the worker picks up his own labor force each morning, puts it into a car, and then, acting as the chauffeur of the commodity the employer has contracted to rent during the eight-hour workday, drives this commodity to the workplace. In addition, this shadow work requires a high level of capital investment. A significant percentage of each workday's wages must be spent by the worker for the purchase and maintenance of the car, and to pay the taxes that finance the construction of the highways on which the car runs. And commuting remains shadow work, whether the vehicle is a car, a bus, or a bicycle. Some small unions won their point. Their members then acted each morning as the chauffeurs employed by the factory to transport their own bodies to work. If, however, this kind of argument were generally accepted and workers were paid for the now unpaid toil expended on "capitalizing themselves" for the job and then transporting themselves to and from it, the industrial system would cease to function.

As these men have done, women can also demand that their shadow work be transformed into paid labor. But as soon as the shadow price of shadow work and the cost of wage labor are compared, the paradoxical nature of the former becomes evident. At least in the non-militarized sector of every modern economy, the shadow-work input required is arguably greater than that of wage labor. The industrial system is based on the assumption that most basic needs must be satisfied for an increasing majority of society's members by the consumption of a bill of goods. Hence, the toil that is connected with the consumption of these commodities is anthropologically more fundamental than the toil connected with their production. This has been hidden, as long as technical imperfections made human hands or memories necessary ingredients in the production process: Consistently productive labor was identified with legitimate work, and toil that was associated with consumption was passed over in silence or associated with satisfaction. Now, the time input in production decreases sharply, while the growing commodity intensity of society increases the time input necessary for consumption. At the same time, more different forms of consumption have become "musts"—they constitute unadulterated toil, full-blown shadow work. The total volume of shadow work rapidly surpasses the total volume of available production-associated work or ritual. No matter how you compute a money equivalent to housework, its total value exceeds the volume of wage labor.

When feminists argue that women should be paid for what they do to ready for consumption what the family income buys, they are mistaken when they ask for wages. The best they can hope for is not a shadow price but a consolation prize. The gratis performance of shadow work is the single most fundamental condition for the family's dependence upon commodities. Even if these commodities were to be produced increasingly by robots, industrial society could not function without shadow work. It is to money what the neutron is to the electron. It is as unlike productive "employment," in which commodities for others are produced, as it is unlike homesteading and traditional household activities, which are performed neither for nor with much money.

* * *

Discrimination against women in formal employment and in shadow work is worldwide, and the same is probably true, although seldom discussed, for women in the unreported or submerged market. Discrimination both on and off the job spreads with a rising GNP, as do other side effects like stress, pollution, and frustration. None of these forms of discrimination is seriously affected by cultural background, politics, climate, or religion. Reports on discrimination follow a pattern not unlike that of reports on cancer of the breast and uterus: When the per-capita GNPs are equivalent, geography influences the way in which the malady is discussed and recognized, rather than the way it occurs. Australian women keep splendid statistics and Italian women cultivate abrasive cynicism. The barriers that keep women from privileged wage labor and the traps that lock them into the kitchen are explained in different ways in Japan and in the USSR, but everywhere they are comparable in height and depth. Again, the educational process provides a good example. Even when, in different countries, it is of equal length, even if the curricula are the same, its consistent result everywhere is a lower lifetime salary for women than for men. Indeed, the more advanced the levels of education scaled, the more tightly are women locked into their place, for they then have less chance than men for a new start on a different track. The battles of the 1970s may have opened the executive suite to women, or have weakened the springs on the traps of the kitchen, but this change has disproportionately benefited "sisters" from privileged backgrounds. A few more women behind the operating table or on the university faculty, an occasional husband domesticated for washing the dishes—these rare tokens only highlight the persistent discrimination against women as a group.

7 | Racism and Poverty

By contemporary American standards a substantial minority of the American population receives less than enough income to keep it adequately fed, clothed, and sheltered. The Census Bureau reported in 1984 that 29 million Americans were living below its officially defined poverty line. Between 1979 and 1984, 8.4 million people were added to the ranks of the poor.[1] There is a clear connection between race, unemployment, and poverty. The poverty rate among minority-group members is three times that among whites. The official data, which tend to underestimate poverty, show that by 1980 one out of every three blacks and one of every four Hispanics in this country were poor. Most of the poor were also unemployed. This is statistical confirmation of the continued existence of racism within one of the wealthiest countries in the world.[2]

What keeps blacks poor in the United States is a combination of semipermanent unemployment for one-quarter of the black labor force and the relegation of many of the rest to lower-paying, menial jobs. The only way out is for the black and white working class together to change the system for their common benefit. This runs into the obstacle of racist attitudes among many white workers, who enhance their feeling of having some status by having another racial group to look down on. A further obstacle to such joint action is the lack of unity within the black community, based on class divisions between the black middle class, the black working class, and what Manning Marable terms the black subproletariat.

The need to survive without jobs in the system has led to the emergence of a black underclass of hustlers, numbers runners, pimps, prostitutes, drug dealers, and petty criminals. The consciousness of this underclass is in-

194

dividualistic, not collective. The very existence of such a philosophy among poor blacks (and other minorities) keeps them from joining in the collective efforts that alone can lead to lasting improvements for their group as a whole. The capitalist society and culture help maintain among the black poor the illusion that social betterment can best be achieved by individuals "making it" for themselves. The existence of a sizable black subproletariat divides blacks from each other, erodes black working-class institutions, increases the number of crimes committed by blacks on another, and promotes a climate of fear in the ghetto. All this, Marable maintains, impedes the development of a black working-class consciousness that could lead to collective action for change.

There have been collective efforts to change the system of racial oppression, exemplified by the civil rights movement of the 1960s that included such groups as the Student Nonviolent Coordinating Committee (SNCC). SNCC organized voter registration drives to obtain political power for blacks in southern communities. The "black power" they sought was power to participate in making the decisions that affected their lives. It meant control by black communities over their police departments, school boards, and so on.

By 1986 much of the fervor of this movement has dissipated, yet some of its goals have been reached. Blacks are able to vote without fear in the South. There are black mayors in Atlanta, Chicago, Philadelphia, Detroit, and Los Angeles, in part a reflection of the exodus of whites from the central cities. There is a black caucus of some 20 members in the U.S. House of Representatives. The black bourgeoisie has access to "good" jobs, and prestigious universities vie for their quota of the brightest black students. Yet the black masses continue to live on the edge of poverty, and half the prison population is black. The intractable problems of black poverty persist because they are part and parcel of the structural features of the capitalist system.

Another response to racism in America has been the development of black nationalism. A rebellion against white values and the white way of life, this nationalism asserts a pride in black culture and identifies with the independent black countries in Africa. Black nationalism appeals most strongly to the black underclass.

Black nationalism is revolutionary insofar as it provides a positive self-image that enables blacks to change their conditions. It is only through black power that the black community can be liberated. However, black power does not automatically lead to black liberation. Black mayors, police chiefs, and school superintendents can be just as bad as their white counterparts unless the people can exercise continuing democratic control over them. Also, full participation in national electoral politics contributes little to black liberation because national politics is only a part of a repressive system in which the most important decisions are monopolized by an elite not answerable to the public.

Black nationalism has its conservative side. Some nationalist groups hold to a doctrine of black supremacy, which by definition is as racist as white supremacy. Also, some groups, instead of demanding an end to capitalism, merely seek to employ it themselves. In contrast, radical groups such as SNCC sought to break free from the confining assumptions of both the white and the black middle class. They rejected white values and white culture, but at the same time they were searching for an entirely new way of life where there would not be room even for black capitalism. SNCC opposed the draft, the Vietnam war, and other interventions against foreign revolutions. It called for a drastic change in the economic system. As Carmichael put it, "The society we seek to build among black people . . . is not a capitalist one. It is a society in which the spirit of community and humanistic love prevail."[3]

Notes

1. In addition to the 29 million poor, another 4.8 million people were raised above the poverty level only by government benefits. *The Philadelphia Inquirer,* (January 26, 1986), p. 1-F.
2. Poverty here is considered only in the context of the United States, in relation to its own general standard of living. This poverty, however, is relative to conditions of poverty in other countries. In Asia, Africa, and Latin America, the poor have nowhere near the material comforts of the poor in the United States, and poverty is a condition not merely of the few but of the majority. In both the Third World and the United States the distance between poverty and wealth is astronomical, and in both the rich keep down the poor; the difference is that in a country with an affluent majority it is possible for the poor to make it in one way or another, whereas in a country where most people are poor poverty means toil from childhood, slow starvation, and an early death.
3. Stokely Carmichael, "Power and Racism," *New York Review of Books,* (September 22, 1966), pp. 5–8.

How Capitalism Underdeveloped Black America

Manning Marable

The Crisis of the Black Working Class

Black people in the United States are the direct product of massive economic and social forces which, at a certain historical juncture, forced the creation of the early capitalist overseas production of staples (rice, sugar, cotton) for consumption by the Western core. The motor of modern capitalist world accumulation was driven by the labor power of Afro-American slaves. In the proverbial bowels of the capitalist leviathan, the slaves forged a new world culture that was in its origin African, but in its creative forms, something entirely new. The Afro-American agricultural worker was one of the world's first proletarians, in the construction of his/or her culture, social structures, labor, and world view. But from the first generation of this new national minority group in America, there was a clear division in that world view. The *Black majority* were those Afro-Americans who experienced and hated the lash; who labored in the cane fields of the Carolina coast; who detested the daily exploitation of their parents, spouses, and children; who dreamed or plotted their flight to freedom, their passage across "the River Jordan;" who understood that their master's political system of bourgeois democracy was a lie; who endeavored to struggle for land and education, once the chains of chattel slavery were smashed; who took pride in their African heritage, their Black skin, their uniquely rhythmic language and culture, their special love of God. There was, simultaneously, a *Black elite*, that was also a product of that disruptive social and material process. The elite was a privileged social stratum, who were often distinguished by color and caste; who praised the master publicly if not privately; who fashioned its religious rituals, educational norms, and social structures on those of the West; who sought to accumulate petty amounts of capital at the expense of their Black sisters and

FROM Manning Marable, *How Capitalism Underdeveloped Black America* (Boston: South End Press, 1983), pp. 24, 27-40, 42-46, 51-69. *Tables omitted.* Reprinted by permission of South End Press, 116 St. Botolph Street, Boston, MA 02115.

brothers; whose dream of freedom was one of acceptance into the inner sanctum of white economic and political power.

* * *

Each member of the Black majority is a prisoner, and shares the marks of oppression upon his/or her shoulders. Each Black worker is a representative of the collective patterns of exploitation, the series of murders, the lynchings, the mutilations. Each has been touched by starvation and unemployment. Each has experienced through his/or her own life or through the lives of others, destitution, illiteracy, prostitution, disease, and death at an early age. Acceptance of bourgeois illusions provides no temporal savlation; the crushing blows of the workplace, the police, and the racists form a chorus which proclaims to the Black majority: *you are not human beings.* The ringing of the racist chorus resounds in the oppressed's ears from cradle to grave. That shrill ringing is the cold aesthetic expression of white capitalist America.[1]

So the basic social impulse of Afro-American workers is more than the search to find meaning within the tedious, often boring labor they are forced to perform to survive. It is a struggle, in part, for retaining collective self-respect in the face of degradation. It is the effort to create the material possibility of a better and more affluent life for future generations. "People are not fighting for ideas, for things in anyone's head," Amilcar Cabral observed. "They are fighting to win material benefits, to live better and in peace, to see their lives go forward, to guarantee the future of their children."[2]

* * *

Over 15 years have now passed since the major upheavals of Black workers, youth, and students which were termed the Black Power and Civil Rights Movements. Black political militancy spread from streets and lunchcounters to factory shops and production lines across the country. Black unrest at the point of production created new and dynamic organizations: the League of Revolutionary Black Workers in Detroit; the Black Panther Caucus at the Fremont, California General Motors plant; and the United Black Brotherhood in Mahwah, New Jersey. In the Deep South, civil rights activists from the Southern Christian Leadership Conference helped to organize sanitation workers' strikes in St. Petersburg, Florida, Atlanta,

Georgia, and Memphis, Tennessee. Ralph D. Abernathy, Hosea Williams, Coretta Scott King and A. Philip Randolph supported the vigorous unionization efforts of the American Federation of State, County and Municipal Employees (AFSCME) in the Deep South . . .

* * *

It cannot be overemphasized that the Civil Rights and Black Power Movements were fundamentally working-class and poor people's movements. From the very beginning, progressive unions were involved in the desegregation campaigns. The United Auto Workers, United Packinghouse Workers, District 65, Local 1199, in New York City, and the Brotherhood of Sleeping Car Porters all contributed funds to Martin Luther King Jr.'s Montgomery County bus boycott of 1955–1956. And in rural areas of the Black Belt, small independent Black farmers risked their families' safety by opening their homes to freedom riders and Student Nonviolent Coordinating Committee (SNCC) workers. Black farm workers, sharecroppers, service workers, and semi-skilled operatives were the great majority of those dedicated foot soldiers who challenged white hegemony at Selma's Pettus Bridge and in the streets of Birmingham.[3] SNCC understood well the importance of Black working-class support for the Civil Rights Movement and thus recognized the need to develop an employment strategy for Blacks.

* * *

A Shift to the Right

By the 1980s much of the political terrain had shifted to the right. White blue-collar workers voted strongly for Ronald Reagan in 1980. The League of Revolutionary Black Workers, the Black Panther Labor Caucuses, and other revolutionary nationalist organizations within the Black working class no longer existed. The late A. Philip Randolph had campaigned for the election of a white racist, neoconservative, Daniel Patrick Moynihan, to the U.S. Senate in 1976. Andrew Young, running for mayor in Atlanta in 1981, advised patience to the Black community's demands in ending the murders of its children. Abernathy and Williams supported Reagan's candidacy. An entire class of Black farmers, sharecroppers, and rural laborers almost completely disappeared, eliminating part of the social foundation for the civil rights struggles in the Deep South a generation ago. As an activist in the Amalgamated Clothing Workers Union, Coleman Young led the creation of the fiercely independent National Negro Labor Council in the 1950s; years later, as mayor of Detroit, he forged a conservative political alliance with corporate capital at the expense of Black and poor constituents.

* * *

The acceleration of Black unemployment and underemployment, the capitulation of many civil rights and Black Power leaders to the Right, the demise of militant Black working-class institutions and labor caucuses, and the growing dependency of broad segments of the Black community upon public assistance programs and transfer payments of various kinds are not mutually exclusive phenomena. These interdependent realities within the contemporary Black political economy are the beginnings of a new and profound crisis for Black labor in America. As Harold Baron once noted, the capitalist class historically has needed "black workers, yet the conditions of satisfying this need compel it to bring together the potential forces for the most effective opposition to its policies, and even for a threat to its very existence. Even if the capitalists were willing to forego their economic and status gains from racial oppression, they could not do so without shaking up all the intricate concessions and consensual arrangements through which the State now exercises legitimate authority."[4] Despite the destruction of *de jure* segregation, the white capitalist class has not abandoned racism. Instead, it has transformed its political economy in such a way as to make the historic "demand for black labor" less essential than at any previous stage of its development. In the production of new goods and services, from semi-conductors to petroleum products, the necessity for lowly paid operatives, semi-skilled laborers, and service workers becomes progressively less with advances in new technology. Simultaneously it has succeeded in developing a strong Black political current against Black participation in unions. Leading representatives of the Black petty bourgeoisie are in outspoken opposition to public-sector union activities in metropolitan centers dominated by newly elected Black officials.

* * *

The historic evolution of the Black working class in advanced capitalism, and the ambiguous relations between Blacks and organized labor, raise a series of difficult questions. Is there any real basis for Black–white working-class unity within the trade union movement, and more generally, within American politics? Does unionization help or hinder Black economic advancement vis-à-vis whites? Are unions "structurally racist" in a racist–capitalist state, unable by their very existence to advance the material interests of Black laborers? To arrive at some conclusions, one must assess whether any real gains in Black income were derived in part from unionization.

Blacks and American Trade Unions

There is no question but that the large majority of the Black working class supports unions. Both in public opinion polls and in their support for "pro-labor" political candidates, most Blacks continue to express support for legislation favorable to union growth, despite organized labor's shoddy record on racial issues. The central reason for this is that the majority of Afro-American people—blue-collar and service workers, public-sector employees and clerical workers—understand that unionization has historically produced higher wages, both in absolute terms and in relative terms compared to white employees with similar educational backgrounds and skills. Unionization means improved working conditions, and a greater likelihood of upward income mobility. . . . Racism still exists within all unions, and most white union leaders tolerate if not encourage the systemic exclusion of their Black members from the highest-paid and skilled positions. Nevertheless, it remains clear that "the relative wages of black workers to those of white workers are considerably better in industries where powerful industrial unions with a militant tradition embrace the majority of production workers, than in industries where craft unions, or weak industrial unions, or no unions at all prevail."[5]

* * *

Racism

Neither the material interests of white workers nor those of labor unions as a whole are advanced by white racism. There are at least several ways to document this. Perhaps the simplest is the lower rate of unionization in the South in virtually every industry. The strength of racial segregation both within the civil society as a whole as well as within broad elements of the trade union movement in the region is commonly recognized by historians as the major reason for Southern labor's failure to organize.[6] Second, racism dilutes the bargaining power of unions for higher wages, fringe benefits and better working conditions. White workers who have greater seniority than many Blacks often accept contracts with decreasing benefits simply to maintain their own positions vis-à-vis Blacks within the labor market. In the long term, however, this racist strategy inhibits "union bargaining strength and militancy," according to economist Michael Reich, "thereby reducing the total income share of labor."[7] Again, the political economy of the South provides an example. By the 1970s, 75 percent of all textile workers in the United States worked in the Southern states. Only 10 percent of this workforce of nearly 600,000 was unionized. The average hourly wage of Southern textile workers in the late 1970s was $3.46, near the bottom of the national wage scale for all industrial workers.[8]

Probably the greatest negative impact of racism upon the material interests of labor and more generally of all workers is in the area of public policy. The massive spending reductions of the Reagan Administration are "racist" in that they have a disproportionately higher affect on Blacks as a group than upon all whites. It is crucial to observe, however, that by far the largest population targeted for cutbacks is the lower-income, white working class.*

* * *

The chief beneficiaries of several decades of liberal and reformist Federal intervention programs have been individuals and families with annual incomes below $20,000 (1982 dollars); those without post-secondary education or technical skills, national minorities; blue-collar and service workers; and the elderly. Mathematically these diverse groupings have the potential for becoming, in the new age of fiscal austerity, a left-of-center coalition that could be forced to articulate minimally a left social democratic public policy agenda, simply for their own survival. Yet the centrifugal forces of white racism, cultural conservatism, and political reaction, embodied in the emergence of the New Right and the election of Reagan, now threaten the realization of such a majority.

The basic issue here is an old problem which can be traced to the very beginnings of U.S. history. White populists, labor leaders, and leftists

---

*Omitted here are data on recipients of food stamps, public housing, and Medicaid. — Ed.

have long made the argument that racism actually reduces the absolute living standards of white workers, retards their unions, and undermines the institutional stability of their communities. Racial divisions within the working class accelerate the processes of exploitation in the workplace for Blacks and whites alike. Yet given clear political options, white workers have frequently sacrificed their own material and political interests to engage in the mass-mania of racist violence, terrorism, and prejudice. White workers have organized lynch mobs, raped Black women, mutilated Black children, engaged in strikes to protest the employment of Black co-workers, voted for white supremacist candidates in overwhelming numbers (e.g., George Wallace in the Democratic Party's presidential primaries in 1972), and have created all-white unions. How and why does this process happen? We can gain some insights here from Georg Lukás. In *History and Class Consciousness,* Lukás writes that "Marx repeatedly emphasized that the capitalist is nothing but a puppet. And when, for example, he compares his instinct to enrich himself with that of the miser, he stresses the fact that 'what in the miser is a mere idiosyncrasy, is, in the capitalist, the effect of the social mechanism, of which he is but one of the wheels.'"[9] In a racist–capitalist state and economy, the instinct among whites to exhibit racist behaviors and practices is not a psychological aberration. To be racist in a racist society is to be normal; to reject racism, denounce lynchings, and fight for Black political and economic rights is to be in a symbolic sense "abnormal." Racism benefits the bourgeoisie absolutely and relatively; working-class whites are usually part of the larger "social mechanism" of racist accumulation and Black underdevelopment, serving as uncritical cogs in the wheels of Black exploitation.

For many working-class whites, the Afro-American is less a person and more a *symbolic index* between themselves and the abyss of absolute poverty. All whites at virtually every job level are the *relative* beneficiaries of racism in the labor force: Blacks, Puerto Ricans, Chicanos, etc., supply the basic "draftees" in the permanent and semi-permanent reserve army of labor. In the capitalist economy's periodic downturns, whites benefit relative to Blacks by not being Black. Moreover, lowly paid white workers, particularly in semi-skilled occupations, can "justify" their low wages, poor working conditions, and deteriorating standards of living with the racist view, "At least I am not living like the niggers."

* * *

The continued suppression of Blacks within the economy and across civil and political societies becomes the means through which many oppressed whites can derive cultural and psychological satisfaction without actually benefiting in an absolute material sense in super profits of racism.

The sad irony is that certain sectors of the white working class are *also* targeted for elimination and radical transformation. The identical processes which threaten the Black proletariat are confronting white autoworkers, steelworkers, rubberworkers, textileworkers, laborers, and many millions more. Whether white workers as a self-conscious mass will *perceive* that their own "benefits" from racism are only relative to the oppressed conditions of Black labor, and that the social and psychological image of the Blacks-as-inferior beings actually promotes their own exploitation as well as that of Blacks, cannot be predetermined. A majoritarian bloc against the New Right and the interests of capital must at some initial point call for the protracted cultural and ideological transformation of the white working class.

* * *

Conclusions

An analysis of the evolution and current status of the Black working class leads us to several conclusions. More than any other social stratum within American society, Black workers would be the direct and immediate beneficiaries of the reorganization of the U.S. political economy. The contemporary and historical crisis which confronts the Black working class primarily, as well as the Black majority, cannot be resolved unless worker self-managed factories and the public ownership of the central means of production, transportation, and the distribution of goods and services is won in our generation. There are two basic contradictions which present barriers to such a solution. The first, and most obvious, is the great (and still unanswered) question: Will labor unions and the white working class wage unconditional war against its own contradictory history? The primitive bigotry, cultural exclusivity, social norms, and explicit ideology of white supremacy have repeatedly undercut Black–white labor unity.[10] If there is no attempt on the part of white labor to engage in extensive self-criticism, and to construct a common program for struggle against capital with nonwhites, the final emancipation of the American working class will be unattainable. The second problem relates to a more recent development within the overall political economy — the growth of a massive number of permanently unemployed men and women. The reserve army of labor is swelling the ranks of the American poor, and has created the socio-economic conditions for an unpredictable "ghetto-class" whose political interests are not always identical to those of employed workers. As the contradictions within the capitalist economy and civil society deepen, millions of unemployed and desperate Americans may continue to ignore socialist alternatives for something that can promise jobs, food and domestic tranquility. That authoritarian alternative could be some form of fascism.

The Black Poor: Highest Stage of Underdevelopment

The citadel of world capitalism, the United States, has never liked to admit that millions of its citizens are poor. Yet the hub of international financial markets, Wall Street, is only blocks from some of the worst urban slums in the world. Atlanta's Omni and glittering convention center is walking distance from delapidated shanties that are mirror images of eighteenth- and nineteenth-century slave quarters. The White House and the posh residential district of Georgetown are respectively less than 20 city blocks from rat-infested, crime-filled squalor. The percentage of the total U.S. population defined as impoverished increased from 11.1 percent in 1972 to 13.0 percent in 1980, the highest figure recorded by the Bureau of the Census since 1966. About 1.3 million New York City residents were defined as poor in 1978, 18.7 percent of the city's populace. Chicago recorded 667,000 poor persons in 1978, 18.4 percent of its total poulation, and Philadelphia had 336,000 poor people, 19.8 percent of the city's total population. There were 3.5 million Latinos, 8.6 million Blacks, and 19.7 million whites who were classified by the Federal government as poor in 1980. In a racist society, poverty is alloted unequally: 32.5 percent of all Blacks in the United States are poor, 25.7 percent of all Hispanics, but only 10.2 percent of all whites. [11]

Poverty and the Class System

Poverty must be understood properly as a comparative relationship between those segments of classes who are deprived of basic human needs (e.g., food, shelter, clothing, medical care) versus the most secure and affluent classes within a social and economic order. It does relatively little good to compare and contrast the family of a Puerto Rican welfare mother in the South Bronx with a poor family in Lagos, Saõ Paulo, or Bombay. Black American living conditions may be superior in a relative material sense to those of working-class families in Poland — but we are not Poles. The process of impoverishment is profoundly national and regional, and it is in the light of capitalism America's remarkable success in producing an unprecedented standard of living for the majority of its indigenous white population that Blacks' and Hispanics' material realities must be judged.

The first dilemma confronting the researcher who explores the dimensions of American poverty involves the definition of class. Traditionally, American bourgeois social scientists have defined one's class status as a function of annual earned income, and not in terms of one's relationship to the means of production. Upper-class Americans are not individuals who own the factories and the corporations, and who live without selling their labor power in the marketplace for a wage. Rather, the capitalist elite is delineated by its annual income of, let us say, $200,000 or more. Of course, this definition could include any number of persons who are not capitalists — from highly successful physicians to lucrative (and illegal) drug dealers. Conversely, the Federal government has established a rather elaborate theoretical construct to define poverty, based again on an individual's or family's annual income — "the sum of the amounts received from earnings; Social Security and public assistance payments; dividends, interest and rent; unemployment and workmen's compensation; government and private employee pensions, and other periodic income." Certain nonmonetary transfers, such as health-care benefits and food stamps, are not counted as income.[12] The Federal government makes a distinction between "nonfarm" and "farm" residence in determining poverty status, weighs its analysis according to the number of persons who are in a particular family, and even considers whether a female is the nominal "head" of a particular household. Thus, widely varying standards emerge on what constitutes "the poor." An 18-year-old Black woman with a small child in Atlanta was considered poor in 1978 if her annual income was $4,268 or less. If she and her child lived in rural Georgia, her "poverty threshold" was $3,614. A Black family of seven persons in Chicago with both male and female parents would be poor at $11,038 or less. If their father was killed by the police, and the family returned to rural North Carolina, its poverty threshold would be $7,462; if it stayed in Chicago, $8,852. A blind and partially crippled 66-year-old widow, living in a dangerous and drafty rowhouse in the slums of North Philadelphia, would not be considered poor if her yearly income exceeded $3,253. Sensible people of all political persuasions would have to admit that no single person can survive on an annual income of under $10,000 in a metropolitan area except at the precipice of despair and hunger. But as everything else in capitalist America, the state defines "poverty" to suit its own needs.[13] Thus, the assertion that the percentage of all Americans who are "poor" declined from 22.4 percent in 1959 to 11.1 percent in 1973 must be viewed with a healthy degree of skepticism.[14]

Race and Poverty in America

Even when one accepts the Federal government's definition of poverty, the general situation for millions of Americans becomes strikingly apparent. For the year 1980, there were 11.1 million children under the age of 18 who lived in families existing below the poverty level. About 3.9 million persons 65 years or older were poor; 12.4 million poor persons, about 42 percent of the nation's total poor population, resided in the South; 62 percent of all poor people lived in metropolitan areas, and almost 60 percent of this population resided in the ghetto or central city.[15]

* * *

Black families throughout the United States, in every region and city, assume the unequal burden of poverty. In suburban districts outside the ghetto, 21.3 percent of all Black families are poor, versus only 5.9 percent of white families. In central cities Black and white families below the poverty level comprise 28.6 percent versus 7.6 percent of their total populations respectively. Outside metropolitan areas 39.1 percent of all Black families are poor, while only 11.2 percent of white families are.[16] When all American families are divided into fifths according to income, a much higher proportion of Blacks and Hispanics are located in the bottom two-fifths, and virtually disappear in the highest fifth of U.S. income earners. Using 1977 figures, 39.6 percent of all U.S. nonwhite families were in the lowest fifth of all income earners. 22.6 percent were located in the second lowest fifth. Only 9.4 percent of all nonwhite families earned yearly incomes to rank in the highest fifth, by way of contrast.[17]

Although Blacks' incomes have increased over the past 10 years, earners generally have not kept pace with inflation. One way of viewing the illusion of black income mobility is by comparing Black median incomes between 1970 and 1977 in current dollars and in constant 1977 dollars. The median Black family income in 1970 was $6279. Seven years later, Black family median income was $9563, an increase of $3284. In constant 1977 dollars, however, $6279 was worth $9799. Thus, the median Black family income actually declined — 2.4 percent in the period 1970 and 1977. Using constant 1977 dollars, a pattern of growing impoverishment becomes clear. The median Black family incomes in Northeastern states declined by 15.2 percent between 1970 and 1977, from $12,132 to $10,285 annually; in the North Central States, the decline was 11.2 percent, $12,045 to $10,690; in the West, 20.6 percent, $12,487 to $9917. Those families that suffered most were located in urban metropolitan areas. In central cities in excess of 1 million persons, Black median family income declined 13.6 percent, from $11,589 to $10,012. Even in the suburbs of major cities, Black median family income dropped 7.1 percent, $14,111 to $13,104. For Black families with no husband present, median incomes increased marginally, from $5581 in 1970 to $5598. Simultaneously, white median family incomes between 1970 and 1977 increased in constant 1977 dollars by 4.8 percent, and white suburban families' median incomes passed to $20,000 mark by 1977.[8]

Although the majority of Black poor families earned something between $3000 and $5000 in 1978, a frightening number of Blacks exist on virtually no financial reserves or resources. About 78,000 Black families reported annual incomes between $1000 and $1499; 45,000 families earned between one dollar to $999 during 1978; 31,000 additional families actually had no cash income at all. For the most oppressed and destitute sector of the permanently unemployed, social services and public programs have provided little in the way of real additional income. Inside poverty areas, residential districts containing at least 20 percent of the population living below the official poverty level, 220,000 Black families survive solely on public assistance plus their meager salaries. 31,000 families in poor communities depend primarily on Social Security income. About one-third of a million Black poor families live in public housing, which reduces the amount of money they must pay toward their rent. 770,000 other Black poor families, however, are forced to find private accommodations usually at exorbitant rates.[19]

Demographically, Black poor people are distinguished from poor whites by certain social characteristics: they are largely more female, younger, and usually reside in the urban ghetto. At all ages, Black women are much more likely to be poor than white females, white males, or Black males.[20]

* * *

Subproletarian status for Black women creates oppressive social conditions that inevitably include an absence of adequate birth control information and support services for young children. In residential areas where at least 20 percent of all persons exist below the poverty level, both birth and infant mortality rates are exceptionally high. In impoverished central cities, the number of Black children under 3 years old per 1000 Black women between the ages of 15 to 44 was 327.93. In rural poverty areas, the rate is a staggeringly high 441.66. Again, these rates must be contrasted with both white and Black women who live above the poverty level, 173.61 and 184.69, respectively. There is a direct relationship between the number of children that are within a Black family with a sole female householder and family's likelihood of being below the poverty level. Only 14.8 percent of all Black women householders without children are in poverty. That percentage increases with each dependent: one child, 42.2 percent in poverty; two children, 59.8 percent; three children, 63.4 percent; four children, 82.5 percent; five children, 86.0 percent.[21]

Poverty is also reinforced within the Black community by educational underdevelopment and academic inequality. By 1978, as an illustration, 74 percent of all Blacks between the ages of 22 to 34 were high school graduates, with 12.6 median years of school completed. Of all whites in this age group, 86.1 percent were high school graduates, with 12.9 median years of education. For Blacks below the poverty level between 22 and 34, both figures were significantly lower — 53.0 percent high school graduates, with 12.1 years of schooling. Overall educational statistics for poor Blacks are much worse. The average poor Black person has completed only 10 years of school. Only 26.8 percent have been graduated from high school . . . about 118,000 Black poor people have never attended school in their lives, 491,000 completed under five years, and another 585,000 had only a sixth- or seventh-grade education.[22]

The strongest roots of Black poverty are anchored firmly in the capitalist marketplace, contrary to the opinions of most social scientists. The process of income erosion for Black families since the 1960s can be examined several ways. Perhaps the most effective is an assessment of the number of salaried workers per family by race, and the ratio of persons to income earners per family . . .

[Between 1967 and 1977, the number of salaried workers per family decreased more among Blacks than among whites. During the same decade] the ratio of persons to earners per family had remained roughly the same for Blacks, while the ratio declined for whites. These figures imply that the recessions of 1969-1970 and 1973-1975 forced at least 550,000 Black workers permanently out of the job market; that Black families who depended upon a second or third job to maintain their homes lost the opportunity to acquire employment; and that whites took the places of Blacks in most of these jobs.[23]

Unemployment statistics provide another key in explaining the steady deterioration of Black economic life. In 1961 the official rate of unemployment for nonwhites and whites in the United States was 12.4 and 6.0 percent respectively. In the mid-1960s, nonwhite unemployment dropped sharply for several reasons: the continued relocation of rural Blacks to the North and West, where more jobs at higher wages were then available; the collapse of legal segregation; the Federal government's implementation of affirmative action guidelines which made jobs available to previously qualified Blacks; and a generally expanding capitalist economy. By 1969 nonwhite unemployment was 6.4 percent. . . .

The crisis of U.S. capitalism in the 1970s contracted the number of available jobs in the labor market, with Black workers usually the first to be dismissed. In 1972 nonwhite unemployment reached 10 percent, and by 1975 the figure was almost 14 percent. . . .

In 1975, 33 percent of all unemployed nonwhites were out of work for 15 weeks or more; 16 percent were jobless for more than half the year. Blacks below the poverty level were particularly victimized. Only 1.6 million of 4.7 million poor Blacks were able to work during 1978. Of this number, less than 950,000 were employed full-time. 508,000 of the employed Black poor held jobs for 26 weeks or less, and 689,000 more could only obtain part-time work. Hardest hit were poor, young Black men and women between 16 and 21 years of age. The mean number of weeks worked in 1978 for this group was a meager 17.2 weeks.[24]

As the crisis of the capitalist economy became more severe, the rules for these unemployed workers, Black and white, to receive compensation became more restrictive. During the recession of 1973–1975, at least three-fourths of the unemployed received some sort of compensation. Workers losing their jobs because of foreign capital's growing shares of the U.S. consumer market were awarded a substantial share of their former wages for up to 18 months, with the passage of the Trade Adjustment Assistance Program. As late as December 1980, almost one-quarter of a million unemployed workers obtained funds through the program; by December 1981, only 12,100 were allowed to collect benefits. By the beginning of 1982, only 37 percent of the jobless were receiving any kind of compensation. Officially, Black overall unemployment reached 17.4 percent in late 1981, a percentage which does not even include those whom the Federal government calls "discouraged workers"—unemployed persons who have not looked for work actively for four weeks. Conservatively, the real rate of Black unemployment in the United States in the early 1980s easily exceeded 20 percent, and might surpass 30 percent under certain economic conditions. In many ghetto communities, Black youth unemployment surpassed 80 percent.[25]

* * *

Summarizing these statistics, one obtains at best a limited insight into the nature of Black poverty in the United States. To grasp the fact that the median annual income of a Black family consisting of one female adult and two children under 18 years of age who are below the poverty level is $3260 does not and cannot tell us how she struggles every day to survive. Statistics report that 10,000 Black families in the United States that include a female householder, no husband, and three small children reported *no cash income* in 1978. Beyond Aid to Families with Dependent Children, and beyond food stamps, how did these 10,000 impoverished Black families purchase school books, new clothing, shoes, and other necessities? Did they have the luxury of going to the cinema on a Saturday afternoon, or jumping into the family automobile to take a leisurely ride down to the beach on a warm summer day? How did they cope when a sudden health problem struck one of the children in their family? What is the possibility of their ever overcoming their massive personal debt, and escaping the harassment of creditors and finance officers? Statistics cannot relate the human face of economic misery.

The Black Underclass

Oppressed people learn strategies for survival: if they do not learn, they perish. The profile above indicates that in 1978 only 10.8 million out of 18.1 million Black persons over 14 years of age could find employment. What do several millions of these workers—the 2.2 million persons who have only found part-time jobs, and the 412,000 Black workers who are unemployed for more than 26 weeks during the years—do to survive? How do the other 7.3 million Black adults provide food, clothing, shelter, medical care, and some measure of security to their families in the age of Reaganomics and racism? At the highest level of underdevelopment, the daily life of the Black poor becomes a continuous problematic, an unresolved set of dilemmas which confront each person at the most elementary core of their existence. The patterns of degradation are almost unrelenting, and thrust upon every individual and family a series of unavoidable choices which tend to dehumanize and destroy many of their efforts to create social stability or collective political integrity.

In recent decades, sociologists have described this growing social stratum as an "underclass" or "ghettoclass." Perhaps the best example of the literature on the subject was written by Douglas G. Glasgow, professor of social welfare at Howard University. Glasgow's *Black Underclass* examines the inner-city Black youth of Los Angeles, from the Watts race uprising of 1965 to the late 1970s. Theoretically, he locates the center of Black unrest in the volatile group of 18- to 34-year-olds who were unified by "their common condition":

> They were jobless and lacked salable skills and opportunities to get them; they had been rejected and labeled as social problems by the police, the schools, the employment and welfare agencies, they were victims of the new camouflaged racism.
>
> Detached from the broader white society, even largely from the seemingly complacent working Blacks around them, they drank, gambled, fought a little, but mostly just generally "hung out." . . . They try to keep body and soul together and maintain a job, but they remain immobile, part of the static poor. Others who could make this adaptation fail to do so, often preferring to remain unemployed rather than accept a job that demands their involvement for the greater part of each day but provides only the barest minimum of financial reward. They seek other options for economic survival ranging from private entrepreneurial schemes to working the welfare system. Hustling, quasi-legitimate schemes and outright deviant activity are also alternatives to work.[26]

Glasgow separates the Black "underclass" from lower-income Blacks by several rough social criteria: an absence of generational socioeconomic upward mobility, the "lack of real opportunities to succeed," and widespread "anger and despair" which "arises from contact with mainstream institutions, which, almost imperceptibly and very impersonally, reject them The author also believes that "racism is probably the most basic cause of the underclass condition."[27]

Conceptually, there are some problems inherent with the term "underclass." Using Glasgow's criteria, literally millions of Black Americans would have to be included with the underclass, since, as I have illustrated previously, they would have absolutely no meaningful prospects for future work. Glasgow emphasizes the subjective and superstructural factors related to underclass status—lack of decent education, widespread alienation from white civil order and society, the disintegration of stability within family life, and so forth. But these factors in and of themselves do not make this massive stratum a "class" in a real and decisive sense. These "subproletarians" include both marginal elements of the working class as well as those of whom Marxists have traditionally termed the lumpenproletariat: pimps and prostitutes, small-time criminals, drug dealers, and numbers runners. The "work" that these elements perform is defined by capitalist society as illegal, but the profits it returns for a few ghetto entrepreneurs can be monumental. Moreover, the question of class must address the issue of consciousness. A class that is neither "self-conscious" nor acts collectively according to its material interests is not worthy of the name. The general philosophy of the typical ghetto hustler is not collective, but profoundly individualistic. The goal of illegal work is to "make it for oneself," not for others. The means for making it comes at the expense of elderly Blacks, young Black women with children, youths, and lower-income families who live at the bottom of working-class hierarchy. The consciousness of the subproletariat is not so much that of a "class," but the sum total of destructive experiences that are conditioned by structural unemployment, the lack of meaningful participation within political or civil society, the dependency fostered by welfare agencies over two or three generations, functional illiteracy, and the lack of marketable skills.

The pimp is one typical representative of inner-city underdevelopment within the subproletariat, the personification of the individualistic hustler. He accumulates petty capital by brutalizing young women, who sell their sexuality on the open market to (usually white middle-class male) "consumers." Methods of "labor discipline" invariably include naked force—rape, threats, physical and psychological assaults. Women who are coerced or who accept these crude terms of "employment" are expected to deliver a certain number of tricks with "Johns" per hour, day, and week. Police in the ghetto are usually an integral part of the trade and expect a regular cut from the women's profits for tolerating the traffic in their precincts. Local Black and white entrepreneurs in the inner-city motel and hotel business find room to expand and even to survive by orienting services to accommodate prostitution. The profits are also used to underwrite other illicit activities, from the ghetto's omnipresent drug traffic in elementary and secondary schools to small-time fencing operations.

Black women with young dependents are invariably touched by the process of lumpenization. A very small percentage may be forced at some point into prostitution simply to put food on the table for their children. Many more, however, supplement their inadequate incomes by a variety of illegal acts which carry relatively low levels of risk. "Boosting" or stealing clothing, shoes, small appliances, and food from retail stores has become a regular and common occurrence. Many poor people who maintain a high degree of public morality, and who actively participate in their churches, find little or no difficulty purchasing clothing, television sets, stereos, washing machines, and even automobiles that they know are stolen. Children even below the age of 12 sometimes become numbers runners or participate in marginal ways in the drug traffic. Teenagers who become skilled in drug transactions can accumulate literally thousands of dollars per month, and annual gross incomes above $20,000 for some high school students are not rare in major cities. In some urban Black communities, especially in Chicago, over one-fourth of all Black youth between the ages of 14 to 25 belong to gangs, which often deal in small robberies, drugs, and prostitution. A great many youth participate in gangs simply to survive daily life in urban high schools. Gang membership usually has little social stigma and carries with it a limited guarantee of safety and security in their neighborhoods. The death of a gang member, the murder of a high school student during classes, or the random arrest of a young Black man by the police are all integral factors of daily life. What is sad about the proliferating incidents of violence within the urban Black community's permanent reserve army of labor is that no one is surprised any more.

Substantial elements of the Black elite do not discuss the unique problems of the "underclass," either with whites or among themselves, because in doing so they would be forced to confront the common realities of racism that underlie the totality of America's social and economic order. They often do not like to be reminded that former friends and family members are on welfare, that their nieces may be prostitutes, or that their cousins peddle drugs, stolen fur coats, and designer jeans. Even the expressions of popular culture among the Black ghetto poor are not seen as having any direct relationship to the Negro upper crust's aesthetics. In *Certain People: America's Black Elite,* author Stephen Birmingham recounts the acute embarrassment of one Black upper-class matron from Washington, D.C., at the sight of a Black young man donning "Super Fly" pimp-type attire. "'Disgusting.' she whispered. 'There is the cause of all our problems.' Her friend, more perceptive, said, 'No, that is the *result* of all our problems.'"[28]

Many Blacks who advanced into highly paid positions in the corporate world intensely dislike the mass cultural expressions of the Black poor and working classes, and refrain from any social relations with Blacks who rely on "transfer payments" to make ends meet. For several generations, the Black elite of Harlem's "Strivers' Row" effectively created a *cordon sanitaire* around their neighborhood to protect themselves and their property from contact with the Black "underclass." As late as the mid-1970s, the Strivers' Row's "two block associations [had] rigid rules which [were] rigidly enforced: no trash or litter thrown in streets; keep hedges uniformly clipped; keep brasswork polished; no children playing in the streets; no peddlers or solicitors; beautify gardens and window boxes." When well-heeled residents contemplated the plight of their distant relatives or neighbors outside Strivers' Row, the nearly universal attitude was one of contempt. The Black poor were characterized repeatedly as "lazy, shiftless, and no good." In employing low-income Blacks as occasional domestic workers, the Negro elite can be every bit as paternalistic as the white ruling class. "One thing that can be said for the black upper class," one affluent Negro lady informed Birmingham, "is that we're always nice to our servants."[29]

A central focus of subproletarian life is fear. Black elderly and handicapped persons are afraid to walk or visit friends in their own neighborhoods at night or travel on public transportation because they are convinced (with good reason) that they will be assaulted. Young Black women are often uncomfortable going to parties or social gatherings by themselves because they will invariably be harassed by Black men and even male youngsters barely into puberty. Parents who live in inner cities are reluctant to send their children several blocks to attend school or to play outside after dark because they are afraid they might be harmed. Black-on-Black crime usually victimizes the working and poor, but it can paralyze virtually all Black people of whatever social class or neighborhood. It produces for capitalism and the state a deep despair, a destructive suspicion we hold against each other. It thwarts Blacks' ability to achieve collective class consciousness, to build political agencies which advance our material and cultural interests, and develop ourselves economically. It forces Black inner-city merchants to strap revolvers on their calves or shoulders, while serving poor patrons behind plexiglass shields. It stops Black doctors from making emergency calls to their patients who live in the midst of a tenement slum or ghetto high-rise complex. It instills a subconscious apathy toward the political and economic hierarchy, and fosters the nihilistic conviction that nothing can ever be changed in the interests of the Black masses.

The permanent reserve army of Black workers, subproletarians, or the "underclass," is the latest social culmination of the process of Black ghettoization, economic exploitation, and urban decay. In one sense, it represents the highest stage of Black underdevelopment because it eliminates millions of Blacks from belonging to working-class organizations. The existence of a massive "ghettoclass" disrupts the internal functions of the mostly working-class Black community, turning Blacks in blue-collar jobs against those who have never had any job. The social institutions created by working-class Blacks to preserve a sense of collective humanity, culture, and decency within the narrow confines of the inner city are eroded and eventually overturned. Subproletarianization and the extension of permanent penury to broad segments of the Black majority provoke the disruption of Black families; increase the number of Black-on-Black murders, rapes, suicides, and assaults; and make terror a way of life for all Blacks of every class background who live in or near the inner city.

Notes

1. Afro-American writers have made this point repeatedly, in various ways. James Baldwin explains: "The history of the American Negro is unique also in this: that the question of his humanity, and of his rights therefore as a human being, being a burning one for several generations of Americans, so burning a question that ultimately became one of those used to divide the nation. It is out of this argument that the venom of the epithet *Nigger!* is derived . . . In America, even as a slave, he was an inescapable part of the general social fabric and no American could escape having an attitude toward him." James Baldwin, *Notes of A Native Son* (New York: Bantam, 1964), pp. 144–145.
2. Amilcar Cabral, *Revolution in Guinea: Selected Texts* (New York: Monthly Review Press, 1969), p. 86.
3. Manning Marable, *From the Grassroots: Social and Political Essays Towards Afro-American Liberation* (Boston: New England Free Press, 1972), p. 39.
4. Harold M. Baron, *The Demand for Black Labor: Historical Notes on the Political Economy of Racism* (Boston: New England Free Press, 1972), p. 39.
5. Victor Perlo, *Economics of Racism USA: Roots of Black Inequality* (New York: International Publishers, 1975), pp. 206–207; see Table 31. "Median Income of Persons 14 Years Old and Over with Income by Sex and Work Experience, for Selected Years: 1956 to 1974," in U.S. Bureau of the Census, *The Social and Economic Status of the Black Population in the United States: An Historical View, 1790–1978* (Washington, D.C.: U.S. Government Printing Office, 1980), p. 47.
6. Ray Marshall, *Labor in the South* (Cambridge, Mass.: Harvard University Press, 1965), and J. Wayne Flint, *Dixie's Forgotten People: The South's Poor Whites* (Bloomington: Indiana University Press, 1979).
7. Michael Reich, *Racial Inequality: A Political Economic Analysis* (Princeton: Princeton University Press, 1981), p. 269. The U. S. Department of Labor reported in 1974 that nonagricultural membership in unions was 26.2 percent in 1974. In the Southeast, the figure

was 14 percent. Mississippi's union membership in 1974 was 12.1 percent, and North Carolina's rate of 6.8 percent was the lowest in the United States. See Douglas Sease, "Many Northern Firms Seeking Sites in South Get Chilly Reception" *Wall Street Journal,* February 10, 1978.

8. Marable, *From the Grassroots,* p. 141. On the plight of Black and white textile workers in the South, see Ed McConville, "The Southern Textile War," *The Nation,* (October 2, 1976), and *The Struggle for Economic Justice at J.P. Stevens* (New York: Amalgamated Clothing and Textile Workers Union, 1977).

9. Georg Lukás, *History and Class Consciousness: Studies in Marxist Dialectics* (Cambridge, Mass.: MIT Press, 1971), p. 133.

10. The thesis expressed in this paper is not a new idea. In 1911, W. E. B. DuBois observed that the liberation of Black Americans was basically an economic, and not simply a political, question. He believed that the material interests of white workers objectively favored Black equality. DuBois stated that the goal of international capital was "to reduce human labor to the lowest depth in order to derive the greatest personal profit." DuBois, "The Economics of Negro Emancipation in the United States," *Sociological Review* 4 (October 1911): 303-313.

11. U.S. Bureau of the Census, *Characteristics of the Population Below the Poverty Level: 1980* (Washington, D.C.: U.S. Government Printing Office, 1982), p. 11; John Herbers, "Poverty Rate on Rise Even Before Recession," *New York Times,* (February 20, 1982).

Perhaps the most obvious manifestation of "lumpenization" in the 1980s was the growing army of homeless women and men who live on America's alleys, sidewalks, and gutters. Gentrification in urban core areas has sharply reduced the number of single-room occupancy hotels for unemployed and poor persons. When the poor are locked out of their boardinghouses, they often have nowhere else to turn except to the street. By 1982, New York City had an estimated 24,000 men and 6000 women who were homeless. Chicago has an estimated 8000 people homeless; Los Angeles 7500; and Washington, D.C., more than 6000. Mary Ellen Schoonmaker, "Home on the Curb," *In These Times,* (April 28-May 4, 1982).

12. *Ibid.,* p. 10.

13. Bureau of the Census, *Social Indicators III: Selected Data on Social Conditions and Trends in the United States* (Washington, D.C.: U.S. Government Printing Office, 1980), p. 417.

14. *Ibid.,* p. 491.

The poverty index was adopted in 1969 to reflect the sex and age of the householder, family size, urban or rural residence, and family composition. Rural standards for poverty are figured at 85 percent of urban or suburban living levels. A number of persons, including prison inmates, are not counted in poverty statistics.

Embarrassed by the recently growing number of poor Americans, the U.S. Commerce Department began to explore statistical maneuvers to redefine "poverty." On April 14, 1982, in what the Bureau of the Census admitted was a "highly exploratory procedure," the government suggested that many noncash benefits might be calculated in the determination of the poverty level. Such benefits under consideration are: food stamps, Medicaid, Medicare, subsidized school lunches, and public housing. The implications of this latest bureaucratic manipulation are alarming. For example, the number of poor persons in 1979 was 23.6 million, 11.1 percent of the total population. If assigned values of noncash government benefits were included in determining poverty status, the number of poor persons would drop between 13.6 million (6.4 percent) and 20.7 million (9.8 percent). For Black Americans, the number of persons classified as being poor would plummet from 7.5 million (30.8 percent of all Blacks) to as low as 3.7 million (15.1 percent). "Including Government Noncash Benefits Would Reduce Number of Poor," U.S. Bureau of the Census, *U.S. Department of Commerce News,* (April 14, 1982).

15. Bureau of the Census, *Characteristics of the Population Below the Poverty Level: 1980,* pp. 1, 11.
16. U.S. Bureau of the Census, *The Social and Economic Status of the Black Population,* p. 201.
17. U.S. Bureau of the Census, *Social Indicators III,* p. 483.
18. Ibid., pp. 486–487.
19. U.S. Bureau of the Census, *Characteristics of the Population Below the Poverty Level: 1978,* p. 97.
20. Ibid., pp. 51, 101, 103.
21. Ibid., pp. 54, 82.
22. Ibid., pp. 56, 58.
23. U.S. Bureau of the Census, *Social Indicators III,* p. 490.
24. U.S. Bureau of the Census, *The Social and Economic Status of the Black Population,* pp. 69–71; and U.S. Bureau of the Census, *Characteristics of the Population Below the Poverty Level: 1978,* p. 71.
25. Conservative estimates of the number of "discouraged workers" ranged from the Bureau of Labor Statistics' figure of 1.2 million in 1981 to over 2 million by independent observers of the labor force. The Federal government's number would still represent the largest total of discouraged workers in the United States since the mid-1940s. About one-third of this group is nonwhite, and almost two-thirds are females.
26. Douglas G. Glasgow, *The Black Underclass: Poverty, Unemployment and the Entrapment of Ghetto Youth* (New York: Vintage, 1981), pp. 1–9.
27. Ibid., pp. 10–11. There is a regrettable oversimplification of the dynamics of racism within the structural realities of late capitalism that mars what is otherwise an important contribution to the field of race relations. At one point, for instance, Glasgow issues this undocumented assertion: "In this country Blacks as a group represent the have-nots, whites the haves. The conflict between the two, although it has shifted from the open confrontation of the sixties, remains constant." This viewpoint all but negates the class component in the racial equation, which in turn creates sharply divergent interests within both the whites and Blacks as groups (p 31).
28. Stephen Birmingham, *Certain People: America's Black Elite* (Boston: Little Brown, 1977), p. 127.
29. Ibid., pp. 127, 192–193, 288.

8 | Power in America

Two rival versions of who holds the power in contemporary American society are the elitist theory and the pluralist theory. A basic question is whether the United States is ruled by a unified power elite, as Mills maintains, or by a plurality of countervailing groups. Both elitists and pluralists agree there are a number of centers of power in America. These include the executive branch of the federal government, the semiautonomous government agencies (the most important and powerful being the CIA), the military establishment, and the major corporations. The question is whether these institutions balance and veto each other or whether they act in concert. A second issue is the degree of power exercised at the "middle" levels of society by state and local governments, Congress, the universities, and the labor unions, and at the "lower" level by ordinary citizens.

The power elite thesis of Mills is that incumbents of key positions in the major corporations, the military, and the executive branch of the federal government form a cohesive interlocking directorate that makes the fundamental decisions governing the course of American society. Members of the power elite are not always in agreement, but the assumptions and interests they share far outweigh their differences. Simply because they are at the top they view the world in a similar fashion. According to the power elite theorists, the more basic issues of national and international consequence are not, as the pluralists maintain, decided at the middle and lower levels.[1]

Following in the footsteps of Mills, Domhoff sees America as dominated by a ruling class—an upper class of the wealthiest families that uses its wealth and power to control the major political and economic decisions

219

in this country. The power elite, he maintains, consists of a leadership group of the economically and politically active members of the ruling class together with their top managerial employees. These high-level employes identify with the interests of the upper class, and many are eventually coopted into this class. Domhoff does not assume that any institutionally based group is *by definition* a member of the power elite.

Domhoff shows how the power elite dominates America through four processes: the special-interest process, whereby the wealthy pressure government to satisfy their needs; the policy-formation process, in which policies beneficial to the upper class in general are adopted; the candidate-selection process, in which the upper class helps determine who runs for public office and buys the allegiance of politicans with campaign contributions; and the ideology process, whereby ideas favorable to the continued domination of this country by the upper class are disseminated through educational institutions and the mass media.

I find the elite theory more convincing than the pluralist theory. The pluralists argue there is no concentration of power because there are disagreements among those at the top, and because many issues are debated and decided on by the legislature. But the pluralists exaggerate the influence of legislators, for the most important issues are decided at the top, and disagreement there concerns tactics rather than goals.

During the 1970s, criticism of the Vietnam war came from inside the cabinet and from business executives, just as today there is dissent among the power elite over continued American support for the "contras" in Nicaragua. Such criticism, however, is based on pragmatic considerations and has rarely touched on the legitimacy of American intervention abroad.

At the apex of power in American society there is a basic agreement on the most vital issues — that "communism" should be contained, that American intervention against revolutions for national liberation may be necessary, that capitalism must be preserved.

Notes

1. For a good exposition of the pluralist view, see Arnold M. Rose, *The Power Structure* (New York: Oxford University Press, 1967). For the power elite view, see C. Wright Mills, *The Power Elite* (New York: Oxford University Press, 1956); G. William Domhoff, *Who Rules America?* (New York: Prentice-Hall, 1967); and G. William Domhoff, *Who Rules America Now? A View for the 80s* (Englewood Cliffs, N.J.: Prentice-Hall, 1983).

The Ruling Class
and the Problem of Power

G. William Domhoff

On top of the gradually merging social layers of blue- and white-collar workers who comprise the working class and make up 85–90 percent of the population, there sits a very small social upper class which comprises at most 0.5 percent of the population and has a very different life style and source of income from the rest of us. Many Americans are not even aware of the existence of this upper class. They are used to thinking of the highly paid and highly visible doctors, architects, television actors, corporate managers, writers, government officials, and experts who stand between the working class and the upper class as the highest level of the social pecking order. The "rich people," if they come to mind at all, are thought of as a few wealthy eccentrics, such as Howard Hughes, who happened to strike it rich; or as the occasional wealthy families, such as the Rockefellers or Mellons or Du Ponts, which are thought to be a remnant of another age, or as the handful of playboys or jet setters who are bent on squandering the little that remains from once-significant family fortunes.

But "the rich" in the United States are not a handful of discontented eccentrics, jet setters, and jaded scions who have been pushed aside by the rise of corporations and governmental bureaucracies. They are instead full fledged members of a thriving social class which is as alive and well as it has ever been. Members of this privileged class, according to sociological and journalistic studies, live in secluded neighborhoods and well-guarded apartment complexes, send their children to private boarding schools, announce their teenage daughters to the world by means of debutante teas and gala ballroom dances, play backgammon and dominoes at their exclusive social clubs, and travel all over the world on their numerous junkets and vacations. They are active as executives and directors in major banks and corporations, as partners in large law firms, as directors of foundations, universities, and cultural centers, and in numerous high-status professions. Some even involve themselves in the political fray, where they are referred

FROM G. William Domhoff, *The Powers That Be* (New York: Random House, 1978), pp. 3–21. Reprinted by permission of the author.

to variously as "patricians," "Brahmins," "aristocrats" and "bourbons," depending upon the "age" of their money and the part of the country from which they come. [1]

There is also in America, as different types of studies show, an extremely distorted distribution of wealth that has remained relatively constant throughout the nineteenth and twentieth centuries. For selected years between 1953 and 1969, the top 1 percent of the population has owned between 25 percent and 30 percent of all privately held material wealth, including from 50–86 percent of all corporate stock. [2] That is not quite the whole story, however, for a closer look at the top 1 percent shows that a mere 0.5 percent have most of the wealth in that category: "The richest 0.5 percent of the United States population has consistently held about 22.0 percent of personal wealth over the last thirty years." [3] The foregoing estimates were developed from studies of the estates of deceased wealthholders; a study for 1962, using survey information developed by the government from interviews with a sample of consumers, estimated that the top 0.5 percent of families held an even higher percent of the wealth, 25.8 percent. [4] Adults with a net worth of $1 million or more in 1969, who are at the core of the wealthy class, make up 0.1 percent of the adult population and have 9.6 percent of the total net worth. [5] All of these figures, it should be stressed, are considered conservative estimates, for good information on this touchy topic is hard to obtain.

As for income, the maldistribution is not quite as bad. In recent years the top 5 percent of income earners, most of whom are wealthy to begin with, have received 14–16 percent of all money income in the United States. [6] Although there are considerable data on income distribution, only one study attempts to estimate the percentage of yearly income that goes to the very wealthy. In that study, for the year 1958, it was estimated that the top 1.5 percent of wealthholders, those with assets of $60,000 or more, received 13 percent of the total income for that year. The percentage rose to 24 if income from capital gains is included. The estimate is considered a conservative one for several reasons, including the allocation of all Social Security income to the lower 98.5 percent of wealthholders. [7]

It is not hard for most of us to imagine that the small social upper class uncovered in sociological research is made up of the top wealthholders revealed in wealth and income studies. However, it is not necessary to rely on our imaginations, for it is possible to do empirical studies linking the one category to the other, thereby demonstrating that the "economic class" of large capitalists is one and the same with the highest "status group" or "social class" in the United States, as would be expected by class-hegemony theorists. The first systematic studies along this line were reported by sociologist E. Digby Baltzell, who showed that the wealthiest people of Philadelphia are also the people who send their children to expensive private schools, belong to exclusive social clubs, and list in the "blue book" of the upper class, the *Social Register,* which is also one of the best indicators of upper-class standing.[8] Looking beyond Philadelphia to the nation as a whole, Baltzell found that 9 of the 10 very richest men at the turn of the century were listed in the *Social Register.* He also found that over 75 percent of the wealthy families in Ferdinand Lundberg's 1937 classic, *America's Sixty Families,* had easily traceable descendants (the same given and surnames as the family founder) in the *Social Register,* and that 87 of the families chronicled in Gustavus Myers' *History of the Great American Fortunes* had descendants listed in that register.[9] Another sociologist, C. Wright Mills, compiled a list of the 90 richest men for the year 1900. He found that roughly half of those on the list had descendants in the New York, Boston, or Philadelphia *Social Register* for 1940.[10]

In most countries, it would be taken for granted that a social upper class with a highly disproportionate amount of wealth and income is a ruling class with domination over the government. How else, it would be argued, could such a tiny network of families possess so much if it didn't have its hooks into government? After all, isn't "power" and "rulership" inferred from various value distributions, such as those for wealth and income, which are merely the outcomes of struggles and conflicts over how the social product is to be produced and how it is to be divided? Isn't politics about "who gets what," with the "when, where, and how" as subsidiary questions when it comes to the shape of the power structure?

Not so in the United States today. In a nation that always has denied the existence of social classes and class conflict, and overestimated the degree of social mobility, systematic information on the persistent inequality of wealth and income tends to get lost from public and academic debate.[11] Besides, most social scientists, being of a pluralist persuasion, believe that many different groups, including organized labor, farmers, consumers, and middle-class environmentalists, have a hand in political decisions—if not since the first years of the republic, at least since the Progressive Era and the New Deal. There is no such thing as a ruling class in America, or so we are assured by leading academicans, journalists, and other public figures.

We can begin to understand this reaction to wealth and income statistics if we realize that the predominant emphasis in American ideology is on the "process" by which things are done—democracy in government, equality of opportunity in education, fairness before the law—and not on "outcomes." The emphasis on outcomes, implying as it does a possible bias toward social egalitarianism, was anathema to most of the founding fathers, and it is anathema to the corporate business community of today. A special commentary in *Business Week* in December 1975 went so far as to charge that the new egalitarian movement of the 1970s was actually authoritarian in nature and would wreck the economic system if it were able to substitute equality of outcomes for equality of opportunity.[12]

The emphasis on process in American thinking appears in the social sciences as a theory of power which insists that power can be known only by seeing it in action. That is, we must study the process of power, rather than infer power from outcomes. Who benefits, the very essence of a power struggle, is hardly considered. This viewpoint is epitomized in the writings of Robert A. Dahl, one of the two or three most eminent political theorists of the past two decades. In a sharp critique of sociologists Floyd Hunter and C. Wright Mills, both of whom believed on the basis of their studies that a small "power structure" or "power elite" dominated in the United States, Dahl rejected their evidence and argument because "I do not see how anyone can suppose that he has established the dominance of a specific group in a community or a nation without basing his analysis on the careful examination of a series of concrete decisions." He went on to say that he found it a "remarkable and indeed astounding fact that neither Professor Mills nor Professor Hunter has seriously attempted to examine an array of specific cases to test his major hypothesis."[13] Not everyone, of course, has held to such an extreme emphasis on process within American social science, but enough have that it was somewhat heretical when a mainstream political scientist, William C. Mitchell, wrote in 1969: "Let us try defining power not as one who makes decisions but as who gets how much from the system. Those who acquire the most goods, services, and opportunities are those who have the most power."[14]

There are philosophical and methodological difficulties with a conceptualization of power and power indicators that focuses exclusively on process. However, rather than enter into an argument over these abstract points, I am going to set aside these differences of philosophy and method for purposes of this book.[15] I will accept the challenge presented by the dominant social-science paradigm and concentrate on the process by which the ruling class in the United States dominates government and subordinates other social classes. Putting aside the argument that we can infer power from the distributions of wealth, income, health, education, and other benefits sought by members of American society, I will suggest that there are four general processes through which economically and politically active members of the ruling class, working with the aid of highly trained and carefully selected employees, are able to dominate the United States at all levels. I call these four processes:

1. *The special-interest process,* which comprises the various means utilized by wealthy individuals, specific corporations, and specific sectors of the economy in influencing government to satisfy their narrow, short-run needs;
2. *The policy-formation process,* which is the means by which general policies of interest to the ruling class as a whole are developed and implemented;
3. *The candidate-selection process,* which has to do with the ways members of the ruling class ensure that they have "access" to the politicans who are elected to office;
4. *The ideology process,* which involves the formation, dissemination, and enforcement of the assumptions, beliefs, and attitudes that permit the continued existence of policies and politicians favorable to the wealth, income, status, and privileges of members of the ruling class.

These four processes are separate from one another, but they do not run simply and smoothly along four isolated and easily observable sociological paths. Although there is some specialization of function among people and institutions, there also is overlap in the sociological networks which sustain each of the processes, as will become clear as the analysis unfolds. Nor do the four processes operate without conflict. Conflict is endemic to much of American political life, even though it must be remembered that there is often more smoke than fire in many of the controversies which engage the attention of newspaper readers and television audiences.[16] Indeed, one of the advantages of the four-process viewpoint to be presented here is that it makes it possible to sort out different kinds of conflicts and assess the degree to which they actually contradict a ruling-class theory of the American power structure. Many conflicts merely involve the division of profits within the ruling class. Some involve sacrificing the short-run interests of specific corporations or industries to the general and long-run interests of big businesspeople as a whole. Others involve no more than personal ambition and personality conflicts among those seeking further fame or fortune. Some involve policy differences between different segments of the ruling class. There are even a few occasions when the ever-present differences between the working class and the ruling class emerge into political conflicts which raise potential challenges to class rule. Within the schema to be presented here, account can be taken of the considerable amount of day-to-day political conflict which many social scientists see as prima facie evidence against a ruling-class perspective.

Before describing each of these four processes and their functioning, it is necessary to define the terms "state," "ruling class" and "power elite." It will then be possible to answer in a brief way several commonly raised objections to ruling-class theory that are preliminary to any discussion of the processes through which an alleged ruling class dominates the state.

"State" is a concept with three levels of meaning. At the most visible level, the state is a "sovereign political territory."[17] It is a nation-state, such as the United States or France. However, the state as a sovereign political territory is maintained by a "governmental system" or "state apparatus." This is the second meaning of "state," and it includes all aspects of the formal system of government — executive, legislative, judiciary, military, and police.[18] Most important, however, the "state" is a state of mind, and its essence involves a common will on the part of the people within a given territory to unite for the common defense of that territory.[19] The "state," then, is ultimately defined by a common allegiance (patriotism), which is expressed in a willingness to accept the governmental system and to defend the common territory. The "state" as governmental apparatus and as a state of mind are thus embodied in the definition of the state as "a sovereign political territory."

By a ruling class I mean a clearly demarcated social class which has "power" over the government (state apparatus) and underlying population within a given nation (state). Evidence for the "power" of a ruling class can be found in such indicators as:

1. A disproportionate amount of wealth and income as compared to other social classes and groups within the state;
2. A higher standing than other social classes within the state on a variety of well-being statistics ranging from infant mortality rates to educational attainments;
3. Control over the major social and economic institutions of the state;
4. Domination over the governmental processes of the country.

This conception of a ruling class does not differ greatly from the views of other social scientists. For example, Marxian definitions of a ruling class speak in terms of a social class that controls the major means of production in a given society, whatever the legal forms of that control may be. A social class than can pass on privileges to its children, direct investments to areas of its choosing, and divide the social product among the classes of society, giving itself a disproportionately large share, is a "ruling class" in a Marxian view.[20] Non-Marxian definitions differ only in that they do not stress ownership or control of the means of production as an integral factor in ruling-class domination. For example, Daniel Bell speaks of a ruling class as a power-wielding group with a continuity of interests and a community of interests.[21] E. Digby Baltzell writes in terms of an upper class that contributes members "to the most important, goal-integrating elite positions." For Baltzell, a ruling class is an upper class which can perpetuate its power "in the world of affairs, whether in the bank, the factory, or in the halls of the legislature."[22]

Generally speaking, then, there is considerable agreement that a ruling class is a social class that subordinates other social classes to its own profit or advantage. However, none of the definitions prescribe how this subordination takes place, nor who is directly involved in the process. To understand the how and who, it is necessary to introduce the concept of a "power elite." I define the power elite as the leadership group or operating arm of the ruling class. It is made up of active, working members of the ruling class and high-level employees in institutions controlled by members of the ruling class. It is members of this power elite or leadership group who dominate within each of the four processes [of domination]. . . .

C. Wright Mills first introduced the concept of a power elite into the sociological literature as a substitute for "ruling class." Mills made this substitution because he thought the ruling class of big property owners and corporate executives had been transformed since the Great Depression and World War II by the addition of "political outsiders" (executive-branch appointees) and "warlords" (military leaders) into the highest circles of leadership and decision.[23] However, in the way I have redefined the term and used it over the past ten years (as the leadership arm of the ruling class), it is more akin to what Baltzell means by "the establishment," for it emphasizes that "while an establishment will always be dominated by upper-class members, it also must be constantly rejuvenated by new members of the elite who are in the process of acquiring upper-class status."[24]

The difference between Mills' definition and mine lies in the fact that (1) I do not assume *a priori* that any institutionally based group is by definition part of the power elite, as Mills did in so designating leaders within corporate, military, and governmental bureaucracies; and (2) I have grounded the power elite in a social class. Using this approach, it is possible to determine empirically which parts of the economy and government can be considered direct outposts of the ruling class by virtue of disproportionate participation by members of the power elite. Proceeding in this fashion I was able to show in earlier research that the power elite as I define it has a membership very similar to that hypothesized by Mills.[25]

Both of these concepts — ruling class and power elite — are important in an exmination of how America is ruled, for they bring together the class-rule and institutional-elite perspectives that are sometimes viewed as separate or even opposing approaches to the analysis of power. Then, too, the simultaneous consideration of ruling class and power elite, as I have defined them, allow us to deal with the everyday observation — which is also the first objection raised by critics of ruling-class theory — that some members of the ruling class are not involved in ruling, and that some of its leaders are not members of the class. Within the present framework, this objection is not a problem at all. There always have been members of ruling classes who have spent much of their time playing polo, riding to hounds, or leading a world-wide social life. A ruling class is a privileged social class which is able to maintain its top position in the social structure, and there is no implication that each and every member of this social class must be involved in ruling, or that a person automatically falls from the class if he or she merely enjoys the disproportionate benefits that are appropriated by the ruling class. At the same time, there always have been carefully groomed and carefully selected employees from lower social classes whose advancement to important positions has been dependent upon their ability to solve problems and attain goals that are determined by the needs and desires of the ruling class.

However, not all upwardly mobile leaders in the United States are part of the power elite. As I have defined it, the power elite does not include labor leaders, even those appointed to government, for they are neither members of the social upper class nor employees of its institutions. Middle-American politicans elected to political office are not members of the power elite by this definition. Nor are leaders of minority-group organizations. These examples are meant to emphasize that strata of the working class and specific social and ethnic groups have leaders too.

From a pluralistic point of view, the existence of these separate sources of leadership may be seen as evidence against the ruling-class view. From a class-hegemony view, however, the problem is not to deny that there are leaders from other classes or social groups, but to demonstrate how the ruling class, through the power elite, is able to impose its policies and ideologies in opposition to the leaders of various strata of the nonpropertied, wage-earning class. To include such people in a definition of the power elite would be to abandon any attempt to support empirically a class-based model of power in America.

With definitional problems clarified, it is possible to turn briefly to several criticisms of ruling-class theory that should be dealt with preliminary to a detailed consideration of the processes of domination. While these criticisms cannot be discussed here in a definitive way, it is possible to indicate the broad outlines of an answer to each of them, thus ensuring that peripheral questions do not detract from the main argument of later chapters.

The first argument against a ruling-class perspective is that the alleged ruling class is never specified in such a way that it can be studied empirically. I have tried to meet this objection by reputational, positional and statistical studies which show that certain social registers, blue books, private schools, and social clubs are good — but by no means perfect — indicators of ruling-class standing.[26] Through the use of these sociological indicators, it is possible to do a wide variety of empirical studies of the ruling class, including studies of its socialization practices, its charitable involvements, its kinship networks, and its historical continuity.

A second common objection is that there is no reason to believe that the alleged ruling class is "cohesive" enough to have the "will" and "class consciousness" to develop class-oriented policies and ideologies, much less to impress them upon the government and general public. This is an important argument, for most pluralists and Marxists have insisted upon social cohesiveness and in-group consciousness as part of their definitional criteria of a social class. In responding to this argument, I have tried to demonstrate the social cohesiveness of the American ruling class by presenting systematic evidence on interregional private school attendance, overlapping club memberships that are nationwide in scope, interlocking corporate directorships, and nationwide attendance at annual retreats such as the Bohemian Grove and Rancheros Visitadores.[27] Others might provide evidence for social cohesion based on intermarriage patterns, intermingling at summer and winter resorts, and clique patterns of a regional nature within the business community.[28]

While educational and social interactions are important evidence for the type of social cohesion from which class awareness can be inferred, it is also important to develop evidence of policy cohesion and a common ideology. Evidence for ruling-class cohesion at these levels also exists. . . .

Many of these common policies and ideologies are developed in specific ruling-class institutions and organizations like the Council on Foreign Relations, Committee for Economic Development, Business Council, Conference Board, Population Council, and National Municipal League. These organizations, in turn, are linked with social clubs and corporations. Quantitative studies which systematically analyze the relationships among large numbers of corporations, social clubs, and policy-planning groups are perhaps most convincing in this regard. The overlaps and clique patterns found among organizations concerned with economic, social and policy matters suggest there is an institutional basis for the kind of generalized world view that is the very essence of class consciousness.[29]

There are many social scientists who would concede that a social upper class exists in the United States. Nonetheless, only a few of them also would agree that this class is a ruling class. One reason many resist this next step is that they believe the upper class no longer controls the banks and corporations that dominate the economy. According to this third objection to ruling-class theory, there has been a separation between the ownership and control of major corporations in the United States. The social upper class reaps the major benefits from large banks and corporations, as the statistics on stock ownership and wealth distribution make very clear, and many of its members sit on corporate boards of directors, but these huge enterprises are allegedly controlled by corporate managers of diverse social origins who remain somewhat separate from the ruling class and sometimes have more "public-regarding," less profit-oriented goals.[30]

The notion of a "managerial revolution" is difficult to refute fully and completely because of an absence of adequate information on corporate ownership and on the functioning of boards of directors. Indeed, the idea itself was able to take hold because its advocates accepted at face value the scanty information on corporate ownership available to them. Rather than assuming that the big rich continued to control corporations unless it was shown otherwise, they assumed from the little information corporations would release that wealthy people no longer controlled them. They then challenged their opponents to prove otherwise. It was a very unusual reversal of investigatory procedure, but the idea has had considerable staying power even in the face of evidence to the contrary. Thus, Robert A. Dahl could write in 1970 that it was a "resounding" and "incontrovertible fact" that ownership and control have been "split apart," even though a careful survey of some of the evidence six years earlier by a traditional social scientist, Earl Chiet, had concluded that "it is far from clear that attenuation of ownership control is as complete as is generally assumed."[31] Sociologist Maurice Zeitlin has chronicled numerous other examples of the persistence of the "pseudo-fact" of a managerial revolution in a detailed survey of the controversy which makes a powerful case for continuing dominance by corporate owners.[32]

The following kinds of evidence controvert the managerial revolution view and the resultant claim that America has been transformed from a class-based, exploitative economic system to a bureaucratic one in which class conflict is a thing of the past and everyone receives rewards in relation to the importance of his or her functional role in various institutional hierarchies:

1. A highly disproportionate number of bank and corporation directors are members of the ruling class according to our sociological criteria of social registers, private schools and social clubs.[33] This suggests that the general direction of these enterprises remains within the ruling class, for there is reason to believe that directors often play a significant role in the major issues that face a corporation. This is particularly the case when the corporation is in crisis, when a merger is being considered or a large-scale change in management is contemplated.[34]

2. There is good evidence for the argument that the highest-level managers of middle-class origins are assimilated into many of the social institutions of the ruling class as they take advantage of stock options and other devices which turn them into significant property owners in their own right. Top managers come to have a common class situation or class position with owners.[35]

3. There is evidence that the firms alleged to be managerially controlled are just as profit-oriented as owner-controlled firms, which deals with the claim that managers have different goals from ruling-class owners and directors.[36]

4. The most careful study of ownership records shows that many more companies are family- or owner-controlled than managerial revolution advocates have claimed.[37]

5. There is evidence that in some industries the corporations are controlled in good measure through financial institutions that are clearly controlled by members of the ruling class.[38]

6. There is reason to believe that studies of the kinship networks, family offices and holding companies of major owning families would show they have much greater involvement in many companies than a superficial glance would indicate.[39]

Notes

1. For various portraits of the upper class, see Dixon Wecter, *The Saga of American Society* (New York: Charles Scribner's Sons, 1937); E. Digby Baltzell, *Philadelphia Gentlemen: The Making of a National Upper Class* (Glencoe, Ill.: Free Press, 1958); and Stephen Birmingham, *The Right People* (Boston, Little, Brown, 1968).

2. Jonathan H. Turner and Charles E. Staines, *Inequality: Privilege and Poverty in America* (Glenview, Ill.: Goodyear, 1976), p. 39, Table 13. This book presents the most recent and careful analysis of the several studies that have been done on wealth. The figures presented in this paragraph as percentage of wealth are in terms of net worth estimates (assets less debt). The most important recent study of top wealthholders reported by Turner and Staines is by James D. Smith and Stephen D. Franklin, "The Concentration of Personal Wealth, 1922-1969," *American Economic Review,* May 1974.

3. Ibid., p. 38.

4. Ibid., p. 22, Table 5.

5. Ibid., p. 43, Table 16.

6. Ibid., p. 51, Table 2.

7. James D. Smith, "An Estimate of the Income of the Very Rich," *Papers in Quantitative Economics* (Lawrence: University of Kansas Press, 1968).

8. Baltzell, *Philadelphia Gentlemen.*

9. Ibid., pp. 36-40.

10. C. Wright Mills, *The Power Elite* (New York: Oxford University Press, 1956), p. 117.

11. For historical information on the stability of the wealth distribution and the modest degree of social mobility, see Jackson Turner Main, *The Social Structure of Revolutionary America* (Princeton:Princeton University Press, 1965); Edward Pessen, ed., *Three Centuries of Social Mobility in America* (Lexington, Mass.: D. C. Heath, 1974); and William Miller, *Men and Business* (Cambridge, Mass.: Harvard University Press, 1952).

12. "Egalitarianism: Threat to a Free Market" *Business Week,* December 1, 1975, p. 62.

13. Robert A. Dahl, "A Critique of the Ruling Elite Model," *American Political Science Review,* June 1958, p. 466.

14. William C. Mitchell, "The Shape of Political Theory to Come: From Political Sociology to Political Economy," in Seymour M. Lipset, ed., *Politics and the Social Sciences* (New York: Oxford University Press, 1969, p. 114.

15. For general discussion of the problems of conceptualizing power, see Steven Lukes, *Power* (Macmillan, 1974); Robert R. Alford and Roger Friedland, "Political Participation

and Public Policy," *Annual Review of Sociology* 1 (1975); and G. William Domhoff, *Who Really Rules,* Chap. 4.

16. Douglass Cater, *Power in Washington* (New York: Random House, 1964), p. 241.
17. Harold Lasswell and Abraham Kaplan, *Power and Society* (New Haven: Yale University Press, 1950), p. 181.
18. Ralph Miliband, *The State in Capitalist Society* (New York: Basic Books, 1969), p. 54.
19. Schlomo Avineri, *Hegel's Theory of the Modern State* (Cambridge: Cambridge University Press, 1972), pp. 40–45.
20. For a consideration of what Marx and Engels wrote on the subject, see Ross Gandy, "More on the Nature of Soviet Society," *Monthly Review,* March 1976, from which several of the phrases in this paragraph are taken. A summary of the Marxist view can be found in Charles H. Anderson, *The Political Economy of Social Class* (Englewood Cliffs, N.J.: Prentice-Hall, 1974).
21. Daniel Bell, *The End of Ideology* (Glencoe, Ill.: Free Press, 1969), Chapt. 2 and 3.
22. Baltzell, *Philadelphia Gentlemen,* p. 405.
23. Mills, *Power Elite.*
24. E. Digby Baltzell, *The Protestant Establishment* (New York: Random House, 1964), p. 8.
25. For a summary of this evidence, see my "The Power Elite and Its Critics," in G. William Domhoff and Hoyt B. Ballard, eds., *C. Wright Mills and the Power Elite* (Boston: Beacon Press, 1968).
26. G. William Domhoff, *The Higher Circles* (New York: Random House, 1970), Chap. 1.
27. Domhoff, *The Higher Circles,* Chaps. 2 and 4; G. William Domhoff, *The Bohemian Grove and Other Retreats* (New York: Harper & Row, 1974).
28. Paul M. Blumberg and P. W. Paul, "Continuities and Discontinuities in Upper-Class Marriages," *Journal of Marriage and the Family,* February 1975; Stephen Birmingham, *The Right Places* (Boston: Little, Brown, 1968); and John Sonquist and Thomas Koenig, "Interlocking Directorates in the Top U.S. Corporations: A Graph Theory Approach," *Insurgent Sociologist,* Spring 1975.
29. G. William Domhoff, "Social Clubs, Policy-Planning Groups, and Corporations: A Network Study of Ruling-Class Cohesiveness," *Insurgent Sociologist,* Spring 1975; Philip Bonacich and G. William Domhoff, "Overlapping Memberships Among Clubs and Policy Groups of the American Ruling Class" (paper presented at the annual meeting of the American Sociological Association, Chicago 1977).
30. E.g., Talcott Parsons, "A Revised Analytical Approach to the Theory of Social Stratification," in Reinhard Bendix and Seymour M. Lipset, eds., *Class, Status, and Power* (Glencoe, Ill.: Free Press, 1953), pp. 122–123; Bell, *End of Ideology,* Chap. 2; and John K. Galbraith, *The New Industrial State,* second ed., (New York: New American Library, 1971), p. xix. For other statements of this view, see the critical review article by Maurice Zeitlin, "Corporate Ownership and Control: The Large Corporations and the Capitalist Class," *American Journal of Sociology* 79, no. 5 (1974): 1073–1119.
31. Robert A. Dahl, *After the Revolution?* (New Haven: Yale University Press, 1970), p. 125; Earl F. Cheit, "The New Place of Business," in Earl F. Cheit, ed., *The Business Establishment* (New York: Wiley & Sons, 1964), p. 172.
32. Zeitlin, "Corporate Ownership and Control."
33. G. William Domhoff, *Who Rules America?* (Englewood Cliffs, N.J.: Prentice-Hall, 1967), Chap. 2.
34. Ibid.
35. Gabriel Kolko, *Wealth and Power in America* (New York: Praeger, 1962); Zeitlin, "Corporate Ownership and Control"; Domhoff, *Who Rules America?* Chap. 2.
36. Zeitlin, "Corporate Ownership and Control".

37. Philip H. Burch, Jr., *The Managerial Revolution Reassessed* (Lexington, Mass.: Heath-Lexington, 1972).

38. Zeitlin, "Corporate Ownership and Control"; Reuben Robertson, III, and Mimi Cutler, Testimony, in *Corporate Disclosure,* Part 1, Hearings Before the Senate Subcommittee on Intergovernmental Relations, 93rd Congress (Washington, D.C.: U.S. Government Printing Office, 1974); *Voting Rights in Major Corporations,* a staff study prepared by the Subcommittee on Reports, Accounting and Management of the Committee on Government Affairs, United States Senate (Washington, D.C.: U.S. Government Printing Office, 1978); David M. Kotz, *Bank Control of Large Corporations in the United States* (Los Angeles: University of California Press, 1978).

39. Charles L. Schwartz and G. William Domhoff, "Probing the Rockefeller Fortune," *Nomination of Nelson A. Rockefeller to be Vice-President of the United States,* Committee on the Judiciary, 93rd Congress (Washington, D.C.: U.S. Government Printing Office, 1974); Marvin G. Dunn, "Kinship and Class: A Study of the Weyerhauser Family" (Ph.D. dissertation, University of Oregon, 1977).

American Imperialism and the Third World

As major American corporations have expanded abroad, they have become increasingly dependent on the aid and protection of their activities by the U.S. government. Such promotion and protection of overseas operations of U.S.-based transnational corporations is known as *imperialism.* After World War II, American corporations extended their overseas operations at an accelerated rate. Transnational companies bought up agricultural land and mineral reserves in the Third World to ensure a source of cheap raw materials and agricultural commodities. They built factories there to produce and assemble consumer goods for American markets using cheap labor, and they found new markets in these countries for their products and services. Such corporate expansion could not have continued without the help provided by the U.S. government, which used its economic and military power to dominate Third World countries and maintain them as profitable places for investment.

James Petras and Morris Morley speak of the U.S. imperial state as a system acting in behalf of the transnational corporations to protect their overseas profits. The imperial state works through its collaborators, the local ruling classes, to maintain a favorable climate for the operation of American-based transnational corporations in Third World countries. This climate (which includes low corporate taxes and extremely low wages) is maintained by repressive regimes, kept in power through American economic and military aid, as well as by loans from agencies such as the World Bank and the International Monetary Fund, and from private American banks.

American economic and military aid is used to prop up dictatorial regimes in many countries in the Third World, and U.S. armed force is deployed, to overthrow socialist governments that might interfere with the flow of profits back to corporate headquarters. Cases in point are the CIA-engineered overthrow of the Arbenz government in Guatemala in 1954; the abortive Bay of Pigs invasion of Cuba in 1961; the U.S. military occupation of the Dominican Republic in 1965; the war in Vietnam, which ended in 1975 after more than a decade of American intervention; the CIA-backed coup that ousted the socialist Allende government in Chile in 1977; the American invasion of Grenada in 1984; and the continuing financing of the "contras," mercenaries hired by the Reagan administration to overthrow the Sandinista government in Nicaragua.

Imperialism begins to make sense if we understand that overseas operations of American-based transnational corporations are generally much more profitable than their domestic ones. The 298 largest global corporations with American headquarters earned 40 percent of all their profits abroad in 1970.[1] The dozen largest American-based global banks received about half their earnings in 1976 from their foreign subsidiaries.[2]

Standard Oil of New Jersey (now Exxon) had one-third of its assets overseas but derived two-thirds of its profits from abroad in 1958. Its international operations were thus four times as profitable as its domestic ones. By 1962, it owned half or more of the stock of 275 subsidiaries in 52 foreign countries, and sold its products in over 100 countries. Before the Cuban revolution, this company owned some $62 million worth of refining and distribution facilities in Cuba where it processed oil purchased at inflated prices from its own subsidiary in Venezuela.[3] These assets were lost when the Castro government nationalized them without compensation. The subsequent U.S. economic and military action against Cuba can be seen as an attempt not only to recover the losses suffered by American companies such as Jersey Standard Oil but to keep the Cuban example from spreading to other countries. American aggression against Cuba was an attempt to deter other Third World nations from engaging in similar revolutions. The same can be said for our military intervention elsewhere in Latin America, in Vietnam, and in other parts of the Third World.

There are some indications that the American imperial state has been weakening since the end of the Vietnam war. Our government has been trying to persuade its Western allies to take over some of the burdens of maintaining the imperial system, but it is not certain they will do so. This may yet provide further opportunities for the dispossessed masses in the Third World to challenge their own ruling classes and initiate an era of participatory socialism and self-reliant development.

Notes

1. Richard J. Barnet and Ronald E. Muller, *Global Reach* (New York: Simon and Schuster, 1974), Chap. 1.
2. James F. Petras, *Class, State and Power in the Third World* (Montclair, N.J.: Allenheld and Osmun, 1981), p. 31, note. 9.
3. Paul A. Baran and Paul M. Sweezy, *Monopoly Capital* (New York: Monthly Review Press, 1966), pp. 193–207.

The U.S. Imperial State

*James F. Petras and
Morris H. Morley*

The U.S. imperial state can be defined as those executive bodies or agencies within the "government" that are charged with promoting and protecting the expansion of capital across state boundaries by the multinational corporate community headquartered in the imperial center. Some imperial agencies, such as the departments of Commerce and the Treasury, are more directly linked to the U.S. private corporate world than others, but the actions of all are directed toward the goal of facilitating U.S. capital accumulation and reproduction on a worldwide scale. The U.S. imperial state essentially exercises two major functions: one economic, the other coercive. Both the coercive and economic apparatuses operate to facilitate capital accumulation on a global basis. Although analytically distinct, these apparatuses perform interrelated functions at the operational level. The imperial state's cumulative economic pressures against the Cuban Revolution during 1959 and 1960, for example, served in part to create the basis for indirect military intervention in mid-1961 as a means of reconstituting the capitalist political order (on one level, through the aegis of large-scale U.S. government economic assistance). In contrast to the failure in Cuba, however, the 1965 U.S. military invasion of the Dominican Republic successfully imposed a proimperial outcome on an internal social struggle that laid the groundwork for renewed U.S. "development" loans and credits from an assortment of public agencies (AID, Export-Import Bank). These

FROM James F. Petras and Morris H. Morley, "The U.S. Imperial State," from James F. Petras with Morris H. Morley, Peter DeWitt, and A. Eugene Havens, eds., *Class, State, and Power in the Third World,* Landmark Studies (Montclair, N.J.: Allanheld, Osmun, 1981). *Reference notes omitted.*

flows of "infrastructure" capital functioned, in turn, to restore an appropriate and secure milieu for foreign capital accumulation. The activities of the U.S. capital state, concerned primarily with the perservation of internal order, are increasingly overshadowed by action directly addressed to the social order within the capitalist world as a whole. The duality of the state — guardian at home and instrument of expansion abroad — reflects distinct, as well as overlapping, jurisdictions of agencies. The Treasury Department, for example, controls the flow of currency inside the country and instructs its representatives in the "international banks" how to vote on loans regarding capitalist development abroad.

As more and more of the largest U.S. industrial and financial corporations have expanded abroad, and as a larger proportion of their total earnings are derived from their overseas operations, the activities of the imperial state have become increasingly important for the maintenance of these "building blocks" of U.S. capitalist economy. The post–World War II imperial state apparatus preceded and initially grew much more rapidly than U.S. corporate capital. While private funds began to advance abroad shortly after 1945, the networks and alliances fashioned by the much more voluminous state and public investments, in the form of foreign aid, were essential in creating the groundwork for the later acceleration of private capital investment.[1] For many writers who adopted a short-term view of these developments, the initial great excess in public expenditures and noneconomic activities over and against private investment and returns was an argument against the theory of imperialism. By emphasizing military organization and spending, they were given a false sense of "autonomy," and their growth was ascribed either to strategic thinking ("national security") or to the "imperatives of bureaucratic organization."

The long-term global impact of massive military and nonmilitary expenditures and activities, however, were soon to be matched and surpassed by the massive flow and accumulation of private capital. From the latter phenomenon, a new group of writers began to assert the "autonomy" of "multinational" capital, forgetting the state's role in providing and sustaining the universe within which "multinational" capital operates. These erroneous conceptions reflect the narrow interpretative focus of the research, which attempts to identify mechanical correlations between economic causes and political effects, or vice versa. The alternative approach is anchored in a wider world-historical analysis of the interplay between the political and economic forces within the capitalist state over time and across regions, emphasizing the role of the imperial state as the organizing force behind the process of world capitalist accumulation. The imperial state embodies the present and future collective interests of the most dynamic sector of capital.

The Imperial System and the Imperial State

The period of global military conflict from 1939 to 1945 produced irrevocable changes within world capitalism, above all the transition from an array of great and medium-size powers to a situation distinguished by the manifest absence of some of the most formidable imperial structures (e.g., British, French, Dutch) of the prewar era. Historically, the "notion" of "the imperial system" and its organizing center, "the imperial state," must be located within a set of processes that were central simultaneously to the emergence of U.S. hegemony ("imperial state") and capital accumulation (uneven development), both on a world scale. Together, these interrelated processes are equivalent to the imperial system, whose locus is formed entirely, at one moment in historical time, by the United States, whose government (or part of it) *thereby* becomes "the imperial state."

In the postcolonial period the U.S. imperial state, by necessity, functions through local intermediaries linked through military and economic alliances or through bilateral ties. These linkages are sustained through reciprocal exchanges that mutually benefit the factions of ruling classes in each country. The conditional nature of imperial state domination is thus based on three sets of factors: the capacity to penetrate another nation's social structure, to create durable linkages, and to sustain collaborator classes.

The superimposition of imperial relations upon the class structure of a target society requires that political ties be matched by sociocultural linkages. The imperial state project requires the "throwing down" of roots into the *society* to create a social and cultural infrastructure to sustain the otherwise narrow and fragile base of external domination. Hence, the imperial state mobilizes social and cultural institutions within its own society to create a multiple series of linkages through which to transmit organizational and ideological instruments to reinforce imperial domination. Insofar as there is a proliferation of relationships, which cover an array of spheres of society, we can begin to speak of "integration into the imperial system." The notion of integration, however, should be seen as a process, although one that is never completed. A subordinate state is never totally assimilated into the imperial system without political, social, and cultural conflicts. The process of integration itself is problematical because the basis for exchanges and exploitation varies, and because there are changes in the class structure, political regime, and legitimating ideology. Redefinitions in the world division of labor and the place that a state occupies within it will also affect the mode of integration.

* * *

In postcolonial societies there is a clear move to diversify economic activity and trading partners. The growth of industry and the diversification of trading partners has caused changes in the world division of labor: Some former colonial countries are increasingly exporting industrial goods with a high labor component, usually from free-trade zones where imperial enterprises exercise quasi-sovereign control. The industrializing Third World countries with free-trade zones thus combine features of the colonial period — special laws that provide exclusive privileges, prerogatives, and tax exemptions to the imperial firms (effectively granting them political autonomy) — with a new position in the world division of labor. Continuities reflected in the type of imperial integration (similar to the colonial period) are harnessed to a new position in the division of labor in which exchange is between high- and low-technology industrial countries. This form of imperial integration is, however, quite fragile, for the economic activity and exchanges are totally dependent on the political relationship: Third World export industries are dependent on maintaining substantial labor cost differentials, which, in turn, are sustained by repressive regimes. The disequilibrium in power between working classes and regime — the favorable correlation in favor of the local ruling classes — sustains this redefinition of the division of labor.

This shift in the imperial system is only superficially the result of the "logic of capital" (capital moves toward low-wage areas to maximize profits). At a deeper level, the shift is a result of the logic of class struggle: The low-wage areas are so defined by the ascendance of the local ruling class — class conflict that redefines the relationship will alter the cost of labor and effect the "logic" of capital. While the (relative) lack of class struggle politics is a necessary but not sufficient condition for the growth and expansion of capital in the periphery, its intensification serves both to inhibit the flow of capital "from the outside" and to accelerate the withdrawal (decapitalization) of capital "from the inside." . . .

The patterns of imperial integration — degree, level, position in the world division of labor — are all premised on high levels of exploitation of labor and cheap, readily accessible strategic materials. These conditions of exploitation/appropriation, moreover, occur in one social formation (periphery), whereas accumulation and elaboration occur in another. This disjuncture between producers and product and the overall adverse sociopolitical conditions that induce inward capital flows can be sustained only by repressive regimes. The coercive apparatus of the imperial state is a far more decisive actor in shaping the state in the periphery than in the metropolis. In the conventional literature on the "capitalist state," coercion is viewed as a factor "in the last instance." In the imperial system coercion is operative in the first instance—and it is sustained over time. The ideological dimensions of rulership so prominently discussed in the literature on the "capitalist state"—meaning in the *metropolitan* capitalist countries—are secondary and subordinated to rule by force. Western-centered studies even speak of periods of repression as "state of exception," whereas this "exception" is the rule in the imperialized countries, thus vitiating any cognitive meaning in the term. The duality of the imperial system—ideologically induced consensus at home and coercively imposed control abroad—was noted some time ago by Franz Fanon.

The multiplicity of coercive regimes and their continual reproduction lead us to identify *force* as the central element in the imperial system—a position obscured by separating out, identifying, and comparing the political regimes of each nation-state. Against this approach, which fragments the notion of power and obscures the real, durable, and substantial linkages that bind the different social formations into one hierarchical unit, is the notion of the imperial system. An imperial system involves a multiplicity of nation-states linked through one or more capitalist states dominating others through exploitative relations sustained by collaborative classes and coordinated by the application of force through the coercive apparatuses of the imperial state. Thus the imperial system is based on a series of asymmetrical relationships that are organized at the state level, but whose roots are essentially located in the organization of production and distribution within the subordinated areas. The imperatives of imperial growth create a worldwide set of interests. Strategic interests are those that have long-term, large-scale importance to the overall operation of the systems. The pursuit of symbolic and tactical interests represents efforts to demonstrate superiority at the level of political or ideological appeal. Indo-China was an area of symbolic/tactical interest to the United States, whose total commitment to military victory and whose subsequent defeat weakened its capacity to intervene in two areas of strategic importance, Angola and

Iran. The development of imperial interests exceeded the capacity of the U.S. imperial state to defend those interests. The *social basis* of imperial mobilization within the imperial state was weakened in the struggle for symbolic gains; and the collaborator *classes* in strategic countries were unable to sustain the condition for their domination. Thus the notion of imperial "state apparatuses" should be used with great care because it involves a mechanical metaphor (the machine), which belies the *social relations* that control the actual flow, operation, and application of the physical tools of repression.

If the imperial state is the central organizing unit of an imperial system, what is its relationship to the class struggle within metropolitan society? No area is more clearly removed from the everyday influences of the electorate and legislative bodies, which might reflect liberal democratic opinion, than the executive agencies that collectively fashion imperial policies. The socialization process and the screening, selection, and promotion procedures that accompany the recruitment of cadres for the permanent line and staff positions within imperial institutions are all guided by the need to defend the foundations and expand the growth of U.S. imperialism.

* * *

The process of accumulation and reproduction and the defense of the class and state structure that conditions and facilitates this process constitute the strategic goals of the decisionmakers. When it comes to protecting the capitalist mode of production, especially in areas where their own imperial economic and military objectives are in question, there is a unity of purpose between the imperial state and classes. The more important the region or social formation to imperial expansion, the greater the coincidence of interest between capital and state, and the more directly will imperial state policy be an expression of class interests. In sum, the more centrally the class struggle affects the overall functioning of the imperial system, the more absolute dependence between state and class structure. The image of the imperial state standing above the class structure that organizes imperialist wars in fact disguises the greatest concentration of social power into the executive agencies of the imperial state and the subordination of civil society to the organized power of the imperial capitalist class.

Within this framework differences among agencies and between the collective decisions of the state and the imperial classes are less a reflection of "autonomy"; rather, they reflect different manners of pursuing the same end. The policy instrumentalities vary, but the imperatives are constant and press upon the decisionmakers to decide in the most rational, direct manner how to maximize imperial interests. In crises, the decision-making process is permeated by the instrumental needs of imperial capital. To exaggerate the relative autonomy of the state is to miss the all-inclusive manner in which the decision makers are immersed in the symbols and substance of capitalist power.

* * *

Postcolonial Imperialism Since World War II

The interrelationship between the U.S. imperial state and capital expansion has been crucial to the development of postcolonial imperialism since World War II. Essentially, we can identify three periods, determined largely by the predominance of three types of investment. In the period between 1945 and 1955 *imperial-state* investment predominated, largely directed toward rebuilding in Europe or constructing, in the Third World, capitalist state structures and economies. Technical aid, large-scale, long-term loans, infrastructure development, and, most of all, massive military spending were directed at forestalling social revolution, to give capital a chance to reemerge. Private investment was of lesser quantity and directed in Europe to industry and in the periphery to agro-mineral areas. Banking capital flows were limited and confined to financing trade and providing credit through isolated groupings.

In the second period, between 1955 and 1969, massive flows of *private investment* circulated throughout the globe — and the multinational conglomerate served as the major vehicle. This wave of investment was directed at all areas of society, but it was especially concentrated in industrial undertakings, both in Europe and in the Third World. Imperial state investments declined, relatively speaking, and were directed toward financing the power, communication, and transport systems, as well as new industrial facilities of advancing industrial capital. Finance capital was still in third position, but it was growing quickly to finance the new import requirements of the Third World, to organize capital markets, and to facilitate transactions among the multiplying capitals. These shifting investment trends are strikingly illustrated in Tables 1 and 2. These figures clearly illustrate the overall investment sequence as outlined above. The ratio of U.S. state overseas economic loans and grants to new U.S. direct private investment overseas declined from $5.7 to $1 billion between 1945 and 1954, to $1.44 to $1 billion between 1955 and 1964, to $0.63 to $1 billion between 1965 and 1974.

TABLE 1

U.S. Direct Private Investment Overseas, 1945-1974
(in billions of dollars, approx.)

1945	8.4	1960	31.9
1946	8.9	1961	34.7
1947	10.0	1962	37.3
1948	11.2	1963	40.7
1949	12.5	1964	44.5
1950	11.8	1965	49.5
1951	13.0	1966	51.8
1952	14.7	1967	56.6
1953	16.3	1968	61.9
1954	17.6	1969	68.1
1955	19.4	1970	75.5
1956	22.5	1971	82.8
1957	25.4	1972	89.9
1958	29.8	1974	110.2

TABLE 2

U.S. Overseas Loans and Grants, 1946–1974
(in billions of dollars, approx.)

	Total Economic Assistance	Total Military Assistance	Assistance from International Organizations
1946-48	12.6	0.5	0.5
1949-52	18.6	3.3	0.8
1953-61	24.1	24.2	5.1
1962-69	33.4	19.3	14.5
1970	3.8	3.1	3.3
1971	3.4	4.6	3.9
1972	4.0	5.3	3.9
1973	4.1	5.3	5.4
1974	4.0	5.1	5.2

The third period, from 1970 to the present, has witnessed the enormous growth of *finance capital,* the massive expansion of banking capital, and the accumulation of massive assets and extension of loans. Between 1960 and mid-1976 the total assets of the overseas branches of U.S. private multinational banks increased from $3.5 billion to $181 billion. By December 1976 the overall Third World external debt was estimated at around $200 billion, of which at least $75 billion was owed to private banks, including an estimated $50 billion of this latter amount to U.S. private banks. This new-found "global reach" of the American private banking community exacerbated an already rising debt service burden under which many peripheral governments labored, which necessitated further loans and an ever-spiraling debt problem. In some cases (e.g., Peru), the ultimate outcome was direct U.S. private bank intervention in the economic decision-making process as a condition for further loans. A substantial proportion of these peripheral government debts to private foreign banks was located in Latin America, principally in the politically and/or economically strategic countries of Brazil, Mexico, and Peru. In 1976 approximately 20 percent of the Third World's total export earnings (an increase of 75 percent over 1973) went to pay the interest and amortization payments on the area's external debt. Finance capital is intimately involved in all aspects of economic activity on a global level, diversifying its activities to all productive areas, and absorbing the huge oil surpluses and redirecting them into controlling farflung activities. Industrial capital continues to expand, interpenetrating in the imperial centers and allying with the state for joint exploitation in the periphery.

Any extended definition of the U.S. imperial state would likely include the leading post–1945 multilateral financial institutions (World Bank, International Monetary Fund, Inter-American Development Bank), whose activities have both overlapped with and complemented the "peak" periods of private investment and finance capital flows on a worldwide basis. The period of greatest expansion of capital assistance from the international banking organizations coincided with the rise of independent states in the periphery of the capitalist world economy. These multilateral capital flows averaged less than $1 billion annually during the 1950s, rising to approximately $2 billion annually during the 1960s, and, as Table 2 shows, peaking in excess of $4 billion annually during the first half of the 1970s. The role this form of assistance has played has tended to be twofold: On the one hand, it has allowed all capitalist governments to assume some responsibility (on a consortium basis) for financing conditions for private capital expansion by all capitalist bloc countries; and on the other, such loans and grants may, in particular conjunctures, have performed the important political function of politically neutralizing or defusing the close, ongoing relationship between U.S. state and private external capital flows.

Imperial state activity continues, in a less central role but an increasingly important source of funding for overextended debtors: The imperial state functions to bail out debtors and to cushion the adverse social consequences generated by industrial and finance capital's expansion. Thus imperial state activity focuses on "social needs," balance of payments problems, and military aid. Public development loans, however, are largely replaced by private ones. The logic of imperialism revealed by this historical succession is largely from imperial state investment to private industrial and finance capital. Massive imperial state activity was the necessary precondition for the development of "economic" imperialism. The development of industrial capital, in turn, was the necessary precondition for the extension of finance capital and the continuous interplay of all three, each with its specific and complementary functions, defines the contemporary imperial system.

The Imperial State: Specialization and Complexity

The imperial state can best be conceptualized as a complex web of interrelated but functionally specific sets of agencies coordinated at the top levels of the executive branch. The agencies can be subdivided into three major functional categories: (1) economic; (2) coercive; and (3) ideological. The economic agencies can, in turn, be divided into two sets: (*a*) those serving particular forms of capital (departments of Agriculture promoting agricultural exports); and (*b*) those performing specific tasks that cut across the different capitals (Treasury and Commerce departments), promoting foreign investment in general. Agencies tied to particular forms of overseas capital expansion develop especially close working relationships between those particular factions and work within the imperial state to maximize the interests of their "client." Similar behavior is evidenced with regard to the specific task-oriented agencies that develop ties within the United States and with their specific collaborator counterparts abroad. Commerce and Treasury department ties with the multinationals and big business abroad occasionally may lead to short-term conflicts with the State Department over policies that may conflict with the short-term interests of their clients.

The second major component of the imperial state, the coercive agencies, includes (1) the military (Defense Department); and (2) intelligence (Central

Intelligence Agency, Defense Intelligence Agency, and the specialized groups within each branch of the military). The military operates in two capacities: (a) to promote and cultivate close relations within the military of target areas, through training schools, aid programs, overseas missions; and (*b*) to intervene directly to forestall social revolution, through military invasions and occupations when their collaborative counterparts are incapable or unwilling to act in concert with U.S. interests. The intelligence agencies usually are heavily involved in recruiting liaisons (contacts for information within regimes and leaders within key organizations of a society) and organizing client groups to manipulate social forces for overt and covert action. The activities of both groups usually are coordinated through agency heads, and their activities usually complement each, although jurisdictional disputes and conflicts over loyalties occasionally emerge.

The third component agency of the imperial state, the ideological, has two aspects: (1) the institutional activities directly tied to the state; and (2) the "subcontracted" activities related to the practices of unofficial groups drawn from imperial society and among collaborator groups. The U.S. Information Agency and the related propaganda arms of the state (Peace Corps, Fulbright-Hayes Program) create favorable images of U.S. imperial activity and denigrate revolutionary action; psychological warfare, including the creation of false consciousness, is a principal activity. In the postcolonial period, however, special importance in the ideological task of defending imperialism is taken on by societal forces — cultural, religious, educational, and so forth. Ideological use is made of their public image of possessing nonofficial status to give them the aura of "objectivity" and "independence," thus increasing the credibility of the propaganda message. These societal auxiliaries of the imperial state are usually "contracted" covertly by the intelligence agencies or overtly through other agencies, ostensibly for some apolitical purpose, i.e., "to promote cultural exchanges." This illusory disjuncture between "state" and "society" obscures the convergence of purpose and allows the imperial state to pursue its ideological goals through a plurality of mutually compatible instrumentalities.

The forward and backward linkages of these agencies create specific ties; the close working relationships within the bureaucratic organization and with collaborator groups frequently leads to policy differences over which instrumentalities should be given priority in any specific circumstances. These and other conflicts are usually resolved within the imperial state and, if serious enough, at the executive level, within the boundaries established by imperial interests.

The Collaborator State

The "collaborator state" possesses several features that facilitate its subordination to the actions of imperial states. First, it is a penetrated society: Political and military organization and cultural institutions contain leaders, formed and loyal to the ideas and definitions of reality formulated in the imperial centers. Crucial sectors of the economy are controlled or managed by multinational capital; thus the class structure is penetrated by imperial interests. State and societal *penetration* is matched by the organization and direction of the economy toward a *complementary role* within the imperial division of labor. Thus the *kind* of goods produced, the terms of exchange, and the direction of exchange all maximize gains to the imperial center and the principal classes and institutional members within the collaborator state.

Two sets of collaborator groups can be identified: the bureaucratic (political) strata and the socioeconomic classes. The bureaucratic-political strata, through their control over the state, receive part of the surplus generated through imperial exchanges and direct exploitation by the multinationals. Private wealth by "indirect relation" means that government officials who don't *own* the means of production appropriate wealth which they later convert to capital; membership on state boards of joint ventures becomes the basis of private entrepreneurship. The bureaucratic-political strata are rewarded by imperial capital for the invitation, insurance, and expeditor functions that they engage in within the exploited country.

Traditional collaborator classes, such as landowners and import-exporters, are now matched by local industrialists and businessmen, who develop joint ventures with the multinationals, become satellite subcontractors, rent technology or managerial skills, and combine and contract with world-marketing and shipping firms. This "collaboration" usually does not reflect a total integration into the imperial system; rather it is a negotiated association subject to bargaining over terms, shifts in market demands, political power, and so forth. The important issue, however, is that postcolonial imperialism expands (and survives) with the growth and incorporation of collaborator groups. In fact, *the strength of the imperial system in large part rests on the influence and control exercised by the collaborative classes and strata within imperialized society.* There are various types of collaborator classes, ranging from those who share power to those who are clearly subordinated to imperial interests. Size, type, and scope of activity, as well as influence and control over the state, affect the relative standing of collaborator classes in relation to imperial classes. Large-scale industrialists involved in production for the local market and with a powerful presence in the state are more likely to be *associate power-sharers* with imperial interests. Import-exporters tied to foreign markets, shipping, and credits are likely to be *dependent power-sharers.* Joint ventures, in which industrialists produce for foreign markets, drawing on foreign technology, capital, and management, and with little direct representation in the state, are likely to be *subordinate collaborators.*

The collaborator classes are oriented toward opening up markets, securing raw materials, and facilitating the recruitment of labor. Their main purpose is, however, *political:* to deal with the state and through their influence to handle "labor relations," repress class conflict, and negotiate labor contracts. Under the slogans of industrialization and development, the collaborator classes purport to "mix" foreign and local, state and private capital into a growth formula—the underlying condition for this growth being the appropriation of resources, the proletarianization of the labor force, and the subordination of the state within the imperial system. The essential policies pursued by collaborator class regimes are directed toward deepening these three processes, without being displaced by their more dynamic imperial partner.

* * *

The Imperial System in Crisis

The post–World War II, postcolonial imperial system has gone through two phases and is now entering a third. The first phase, roughly between 1945 and 1960, was the period in which the United States was the overwhelmingly dominant direct actor throughout the system: investor, military intervener, financier. In a word, the imperial system was *coterminus* with the imperial state of the United States: Power and decision were concentrated in the hands of Washington[2]; officials of imperialized states were informed of decisions or told what to do.

The second phase of the imperial system can be dated from the early 1960s and can be located approximately in the period between 1961 and 1976. In this period the growth of European and Japanese power and the growth of OPEC and, to a much lesser degree, other commodity producers forced the United States into a consultive relationship with "allies": While the United States still is "first among equals," it is increasingly obliged to accommodate the interests of other states and capitals. More important, the U.S. commitment in Vietnam drained resources from the economic to the coercive apparatus, improved the relative trade and investment position of Europe in relation to the United States, and created a flood of Eurodollars at a time when the U.S. productive base was unable to sustain them—thus threatening the U.S.-centered imperial financial system. The inability of the United States to commit its allies in Vietnam was a consequence of their growing independence and had, as a further consequence, the result of strengthening their competitive position within the U.S. imperial umbrella. As this phase ended, the United States began its reach for means of delegating authority, of finding power surrogates ("regional influentials") in recognition of its limited capacity to defend the imperial system and its unwillingness to bear all the costs while its allies reap all the benefits.

The third phase of the imperial system is highlighted by the steady erosion of the imperial system, both the outer fringes and inner fortresses: The defeat in Indo-China was followed by Angola, thus opening up southern Africa, and then the Middle Eastern regional power anchored in the Shah's regime.

At certain historical moments the imperial system is made vulnerable by a weakened capacity on the part of the imperial state to sustain a level of cohesion that the system requires. Between 1945 and 1965 the U.S. imperial state could count on a public opinion unified in support of its actions, an organized and mobilized military fighting force, and a high degree of cooperation from its allies in Western Europe, Japan, and the Third World. The U.S. involvement in Indo-China during the late 1960s and early 1970s substantially weakened the interventionary capacities of the imperial state consequent upon growing internal divisions among the populace at large, the decline of institutional solidarity and *esprit de corps* within the armed forces, and their increasing loss of legitimacy on the "home front," and widespread defections among allied opponents of the imperial state enterprise.[3]

In the post-Vietnam period the acceleration of national liberation and revolutionary struggles in the periphery of the capitalist world economy increasingly reflects the fact that the United States has lost its capacity to hold together the imperial system, while, at the same time, no other country has emerged to replace it. What we have is a series of state-by-state policy improvisations, unsuccessful annual trilateral meetings and the fragments of power, and the potent leftovers and linkages of the U.S. imperial state that still operate. Europe and Japan, imperial competitors, have been strong enough to weaken the United States but totally incapable of assuming the responsibility of creating the apparatuses and sustaining the universe in which competition and growth occur. They have operated under the mistaken assumption that (*a*) the United States will bail them out in crisis circumstances; (*b*) their economic relations and "strength" are sufficient to guarantee favorable access in the operating environment; and (*c*) the existing state and class configurations that are functioning to their satisfaction are capable of enduring over time.

Recent events in Iran and Afghanistan, however, have generated a sustained U.S. effort to pressure West Germany, France, and Japan, in particular, to assume a greater share of the risks and costs inherent in fashioning a global, interventionary foreign-policy response for the imperial system as a whole. At the same time, Western Europe and Japan remain critically dependent on Middle East oil for the day-to-day operations of their economies, but their lack of military strength and limited economic leverage render them incapable of exercising any substantive control over OPEC pricing policies. Meanwhile, the overthrow of the Shah in Iran (a major capitalist-bloc petroleum supplier) has been followed by the appearance of fissures within the Saudi Arabian polity and an overall increase in the level of economic and political instability throughout the Persian Gulf region. These new imperial rivals thus overestimate U.S. capability, underestimate the importance of imperial state linkages for sustaining "economic" dimensions of the imperial system, and miscalculate the sources of strength among collaborator classes in the Third World.

This profound misjudgment, however, is rooted in the structural constraints that have facilitated growth: The capacity to contain class struggle and promote capital growth has been based precisely on avoiding expenditures in sustaining coercive apparati and costly military intervention. For Western Europe and Japan to assume the political and military responsibilities commensurate with their expanded economic power would eventually result in a radical restructuring of the economic and political system with many unforeseen and dangerous consequences. It would, at minimum, require a redirection of national budget allocations away from economic development and toward increased military spending, which would likely presage a growing role for the political right in these countries and the emergence of the armed forces as a central actor in the political system. These events, in turn, could conceivably lead to the revival of militarism, territorial expansionist ambitions, and possible open military conflicts not only with the socialist bloc countries and the Third World, but with the United States as well.

In summary, the imperial system is in crisis. The capacity of the United States to hold together the imperial system and sustain its position as the dominant imperial power in the capitalist world economy has been severely strained, beginning with the recovery of its capitalist rivals in the early 1960s, deepening with the Vietnam war, and continuing in its aftermath. The subordinated allies in Europe and Asia, namely West Germany and Japan, who previously concentrated on internal rebuilding, have successfully branched out, capturing important markets and eagerly challenging U.S. economic domination. Client-states have broken out of the imperial system, and a key regional influential base has been destroyed, increasing the cost of key energy resources and destablizing regional hegemony. The close linkages between imperial state policies and the populace have been weakened, with the resultant constraints on the interventionary capacity of the coercive components of the state. Nonetheless, this process of declining U.S. imperial state capacities is not an irreversible one, as evidenced by the political-military propaganda campaign against the Soviet Union originating in the highest echelons of the Carter Administration as part of a concentrated effort to, at least temporarily, re-create the old bonds of the imperial system and reassert the preeminent role of the U.S. imperial state within that system.

The imperial state provided a protective nest within which U.S. capital operated in a manner *not* conducive to developing a competitive edge. Tied foreign aid guaranteed U.S. sales — until imperial rivals could match the aid and underbid U.S. sellers. U.S. firms paid high dividends and ran down capital stock, while its competitors did the opposite. Military and political collaborators in client-states facilitated access to local markets for overpriced U.S. goods until changes in regime and/or personnel altered the balance toward alternative, more efficient sellers. Undisputed domination conditioned directors of U.S. multinationals to resist joint ventures where they held minority control, while their competitors eagerly seized the chance. In a word, the imperial system created a series of structural and sociopsychological conditions that *initially* greatly improved U.S. capital's position, but which later greatly reduced its competitive capability. Competition from Japan and West Germany, the equalization of exchange between petroleum and industrial goods established by OPEC, the internal constraints imposed by the class structure in the United States, and the revolutionary ferment in the Third World — beginning in Southeast Asia, continuing to southern and central Africa, and extending to the Middle East — have all created deepening fissures in the imperial system.

The relative decline of the United States, linchpin of the overall system, is manifest in the economic sphere by the relative deterioration in its share of world exports, production of industrial goods, and share of overseas investments, as well as by the relative increase in the cost of energy. In the military sphere this relative decline has been manifested in the weakening in military interventionary capacity in southern and central Africa and the Middle East. Concomitantly, class struggle has weakened the role both of "old" (export-importers, landowners) and "new" (industrialists) collaborator classes in key areas. In Iran, Angola, and Afghanistan these classes have been overthrown. In Ethiopia and Rhodesia they are subject to substantial challenges, as is the case in Nicaragua and to a lesser degree in Brazil, Peru, Bolivia, El Salvador, Guyana and Grenada. The network of economic and military strategic areas encompassing large and small countries, whose regimes collectively are an essential part of the imperial system, threatens to be torn asunder. This multiple challenge is both cause and consequence of the United States' declining capacity to intervene militarily. This illustrates the critical importance of the linkage between imperial state *and* internal classes in sustaining the imperial system. The declining global position of the United States, its internal manifestation, *and* the shift in class forces within the collaborator states combine to weaken the coercive apparatuses that sustain the imperial system.[4]

In the sociopolitical sphere the relative decline of the United States and the fissures in the imperial system have contributed to a decline in the standard of living for substantial sectors of the wage and salaried groups within the United States. The combined effects of an inflation rate that exceeds wage increases and chronic high rates of underemployment and unemployment have highlighted the fact that the substantial improvements during the decades immediately after World War II were not outcomes inherent in "welfare capitalism"; rather, they were specific features resultant from the strength of the imperial system and the undisputed domination of the United States within that system. The internal manifestation of imperial crisis manifested itself in the contradiction between the decline of external opportunities and the socially defined high level of existence deemed necessary to reproduce labor.

The state's response is to impose a selective austerity plan to cushion the effects of the imperial crisis for capital by lowering the historic gains of wage and salaried workers. The long-term accommodation and collaboration between imperial capital and the labor bureaucracy, based on external exploitation and internal reforms, begins to crumble. No longer able to provide improvements, and yet bureaucratized beyond the capacity to engage in sustained and all-encompassing struggles, the executive directorate of the trade unions is under increasing attack by the rank and file in major unions, including coal, steel, teamsters, and auto. The consensus between the labor bureaucracy and imperial capital built during the heyday of the imperial system is beginning to break down—opening the possibility for the emergence of class politics.

Thus the military, economic, and sociopolitical foundations of the imperial systems have begun to be affected, eroded but not undermined. While the crisis to imperialism is real, it should not be exaggerated: The military and intelligence networks still exist; traditional collaborator regimes are still strong in many areas (South Korea, Phillippines, Thailand, Indonesia, Israel, South Africa, Zaire, Senegal, Kenya, Paraguay), and some additions have been added (Argentina, Egypt, Uruguay, Chile). Moreover, the growth of debt financing has strengthened the financial arms of the imperial system,[5] allowing the imperial states to restructure economies and societies through loans conditioned by meeting specific capital requirements. While the standard of living has declined in the United States, it has not been precipitous as yet, and, more important, it has been accompanied by a declining percentage of organized workers and the almost total absence of any class-based *political* challenge from among the militant trade unionists. Finally, while interimperial relations have led to increasing inroads by Europe and Japan on U.S. economic turf, they are still more dependent on the United States than vice versa. And in a pinch the U.S.'s decisions still have a central importance to the performance of their economies.

Conclusion

While U.S. imperial state power continues to be formidable in relation to its main competitors within the imperial system, long-term structural and operational trends are countering that power. The long-term relative decline in productivity is an indicator of the weakening position of non-financial capital in the United States. The incapacity of U.S. capital to sustain its competitive position is the result of investments and profit-taking decisions that hinder the continual rationalization and transformation of U.S. productive capacity to meet the terms of competition emerging from other capital. It is not labor, the loss of the work ethic, or wage levels that have been forcing down productivity and weakened the U.S. market position, but the behavior and movement of capital.

The deterioration of the U.S. balance of trade, beginning in the late 1950s, was not solely a function of competition from the revitalized postwar economies of Western Europe and Japan. "The United States," as Fred Block reminds us, "had the resources—capital, skilled labor, technological sophistication, and entrepreneurial competence—to meet the competitive challenge directly and successfully." What was lacking, however, was any substantial impulse toward modernization of local industry on the part of American exporters, who continued to operate behind protective high tariffs. Instead of concentrating on increased productive capacity at home to meet the new challenge, they began to invest in the setting up of overseas branch plants, principally in Western Europe. As a result, they suffered a long-term decline in their competitive position on a global scale. Between 1968 and 1971 the U.S. trade figures spoke to an average annual deficit of approximately the same amount.

The extent of the declining U.S. export competitiveness is further revealed if we compare the changing patterns of U.S., Japanese, and West German exports of manufactured goods over the period 1963 to 1976 (see Table 3).

TABLE 3

World Trade Pattern
(percentage distribution of manufactured exports)[a]

	1963	1976
U.S	17.24	13.55
Japan	5.98	11.38
West Germany	15.53	15.81

[a] Figures in each column are percentages of total world manufactures exported by each country within the time period. —Ed.

The United States experienced an absolute *and* a relative decline in its position vis-à-vis its major capitalist-bloc export competitors. While American exports as a percentage of the world total fell substantially, of even greater importance was that, whereas Japanese and West German exporters together sold approximately 30 percent more manufactured goods than their American counterparts in 1963, some 13 years later they accounted for almost double the amount of manufactured goods entering the world market from U.S. sources.

While U.S. economic positions in world trade have declined, the costs of sustaining the political-military umbrella (the coercive components of the imperial state) have increased, leaving the U.S. political economy to pay the major share of the costs. Japanese and West German imperial policymakers concentrate almost exclusively on the economic functions of the imperial state, while U.S. policymakers divide their time and energies in coercive components. Thus while Washington tries to deal with problems of societal control and order ("stability and security"), Bonn and Tokyo concentrate on promoting capitalist development. The U.S. imperial state furnished stability, and its competitors exploit the development opportunities. This schism between expansion and maintenance of the imperial system, a costly imperial state and declining economic benefits, has its consequences: the growth of inflation and a declining standard of living.

This state of affairs presents U.S. imperial state policymakers with the following most likely choices: a combination of (1) exercise coercive and economic power to muscle out competitors in the periphery, as well as freezing out rivals dependent on U.S. markets; (2) pressure imperial competitors to share the cost of the coercive umbrella, thus vastly increasing their military commitments and intelligence networks; (3) increase the recruitment and responsibility of regional influentials among the collaborator regimes in the Third World, delegating costs and responsibilities for policing the imperial system; and (4) some combination of the above.

The policy of "exercising power" is a two-way street: Showing muscle invites similar responses elsewhere. Closing markets could lead to retaliatory measures and eventually to uncontrollable protectionism, cut-throat competition, and the demise of capitalist allies/rivals. Proponents of this "will to power" overlook the fact that U.S. economic interests are intertwined abroad with local and imperial competitors, and adversaries such as the Soviet Union, and many are fairly well entrenched and could effectively resist coercive efforts. In this circumstance, the degree of direct force and the ongoing control that would be required to displace and contain global and local rivals far exceeds U.S. capability at this time and in the foreseeable future.

The second, more modest proposal to pressure rivals to assume more of the costs of the maintenance of the imperial system is being applied, and some gains have been registered. Japan and West Germany are paying more but have hardly made a commitment commensurate to what the United States would like them to assume. In any case, this proposal does not directly affect the issue of competition (it tries to equalize the conditions for it), but rather institutionalizes the positions of all participants within the system. As such, it may strengthen the independence of the competitors, increase their challenge to U.S. hegemony, and raise their influence over collaborator regimes and classes in target countries.

With regard to the policy of promoting regional influentials, the Iranian experience points directly to the problems. The overextension of an internally vulnerable regime led not only to the demise of regional influence, but to the overthrow and transformation of a collaborator regime. Vast disproportions between expenditures on arms and social welfare and between the concentration of political power in the autocratic ruler and the lack of organs of popular representation combined to provoke a sociopolitical crisis that could not be contained by the regime. Apart from exacerbating the internal contradictions of collaborator regimes, the delegation of regional authority could whet their appetite for independent action, setting off a series of activities that could convert the subordinate collaborator into a competitive ally or at least threaten the security of neighboring collaborator regimes and classes.

Notes

1. In using the terms "public capital" to describe U.S. government funds and "private (corporate) capital" to describe U.S. corporate funds, we are of course cognizant that both are agencies of "capital" and that none of the "funds" at any time leaves the realm or circuits of capital. We make this distinction, however, to serve a very specific purpose, viz., to provide a basis to differentiate between state and society, between class and state. Otherwise, the particular relationship between state and (civil) society is fundamentally obscured, and, therefore, one cannot comprehend the nature of that relationship. Nor can one understand the basis on which the state as a product of class society and class struggle is, at the same time, not identical with that society.
2. We do not here discuss the role of the dominant social class in the United States (owners and controllers of major corporations, banks, financial institutions) in making of U.S. imperial state policy, but a central assumption that informs our analysis is that capitalist social forces are crucial to fashioning the boundaries within which the U.S. imperial state operates and to shaping the direction and goals of imperial state policy.
3. At present, the U.S. imperial state is attempting to use the Soviet Union intervention in Afghanistan and its purported threat to Iran, Pakistan, and the Persian Gulf area in general as a pretext to create the basis for reconstructing the U.S. imperial capacity and mobilizing the population for future military interventions around the world. The multiple political-military response (reinstitution of the draft, massive increase in the military budget, expansion of the U.S. military forces abroad, creation of new regional, counterrevolutionary alliances with Egypt, Saudi Arabia, Pakistan, the application of enormous diplomatic pressures on Western Europe and Japan to "line up" with the U.S. position) cannot be understood in all its ramifications unless located in the context of previous U.S.

imperial state vulnerabilities and the renewed efforts to reconstruct imperial capacities to a level appropriate to the desired operations of a U.S.-dominated imperial system.

4. While increased "competition" among "states" within the interstate system does not, of course, bring the processes of capital accumulation and centralization to an abrupt halt, the weakened role of government as a cohesive factor does make the multi-national corporations increasingly vulnerable — to the extent that they may be forced to more directly confront new anticapitalist antagonists (workers, peasants, and other adversaries), who embody a fundamental challenge to the accumulation process itself. Our principal concern, however, is with an evolving (dialectical) process that creates contradictions which are ultimately resolved in the confrontation of classes on a world scale, even though the particular locus of struggles are found in particular national political economies. . . .

5. While it is conceivable that countries theoretically could raise the issue of debt repudiation, the almost certain likelihood of international pariah status within the capitalist world economy (in the areas of trade and financial resources) acts to circumscribe sharply the capacity of governments in these resource-scarce countries to contemplate seriously carrying through such an action. In the event that a country does possess alternative sources of trade and external funding, this type of threat may be useful, but only as a one-shot bargaining tool. Finally, with the exception of Brazil and perhaps a few other Third World countries, it is not clear that debt repudiation would have anything but a very minimal impact within the affected capitalist economies.

Part III | Visions and Strategies of Change

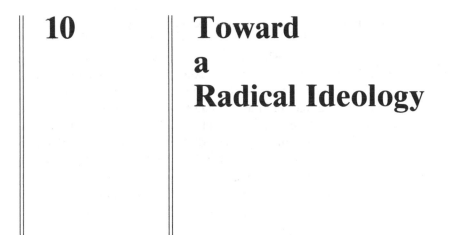

10 Toward a Radical Ideology

Two of the most important ideologies of social change are Marxist socialism (or communism) and anarchism. The two theories are alike insofar as both insist on the abolition of private property and look forward to a society where people contribute and produce what they are able and receive what they need. Anarchists, however, insist on the abolition of government, whereas communists leave room for a "temporary" dictatorship after the revolution. Anarchists point out that this state will not just "wither away" and that the history of Russia has proved them correct.

Marxist theory holds that there is an inherent contradiction in the capitalist system, an imbalance between its ever-increasing production and the consumption that lags behind it. As Paul Sweezy explains, the boss pays the worker only part of the value the worker creates and keeps the surplus. The surplus accumulates and is invested in further production. Output expands, but the purchasing power of the workers is not enough to buy more than a portion of it. This process is accelerated by the introduction of labor-saving machines that create more goods with fewer workers. The imbalance between production and consumption and other contradictions inherent in the economic system will force it to break down and enable the workers to take over the means of production. The industrial working class, according to Marx, was to be the main lever of social change. Both Sweezy and Dwight Macdonald point out that the proletarian revolution Marx believed would take place in the advanced industrial nations has not occurred. The communist revolutions that *did* sweep Russia, China, and Cuba were led by intellectuals and supported mainly by the peasants.

261

Anarchists in the past shared the Marxist belief that factory workers were to be the main agency of social change in the highly industrialized countries. Many contemporary anarchists have shifted their hopes to other groups: students, ethnic minorities, intellectuals, and the "new working class" of teachers, technicians, and other middle-level white-collar workers.

I would add that whether Marx's predictions were correct is less important than how they have been used. National leaders in the Third World have been able to use Marxism to organize the people to destroy the system that had kept them hungry and exploited. On the other hand, revolutionary leaders have used Marxist doctrine to justify repressive policies of their own once they have obtained power.

Macdonald proposes an ideology in which "the root is man." He agrees with the ethical goals originally stated by Marx: the withering away of the state, production for use instead of profit, distribution on the basis of need instead of work, abolition of toil. He criticizes Marxism for its illusion that the victory of one side or the other in a modern war may advance the cause of socialism, and for its belief that progress is inevitable. He also criticizes the belief shared by some Marxists, liberals, and progressives that the development of science and technology will necessarily lead to a better world. As an anarchist, Macdonald feels it is important to refrain from the political game of choosing between the lesser of two evils, as represented by the major political parties. He suggests that dissenters go beyond electoral politics and engage in direct action, such as draft refusal and sabotage.

The anarchist position seems the more appropriate one for solving the difficult issue of international war. (This was perceived clearly by Macdonald at the time he wrote the selection reprinted below, although he later retreated from his pacifist outlook.) If we could abolish nation-states, there would be a far lower probability of large-scale conflicts such as World War II.[1] There will probably always be religious, ideological, and other conflicts between various social groups, but only when these groups take the form of the modern nation-state do genocide and mass murder become likely consequences. The world superpowers, the United States and the Soviet Union, have assembled large armies and nuclear arsenals capable of destroying all life on this planet. The view that war will be abolished when governments are controlled by socialist rather than capitalist leaders has little credibility. There are continuing hostilities between contiguous "socialist" states such as China and Vietnam; the escalating international arms race includes both "socialist" governments (as in Russia) and "democratic socialist" governments (as in Western Europe).

Another anarchist represented in this chapter is the Italian revolutionary Errico Malatesta, who was active from the turn of the century until his death in 1932. In common with the socialists, Malatesta believes that private ownership of the means of production should be abolished, and he agrees with them that governments in capitalist society represent the interests of a ruling capitalist class. He does not, however, see the solution in establishing a socialist government that would manage industry and truly represent working-class interests. Since all government is based on the domination of the majority by a minority, the anarchist solution is to abolish government and rely instead on voluntary association and mutual aid.

Anarchists see the need to destroy the power of the existing state, its military machines, and the giant corporations. Unlike the Marxists, they do not see this change as coming about through the leadership of a centralized party, but through the decentralized, loosely coordinated efforts of many small groups. Anarchists see government as necessarily repressive, and thus cannot share the Marxist idea that the revolution must set up a temporary dictatorship. They call for immediate decentralization — direct control of production by the people at the local level. Anarchists believe not only in working for the future revolution but also in living as free people here and now.

Notes

1. The same would be true if there were a world government, but there seems little chance of creating such a government unless it is imposed by force on the rest of the world by a military superpower state.

Marxism Socialism

Paul M. Sweezy

Marxism is a body of ideas about the nature of the universe, of man, of society, and of history. It bears the name of Karl Marx, a German who was born in 1818 and died in 1883, and who lived the latter half of his life in

FROM *Monthly Review* Pamphlet Series (Number 13), pp. 6–13. Copyright © 1956 by Monthly Review Inc. Reprinted by permission of the Monthly Review Foundation.

London. Marx was a man of prodigious learning and enormously powerful intellect, one of the greatest thinkers not only of the nineteenth century but of all recorded history.

Marx combined in his system of ideas the realistic philosophy of the English and French Enlightenment, the comprehensive and dynamic point of view of the German idealists and particularly of Hegel, and the hard-headed analysis of the capitalist economy which we owe to the great British classical economists. The result was a brilliant new synthesis which is both highly original and at the same time stands squarely in the mainstream of modern intellectual development from the Renaissance onward. Here, in desperate brevity, are what I understand to be the central elements of the Marxian view of society and history:

The universe is real and existed for eons before there was human life, or for that matter life of any kind, on our planet. Life here on the earth is a natural by-product of the earth's cooling, and humanity is the result of a long process of evolution. In the earliest stages of society, human labor was still so unproductive that it yielded no surplus over and above the requirements of life and reproduction. As long as this was true, men lived in a state of primitive communism — cooperating, sharing, fighting, but not yet exploiting each other.

Later, techniques improved so much that a man could produce a surplus over and above what he needed for himself, and from this dates the beginning of economic exploitation and social classes. When one tribe fought and defeated another, it was now worthwhile to take captive the vanquished and force them to work for the victors. Some men became rulers living off the surplus produced by others; while the actual producers lost their independence and spent their lives toiling for their masters. It was in this way that exploitation of man by man and the division of society into classes originated.

But the form of exploitation has not remained unchanged — indeed, nothing remains unchanged, everything is in a constant state of flux. The exploiters seek to expand the surplus at their disposal, and with this end in view they invent and introduce new and better techniques of production; the exploited seek to improve their condition and therefore carry on a never-ending struggle to enlarge their share of the product. As a result the forms of exploitation change, and with them the whole structure of society. At first it was slavery, in which the laborer is the property of his master. Next came serfdom, in which the laborer has attained a certain degree of freedom but is still tied to the soil. And finally there is wage labor, in which the laborer is legally entirely free but must work for the profit of others because he lacks means of production of his own.

A society based on private ownership of the means of production and wage labor is called capitalism. It came into the world first in England and certain parts of Western Europe, not all at once but gradually and painfully between the sixteenth and nineteenth centuries. It brought with it social and political upheavals, new ways of thinking, and a deep awareness of the vast creative potentials of human labor and industry. Historically speaking, capitalism was a long leap forward. In the words of the *Communist Manifesto:* "It has been the first to show what man's activity can bring about. It has accomplished wonders far surpassing Egyptian pyramids, Roman aqueducts, and Gothic cathedrals; it has conducted expeditions that put in the shade all former migrations and crusades."

But capitalism contains within itself what Marx called contradictions which prevent it from fully realizing the potentials which it was the first to uncover. The capitalist class, comprising those who own the instruments of production and set them in motion, is and must be concerned with making profits, not with the general welfare. Capitalists subordinate other aims to the maximization of profit. In pursuit of this objective, they pay workers as little as they can get away with and steadily introduce labor-saving machinery. The consequence, of course, is to hold down the consuming power of the working class. At the same time, the capitalists restrict their own consumption in the interests of accumulating more and more capital. But accumulating more and more capital means adding to society's productive capacity. We, therefore, have the paradox that capitalism steps on the brake as far as consumption is concerned and on the accelerator as far as production is concerned. This is its basic contradiction, and it cannot be eliminated except through changing the system from one of production for profit to one of production for use.

On the basis of this analysis, Marx believed that it was to the interest of the workers to organize themselves politically in order eventually to gain power and replace capitalism by a system based upon common ownership of the means of production and economic planning, a system to which he and his followers came in time to give the name of socialism. Moreover, Marx had no doubt that the workers would in fact follow this course, and that their growing numbers, importance, and discipline under capitalism would sooner or later ensure their victory. As to *how* the transition would be effected, Marx at first thought that it would have to be everywhere by means of a violent revolution. But as political democracy spread, especially in the English-speaking countries, he modified this view and in the last decades of his life believed that a peaceful and legal transition was quite possible in some countries and under some conditions. "We know," he said in a speech at Amsterdam in 1872, "that special regard must be paid to the institutions, customs, and traditions of various lands; and we do not deny that there are certain countries, such as the United States and England, in which the workers may hope to achieve their ends by peaceful means."

What Is Socialism?

So much then for Marxism. Naturally, my account is oversimplified and very incomplete, but I hope it may serve to give you some idea of the scope and quality of Marx's thought — so different from the impressions which demagogic opponents have always sought to convey. Let us now ask: What is socialism?

Socialism, according to Marx, is the form of society which will succeed capitalism, just as capitalism is the form of society which succeeded feudalism.

The fundamental change would consist in the abolition of private ownership of the means of production. Please note that neither Marx nor (so far as I know) any other modern socialist of importance ever advocated or expected that private ownership of consumer goods would or should be abolished. On the contrary, he favored the multiplication of consumer goods in the hands of the lower-income groups, hence a great extension of private ownership in this sphere.

As to the form of ownership of the means of production which would characterize socialism, Marxists have never been dogmatic. Ownership must be by public bodies, but that does not necessarily mean only the central government: local governments, special public authorities of one sort or another, and cooperatives can also own means of production under socialism. And there can even be a certain amount of private ownership, provided it is confined to industries in which production takes place on a small scale.

A corollary of public ownership of the means of production is economic planning. The capitalist economy is governed by the market, that is to say, by private producers responding to price movements with a view to maximizing their own profits. It is through this mechanism that supply and demand are adjusted to each other and productive resources are allocated to various industries and branches of production. But public bodies have no compelling reason to maximize their profits (though, admittedly, under certain circumstances they may be *directed* to make as much profit as they can). In general, therefore, they must have some other principle to guide their economic conduct, and this can only be the following of a plan which coordinates the activities of all the public bodies.

Now socialists claim that it is precisely the freedom from the necessity to make profits and the coordination of all economic activities by a general plan which allows socialism to overcome the contradictions of capitalism and to develop its resources and technology for the greatest good of the people as a whole. Under such a system, crises and unemployment could only result from bad planning; and while bad planning is certainly not impossible, especially in the early stages of socialist society, there is no reason why planners should not learn to correct their mistakes and to reduce the resulting maladjustments and disproportions to smaller and smaller dimensions.

What about the non-economic aspects of socialism? Here Marx had a well-developed theory. He expected socialism to come first in the more advanced industrialized countries and to build on the political foundations which they had already achieved. Since in such countries the workers were in a majority, he believed that the taking of political power by the working class would mean full democracy and liberty for most of the people, though he also expected that there would be a period of greater or lesser duration when the rights and freedoms of the former exploiters would be subject to certain restrictions. As to the longer-run future, he reasoned that the full development of society's economic potential under socialism would gradually raise the well-being and education of everyone so that eventually all classes and class distinctions would be done away with. When that happened — but not before — the state as a repressive apparatus for dealing with class and other forms of social conflict would "wither away." The final goal of Marx and his followers can therefore be said to be the same as that of the philosophical anarchists. It would be a state of society in which, to quote Marx's words, "the free development of each is the condition for the free development of all" and in which distribution takes place according to the principle "from each according to his ability, to each according to his need."

Others before Marx had had a similar vision of a good society to come — a society of abundance and brotherhood in place of the society of scarcity and alienation which the human race had always been condemned to live in. What particularly distinguished Marx from his predecessors is that he purported to prove that this society of the future, which he called socialism, is not only a dream and a hope but is in fact the next stage of historical evolution. It would not come automatically, to be sure — not as the result of the blind decrees of fate. It would come rather as the result of the conscious, organized activity of working people, the vast majority of mankind. Given this perspective, the task of the humanitarian could only be to devote his energies to educating and organizing the working class to fulfill its historic mission. That, in a word, is what Marxists have been trying to do for nearly a hundred years now.

Was Marx Right?

Marx's prophetic forecast of the end of capitalism and the opening of a new era in human history was given to the world in the *Communist Manifesto* in 1848. More than a century has passed since. Do the facts of this intervening period permit us to say whether Marx was right or wrong?

In the broadest sense, I do not see how it can be denied that Marx has been brilliantly vindicated. A mighty socialist movement based on the working class grew up during his lifetime. The crises of capitalism, far from abating, grew in intensity and violence, culminating in the holocausts of two world wars. Beginning with the Russian Revolution of 1917, more and more of the earth's population has withdrawn from the orbit of capitalism and has undertaken to reconstruct its economy and society on the basis of public ownership and planning. Today, something like a third of the human race has definitively abandoned private enterprise and, under Communist leadership, is building up a network of planned economies.

But it is not only in Communist-led countries that this is happening, though elsewhere the pace is slower. Since World War II, Great Britain has moved a considerable distance along the road to a socialized economy, and one of the two big political parties is a socialist party. Even more recently, India, next to Communist China the most populous country in the world, has adopted a Five Year Plan which the sober London *Times* calls "India's Socialist Plan."

The fact is that over most of the world's surface the trend is now visibly away from private enterprise and toward public ownership of the means of production, away from market-dominated economies and toward economic planning. Only in the United States and a few countries closely allied to the United States does the trend seem to be in the other direction. Here, it is true, the socialist movement is at a low ebb, and private enterprise is very much in the saddle.

Should we perhaps conclude that Marx was right for the rest of the world but wrong for the United States? Are we the great exception? Or are we merely lagging somewhat behind in a movement which eventually will be as universal as Marx predicted it would?

These are crucial questions, especially for us Americans. In what time remains to me, I shall attempt to indicate some possible answers.

There is one respect, and it is an important one, in which Marx was certainly wrong. As I noted earlier, he expected socialism to come first in the most advanced industrial countries. It did not. For reasons having to do with the late nineteenth and early twentieth-century development of relations between the advanced countries and the colonial and semi-colonial backward countries, the revolutionary movement grew more rapidly and had more opportunities in the backward than in the advanced regions. When the capitalist system was wracked by the destruction and disasters of the two world wars, it broke at its weakest points not at its strongest. Socialism came first to the Tsarist Empire, and spread from there to Eastern Europe and China.

This has, of course, meant that the early stages of the development of socialism have been very different from what Marx foresaw.

The new order could not build directly on the achievements of the old. It had no developed industrial base, no educated and trained labor force, no political democracy. It had to start from scratch and work under conditions of utmost difficulty.

Many people, including Marxists, expected socialism to proceed at once, or at any rate within a short time, to achieve its great goals: an economy of abundance, increasing democracy and freedom for the workers, a richer life for all. It could have happened that way if Britain, Germany, and the United States had been the first socialist countries. But it could not possibly happen that way in backward Russia standing alone for a whole generation. The industrial base had to be built, and that meant belt-tightening. The Russians had no traditions of democracy and civil liberty, and under the difficult conditions of the 1920s and 1930s it was natural that a new police state should arise on the foundations of the old Tsarist police state. Moreover, like all police states this one committed excesses and horrors which had little if anything to do with the central tasks of construction the regime had set itself.

Under these circumstances, socialism in practice had little attraction for the people of the advanced countries. The standard of living of those living under it remained abysmally low, and political conduct, both among leaders and between leaders and people, often seemed closer to oriental despotism than to enlightened socialism. It was widely assumed in the West either that the Soviet Union was not socialist at all, or that socialism had been tried and failed.

In the underdeveloped countries, however, the USSR made a very different impression. They saw rapid economic advance, a vast process of popular education, some improvement in living standards — and never having experienced democracy themselves, they hardly noticed its absence in Russia. Communism was imposed on Eastern Europe by the Red Army chasing Hitler back to Berlin, but in China it was the product of a great popular revolution. And it is now expanding its influence throughout the underdeveloped regions of the world.

The Competition of the Systems

The two systems of capitalism and socialism exist side by side in the world today. They are competing for the support and emulation of the backward and uncommitted countries. They are also competing in terms of absolute performance. How will this contest turn out? Will those now in the capitalist camp remain there? Or will they tend to join the socialist camp as time goes on? And finally, what about the United States, the leader of the capitalist camp?

These are questions which every serious person in the world is asking today. I predict that they will be increasingly the center of attention in the years and decades ahead.

The answers, I think, will depend very largely on the relative success of the two systems in the following fields: production and income, education, and liberty.* I believe that socialism will win out in this great world-shaking contest, and I am going to conclude . . . by trying to give you some of the reasons why I hold this view. I should add perhaps that I don't expect you to agree with me at this stage of the game. The decisive forces and trends are still operating for the most part below the surface, and it will be some time yet before they can be seen and evaluated by all. But I hope that I may succeed in making you *think* seriously about these matters.

---

*The concluding section of Sweezy's pamphlet is omitted here. In it, he compares the performance of the United States and the Soviet Union in these areas. — Ed.

The Root Is Man

Dwight Macdonald

We Need a New Political Vocabulary

Between the French Revolution (1789) and 1928, political tendencies could fairly accurately be divided into "Right" and "Left."

* * *

The Left comprised those who favored a change in social institutions which would make the distribution of income more equal (or completely equal) and would reduce class privileges (or do away with classes altogether). The central intellectual concept was the validity of scientific method; the central moral concept was the dignity of Man and the individual's right to liberty and a full personal development. Society was therefore conceived of as a means to an end: the happiness of the individual. There were important differences in method (as, reform vs. revolution, liberalism vs. class struggle) but on the above principles the Left was pretty much agreed.

The Right was made up of those who were either satisfied with the status quo (conservatives) or wanted it to become even more inegalitarian (reactionaries). In the name of Authority, the Right resisted change, and in the name of Tradition, it also, logically enough, opposed what had become the cultural motor of change: that willingness, common alike to Bentham and Marx, Jefferson and Kropotkin, to follow scientific inquiry wherever it led and to reshape institutions accordingly. Those of the Right thought in terms of an "organic" society, in which society is the end and the citizen the means. They justified inequalities of income and privilege by alleging an intrinsic inequality of individuals, both as to abilities and human worth.

This great dividing line has become increasingly nebulous with the rise of Nazism and Stalinism, both of which combine Left and Right elements

FROM *The Root Is Man,* by Dwight Macdonald (Alhambra, Calif.: The Cunningham Press), pp. 17–54. Copyright © 1953 by Dwight Macdonald. Reprinted by permission of The Cunningham Press.

in a bewildering way. Or, put differently, both the old Right and the old Left have almost ceased to exist as historical realities, and their elements have been recombined in the dominant modern tendency: an inegalitarian and organic society in which the citizen is a means, not an end, and whose rulers are antitraditional and scientifically minded.

* * *

In this Left-Right hybrid, the notion of Progress is central. A more accurate terminology might therefore be to reserve the term "Right" for such old-fashioned conservatives as Herbert Hoover and Winston Churchill and to drop the term "Left" entirely, replacing it with two words: "Progressive" and "Radical."

By "Progressive" would be understood those who see the Present as an episode on the road to a better Future; those who think more in terms of historical process than of moral values; those who believe that the main trouble with the world is partly lack of scientific knowledge and partly the failure to apply to human affairs such knowledge as we do have; those who, above all, regard the increase of man's mastery over nature as good in itself and see its use for bad ends, as atomic bombs, as a perversion. This definition, I think, covers fairly well the great bulk of what is still called the Left, from the Communists ("Stalinists") through reformist groups like our own New Dealers, the British Laborites, and the European Socialists to small revolutionary groups like the Trotskyists.

* * *

"Radical" would apply to the as yet few individuals — mostly anarchists, conscientious objectors, and renegade Marxists like myself — who reject the concept of Progress, who judge things by their present meaning and effect, who think the ability of science to guide us in human affairs has been overrated and who therefore redress the balance by emphasizing the ethical aspect of politics. They, or rather we, think it is an open question whether the increase of man's mastery over nature is good or bad in its actual effects on human life to date, and favor adjusting technology to man, even if it means — as may be the case — a technological regression, rather than adjusting man to technology. We do not, of course, "reject" scientific method, as is often charged, but rather think the scope within which it can yield fruitful results is narrower than is generally assumed today. And we feel that the firmest ground from which to struggle for that human liberation which was the goal to the old Left is the ground not of History but of those non-historical values (truth, justice, love, etc.) which Marx has made unfashionable among socialists.

The Progressive makes History the center of his ideology. The Radical puts Man there. The Progressive's attitude is optimistic both about human nature (which he thinks is basically good, hence all that is needed is to change institutions so as to give this goodness a chance to work) and about the possibility of understanding history through scientific method. The Radical is, if not exactly pessimistic, at least more sensitive to the dual nature of man; he sees evil as well as good at the base of human nature; he is sceptical about the ability of science to explain things beyond a certain point; he is aware of the tragic element in man's fate not only today but in any conceivable kind of society. The Progressive thinks in collective terms (the interests of Society or the Workingclass); the Radical stresses the individual conscience and sensibility. The Progressive starts off from what actually is happening; the Radical starts off from what he wants to happen.

* * *

The Question of Marxism

The Ambiguity of Marxism

Marxism is not simply, or even primarily, an interpretation of history. It is a guide to political action. The worst fate that can befall a philosophy of action is for it to be ambiguous. This is what has happened to Marxism. Its ambiguity stems from the fact that Marx's ethical aims have not been realized — quite the contrary! — while the historical process by which he thought they would be realized has to a large extent worked out as he predicted it would. It is possible to reach opposite conclusions, on the basis of Marxism, about Soviet Russia, depending on whether one emphasizes Marx's ethical values or his idea of the historical process. Since Marx himself made the process significant rather than the values, the Stalinists would seem to have a somewhat better claim to be the "real" Marxists than their more ethically minded opponents. But the point is not which is "really" the Marxist view; the point is that each view may be maintained, on the basis of Marx's thought, with a good deal of reason. There is an ambiguity here, fatal to a philosophy conceived as a basis for action, which was not apparent during Marx's lifetime, when history seemed to be going his way, but which is all too clear now that history is going contrary to socialist values.

What Marx Wanted

Marx's vision of a good society was essentially the same as that of the anarchists, the Utopian socialists, and the great eighteenth-century liberals — also as that of those today whom I call "Radicals." The same theme runs through his writings from beginning to end. The *Communist Manifesto* (1848): "An association in which the free development of each is the condition for the free development of all." *Capital,* Vol. 1 (1867): "a society in which the full and free development of every individual becomes the ruling principle . . . production by freely associated men." The *Critique of the Gotha Program* (1875) gives us the most explicit and famous formulation:

> In a higher phase of communist society, after the enslaving subordination of individuals under division of labor, and therewith also the antithesis between mental and physical labor, has vanished; after labor, from a means of life, has itself become the prime necessity of life; after the productive forces have also increased with the all-round development of the individual, and all the springs of cooperative wealth flow more abundantly — only then can the narrow horizon of bourgeois right be fully left behind and society inscribe on its banners: from each according to his ability, to each according to his needs.

The political seal of this future society would be the elimination of all forms of coercion, i.e., the withering away of the State.

* * *

How He Thought It Would Come About

So much for Marx's ethical aims. I think it needs no demonstration that such a society is farther off today than it was in Marx's time. Now what about the way Marx conceived the historical process that would realize these aims? Two passages will give us the grand outlines:

At a certain stage of their development, the material forms of production in society come into conflict with the existing relations of production or — what is but a legal expression for the same thing — with the property relations within which they had been at work before. From forms of development of the forces of production, these relations turn into their fetters. Then comes the period of social revolution. With the change of the economic foundation, the entire immense superstructure is more or less rapidly transformed. . . . In broad outline we can designate the Asiatic, the ancient, the feudal, and the modern bourgeois methods of production as so many epochs in the process of the economic formation of society. The bourgeois relations of production are the last antagonistic form of the social process of production — antagonistic not in the sense of individual antagonism, but of one arising from conditions surrounding the life of individuals in society. At the same time, the productive forces developing in the womb of bourgeois society create the material conditions for the solution of that antagonism. This social formation constitutes, therefore, the closing of the prehistoric stages of human society" (Marx's Preface to *A Contribution to the Critique of Political Economy*).

Along with the constantly diminishing number of magnates of capital . . . grows the mass of misery, oppression, slavery, degradation, exploitation; but with this too grows the revolt of the workingclass, a class always increasing in numbers, and disciplined, united, organized by the very mechanism of the process of capitalist production itself. The monopoly of capital becomes a fetter upon the mode of production. . . . Centralization of the means of production and socialization of labor at last reach a point where they become incompatible with their capitalist integument. This integument is burst asunder. The knell of capitalist private property sounds. The expropriators are expropriated. . . . The transformation of scattered private property, arising from individual labor, into capitalist private property is, naturally, a process incomparably more protracted, violent and difficult than the transformation of capitalistic private property, already practically resting on socialised production, into socialised property. In the former case, we had the expropriation of the mass of the people by a few usurpers; in the latter, we have the expropriation of a few usurpers by the mass of people" (*Capital,* Vol. 1).

How It Really Is Coming About

Two aspects of these passages concern us here: (1) the assumption that there is a progressive evolution in history from worse to better; (2) the description of how the overthrow of capitalism, the final step in this evolution, would come about.

1. The belief in Progress is central to Marx's thought, although his more sophisticated followers today, for understandable reasons, say as little as possible about it. As I shall show later on, Marx's concept of historical Progress has not only proved to be empirically false, but it has also been used by the Communists as an ideology to justify the most atrocious policies. So long as we are bemused by the will-o-the-wisp of Progress, we can never become truly radical, we can never make man the root.

2. Marx predicted that the contradiction between the increasing productivity of industry and the forms of private property would "burst asunder" the capitalist "integument" and lead to "socialised property." The agency that would accomplish this change would be the proletariat, lashed to the task by increasing misery and historically fitted for it by the fact that collectivism was to its interest as a class (and, so far as Marx ever states, to the interest of no other class). The result of the change would be a non-antagonistic form of social production in which, for the first time in history, the masses would expropriate "a few usurpers" instead of the other way around. As we have seen already in this article, private capitalism is indeed decaying and the bourgeoisie are being expropriated, but the agency is not the proletariat but rather a new *political* ruling-class which is substituting its rule for the old ruling class in the time-honored way. The process on which Marx banked so heavily is being brought about from the top, not the bottom, and is directed toward nationalism and war. The result is not the

liberation of the masses but their even more complete enslavement, not the coming of the Kingdom of Freedom but
the creation of an even more crushing Kingdom of Necessity.
The external process is working out, but the inner spirit is
the reverse of what Marx expected.

The weakness of Marxism seems to me to be precisely its most distinctive contribution to socialist thinking: the expectation that external,
materialistic factors (such as changes in class and property relationships)
will bring about certain desired results with "iron necessity." Ends, values,
cannot safely be treated only as functions of materialistic factors but must
be defined and communicated in their own terms.

* * *

The Rock That Turned Out to Be Sand

When Marx concentrated his great intellectual powers on the economic
process of capitalism, he thought he was building on a rock. In the preface to
Capital he quotes approvingly from a Russian review: "The one thing which
is of moment to Marx is to find the law of the phenomena with whose investigation he is concerned. . . . This law once discovered, he investigates in
detail the effects in which it manifests itself in social life. Consequently, Marx
only troubles himself about one thing: to show, by rigid scientific investigation, the necessity of successive determinate orders of social conditions. . . .
Marx treats the social movement as a process of natural history, governed by
laws not only independent of human will, consciousness and intelligence, but
rather on the contrary, determining that will, consciousness and intelligence.
. . . The scientific value of such an inquiry lies in the disclosing of the special
laws that regulate the origin, existence, development and death of a given
social organism and its replacement by another and higher one." The op-
timism of the nineteenth century, both about Progress and about the
possibilities of scientific inquiry, is strikingly expressed here. Also the influence of Darwin's evolutionary theory on Marx, with its reinforcement of
the idea of Progress that had arisen in the eighteenth century and its emphasis
on external environmental factors over human consciousness. In the same
preface, Marx grandiosely writes of "the natural laws of capitalist production
. . . working with iron necessity towards inevitable results." The necessity has
proved to be putty, the results quite evitable. The rock of Historical Process
on which Marx built his house has turned out to be sand. . . .

In the following three sections, I try to show that (1) the working class has "come of age" without advancing us toward socialism; (2) a great shift away from capitalism is taking place without advancing us toward socialism; (3) modern war, far from offering "revolutionary opportunities" for socialism, is creating new conditions which make the struggle for socialism even more difficult. This failure of history to take the anticipated course might not be fatal to some systems of political thought but it is so to Marxism, because that system is built not on ethical principles but on the historical process itself.

The Mirage of the Proletarian Revolution

It was to the working class that Marx looked to bring in a better society.

* * *

Economic: The Unions

Instead of broadening their objectives, as Marx expected them to, and aspiring finally to "the emancipation of the downtrodden millions," unions have usually followed precisely the opposite course.

. . . The early struggle to establish unions had an anti-capitalist character which more and more disappeared as time went on. The evolution has been at first into simple pressure groups fighting for labor's interests *against* the rest of society (which does not by any means consist only of bankers in silk hats) and with an attitude of devil take the hindmost so long as "we get ours"; Lewis' United Mine Workers and the old-line AF of L unions are still in this stage. There is also a later stage, more typical of mature capitalism, which indeed involves the assumption of a broad social responsibility, but as an integral part of capitalism rather than as a force for labor's emancipation *from* capitalism. Industrialists often find it advantageous to have their work force controlled by a "responsible" union bureaucracy with whom they can deal on a "reasonable" basis — in England, for example, the employer himself often makes union membership a condition of employment. The State also finds unions of great value as agencies of control, especially in wartime. In short, the modern union is a bureaucratized mass-organization which simply extends the conventional patterns of society into the working class and has little significance as an expression of a specific workingclass consciousness. It may be a narrowminded economic pressure-group, or, more typically, the kind of a prop to a disintegrating status quo the Social Democracy was in Weimar Germany and the TUC is today in somewhat similar circumstances in England. In either case, what it has to do with either socialism or revolution is obscure.

Political: The Parties

The most obvious fact about the Proletarian Revolution is that it has never occurred.[1] Such revolutions as have taken place have not followed the working class pattern which Marxism anticipated. The Paris Commune had a very mixed class character and materialized more along the lines of Blanqui or Proudhon than of Marx. The other revolutionary upheavals have been in the least advanced, not the most advanced, countries, and have therefore had a mixed peasant-worker character (Russia, China, Spain). These revolutions in backward lands have either failed or have produced new tyrannies; the Marxist explanation is that the low level of economic development made socialism impossible. But when countries are highly developed, their workers don't make revolutions at all.

The proletarian revolution today is even less of a historical possibility than it was in 1900. World War I was the turning point. The reformist-socialist movements of Europe, by supporting their capitalist governments in that war, permanently discredited the Second International.*

* * *

Modern War and the Class Struggle

In the century after Waterloo (1815-1914), there was only one war in Europe between first-class powers: the Franco-Prussian War. In the first half of the twentieth century, there have already occurred two world wars which involved not only all the great European powers but also the United States, Russia, and Japan; and a third world war is generally anticipated. Furthermore, World War II was much more destructive of lives, property, and culture than World War I, and the atomic bomb promises to make World War III devastating beyond any historical parallel.

* * *

From these facts, two conclusions emerge: (1) The preparation and waging of war is now the normal mode of existence of every great nation; the creation of military force is no longer one among other means of advancing the national interest but rather, it *is* now the national interest. (2) Since

---

*A worldwide association of socialist and labor parties active between 1889 and 1914 — Ed.

the chronic world warfare of our day was unknown to them, the theoreticians of socialism devoted their attention mainly to the internal class struggle and failed to work out an adequate theory of the political significance of war; this gap still remains to be filled; until it is, modern socialism will continue to have a somewhat academic flavor.[2]

The Inadequacy of the Marxian View of War

Marxism regards war as a means to an end, a method of advancing certain definite class interests; as a means, it is subordinated to its end, so that if the destruction it causes seems likely to exceed the gains to those groups using this means, they will presumably not use it; there is implied in this whole view a certain rationality, even moderation and limit, to warfare, so that one can say that a given war may offer a "revolutionary opportunity" or that the victory of one side may be more advantageous to the cause of socialism than the victory of the other.

There was some truth in these ideas in Marx's time, but they are now obsolete. War has become an end in itself; instead of advancing certain class or national interests at the expense of others, war tends more and more to make the situation of the "victors" indistinguishable from that of the "defeated," as in post-World War II Europe the effects of the technical measures that must be taken to fight a modern war have become more important than any political effect of the war's outcome. In a word, war seems to have lost its rationality, so that one might say there will probably be a third world war because there has been a second world war; that is, the existence of powerful warmaking apparatuses, with economies and social institutions deformed to support them, and the quite justified fears of every nation of attack from every other nation—these factors are the key to the problem, . . .

Economic: "More Work, Better Pay"

Marx and Engels regarded the periodic economic crises which they predicted would occur under capitalism as the immediate causes of revolutions. "We can almost calculate the moment," wrote the latter in his preface to the first volume of *Capital*, "when the unemployed, losing patience, will take their own fate into their hands." And Marx, in *The Class Stuggles in France,* noted that "a real revolution is only possible in the periods when these two factors, the modern productive forces and the bourgeois production forms, come into collision with each other. . . . A new revolution is only possible in consequence of a new crisis. It is, however, just as certain as this." How do these crises arise? Marx sums it up in *Capital* (V. 3, p. 568):

"The last cause of all real crises always remains the poverty and restricted consumption of the masses as compared to the tendency of capitalist production to develop productive forces in such a way that only the absolute power of consumption of the entire society would be the limit."

In a fully-developed Bureaucratic Collectivist society like that of Russia, none of the above applies: crises may occur, but they have a political character and cannot be shown—or at least have not been shown—to arise from the kind of periodic and automatic economic imbalance described by Marx. The forms of production still conflict with the productive forces—but along new lines. In societies like our own and England, which are still capitalist but in which Bureaucratic Collectivism is spreading, techniques of State spending, economic control, and deficit financing have been developed which in practice *have* avoided crises and in theory *should* be able to do so. These new economic forms are closely related to preparation for warfare.

* * *

The modern warmaking State, even if it is still mainly capitalist, thus avoids Marx's "inevitable" economic crises. Through deficit spending, it enlarges the purchasing power of the masses. And it brings to bear "the power of consumption of the entire society" through vast orders for munitions (a form of buying which has the further advantage of removing the goods entirely outside the market sphere so that they don't compete for a share of the public spending power: the ultimate consumer of munitions   and the adjective is most fitting—is the Enemy soldier). There is also largely eliminated another one of the factors to which Marx looked for the self-disintegration of capitalism: the "industrial reserve-army of the unemployed." In wartime, this becomes a real army. In peacetime, it gets employment through the measures just noted. For, while Marx was able to demonstrate how essential "an industrial reserve army" was to the bourgeoisie to keep down the price of labor, such an army is of no advantage to the rulers of a warmaking society, which needs two things above all: "National unity" and full production. Unemployment, with its idle and discontented millions, from this standpoint has only disadvantages.

Finally, nothing improves the economic position of the working class and strengthens its trade unions more than a really good war.

* * *

Political: The Dominance of Foreign Policy

The more war becomes dominant, the more the ruling classes can monopolize continually—not just in time of actual hostilities—the most powerful ideological weapon they have ever grasped: the appeal for "unity" of the whole nation against a threat from outside. This weapon is powerful psychologically, because it plays on very deep fears and in-group loyalties. It is also powerful in rational terms, because it is perfectly true that national defeat is catastrophic for *all* classes, not just for the ruling class. Thus the strongest appeal of the Nazis in the terrible final year of the war was their picture of what the consequences of defeat would be for the German people. . . .

One striking confirmation of the way war rather than class struggle has become the center of our world is the importance that foreign policy now assumes. The disagreements between "Left" and "Right" on domestic policy, unsubstantial enough precisely because of the needs of "national unity" in order to present a strong front to competing nations, vanish completely when the really vital question of foreign policy arises. . . .

Now that the national State has become the great menace, and war and foreign policy the great issues, the "realistic" attitude that has always distinguished Marx and his followers on these matters has become quite unrealistic (if one's aim is not effective warmaking or the furtherance of nationalistic ambitions). The Anarchists' uncompromising rejection of the State, the subject of Marxian sneers for its "absolutist" and "Utopian" character, makes much better sense in the present era than the Marxian relativist and historical approach.[3] The pacifists also seem to be more realistic than the Marxists both in their understanding of modern war and also in their attempts to do something about it.

* * *

Wanted: A New Concept of Political Action

It is not difficult to sketch out the kind of society we need to rescue modern man from his present alienation. It would be one whose only aim, justification and principle would be the full development of each individual, and the removal of all social bars to his complete and immediate satisfaction in his work, his leisure, his sex life, and all other aspects of his nature. (To remove all social bars does not, of course, mean to remove all bars; complete happiness and satisfaction is probably impossible in any society, and would be dull even if possible; regardless of the excellence of social institutions, there will always be, for example, persons who are in love with others who aren't in love with them.) This can only be done if each individual understands what he is doing and has the power, within the limitations of his own personality and of our common human imperfection, to act exactly as he thinks best for himself. This in turn depends on people entering into direct personal relationships with each other, which in turn means that the political and economic units of society (workshops, exchange of goods, political institutions) are small enough to allow the participants to understand them and to make their individual influence felt. If effective wars cannot be fought by groups the size of New England town meetings, and I take it they cannot, this is one more reason for giving up war (rather than the town meeting). If automobiles cannot be made efficiently by small factories, then let us make them inefficiently. If scientific research would be hampered in a small-unit society, then let us by all means hamper it. Said the young Marx: "For Hegel, the starting-point is the State. In a democracy, the starting-point is man . . . Man is not made for the law, but the law is made for man."

This is all clear enough. What is not so generally understood is that the traditional Progressive approach, taking History as the starting-point and thinking in terms of mass political parties, bases itself on this same alienation of man which it thinks it is combating. It puts the individual into the same powerless, alienated role vis-à-vis the party or the trade union as the manipulators of the modern State do, except that the slogans are different.

* * *

From all this one thing seems to follow: We must reduce political action to a modest, unpretentious, personal level — one that is real in the sense that it satisfies, here and now, the psychological needs, and the ethical values of the particular persons taking part in it. We must begin way at the bottom again, with small groups of individuals in various countries, grouped around certain principles and feelings they have in common. These should probably not be physically isolated as was the case in the 19th century since this shuts one off from the common experience of one's fellow men. They should probably consist of individuals — *families*, rather — who live and make their living in the everyday world but who come together often enough and intimately enough to form a *psychological* (as against a geographical) community. The purpose of such groups would be twofold. Within itself, the group would exist so that its members could come to know each other as fully as possible as human beings (the difficulty of such knowledge of others in modern society is a chief source of evil), to exchange ideas and discuss as fully as possible what is "on their minds" (not only the atomic bomb but also the perils of child-rearing), and in general to learn the difficult art of living with other people. The group's purpose toward the outside world would be to take certain actions together (as, against Jim Crow in this country, or to further pacifism), to support individuals whether members of the group or not who stand up for the common ideals, and to preach those ideals — or, if you prefer, make propaganda — by word and by deed, in the varied everyday contacts of the group members with their fellow-men. . . .

The ideas which these groups would advance, by word and deed, would probably run along something like the following lines:

1. The dominance of war and the development of weapons atrocious beyond all past imagination make pacifism, in my opinion, a sine-qua-non of any Radical movement. The first great principle would, therefore, be that killing and hurting others is wrong, always and absolutely, and that no-member of the group will use such methods or let himself be drafted to do so.[4]

2. Coercion of the individual, whether by the State or by a revolutionary party, is also wrong in principle, and will be opposed with sabotage, ridicule, evasion, argument, or simple refusal to submit to authority — as circumstances may require. Our model here would be the old IWW* rather than the Marxist Internationals.[5]

3. All ideologies which require the sacrifice of the present in favor of the future will be looked on with suspicion. People should be happy and should satisfy their spontaneous needs here and now.[6] If people don't enjoy what they are doing, they shouldn't do it. (This includes the activities of the group.) This point is a learning, a *prejudice* rather than a principle; that is, the extent to which it is acted on would be relative to other things.

4. Socialism is primarily an ethical matter. The number of people who want it at any given moment has nothing to do with its validity for the individual who makes it his value.

---

*Industrial Workers of the World, a radical American-labor organization founded in 1905 and most active just before World War I. Militantly anti-capitalist and pro-socialist, it used direct action tactics such as sudden strikes, slow-ups and sabotage. — Ed.

What *he* does, furthermore, is considered to be just as "real" as what History does.

5. Members of the groups would get into the habit, discouraged by the Progressive frame of mind, of acting here and now, on however tiny a scale, for their beliefs. They would do as the handful of British and American scientists did who just refused, as individuals and without any general support, to make atomic bombs; not as Albert Einstein and other scientists are now doing—raising money for an educational campaign to show the public how horrible The Bomb is, while they continue to cooperate with General Groves in making more and bigger bombs.

6. They will think in human, not class terms. This means they will free themselves from the Marxian fetishism of the mass, preferring to be able to speak modest meaningful truths to a small audience rather than grandiose empty formulae to a big one. This also means, for the moment, turning to the intelligentsia as one's main supporters, collaborators and audience, on the assumption that what we are looking for represents so drastic a break with past traditions of thinking and behaving that at this early stage only a few crackpots and eccentrics (i.e., intellectuals) will understand what we're talking about, or care about it at all. We may console ourselves that all new social movements including Marxism, have begun this way: with a few intellectuals rather than at the mass level.

Five Characteristics of a Radical

While it is still too soon to be definite about what a Radical *does* (beyond the vague suggestions just indicated), it is possible to conclude with a more concrete idea of what he is. What are his attitudes toward politics? They may be summed up under five heads:

1. Negativism
2. Unrealism
3. Moderation
4. Smallness
5. Self-ishness

* * *

The Positiveness of Negativism

The only way to be positive vis-à-vis the modern State is to be negative, i.e., refuse to do what it wants one to do. The situation might be compared to a group of people being driven in a high-powered automobile along a road that ends in a precipice. They see the Radicals sitting by the side of the road—just sitting. "Yaahh, negativists!" they cry. "Look at us! *We're* going somewhere, *we're* really *doing* something!" (There is no space here to develop the relevance of Lao-Tse's principle of "non-acting"—and perhaps it is not necessary.)

The Realism of Unrealism

The Progressive insists that one has a duty in every situation to choose between what he calls "real" alternatives, and that it is irresponsible to refuse to make such a choice. By "real" he means an alternative which has a reasonably good chance of success. Thus, in World War II, he saw two real alternatives: to support the Allies or to support Hitler. He naturally chose the former. The trouble with his "real" alternatives is that each of them is part of the whole system of war and exploitation, to put an end to which is the very justification of his choice. The Radical believes—and I think logic is on his side—that only an alternative which is antithetical to the existing system can lead one to the abolition of that system. For him, it is unrealistic to hope to secure a peaceful world through war, to hope to defeat the brutality and oppression of Hitler by the brutality and oppression of the American and Russian political systems.

* * *

Against the Fetishism of the Masses

To Marx's "fetishism of commodities" I would counterpoise our modern fetishism—that of the masses. The more Progressive one's thinking, the more one assumes that the test of the goodness of a political program is how wide a popular appeal it makes. I venture to assert, for the present time at least, the contrary: that, as in art and letters, communicability to a large audience is in inverse ratio to the excellence of a political approach. This is not a good thing: as in art, it is a deforming, crippling factor. Nor is it an external rule: in the past, the ideas of a tiny minority, sometimes almost reduced to the vanishing-point of one individual, have slowly come to take hold on more and more of their fellow-men; and we may hope that our own ideas may do likewise.

* * *

Individual actions, based on moral convictions, have *greater* force today than they had two generations ago. As an English correspondent wrote me recently: "The main reason for Conscientious Objection is undoubtedly that it does make a personal feeling have weight. In the present world, the slightest sign of individual revolt assumes a weight out of all proportion to its real value." Thus in drafting men into that totalitarian society, the U.S. Army, the examiners often rejected anyone who stated openly that he did not *want* to enter the Army and felt he would be unhappy there. We may assume this action was not due to sympathy, but rather to the fact that, as practical men, the examiners knew that such a one would "make trouble" and that the smooth running of the vast mechanism could be thrown out by the presence of such a gritty particle precisely because of the machine's delicately-geared hugeness.

Another conclusion is that group action against The Enemy is most effective when it is most spontaneous and loosest in organization. The opposition of the romantic clubs of German youth ("Edelweiss," "Black Pirates") was perhaps more damaging to the Nazis than that of the old parties and unions. So, too, World-over Press reports that a recently discovered secret list of British leaders to be liquidated by the Nazis after the invasion of England gave top priority not to trade unionists nor to leftwing political leaders but to well-known pacifists.

What seems necessary is thus to encourage attitudes of disrespect, scepticism, ridicule towards the State and all authority, rather than to build up a competing authority. It is the difference between a frontal attack all along the line and swift flanking jabs at points where The Enemy is weakest, between large-scale organized warfare and guerrilla operations. Marxists go in for the former: the Bolsheviks emphasize discipline and unity in order to match that of The Enemy; the reformists try to outweigh The Enemy's power of shepherding great masses of voters and trade unionists into the scales. But the status quo is too powerful to be overthrown by such tactics; and, even worse, they show a disturbing tendency to lead one over to the side of The Enemy.

Self-ishness, or the Root Is Man

Granted that individual actions can never overthrow the status quo, and also that even spontaneous mass rebellion will be fruitless unless it has some kind of conscious program and also unless certain elementary steps of coordination and organization are taken. But today we confront this situation: the masses just do not act toward what most of the readers of this magazine* would recognize as some fundamental betterment of society. The only way, at present, of so *acting* (as against just "making the record" for the muse of Marxian history by resolutions and manifestoes "against imperialist war," "for the international proletarian revolution," etc.) seems to be through symbolic individual actions, based on one person's insistence on his own values, and through the creation of small fraternal groups which will support such actions, keep alive a sense of our ultimate goals, and both act as a leavening in the dough of mass society and attract more and more of the alienated and frustrated members of that society. These individual stands have two advantages over the activities of those who pretend that mass action is now possible:

1. They make a dramatic appeal to people, the appeal of the individual who is bold enough and serious enough to stand alone, if necessary, against the enormous power of The State; this encourages others to resist a little more than they would otherwise in *their* everyday life, and also preserves the living seeds of protest and rebellion from which later on bigger things may grow.
2. They at least preserve the revolutionary vitality and principles of the few individuals who make such stands, while the mass-actionists become, if they stick by their principles, deadened and corrupted personally by their constant submission in their own personal behavior to the standards of The Enemy.

* * *

The first step toward a new concept of political action (and political morality) is for each person to decide what he thinks is right, what satisfies *him*, what *he* wants. And then to examine with scientific method the environment to figure out how to get it — or, if he can't get it, to see how much he can get without compromising his personal values. Self-ishness must be restored to respectability in our scheme of political values. Not that the individual exists apart from his fellow men, in Max Stirner's sense. I agree with Marx and Proudhon that the individual must define himself partly in his social relations. But the point is to make these real *human* relations and not

*Reference is to *Politics,* in which the article originally appeared. — Ed.

abstract concepts of class or history. It has often been observed that nations — and, I might add, classes, even the proletariat — have a lower standard of ethical behavior than individuals do. Even if all legal constraints were removed, I take it we can assume that few people would devote themselves exclusively to murder or would constantly lie to their friends and families; yet the most respected leaders of present societies, the military men and the political chieftains, in their public capacities become specialists in lying and murder. Always, of course, with the largest aims, "for the good of humanity."

A friend put it well in a letter I received several months ago: "So long as morality is all in public places — politics, Utopia, revolutions (nonviolent included), progress — our private mores continue to be a queasy mixture of chivalry and cynicism: all in terms of *angles*, either for or against. We're all against political sin, we all love humanity, but individuals are sort of tough to love, even tougher to hate. Goldenhaired dreams, humanitarian dreams — what's the difference so long as they smell good? Meanwhile, patronize any whore, fight in any war, but don't marry the girl and don't fight the boss — too dangerous . . . No. Damn, our only chance is to try to get as small, private, honest, selfish as we can. Don't you agree that one can't have a moral attitude toward Humanity? Too big."

Or to put it more generally. Technological progress, the organization from the top of human life (what Max Weber calls "rationalization"), the overconfidence of the past two centuries in scientific method — these have led us, literally, into a dead end. Their trend is now clear: atomic warfare, bureaucratic collectivism, "the crystallization of social activity into an objective power above us, growing out of our control, thwarting our expectations, bringing to naught our calculations . . ." To try to fight this trend, as the Progressives of all shades do, with the same forces that have brought it about appears absurd to me. We must emphasize the emotions, the imagination, the moral feelings, the primacy of the individual human being, must restore the balance that has been broken by the hypertrophy of science in the last two centuries. The root is man, here and not there, now and not then.

Notes

1. And probably never will occur.
2. For some nonacademic thinking on modern war and politics, see Simone Weil's "Reflections on War" (*Politics,* Feb. 1945) and "Words and War" (*Politics,* March 1946); also two remarkable and not-enough-noticed-at-the-time pieces by "European" in *Politics:* "Is a Revolutionary War a Contradiction in Terms?" (April 1946) and "Violence and Sociability" (Jan. 1947); also, of course, that little classic from the First World War, Randolph Bourne's *The State,* with its sombre refrain: "War is the health of the State."

3. "Bakunin has a peculiar theory," Engels wrote to Cuno in 1872, "the chief point of which is that he does not regard capital, and therefore the class contradiction between capitalists and wage earners . . . as the main evil to be abolished. Instead, he regards the State as the main evil. . . . Therefore, it is above all the State which must be done away with, and then capitalism will go to hell of itself. We, on the contrary, say: do away with capital, the appropriation of the whole means of production in the hands of the few, and the State will fall away of itself. The difference is an essential one." It is indeed.

4. Again, I am now more moderate in my absolutism. Under certain extreme circumstances, I would use force, personally and even as a soldier.

5. Though I still hold to the *tendency* expressed here, the actual formulation now seems to me absurdly overstated. Even the Wobblies [members of the IWW — Ed.], after all, since they lived in a world of cops and judges, must have submitted to authority far more often than they rebelled against it or evaded it — or else, they would have spent *all* their time in jail (where, again, if they consistently flouted authority, they would have spent *all* their time in solitary confinement if not worse). Also certain kinds of social authority — as, traffic laws, sanitary regulations — are from even the purest anarchist viewpoint not objectionable and indeed useful. Proudhon drew the line sensibly: he was willing to submit to the State in matters which did not seem to him to importantly affect his interests adversely.

6. "To make such a statement," a friend wrote me, "amounts to saying in so many words that one doesn't give a damn about moral ideals. Morality, in fact, is nothing at all if it is not giving up something in the present in favor of something not only of the future but even of the purely 'ideal.' And it isn't even a question of morality: no intelligent activity of any kind would be possible if your statement, and your demand for immediate satisfaction, had to be taken seriously." Even though I qualify this statement as "a leaning rather than a principle," I still must admit it is onesided as put here, and that acting out an ethical ideal may often involve some sacrifice of the present to the future and perhaps also of one's spontaneous, or at least immediate needs. . . .

Anarchy

Errico Malatesta

What is the government? There is a disease of the human mind called the metaphysical tendency, which causes man, after he has by a logical process abstracted the quality from an object, to be subject to a kind of hallucination which makes him take the abstraction for the real thing. This metaphysical tendency, in spite of the blows of positive science, has still strong root in the minds of the majority of our contemporary fellow-men. It has such influence that many consider government an actual entity, with

FROM Malatesta, *Anarchy* (London: Freedom Press, 1907). Portions of the original text have been omitted.

certain given attributes of reason, justice, equity, independently of the people who compose the government.

For us, the government is the aggregate of the governors, and the governors — kings, presidents, ministers, members of parliament, and what not — are those who have the power to make laws regulating the relations between men, and to force obedience to these laws. They are those who decide upon and claim the taxes, enforce military service, judge and punish transgressors of the laws. They subject men to regulations, and supervise and sanction private contracts. They monopolize certain branches of production and public services, or, if they wish, all production and public service. They promote or hinder the exchange of goods. They make war or peace with the governments of other countries. They concede or withhold free trade and many things else. In short, the governors are those who have the power, in a greater or lesser degree, to make use of the collective force of society, that is, of the physical, intellectual, and economic force of all, to oblige each to their (the governors') wish. And this power constitutes, in our opinion, the very principle of government and authority.

* * *

Many and various are the theories by which men have sought to justify the existence of government. All, however, are founded, confessedly or not, on the assumption that the individuals of a society have contrary interests, and that an external superior power is necessary to oblige some to respect the interests of others, by prescribing and imposing a rule of conduct, according to which the interests at strife may be harmonized as much as possible, and according to which each may obtain the maximum of satisfaction with the minimum of sacrifice. If, say the theorists of the authoritarian school, the interests, tendencies, and desires of an individual are in opposition to those of another individual, or perhaps all society, who will have the right and the power to oblige the other to respect the interests of the other or others? Who will be able to prevent the individual citizen from offending the general will? The liberty of each, they say, has for its limit the liberty of others; but who will establish those limits, and who will cause them to be respected? The natural antagonism of interests and passions creates the necessity for government, and justifies authority. Authority intervenes as moderator of the social strife, and defines the limits of the rights and duties of each.

This is the theory; but to be sound the theory should be based upon an explanation of facts. We know well how in social economy theories are too often invented to justify facts, that is, to defend privilege and cause it to be accepted tranquilly by those who are its victims. Let us here look at the facts themselves.

In all the course of history, as in the present epoch, government is either brutal, violent, arbitrary domination of the few over the many, or it is an instrument devised to secure domination and privilege to those who, by force, or cunning, or inheritance, have taken to themselves all the means of life, and first and foremost the soil, whereby they hold the people in servitude, making them work for their advantage. . . .

Every time that, by military enterprise, physical brute force has taken the upper hand in society, the conquerors have shown the tendency to concentrate government and property in their own hands. In every case, however, because the government cannot attend to the production of wealth, and overlook and direct everything, it finds it necessary to conciliate a powerful class, and private property is again established. With it comes the division of the two sorts of power, that of the persons who control the collective force of society, and that of the proprietors, upon whom these governors become essentially dependent, because the proprietors command the sources of the said collective force.

Never has this state of affairs been so accentuated as in modern times. The development of production, the immense extension of commerce, the extensive power that money has acquired, and all the economic results flowing from the discovery of America, the invention of machinery, etc., have secured such supremacy to the capitalist class that it is no longer content to trust to the support of the government, and has come to wish that the government shall emanate from itself; a government composed of members from its own class, continually under its control and specially organized to defend it against the possible revenge of the disinherited. Hence the origin of the modern parliamentary system.

In many countries, the proletariat participates nominally in the election of the government. This is a concession which the bourgeois (i.e., proprietory) class have made, either to avail themselves of popular support in the strife against royal or aristocratic power, or to divert the attention of the people from their own emancipation by giving them an apparent share in political power. However, whether the bourgeoisie foresaw it or not, when first they conceded to the people the right to vote, the fact is that the right has proved in reality a mockery, serving only to consolidate the power of the bourgeoisie, while giving to the most energetic only of the proletariat the illusory hope of arriving at power.

So also with universal suffrage—we might say, especially with universal suffrage—the government has remained the servant and police of the bourgeois class. How could it be otherwise? If the government should reach the point of becoming hostile, if the hope of democracy should ever be more than a delusion deceiving the people, the proprietory class, menaced in its interests, would at once rebel, and would use all the force and influence which come from the possession of wealth, to reduce the government to the simple function of acting as policeman.

In all times and in all places, whatever may be the name that the government takes, whatever has been its origin, or its organization, its essential function is always that of oppressing and exploiting the masses, and of defending the oppressors and exploiters. Its principal characteristic and indispensable instrument are the policeman and the tax-collector, the soldier and the prison. And to these are necessarily added the time-serving priest or teacher, as the case may be, supported and protected by the government, to render the spirit of the people servile and make them docile under the yoke.

Certainly, in addition to this primary business, to this essential department of governmental action other departments have been added in the course of time. We even admit that never, or hardly ever, has a government been able to exist in a country that was at all civilized without adding to its oppressing and exploiting functions others useful and indispensable to social life. But this fact makes it none the less true that government is in its nature a means of exploitation, and that its origin and position doom it to be the defense of a dominant class, thus confirming and increasing the evils of domination.

With all this, the government does not change its nature. If it acts as regulator or guarantor of the rights and duties of each, it perverts the sentiment of justice. It justifies wrong and punishes every act which offends or menaces the privileges of the governors and proprietors. It declares just and *legal,* the most atrocious exploitation of the miserable, which means a slow and continuous material and moral murder, perpetrated by those who have on those who have not. Again, if it administers public services, it always considers the interests of the governors and proprietors, not occupying itself with the interests of the working masses, except insofar as is necessary to make the masses willing to endure their share of taxation. If it instructs, it fetters and curtails the truth, and tends to prepare the minds and hearts of the young to become either implacable tyrants or docile slaves, according to the class to which they belong. In the hands of the government everything becomes a means of exploitation, everything serves as a police measure, useful to hold the people in check. And it must be thus. If the life of mankind consists in strife between man and man, naturally there must be conquerors and conquered, and the government, which is the means of securing to the victors the results of their victory, and perpetuating those results, will certainly never fall to those who have lost, whether the battle be on the grounds of physical or intellectual strength, or in the field of economics. And those who have fought to secure to themselves better conditions than others can have, to win privilege and add dominion to power, and have attained the victory, will certainly not use it to defend the rights of the vanquished, and to place limits to their own power and to that of their friends and partisans.

* * *

In the present condition of society, the vast solidarity, which unites all men, is in a great degree unconscious, since it arises spontaneously from the friction of particular interests, while men occupy themselves little or not at all with general interests. And this is the most evident proof that solidarity is the natural law of human life, which imposes itself, in spite of all obstacles, even those artifically created by society as at present constituted.

On the other hand, the oppressed masses, who were never wholly resigned to oppression and misery, and who today more than ever show themselves ardent for justice, liberty, and well-being, are beginning to understand that they can emancipate themselves only by uniting in solidarity with all the oppressed and exploited over the whole world. And they understand also that the indispensable condition of their emancipation is the possession of the means of production, of the soil, and of the instruments of labor, which involves the abolition of private property. Science and the observation of social phenomena show that this abolition would, in the end, be of immense advantage even to the privileged classes, if only they could bring themselves to renounce the spirit of domination and concur with all their fellows in laboring for the common good.

Now, should the oppressed masses one day refuse to work for their oppressors; should they take possession of the soil and the instruments of labor, and apply them for the use and advantage of all who work; should they no longer submit to the domination, either of brute force or economic privilege; should the spirit of human fellowship and the sentiment of human solidarity, strengthened by common interests, grow among the people and put an end to strife between nations; what ground would then remain for the existence of a government?

When private property is abolished, government — which is its defender — must disappear. Should it survive, it would continually tend to reconstruct, under one form or another, a privileged and oppressing class.

But the abolition of government does not signify the doing away with human association. Far otherwise, for that cooperation which today is enforced, and directed to the advantage of the few, would be free and voluntary, directed to the advantage of all. Therefore it would become more intense and effective.

The social instinct and the sentiment of solidarity would develop to the highest degree; and every individual would do all in his power for the good of others, as much for the satisfaction of his own well-understood interests as for the gratification of his sympathetic sentiments.

By the free association of all, a social organization would arise through the spontaneous grouping of men according to their needs and sympathies, from the low to the high, from the simple to the complex, starting from the more immediate to arrive at the more distant and general interests. This organization would have for its aim the greatest good and fullest liberty of all; it would embrace all humanity in one common brotherhood, and would be modified and improved as circumstances were modified and changed, according to the teachings of experience.

This society of free men, this society of friends would be Anarchy.

We have hitherto considered government as it is, and as it must necessarily be in a society founded upon privilege, upon the exploitation and oppression of man by man, upon antagonism of interests and social strife, in a word, upon private property.

We have seen how this state of strife, far from being a necessary condition of human life, is contrary to the interests of the individual and of the species. We have observed how cooperation, solidarity of interest, is the law of human progress, and we have concluded that, with the abolition of private property and the cessation of all domination of man over man, there would be no reason for government to exist — therefore it should be abolished.

But, it may be objected, if the principle on which social organization is now founded were to be changed, and solidarity substituted for strife, common property for private property, the government also would change its nature. Instead of being the protector and representative of the interests of one class, it would become, if there were no longer any classes, representative of all society. Its mission would be to secure and regulate social cooperation in the interests of all, and to fulfill public services of general utility. It would defend society against possible attempts to reestablish privilege, and prevent or repress all attacks, by whomsoever set on foot, against the life, well-being, or liberty of the individual.

There are in society certain matters too important, requiring too much constant, regular attention, for them to be left to the voluntary management of individuals, without danger of everything getting into disorder.

If, there were no government, who would organize the supply and distribution of provision? Who regulate matters pertaining to public hygiene, the postal, telegraph, and railway services, etc.? Who would direct public instruction? Who undertake those great works of exploration, improvement on a large scale, scientific enterprise, etc., which transform the face of the earth and augment a hundredfold the power of man?

Who would care for the preservation and increase of capital, that it might be transmitted to posterity enriched and improved?

Who would prevent the destruction of the forests, or the irrational exploitation and impoverishment of the soil?

Who would there be to prevent and repress crimes, that is, antisocial acts?

What of those who, disregarding the law of solidarity, would not work? Or of those who might spread infectious disease in a country by refusing to submit to the regulation of hygiene by science? Or what again could be done with those who, whether insane or not, might set fire to the harvest, injure children, or abuse and take advantage of the weak?

To destroy private property and abolish existing government without reconstituting a government that would organize collective life and secure social solidarity, would not be to abolish privilege and bring peace and prosperity upon earth. It would be to destroy every social bond, to leave humanity to fall back into barbarism, to begin again the reign of "each for himself," which would reestablish the triumph, first, of brute force, and, second, of economic privilege.

Such are the objections brought forward by authoritarians, even by socialists, who wish to abolish private property and class government founded upon the system of private property.

We reply:

In the first place, it is not true that with a change of social conditions the nature of the government and its functions would also change. Organs and functions are inseparable terms. Take from an organ its function, and either the organ will die, or the function will reinstate itself. Place an army in a country where there is no reason for or fear of foreign war, and this army will provoke war, or, if it did not succeed in doing that, it will disband. A police force, where there are no crimes to discover, and delinquents to arrest, will provoke or invent crimes, or will cease to exist.

For centuries there existed in France an institution, now included in the adminstration of the forests, for the extermination of the wolves and other noxious beasts. No one will be surprised to learn that, just on account of this institution, wolves still exist in France, and that, in rigorous seasons, they do great damage. The public take little heed of the wolves, because there are the appointed officials, whose duty it is to think about them. And the officials do hunt them, but in an intelligent manner, sparing their caves, and allowing time for reproduction, that they may not run the risk of entirely destroying such an interesting species. The French peasants have indeed little confidence in these official wolf-hunters, and regard them rather as the wolf-preservers. And, of course, what would these officials do if there were no longer any wolves to exterminate?

A government, i.e., a number of persons deputed to make the laws, and entitled to utilize the collective forces of society to make every individual respect these laws, already constitutes a class privileged and separated from the rest of the community. Such a class, like every elected body, will seek instinctively to enlarge its power; to impose its tendencies, and to make its own interests predominate. Placed in a privileged position, the government always finds itself in antagonism to the masses, of whose force it disposes.

In order to understand how society could exist without a government, it is sufficient to turn our attention for a short space to what actually goes on in our present society. We shall see that in reality the most important social functions are fulfilled even nowadays outside the intervention of government. Also that government only interferes to exploit the masses, or defend the privileged, or, lastly, to sanction, most unnecessarily, all that has been done without its aid, often in spite of and in opposition to it. Men work, exchange, study, travel, follow as they choose the current rules of morality, or hygiene; they profit by the progress of science and art, have numberless mutual interests without ever feeling the need of any one to direct them how to conduct themselves in regard to these matters. On the contrary, it is just those things in which there is no governmental interference that prosper best and give rise to the least contention, being unconsciously adapted to the wish of all in the way found most useful and agreeable.

Nor is government more necessary for large undertakings, or for those public services which require the constant cooperation of many people of different conditions and countries. Thousands of these undertakings are even now the work of voluntarily formed associations. And these are, by the acknowledgment of every one, the undertakings which succeed the best. We do not refer to the associations of capitalists, organized by means of exploitation, although even they show capabilities and powers of free association, which may extend until it embraces all the people of all lands, and includes the widest and most varying interests. We speak rather of those associations inspired by the love of humanity, or by the passion for knowledge, or even simply by the desire for amusement and love of applause, as these represent better such groupings as will exist in a society where, private property and internal strife between men being abolished, each will find his interests compatible with the interests of everyone else, and his greatest satisfaction in doing good and pleasing others. Scientific societies and congresses, international life-boat and Red Cross associations, laborers' unions, peace societies, volunteers who hasten to the rescue at times of great public calamity, are all examples, among thousands, of that power of the spirit of association, which always shows itself when a need arises, or an enthusiasm takes hold, and the means do not fail. That voluntary associations do not cover the world, and do not embrace every branch of material and moral activity, is the fault of the obstacles placed in their way by governments, of the antagonisms created by the possession of private property, and of the impotence and degradation to which the monopolizing of wealth on the part of the few reduces the majority of mankind.

The government takes charge, for instance, of the postal and telegraph services. But in what way does it really assist them? When the people are in such a condition as to be able to enjoy and feel the need of such services they will think about organizing them, and the man with the necessary technical knowledge will not require a certificate from a government to enable him to set to work. The more general and urgent the need, the more volunteers will offer to satisfy it. Would the people have the ability necessary to provide and distribute provisions? Never fear, they will not die of hunger, waiting for a government to pass laws on the subject. Wherever a government exists, it must wait until the people have first organized everything, and then come with its laws to sanction and exploit what has already been done. It is evident that private interest is the great motive for all activity. That being so, when the interest of every one becomes the interest of each (and it necessarily will become so as soon as private property is abolished) then all will be active. If they work now in the interest of the few, so much more and so much better will they work to satisfy the interests of all. It is hard to understand how anyone can believe that public services indispensable to social life can be better secured by order of a government than through the workers themselves who by their own choice or by agreement with others carry them out under the immediate control of all those interested.

* * *

There are two methods by which the different parties opposed to Anarchism expect, or say they expect, to bring about the greatest good of all. These are the authoritarian or State Socialist, and the individualist methods. The former entrusts the direction of social life to a few, and would result in the exploitation and oppression of the masses by that few. The second method trusts to the free initiative of individuals, and proclaims, if not the abolition, the reduction of government. However, as it respects private property, and is founded on the principle of each for himself, and therefore on competition, its liberty is only the liberty of the strong, the license of those who have to oppress and exploit the weak who have nothing. Far from producing harmony, it would tend always to augment the distance between the rich and the poor, and end also, through exploitation and domination, in authority. This second method, Individualism, is in theory a kind of Anarchy without cooperation. It is therefore no better than a lie, because liberty is not possible without equality, and true Anarchy cannot exist without solidarity, without cooperation. The criticism which Individualists pass on government is merely the wish to deprive it of certain functions, to hand them over virtually to the capitalist. But it cannot attack those repressive functions which form the essence of government, for without an armed force the proprietary system could not be upheld. Even more, under Individualism, the repressive power of government must always increase, in proportion to the increase, by means of free competition, of want, inequality, and disharmony.

Anarchists present a new method: the free initiative and free agree-ment of all. Thus, after the revolutionary abolition of private property, everyone will have equal power to dispose of social wealth. This method, not admitting the re-establishment of private property, must lead, by means of free association, to the complete triumph of the principles of solidarity.

Thus we see that all the problems put forward to combat the Anarchist idea are on the contrary arguments in favor of Anarchy, because it alone in-dicates the way in which, by experience, those solutions which correspond to the dicta of science, and to the needs and wishes of all, can best be found.

How will children be educated? We do not know. What then? The par-ents, teachers, and all who are interested in the progress of the rising generation, will meet, discuss, agree, and differ, and then divide according to their various opinions, putting into practice the methods which they respectively hold to be best. That method which, when tried, produces the best results will triumph in the end.

And so for all the problems that may arise.

According to what we have said, it is evident that Anarchy, as the Anarchists conceive it, and as it can alone be comprehended, is based on socialism. Furthermore, were it not for that school of socialists who ar-tificially divide the natural unity of the social question, considering only some detached points, and were it not also for the equivocations with which they strive to hinder the social revolution, we might say right away that Anarchy is synonymous with socialism, for both signify the abolition of ex-ploitation and of the domination of man over man, whether maintained by the force of arms or by the monopolization of the means of life.

Anarchy, like socialism, has for its basis and point of departure *equality of conditions.* Its aim is *solidarity,* and its method *liberty.* It is not perfect, nor is it the absolute ideal, which, like the horizon, always recedes as we ad-vance toward it. But it is the open road to all progress and to all improve-ment made in the interest of all humanity.

With the abolition of this negative power constituting a government, society will become what it can be with the given forces and capabilities of the moment. If there are educationalists desirous of spreading education, they will organize the schools, and will be constrained to emphasize the use and enjoyment to be derived from education. And if there are no such men, or only a few of them, a government cannot create them. All it can do, as in fact it does nowadays, is to take these few away from practical, fruitful work in the sphere of education, and put them to direct from above what has to be imposed by the help of a police system. So they make out of intelligent and impassionate teachers mere politicians, who become useless parasites, entirely absorbed in imposing their own hobbies, and in maintaining themselves in power.

If there are doctors and teachers of hygiene, they will organize themselves for the service of health. And if there are none, a government cannot create them; all that it can do is to discredit them in the eyes of the people, who are inclined to entertain suspicions, sometimes only too well-founded, with regard to everything which is imposed upon them.

If there are engineers and mechanics, they will organize the railways, etc.; and if there are none, a government cannot create them.

The revolution, by abolishing government and private property, will not create energy which does not exist, but it will leave a free field for the exercise of all available energy, and of all existent capacity. While it will destroy every class interested in keeping the masses degraded, it will act in such a way that everyone will be free to work and make his influence felt, in proportion to his own capacity, and in conformity with his sentiments and interests. And it is only thus that the elevation of the masses is possible, for only with liberty can one learn to be free, as it is only by working that one can learn to work. A government, even had it no other disadvantages, must always have that of habituating the governed to subjection, and must also tend to become more oppressive and necessary, in proportion as its subjects are more obedient and docile.

But suppose government were the direction of affairs by the best people. Who are the best? And how shall we recognize their superiority? The majority are generally attached to old prejudices, and have ideas and instincts already outgrown by the more favored minority. But of the various minorities, who all believe themselves in the right, as no doubt many of them are in part, which shall be chosen to rule? And by whom? And by what criterion, seeing that the future alone can prove which party among them is the most superior? If you choose a hundred partisans of dictatorship, you will discover that each one of the hundred believes himself capable, if not of being sole director, at least of assisting very materially in the dictatorial government. The dictators would be those who, by one means or another, succeeded in imposing themselves on society. And, in course of time, all their energy would inevitably be employed in defending themselves against the attacks of their adversaries, totally oblivious of their desire, if every they had had it, to be merely an educative power.

Should government be, on the other hand, elected by universal suffrage, and so be the emanation, more or less sincere, of the wish of the majority? But if you consider these worthy electors as incapable of providing for their own interests, how can they ever be capable of themselves choosing directors to guide them wisely? How solve this problem of social alchemy: to elect a government of geniuses by the votes of a mass of fools? And what will be the lot of the minority, who are the most intelligent, most active, and most advanced in society?

To solve the social problem to the advantage of all, there is only one way. To expel the government by revolutionary means, to expropriate the holders of social wealth, putting everything at the disposal of all, and to leave all existing force, capacity and goodwill among men free to provide for the needs of all.

We fight for Anarchy and for socialism because we believe that Anarchy and socialism ought to be brought into operation as soon as possible. This means that the revolution must drive away the government, abolish private property, and entrust all public service, which will then embrace all social life, to the spontaneous, free, unofficial, and unauthorized operation of all those interested and of all willing volunteers.

11 Visions of a New Society

Prophets and visionaries help us to imagine utopias, possible future societies. By picturing what the world could be like, these utopias provide inspiration and direction for social-change movements. Such visions can be found in literary as well as in political writings.[1] One vital issue dealt with in such utopias concerns the organization of work, of production and distribution, because the way these are dealt with influences many other aspects of the society. A common theme in many utopias is the abolition of class privileges and distinctions, and the attainment of freedom for all through the abolition of toil and wage labor. Such was the vision that inspired Karl Marx, who dreamed of a communist society that would transcend the division of labor and in which each person would work according to his or her ability and receive what was needed.

The two visions represented in this chapter are (1) a model of a society in which production and consumption are integrated with regional economies; and (2) a dual-economy model with a subsistence sector where mass produced basic necessities are distributed free to all and a luxury sector where craftsmen, cooperatives, and entrepreneurs produce a wide variety of goods and services for sale or trade.

Starting from an ecological viewpoint, Kirkpatrick Sale depicts a model of bioregional self-sufficiency in which artificial political boundaries are replaced by "natural" ones, marking self-sustaining, human-scale regions. The economies of these regions would be governed by the principles of conservation of natural resources and the maintenance of a stable, steady-state economic balance. Regions might trade with each other without becoming dependent on such trade, however. Self sufficient bioregions

303

would sustain diverse and complex economic activities, and their inhabitants would be able to enjoy a more satisfying life than that provided by the extremely specialized division of labor.

One of the two paradigms offered by Paul and Percival Goodman is quite similar to that of Sale, namely, the vision of an economy where production and consumption are integrated within small, relatively self-sufficient economic areas. In such an economy, residences would be closer to places of work; in fact, considerable production would take place in home workshops. There would be greater integration of farm and factory. There would be far less emphasis on punctuality. Workers would have a greater say than they do at present in all aspects of production, and human beings would be considered as ends in themselves so that the emphasis would be shifted from efficiency of production to the happiness and well-being of the producers.

The other paradigm of the Goodmans is a dual economy. The enormous productive capacity of modern technology would be used for the mass production of basic necessities within a state-run subsistence sector. There would be universal conscription of all to work a few years for their subsistence. In exchange, all members of the society would be entitled to free distribution of basic necessities for the rest of their lives. A separate luxury sector of the economy would encompass all other economic activities. In this sector, people would work for wages as they do now, to buy luxury goods or services. There would be absolutely no compulsion for people to work after they had completed their service to society in the subsistence sector. Men and women would be free to engage in craft activities, to join together in cooperatives, or to work for others. This is an attractive vision, though it should be possible to organize labor needed for the subsistence sector without resorting to conscription. Many persons would volunteer for such work, for the same reasons that people have volunteered for the Peace Corps. If there were not enough volunteers, a tax could be imposed on the luxury sector to provide attractive wages for subsistence workers.

A related issue concerns the possibility of transforming hierarchical social relations in the workplace into participatory-democratic ones, substituting cooperative decision making for top-down orders. This topic is dealt with in Chapter 12.

Notes

1. See, for example, William Morris, *News From Nowhere;* Aldous Huxley, *Island;* Robert Heinlein, *Stranger in a Strange Land;* and the novels of Ursula LeGuin.

A Vision of Bioregional Self-Sufficiency

Kirkpatrick Sale

The human-scale vision is based on the idea of *bioregional self-sufficiency*—a North America, a world, made up of autonomous and empowered regions whose boundaries and activities are determined, not arbitrarily by governments, but organically by nature. *Bioregional self-sufficiency:* in other words, the break-up of the American system—to cure the breakdown of the American system.

Let me, briefly, examine the two parts of that phrase, and suggest in some very preliminary ways what they might entail.

A bioregional economy takes its guiding principles from ecodynamics and its form from nature. The first law of ecodynamics is that conservation, preservation, sustenance is the central goal of the natural world, hence its resistance to large-scale structural change (such as the industrial world has been trying to foist upon it for a century). The second law is that, far from being entropic—as is fashionable for many of the ignorant to claim—nature is inherently stable and works always toward what ecologists call a *climax,* that is to say, a balanced, communal, integrative state of maturity.

Now you will note that these two natural laws do not sit well with the imperatives of capitalism—but it is not hard to imagine an economy based upon them, as many economists from John Stuart Mill on down have done. It would be one in which one sought to maintain rather than exploit the natural world, to encourage rather than resist the process of nature, to try to understand and accommodate to the character of the environment rather than to run blindly and stupidly up against it.

An environmentally conscious bioregional economy would be what is now fashionable to call a steady-state economy—in other words, like nature, one which would seek a climax, a balance, a stability, not seeking growth and change and "progress"; one which would minimize resource use, emphasize conservation and recycling, avoid pollution and waste; one which would adapt its systems to the natural *givens*—energy based on wind,

FROM *Green Revolution*, Summer 1983, pp. 3–7. Reprinted by permission of the author.

for example, where nature called for that, or wood where that was appropriate; one which, like nature, would seek to bring each individual, each community, to its healthiest and richest—knowing that the maximum health of the system derives from the maximum health of each part.

As to the form, the setting of such an economy, that, too, is determined by nature. A bioregion is part of the earth's surface where there is a more or less distinct geographical, biological, horticultural, and climatic identity, from which the human inhabitants have developed a more or less distinct economic, social, and cultural identity. A watershed, or river basin, is perhaps the most obvious type of bioregion, though there can be many others—a valley, say, or a desert or a plateau. The borders between them are usually not rigid—and that is another rather lovely feature of the bioregion as a political concept—but the regions themselves are not hard to identify, when once we pay attention to nature's patterns rather than those of some government.

I have spent considerable time in recent months trying to determine just what the map of North America might look like if based on a bioregional concept, weighing such things as geological substrata, soil patterns, rainfall contours, biotic spreads, and a great deal more. And the remarkable thing is that not only do the bioregions begin to take a rough shape, but a surprising number of them conform to the pattern of Native American (Indian) settlements as near as we know it to have been. Well, maybe that is not so surprising because the Indians understood the concept of the bioregion, almost viscerally as it were, long before we came and imposed our own concepts upon them; like most preliterate people, they specialized in understanding what nature was like, what she had to teach, what she could tolerate, what she demanded, and so it was only natural that they would settle themselves—and in general with great success—in bioregional patterns.

The bioregions, then, are nature's givens, the ecological truths of our earth. It would behoove us to pay attention to them, and soon.

As to how we pay attention, that takes us to the second part of my phrase, to "self-sufficiency." A bioregion with a self-sufficient economy would find ways of providing for all its essentials within that region, within what nature has provided—not a difficult task at all, when you come down to it, and again it was essentially how the Indians lived. There is not a single bioregion in this country that would not, if it looked to all its resources, be able to provide its own abundant food, its own energy, its own shelter and clothing, its own health and medical care, its own arts and manufactures and industries. Most parts of this country are singularly fitted to depend on their own natural endowments—and where this or that material or resource may be missing, it is not long before human ingenuity is able to contrive a substitute—as, for example, this country learned to get rubber from the guayule plant during World War II when rubber supplies from abroad were threatened. If necessity is the mother of invention, I've long insisted, then self-sufficiency is the grandmother.

Does it make sense, I ask you, for New York City to import 29,000 tons of broccoli a year from California when it could just as easily get that amount of broccoli from its own bioregion provided it were developed sensibly? Does it make sense for my Manhattan to be totally dependent on the Sacramento and San Joaquin valleys for almost all its vegetables and much of its fruit? Among the consequences: It means higher prices, obviously, for transportation, storage, and distribution; it means the expenditure of immense amounts of fossil fuels—all the stuff comes by truck—and a heavy toll on the already crumbling highways; it means increased pollution right straight across the country, but particularly in New York, and increased congestion too; it means a decline in nutritional quality, inevitably, and often the addition of chemicals put in just so that the stuff can travel so far so long; it means that farmers in New York and New Jersey are squeezed out of business, their lands sold and turned into shopping malls and condominiums, and more people moving into the already crowded metropolitan areas, with the concomitant impoverishment of vast rural areas; and in California it means ripping up the countryside for the demands of agribusiness, the death of the family farmer, the depletion of topsoil and water resources, the overuse of pesticides and fertilizers, with a great risk to both grower and consumer, and the creation of fragile monocultures and risk of pest and disease attack. Does that—by any measure—make sense?

There may be certain difficulties with this idea of self-sufficiency—it does usually demand some extra work (though obviously that is just what is needed in a land of such high unemployment); it may require some change in eating habits (though only in the direction of fresher, more nutritional, more healthful foods); it does mean giving up certain imports (though almost any that are truly valuable can be produced locally or substituted for in one way or another). Some difficulties perhaps, but the fact is that haphazard trade, and the kind of *dependent* trade that we have developed—New York is dependent on California fruit, New England is dependent on southern natural gas, the United States is dependent on foreign oil (and uranium, manganese, cobalt, chromium, copper—and almost

everything else except wheat) — has many more difficulties. There is no way
to escape from the *vulnerability* of dependence, as we discovered during the
oil crisis; nor from the enslavement of one part of the earth in service to
another, as the cocoa growers of Ghana or the rubber workers in Malaysia
could testify; nor from the employment of some significant part of the local
economy, not for any useful goods or services but solely to create the
money to pay for imports.

A self-sufficient bioregion is, in short, healthier than a dependent one.
It is more stable, it has more control over its economy, it is not at the mercy
of boom-and-bust cycles and distant political crises. It is not in economic
vassalage to distant and uncontrollable political forces. It is able to plan, to
allocate its resources, to develop what it wants to develop at the safest pace,
in the most ecologically sound manner. It does not ship its money off to distant and uncontrollable transnational corporations. And it is of necessity a
more cohesive, more self-regarding, self-concerned region, with a sense of
place, of comradeship, of community, with the kind of character that
comes from stability, pride, competence, control, and independence.

Lastly — and I find this of special interest — that self-sufficient region has a
greater *diversity* than the dependent one, largely because it is thrown on its own
resources; and just as the self-reliant individual had best be able to cook and
sew and harvest and chop wood and build and repair and play a little music at
night, so the self-sufficient region would have to develop in highly diverse
ways; it would have to complexify rather than simplify. The dangers of the
world around us today are those of simplicity, of monolithicity, of monopoly,
of monotony, of monochromality: whole nations given over to a single crop,
cities to a single industry, farms to a single culture, factories to a single product,
people to a single job, jobs to a single motion, motions to a single purpose.
Diversity is the rule of human life, not simplicity; the human animal has succeeded precisely because it has been able to diversify, not specialize: to climb
and swim, hunt *and* nurture, work alone *and* in packs. The same is true of
human organizations: they are healthy and they survive when they are diverse
and differentiated, capable of many responses; they become brittle and
unadaptable and prey to any changing conditions when they are uniform and
specialized. It is when an individual is able to take on many jobs, learn many
skills, live many roles, that growth and fullness of character inhabit the soul; it
is when a region complexifies and mixes, when it develops the multiplicity of
ways of caring for itself that it becomes textured and enriched.

What I am suggesting, then, what I leave with you as a *vision* of a sen-
sible economic alternative, is the human-scale economy built around the

principles of bioregionalism and self-sufficiency, both of which go together, are in fact dependent on one another. Now I do not want to claim that this idea, which may still be somewhat new to you, is both divine and eternal, but I would like to share with you a story about the great English biologist J. B. S. Haldane.

It seems that once, at the end of his long and distinguished career, Haldane was invited to a luncheon of renowned theologians at Cambridge, at the end of which he was asked, on the basis of his immense knowledge about the nature of the universe, what he would say was the chief characteristic of the Supreme Being who created it all. The old man thought for a moment, bent forward, and replied: "An inordinate fondness for beetles."

That's right, beetles. And, upon reflection, that seems very nearly to be the case. For, of the million or so animal species that have been identified, some 75 percent are insects, of which about 60 percent are . . . beetles.

Now I know very little about God and I will not presume to guarantee what His plan really is. But I do know a little about nature, and I think it is safe to say that in the beetle we behold two essential truths about the natural world. The first is smallness, for almost all beetles are quite small, most not as big as a finger joint, and small species outnumber large species by about 10 to 1. The second is diversity, for it is a fact that there are something like 400,000 different kinds of beetles, more different kinds than of any other animal species by far.

And so I would suggest that nature has a lesson for us, and it is simple: that she looks with special favor upon a world of smallness and diversity. A world, in other words, of bioregional self-sufficiency.

Community Paradigms

Paul and Percival Goodman

The Elimination of the Difference between Production and Consumption

Men like to make things, to handle the materials to see them take shape and come out as desired, and they are proud of the products. And men like

CONDENSED FROM *Communitas: Ways of Livelihood and Means of Life,* by Paul and Percival Goodman. Copyright 1947, © 1960 by Paul and Percival Goodman, pp. 153–160; 188–194; 199-203. Reprinted by permission of Random House, Inc.

to work and be useful, for work has a rhythm and springs from spontaneous feelings just like play, and to be useful makes people feel right. Productive work is a kind of creation, it is an extension of human personality into nature. But it is also true that the private or state capitalist relations of production, and machine industry as it now exists under whatever system, have so far destroyed the instinctive pleasures of work that economic work is what all ordinary men dislike. (Yet unemployment is dreaded, and people who don't like their work don't know what to do with their leisure.) In capitalist or state-socialist economies, efficiency is measured by profits and expansion rather than by handling the means. Mass production, analyzing the acts of labor into small steps and distributing the products far from home, destroys the sense of creating anything. Rhythm, neatness, style belong to the machine rather than to the man.

The division of economy into production and consumption as two opposite poles means that we are far from the conditions in which work could be a way of life. A way of life requires merging the means in the end, and work would have to be thought of as a continuous process of satisfying activity, satisfying in itself and satisfying in its useful end. Such considerations have led many moralist-economists to want to turn back the clock to conditions of handicraft in a limited society, where the relations of guilds and small markets allow the master craftsmen a say and a hand in every phase of production, distribution, and consumption. Can we achieve the same values with modern technology, a national economy, and a democratic society? With this aim, let us reanalyze efficiency and machine production.

Characteristic of American offices and factories is the severe discipline with regard to punctuality. (In some states the law requires time clocks, to protect labor and calculate the insurance.) Now no doubt in many cases where workers cooperate in teams, where business is timed by the mails, where machines use a temporary source of power, being on time and on the same time as everybody else is essential to efficiency. But by and large it would make little difference at what hour each man's work began and ended, so long as the job itself was done. Often the work could be done at home or on the premises indifferently, or part here part there. Yet this laxity is never allowed, except in the typical instances of hack-writing or commercial art—typical because these workers have an uneasy relation to the economy in any case. (There is a lovely story of how William Faulkner asked M-G-M if he could work at home, and when they said, "Of course," he went back to Oxford, Mississippi.)

Punctuality is demanded not primarily for efficiency but for the discipline itself. Discipline is necessary because the work is onerous; perhaps it makes the idea of working even more onerous, but it makes the work itself much more tolerable, for it is a structure, a decision. Discipline establishes the work in an impersonal secondary environment where, once one has gotten out of bed early in the morning, the rest easily follows. Regulation of time, separation from the personal environment: these are signs that work is not a way of life; they are the methods by which, for better or worse, work that cannot be energized directly by personal concern can get done, unconfused by personal concern.

In the Garden City plans, they "quarantined the technology" from the homes; more generally, we quarantine the work from the homes. But it is even truer to say that we quarantine the homes from the work. For instance, it is calamitous for a man's wife or children to visit him at work; this privilege is reserved for the highest bosses.

Reanalyzing Production

In planning a region of satisfying industrial work, we therefore take account of four main principles:

1. A closer relation of the personal and productive environments, making punctuality reasonable instead of disciplinary, and introducing phases of home and small-shop production; and vice versa, finding appropriate technical uses for personal relations that have come to be considered unproductive.
2. A role for all workers in all stages of the production of the product; for experienced workers a voice and hand in the design of the product and the design and operation of the machines; and for all a political voice on the basis of what they know best; their specific industry, in the natural economy.
3. A schedule of work designed on psychological and moral as well as technical grounds, to give the most well-rounded employment to each person, in a diversified environment. Even in technology and economics, the men are ends as well as means.
4. Relatively small units with relative self-sufficiency, so that each community can enter into a larger whole with solidarity and independence of viewpoint.

These principles are mutually interdependent.

1. To undo the present separation of work and home environments, we can proceed both ways: (*a*) Return certain parts of production to homeshops or near home; and (*b*) introduce domestic work and certain productive family-relations, which are now not considered part of the economy at all, into the style and relations of the larger economy.

   a. Think of the present proliferation of machine-tools. It could once be said that the sewing machine was the only widely distributed productive machine; but now, especially because of the last war, the idea of thousands of small machine shops, powered by electricity, has become familiar; and small power-tools are a best-selling commodity. In general, the change from coal and steam to electricity and oil has relaxed one of the greatest causes for concentration of machinery around a single driving-shaft.

   b. Borsodi, going back to the economics of Aristotle, has proved, often with hilarious realism, that home production, such as cooking, cleaning, mending, and entertaining has a formidable economic, though not cash, value. The problem is to lighten and enrich home production by the technical means and some of the expert attitudes of public production, but without destroying its individuality.

   But the chief part of finding a satisfactory productive life in homes and families consists in the analysis of personal relations and conditions: e.g., the productive; cooperation of man and wife as it exists on farms, or the productive capabilities of children and old folk, now economically excluded. This involves sentimental and moral problems of extreme depth and delicacy that could only be solved by the experiments of integrated communities.

2. A chief cause of the absurdity of industrial work is that each machine worker is acquainted with only a few processes, not the whole order of production. And the thousands of products are distributed he knows not how or

where. Efficiency is organized from above by expert managers who first analyze production into its simple processes, then synthesize these into combinations built into the machines, then arrange the logistics of supplies, etc., and then assign the jobs.

As against this efficiency organized from above, we must try to give this function to the workers. This is feasible only if the workers have a total grasp of all the operations. There must be a school of industry, academic and not immediately productive, connected with the factory. Now let us distinguish apprentices and graduates. To the apprentices, along with their schooling, is assigned the more monotonous work; to the graduates, the executive and coordinating work, the fine work, the finishing touches. The masterpiece that graduates an apprentice is a new invention, method, or other practical contribution advancing the industry. The masters are teachers, and as part of their job hold free discussions looking to basic changes.

Such a setup detracts greatly from the schedule of continuous production; but it is a question whether it would not prove more efficient in the long run to have the men working for themselves and having a say in the distribution. By this we do not mean merely economic democracy or socialist ownership. These are necessary checks but are not the political meaning of industrialism as such. What is needed is the organization of economic democracy on the basis of the productive units, where each unit, relying on its own expertness and the bargaining power of what it has to offer, cooperates with the whole of society. This is syndicalism, simply an industrial town meeting. To guarantee the independent power of each productive unit, it must have a relative regional self-sufficiency; this is the union of farm and factory.

3. Machine work in its present form is often stultifying, not a "way of life." The remedy is to assign work on psychological and moral as well as technical and economic grounds. The object is to provide a well-rounded employment. Work can be divided as team work and individual work, or physical work and intellectual work. And industries can be combined

in a neighborhood to give the right variety. For instance, cast glass, blown glass, and optical instruments; or more generally, industry and agriculture, and factory and domestic work. Probably most important, but difficult to conjure with, is the division in terms of faculties and powers, routine and initiation, obeying and commanding.

The problem is to envisage a well-rounded schedule of jobs for each man, and to arrange the buildings and the farms so that the schedule is feasible.

4. The integration of factory and farm brings us to the idea of regionalism and regional relative autonomy. These are the following main parts:

   a. Diversified farming as the basis of self-subsistence and, therefore, small urban centers (200,000).

   b. A number of mutually dependent industrial centers, so that an important part of the national economy is firmly controlled. (The thought is always to have freedom secured by real power.)

   c. These industries developed around regional resources of field, mine, and power.

Diversified farmers can be independent, and small farms have therefore always been a basis of social stability, though not necessarily of peasant conservatism. On the other hand, for the machines now desirable, the farmer needs cash and links himself with the larger economy of the town.

The political problem of the industrial worker is the reverse, since every industry is completely dependent on the national economy, for both materials and distribution. But by regional interdependence of industries and the close integration of factory and farm work — factory workers taking over in the fields at peak seasons, farmers doing factory work in the winter; town people, especially children, living in the country; farmers domestically making small parts for the factories — the industrial region as a whole can secure for itself independent bargaining power in the national whole.

* * *

Planned Security with Mininum Regulation: The Dual Economy

Our economy is gigantic by the quantity and number of kinds of goods and services, but as such it is not out of human scale, for to the immense civilized population the immense quantity of goods is appropriate. The increase of useless wealth of individuals, in the form of gadgets sold by advertising, may not add to human virtue, but then it adds to folly, which is equally human. The inequitable distribution of wealth, especially considered internationally, is a subject of resentment, and this is an intensely human proposition.

But we have grown out of human scale in the following way: Starting from the human goods of subsistence and luxury, the increment of profit was reinvested in capital goods in order to earn more profits, to win for the enterprisers more luxury and power; this is still human motivation. But in recent decades the result has been that the center of economic concern has gradually shifted from either providing goods for the consumer or gaining wealth for the enterpriser, to keeping the capital machines at work and running at full capacity; for the social arrangements have become so complicated that, unless the machines are running at nearly full capacity, all wealth and subsistence are jeopardized, investment is withdrawn, men are unemployed. That is, when the system depends on all the machines running, unless *every* kind of goods is produced and sold, it is also impossible to produce bread. Then an economy is out of human scale.

Social Insurance Versus the Direct Method

But elementary subsistence and security cannot be neglected by any social order; they are political needs, prior to economic needs. So the governments of the most highly capitalized states intervene to assure elementary security which is not longer the first business of the economy. And the tack they take is the following: to guarantee social security by subsidizing the full productivity of the economy.

Security is provided by insurance paid in the money that comes from the operation of the whole economy. The amazing indirectness of this procedure is brilliantly exposed by the discovery of a new human "right" – as if the rights of man could be so easily amended. This is the "right to employment," failing which one gets the insurance. Full employment is the device by which we flourish; and so the old curse of Adam, that he must work in order to live, now becomes a goal to be struggled for, just because we have the means to produce a surplus, cause of all our woes. This is certainly out of human scale, yet the statesmen of America and England talk this way with absolute conviction; and anyone who spoke otherwise would be voted out of office.

The immediate result of such a solution, of insurance, social credit, or any other kind of give-away money, is to tighten even closer the economic trap. Whatever freedom used to come from free enterprise and free market — and they are freedoms which were indeed fought for with blood — is now trapped in regulation and taxes. The union of government and economy becomes more and more total; we are in the full tide toward statism. This is not a question of anybody's bad intentions, but follows from the connection of the basic political need of subsistence with the totality of an industrial economy.

So much for the indirect solution.

The direct solution, of course, would be to divide the economy and provide the subsistence directly, letting the rest complicate and fluctuate as it will. Let whatever is essential for life and security be considered by itself, and since this is a political need in an elementary sense, let political means be used to guarantee it. But the rest of the economy, providing wealth, power, luxury, emulation, convenience, interest and variety, has to do with varying human wishes and satisfactions, and there is no reason for government to intervene in it in any way. The divided economy has, therefore, the twofold advantage that it directly provides the essential thing that is in jeopardy, without having to underwrite something else; and it restricts the intervention of government to this limited sphere.

Up to, say 60 years ago, more than half of the productive capacity of our economy was devoted to subsistence; subsistence could be regarded as the chief end of the economy; and whatever their own motives, most enterprisers served the subsistence market. Now, however, in the United States less than a tenth of the economy is concerned with subsistence goods. (Probably nearer a fifteenth; the exact figure would depend on what one considers an adequate minimum.) Except for the biological and political factors involved, the economic machinery could roll almost as usual though everybody were dead of starvation, exposure, and disease. When the situation is viewed in this way, one of the causes is at once clear why prosperity and surplus lead precisely to insecurity: namely, that too few people are busy about subsistence, and as we know from recent farming history, those who are busy about it try to get out of it; there's no real money in meat and potatoes.

But once the economy would be divided as we are suggesting, the very techniques of industry that, when applied incidentally to subsistence, lead to insecurity, would, applied directly to subsistence, produce it with an even smaller fraction of the social labor than at present.

Probably there are various political means by which this small fraction of production could be effectuated, and we will soon develop an obvious one, direct state production of subsistence by universally conscripted labor, run as a state monopoly like the post office or the army, but paying not money but its own scrip, exchangeable only for subsistence goods made by this same enterprise.

(This is a vast undertaking. It would be apparently simpler to effect approximately the same end by using private semi-monopolistic concessionaires in the state nonprofit subsistence-business. But if indeed the production cost is absolutely minimum and the types absolutely standard and non-competitive, how could a private firm profit? Further, it is intolerable, and unconstitutional, to *have* to work for a private concessionaire. Therefore we prefer the state production — taking over relevant private plant and building its own plant — because of its purity of method. It takes subsistence *out of the economy.* Subsistence is not something to profit by, to invest in, to buy or sell. On the part of the consumer, it is not something to choose or reject or contract for or exchange his labor for, but simply to work for.)

On whatever method — and there are no doubt possibilities we have not thought of — there is one principle: to assure subsistence by specific production of subsistence goods and services rather than by insurance taxed from the general economy. This involves a system of double money: the "money" of the subsistence production and consumption and the money of the general market. The subsistence-certificates are not money at all, for by definition a man's subsistence leaves nothing to exchange; this "money" is like wartime ration stamps, which are likewise not legally negotiable. A man's right to life is not subject to trade.

A major moral advantage of this proposal is that every person can know that the work he does for a living is unquestionably useful and necessary, and unexploited. It is life itself for himself and everybody else. In our times of so much frivolous production and synthetic demand, and the accompanying cynicism of the producers, the importance of such a moral cannot be overestimated.

Another consequence: To everyone, but especially to the small wage earner, the separation of his subsistence, employing a small fraction of his labor time, from the demands and values of the general economy employing most of his labor time, would give a new security, a breath of freedom, and the possibility of choice. He is independent. He has worked directly for what he absolutely needs; he does not feel the pressure of being a drain on society; he does not fear that his insurance payments will cease. By the same token, people in general, including the small enterpriser, would be more fearless, for their risks are less fatal. But indeed, these things imply a change of social attitude so profound that we must think deeply about both the dangers and the opportunities.

The retrenchment of government from economic interference in the general part, again, might go very far, relaxing kinds of regulation that are now indispensable — protection of women and children, protection of unions, and so forth. For where the prospective wage earner has a subsistence independently earned, the conditions under which he agrees to work can be allowed to depend on his own education rather than on the government's coercion of the employer.

Let us sum up by contrasting the actual plans offered by present-day governments with the plan here suggested. They propose:

Security of subsistence

A tax on the general economy

Necessity to maintain the economy at full production to pay the tax: therefore, governmental planning, pump-priming, subsidies, and made work; a still further tax, and possibly a falling rate of profit

Insistence on the unemployed worker's accepting the third or fourth job available, in order to prevent a continuing drain on the insurance fund

Protection of the workers thus coerced by regulating the conditions of industry and investment

Against this we propose:

Security of subsistence

Loss to the industrialist and merchant of the subsistence market and a small fraction of the social labor

Coercion of a small fraction of the social labor to produce the subsistence goods and services

Economic freedom in all other respects

Now financially, the choice between these two plans would depend on the comparison between the insurance and subsidies tax and the loss of labor time and market. (Unfortunately, for reasons explained below, this comparison is hard to make accurately — at least by us.) Socially and morally, however, there seems to be no comparison at all: our way is direct, simple, liberating, and allows people a quiet interim to make up their minds about things.

* * *

The Standard of Minimum Subsistence

What is the minimum standard on which a person will feel himself secure and free, not struggling to get more in the private economy, unless he chooses? The problem is subtle and difficult, for although as a medical problem it has a definite solution, as a psychological and moral problem it depends on emulation, and who is emulated, and these things themselves are subject to alteration good or bad. What is minimum for even a poor Southern sharecropper might be spendthrifty to an indio of Yucatan (who, however, has other satisfactions).

We are speaking always of a going surplus technology. This technology which can provide all manner of things for everybody can also, in a different way, produce a few things of a very few kinds accompanied by a minimum regulation of time, living arrangements, and habits of life. How seriously are people willing to dispense with many things in order to have the freedom which they also think they want?

When combined with freedom, a minimum standard would be far less than what is estimated minimum in our present society. Let us give a single example. In estimating minimum standards of decency and safety, Stuart Chase finds it indispensable for every home to have a radio, because in an integrated society — especially during a total war — a person must have instant communications (and how desirable to have it one way!) But if the very point of our minimum standard is to free people from "integration," a radio is a convenience which a person might think twice about.

Other examples of reducing the "necessary" minimum could be found by considering how much of decency of appearance and how many contacts are required solely by the fact that we live in a society competitive through and through.

On the other hand, when combined with freedom, our minimum is far higher than exists in a scarcity economy, for instance China, where a person subsists in time-bound service to field or commune (and that standard too, since inevitable, is socially acceptable). But if the very point of our minimum is to free people for a selective choice of how they will regulate their time, mobility and independence of location are indispensable.

The minimum is based on a physiological standard, heightened by the addition of whatever is necessary to give a person a true possible freedom of social choice, and not violating our usual mores.

If freedom is the aim, everything beyond the minimum must be rigorously excluded, even if it should be extremely cheap to provide; for it is more important to limit political intervention than to raise the standard of living.

Then, the minimum economy must produce and distribute:

1. Food sufficient in quantity and kind for health, palatable but without variety
2. Uniform clothing adequate for all seasons
3. Shelter on an individual, family, and group basis, with adequate conveniences for different environments
4. Medical service
5. Transportation

but *not* primary education, which is a public good taxed from the general economy.

Of these, food, clothing, and shelter are produced by absolute mass production in enormous quantities, without variation of style. Medicine and transportation are better provided by some arrangement between the subsistence and general economies.

The Cost of Subsistence

The extent and cost of the proposed subsistence system, measured in current money, is very hard to determine — and therefore it is hard to name, except by guesswork, the number of years of labor service that are bartered away for economic freedom.

In the first place, although the number of laborers is fixed — for even those who would buy off must furnish a laborer as a substitute — the amount of goods to be produced is fluctuating. For, obviously, though all are entitled to the minimal goods, many, and perhaps most, of the people who are used to better and can afford better, will not take them. There is no advantage in taking and wasting, for the less that needs to be produced, the less the exaction of universal service. Different kinds of goods will differ in demand: fewer will use the minimal housing and clothing; most perhaps can use some of the minimum food; very many will use the transportation and medical service. After a sufficient reserve is built up, production is geared to the prospective use of the next year. But further, this demand will fluctuate with the fluctuation of the general economy, though less sharply: in times of general economic crisis, the demand for subsistence goods increases; in times of prosperity, it diminishes. (The fluctuation is less sharp because of the ratio of minimum goods to substitutes of a higher standard, because of the ratio of the number of unemployed to the universal labor service, and because the reserve functions as an ever-normal granary.)

But secondly and most importantly, the price of goods under such a system of absolute mass production is impossible to estimate. It would be unbelievably cheap. . . .

12 | Economic Alternatives

Hierarchically structured bureaucracies, based on job specialization and designed to facilitate control by a few managers at the top, are the major form of organization in the contemporary industrialized world. There are, however, democratic alternatives based on workers' control. The alternatives include small-scale collectives of from 2 to 12 members where major decisions are made by the entire group deliberating together, as well as larger, democratically structured organizations. A major form of the latter is the workers' cooperative in which democratically chosen committees make policy decisions and hire and fire managers, and in which the membership as a whole retains final authority and veto power on the basis of one person, one vote. Such organizations seem to function best when they are of *medium* size, up to 500 members. With advances in microcomputer technology, work organizations of such size are capable of providing most socially necessary goods and services in a cost-efficient manner.

An example of a small collective is the Little People's Center described by Scott Brown, where women and men run a day-care center for about 40 preschool children. The center is coordinated by two staff members who serve as co-directors. These positions rotate among the staff and are held for about 18 months. All staff members get the same hourly wage. An elected board of directors, consisting of staff, parents, and community members, is the final authority in disputes, but in practice the board acts in an advisory capacity and concentrates on fund raising. Most day-to-day decisions are made by meetings of the entire staff, in a consensual process. There are today thousands of organizations in the United States like the Little People's Center, though few have been able to match its longevity of 15 years. These democratically organized collectives include food cooperatives, alternative schools, restaurants, magazines, radio stations, construction crews, and printing shops. Organizations with both worker members and consumer or client members, such as food co-ops and schools often have a policy-setting board with elected representatives of *both* groups; some, like the Little People's Center, have community representatives as well.

There are also medium-size workers' cooperatives in this country, such as the Atlas Chain Company described by Robert Pankin and the O&O supermarkets discussed by Frank Lindenfeld. Although not as numerous as the more ubiquitous collectives, these co-ops show that workplace democracy is feasible in many industries. There are tree-planting cooperatives and cooperatively owned and managed plywood factories, as well as democratically organized insurance companies, supermarkets, and manufacturing plants.[1] Such organizations have a managerial staff that coordinates production and supervises the work, but there are democratic checks and balances on managerial power; such co-ops maximize the possibility of workers' control. In most cases, working conditions are better and worker members are more satisfied in co-operative organizations than in comparable ones run by capitalist or state-appointed managers. A number of workers' cooperatives, including the first two O&O super-markets and the Atlas Chain Company, were developed in reaction to plant closings that treatened to eliminate jobs. (Shutdowns are often attempts by conglomerate giants to divest themselves of acquired subsidiaries that do not provide them with a high enough rate of profit.) Such enterprises can be viable when taken over by workers interested *primarily* in preserving their jobs and only secondarily in sharing profits. Technical assistance organizations can play a large part in ensuring the success of such cooperatives by providing them with feasibility studies, cooperative education, and access to loans.

Ana Gutierrez-Johnson describes a highly developed network of coop-eratives near Mondragon, Spain, which provides employment for over 20,000 persons. There are 93 industrial cooperatives, 7 agricultural ones, 14 housing co-ops, 44 educational organizations, 3 service co-ops, and a net-work of consumer co-ops serving 75,000 members. At the center of the net-work is a bank, the *Caja Laboral Popular*, with some $1 billion in assets contributed mainly by savings from some 200,000 members. The bank sup-plies feasibility studies and technical assistance for the opening of new cooperative ventures. The bank's entrepreneurial role has been crucial to the success of its associated co-ops.

Some of the industrial cooperatives produce high-technology items, and the largest, Ulgor, is a major exporter of such consumer items as refrigerators. With the exception of one fishing co-op, none of the organizations in the network has failed. The pay is linked to average wages in comparable industries in Spain. The highest-paid managers, however, receive no more than three times the compensation of the lowest-paid workers. Unemployment is virtually non-existent; when there is a business turndown, the hours of work are cut back equally, insted of laying off workers. Profit is used for reinvestment to create new jobs, for member education, and a portion is credited to members' "internal accounts" where it earns interest and can be withdrawn on retirement.

The Mondragon network is impressive. Chris Axworthy raises some disturbing questions, however. Is the system overdependent on central direction by the Caja Laboral? To what extent have working conditions been humanized ? Do managers and workers really treat one another as equals? Why does the Caja Laboral invest two-thirds of its money in the private sector, instead of using all of it to fund further cooperative development? Such questions deserve detailed answers so that others can benefit from the mistakes as well as the pioneering innovations of Mondragon, and be better prepared for the task of building a participatory socialist economy..

Notes

1. See Frank Lindenfeld and Joyce Rothschild-Whitt, eds. *Workplace Democracy and Social Change* (Boston: Porter Sargent, 1982); and Christopher E. Gunn, *Workers' Self Management in the United States* (Ithaca: Cornell University Press, 1984).

Little People's Center

Scott Brown

The day begins at 7:30 a.m. Larry arrives just a little early to open the building and meet the first arrivals, people whose parents need to get to work or school by 8:00 a.m. Slowly, the activity level builds. By 8:15, Holly

FROM *Changing Work*, Spring/Summer 1985, pp. 28 – 32. Reprinted by permission.

is at work in the kitchen fixing breakfast, Joanna discusses a scheduling conflict with a parent, and several of the older children—4- and 5-year olds—surround Tim and clamor for adventure on the climbing structure in the side yard. Chuck and Jan each gather two or three little ones and head for a quiet corner to read and imagine. Ginny arrives and begins to collect the small group that will spend the day at her home a short distance away.

Adults who work with preschool children know there are no typical days, but for the past 15 years this sort of scene has been repeated nearly every weekday at the Little People's Center (LPC) in Durham, New Hampshire.

LPC was founded in 1970 by a small group of women who were returning to school at the University of New Hampshire in Durham. For them, if school was going to work, dependable, affordable, high-quality child care was necessary. So they created it themselves.

Their first step was to organize themselves, and although the organization they formed, Disadvantaged Women for Higher Education, no longer exists, one of its first projects—LPC—is a thriving legacy 15 years later.

More Than Custodial Service

These women envisioned day care that was more than custodial service; there was active recognition of the important role played by child-care centers in transmitting attitudes and values. As a result, a staff was developed with balanced numbers of men and women who shared a commitment to cooperation, nonviolence, and nonsexist role modeling. Perhaps because personal empowerment was a concern of the founding group, LPC was organized as a staff collective. Thus, all decisions affecting the operating of the center are made by the working staff. All workers are paid the same hourly wage, and all are encouraged to participate in as many aspects of the center's operations as their interest allows.

Not only has LPC survived; it has developed a strong reputation for expert as well as socially conscious approaches to child care. Part of this success is certainly due to the high levels of worker satisfaction reported by staff members and reflected in an extremely low turnover rate in an occupation noted for low wages, worker exploitation, and brief job tenure. At the same time, workers report substantial amounts of personal and professional development, which can be attributed to the organizational structure of the center. The LPC model encourages workers to build new skills, whether that involves planning and cooking meals for 40 or delivering a talk about important day-care issues to a local community group.

The difficulties and tensions highlighted in a discussion of child care by Kris Cail and Jayne Port (see *Changing Work,* Winter 1984) are experienced by many day-care providers. Still, through its collective process LPC has developed an alternative that mitigates much of the unpredictable and violent tugging that constantly threatens to pull actors in the day-care game into the danger zone. The 15-year-old model, therefore, should be of interest to day-care providers, feminists, and advocates of workplace democracy.

My primary focus, then, will be the organizational and management structure of the center, rather than care-related issues. Information for this article was obtained from interviews with workers, my long-standing association with the LPC staff, and from the firsthand experience of substituting for regular staff members who were sick or temporarily unavailable for work.

Organization

Currently, LPC maintains three programs: nursery for children 1 to 3 years of age, preschool for 3- to 6-year-olds, and home day care. LPC has always given priority to low-income, single-parent households, and has recently begun its own scholarship fund to bridge gaps left by federal cut-backs in support for social programs.

LPC is licensed to accommodate 38 children at one time. Because some children only attend half-days, the center services 42 little people, 10 of whom are toddlers.

There are 9 full-time staff members with a 2:1 female to male ratio. Two workers spend a major portion of their time as "co-directors," a rotating position that focuses on administrative chores. One worker is designated a teacher, and leads three formal periods of instruction per week for the older children. Specific recurring tasks, such as meal planning, shopping, liaison with the USDA, and bookkeeping are assigned to specific individuals for fixed periods of time.

LPC is legally organized as a New Hampshire nonprofit corporation and has qualified for 501c3 tax-exempt status. As a corporation, it is legally governed by its Board of Directors. LPC's bylaws specify that the board will number between 9 and 15 people and consist of equal numbers of staff, parents, and community people (often former staff and parents). The board meets eight times per year, primarily to deal with fund raising. Practical authority and management responsibility resides by intent and tradition with the staff itself, which does all the hiring, child enrollment, evaluation, program development, scheduling, and administrative work. While the board is the legal arbiter of last resort, there has never been an issue that the staff has not resolved itself. The board serves only as an advisory committee, and works to build the scholarship fund endowment which is LPC's response to the cutbacks of Reaganomics.

All the decisions that affect the operation of the center are made through a collaborative and consensus-seeking process. Even a group as small and cohesive as this nine-member collective must delegate responsibility for certain tasks, but ultimate authority rests in the weekly staff meeting. The two "co-directors" are the principal administrative agents of the staff, serve as liaison people to state agencies and parents, and perform other tasks, such as budget monitoring.

Attendance at weekly meetings is mandatory, and all staff are paid for the first three hours, although it is not unusual for meetings to run as late as 10:00 p.m. Since LPC seeks to make decisions that reflect the consensus of the entire staff, discussions can be long.

The staff meeting is the organized forum not only for resolution of issues but for the education of new staff in the history and operation of the center. Since co-directors are selected from among the staff and typically serve an 18-month tenure, there are often a number of staff members who have the experience of dealing with the various agencies and funders that the center has contact with. The depth of staff knowledge is particularly important when difficult decisions need to be made, such as determining the composition of a certain group of children or dealing with funding cutbacks and unfavorable legislation. Depth of experience is due to LPC's record in maintaining a stable workforce with low turnover and diverse job functions. Above all, sensitivity to the needs of the children comes from the fact that all LPC staff work with kids every week.

Each of the co-directors has important responsibilities and generally spends less time with children than other workers. They do not, however, *run* the center or the staff meetings. They function more like resource people or consultants who provide technical data or summarize a problem so that others who are less familiar can participate in reaching a decision.

Meeting agendas are developed in two ways. Topics are often scheduled in advance (such as staff evaluations) or carried forward from previous meetings. A paper listing agenda items for the next meeting is posted near the kitchen area all week long. As new issues arise, they are added to the agenda. The first order of business in each meeting is to select a facilitator for the evening and to rank agenda items.

Coping with Conflicts

In many ways LPC functions like a partnership. As in any small business, the needs of the clients have come first, and there is always extra work that has to be done without direct compensation. At LPC there is a sense of ownership and responsibility among the staff, but each person is also an hourly wage earner. According to some, this is an area that can cause difficulty when the needs of the center conflict with personal needs. One staff member pointed out that many jobs require uncompensated work, but at LPC there is much more potential to *negotiate* the type of activity that will be performed so that it can be smoothly integrated into one's schedule. Most workers agree that the overall sense of empowerment and control fostered by the organizational structure more than compensates for the sacrifices required from time to time. There seems to be agreement that, over time, the less desirable tasks are shared equitably among the workers.

Besides extracurricular work, scheduling is the other main area of conflict between organizational and individual needs.

Since its inception in 1970, LPC has maintained a strong commitment to principles that directly affect scheduling and enrollment decisions. Continuity and stability are important to early childhood development, and LPC seeks to foster these in two ways. The week is divided into morning and afternoon sessions, a total of 10 "slots." Children are organized into groups that are fairly stable for extended periods of time. Perhaps of more importance is the center's goal of assigning the same staff person to work with the same group every morning or afternoon period so that familiarity and trust develops between adult and child. While this is a sought-after ideal, developing work schedules three times a year that seek to meet this goal and accommodate personal needs of workers is a complex and challenging process. Many workers cite this as the most difficult issue they have had to confront at the center. Continuing resolution of this issue is attributed to the sense of participation that each worker exercises in the development of the schedule, and an understanding of the needs of children that comes from all staff members having "hands on" experience.

Staff members make several points about LPC's structure and the way it affects the quality of childcare provided in the center.

First, although more is demanded of each employee since they must attend to management as well as to program issues, the control that each worker can exercise in all aspects of the enterprise stimulates interest, excitement, and commitment. The current staff has a cumulative total of more than 25 years' experience at LPC, and it is not uncommon for workers to stay on the job for 6 – 10 years. The average tenure is in the range of 4 years. As a result, children entering the program as toddlers often have contact with the same adult throughout their stay at the center (up to 5 years). Strong relations are formed that can add stability to families that are often under stress from other sources.

Second, staff also have the ability to try out new ideas, in consultation with co-workers and parents. Since the feedback loop is so short and direct, success or failure is quickly recognized and easily encouraged or corrected. The absence of a bureaucratic hierarchy fosters creativity and innovation.

Several LPC workers have worked in other human service settings. They report a very high level of awareness and appreciation of the flexibility and democracy found in the LPC work environment. The opportunity to affect policy on any level is often cited as a major benefit of the job.

On the other hand, it is pointed out that traditional agencies and organizations (some who have dealt with LPC for 15 years) still have difficulty understanding and dealing with an organization that has no clearly defined management hierarchy. One staff member related that the monitor assigned by the state Division of Social Services was initially skeptical, believing that the LPC system deflected competent people from their specific area of skill into activities where they were less competent. After several years' contact with LPC, however, the monitor now enthusiastically supports the center in terms of both program and structure. While the monitor's initial perception may have had plausibility, it did not take into account the strong commitment to share skills and support personal growth that is at the heart of the LPC philosophy.

Wages and Benefits

Workers are paid the same wage regardless of length of service, training, or responsibility – and there is a conscious effort to share all responsibilities. The current regular wage is $5.75 per hour. This is well above the rate paid to the typical child-care worker in our area, who generally receives less than $4 per hour. Benefits include two-thirds paid health insurance for the worker and family (through Co-Op America and Consumers United), two weeks paid vacation after one year of service, three thereafter, and two personal leave days per year.

LPC also has a unique arrangement to provide paid sick leave when necessary. It is recognized that stress can accompany child-care work, along with increased exposure to colds and infections. But instead of apportioning 10 sick days to each employee, the total number of days budgeted for the entire staff is pooled. Sick days are not viewed as a finite personal benefit that are used up or lost, as in most work situations. When staff miss a work shift for health reasons, sick pay is drawn from the fund of pooled benefit days. At the end of the fiscal year any unused money in the pool is either paid in bonuses to staff members (in equal portions) or turned back to the general operating fund. This system places the health of the worker *and* child above the economics that might motivate an individual to work when ill, if his or her allocated sick time had already been used.

Sick-day benefits are an especially important element in the success of the home day-care component of LPC's program. In conventional home day care, health issues have tremendous potential for pulling parents, children, and providers into the danger zone. A home day-care provider can be forced to sacrifice either health or income, jeopardizing children, parents, or themselves. Parents I know who place their children in home day care often talk about the stress of never knowing when their child-care provider might be sick and unavailable. At LPC, the children who normally attend the home-care program spend the day at the center if the regular provider is ill. This takes the pressure off everybody. Not only can the provider rest and recuperate when necessary (and not expose the children to illness), but parents have the security of knowing there will always be reliable care available. Schedules are not disrupted, and a responsible employment arrangement is maintained for the worker.

To provide additional protection from unforeseen financial emergencies, LPC has created a special loan fund that each worker contributes to at the rate of $1 per week. If an emergency arises, workers can borrow against the fund without interest. Loans are paid back, but in extreme cases can be waived. Self-monitoring is the principal control that allows this arrangement to succeed.

Although LPC workers are paid a relatively acceptable hourly wage and receive other important benefits, none earns more than a modest annual income. One reason for this is the average "full-time" workweek is in the range of 30−32 hours. (The minimum week is 25.5 hours, 5 shifts plus 3 hours of staff meetings.) There has always been a feeling that the center could not maintain the quality of child care that it aspired to if workers put in 40−45 hours per week. The work is just too demanding.

In the early days of the center, staffers worked 25 hours per week, and many if not all held part-time jobs elsewhere. At least one worker found it necessary to leave LPC because of the need to make more money to support a family. As the staff matured and many acquired more dependents, it became obvious that the salary provided by the center was no better than a second income. This led to tension. As a result of the real financial needs of workers and the center's commitment to maintain a gender-balanced, experienced, stable workforce, the decision was reached to reduce staff by attrition, thereby allowing the remaining workers to increase their weekly hours at work. The current annual salary is in the neighborhood of $9000, but additional LPC responsibilities impede taking on part-time, outside work. There is little doubt that LPC staffers have "subsidized" the center with their commitment. Like other child-care centers, LPC has also relied on various subsidies provided by the state, the federal government, and the local community.[1]

LPC has made only modest attempts to spread its model to other child-care centers or communities, generally in response to outside requests. Interest was stronger in the mid-to-late 1970s than in today's climate of fiscal austerity and social reaction.

There is, however, at least one other child-care center closely modeled on LPC. My School, in nearby Newburyport, Massachusetts, has recently celebrated its tenth anniversary. Similar to LPC in terms of staff size and philosophy, decision-making structure, and licensed enrollment, My School obtained technical assistance from LPC when it first began operation. A former LPC staff member went to work at My School and has been there for nine years.

It was reported by one LPC worker with more than nine years' experience at the center that directors of other centers in the area were skeptical of the model's usefulness. The significant differential between LPC wages and the typical salary paid to center administrators cannot be ignored as a reason for the model's failure to spread. Given this, it probably makes more sense to start new centers using LPC principles rather than attempting to convert existing facilities.

Perhaps, though, this begs the original question. If the LPC model is so effective, why has it failed to spread? Is the model only an isolated and unique case, or can it be translated to other localities and environments?

Size, and the companion economic issues implied for workers and parents, are important limits. Direct democracy probably would not work very well once the decision-making group exceeded 20 or 25 members, especially where decisions that seek to reflect near unanimity are sought. Large day-care centers enjoy economies of scale that can result in improved services and more affordable rates — a key issue for the consumer. Economies of scale will be increasingly important if centers that now enjoy subsidized tenancy look to ownership of their facilities, or lose their subsidies.

Several alternatives may offer promising solutions to this dilemma. A center could develop a representative democracy with policies and procedures designed to protect worker interests. Another possibility would be a network of "service locations" organized under one umbrella organization, or a federation of smaller, independent centers that could achieve economic benefits by consolidating purchases and by sharing resources. Both of these latter possibilities would preserve the self-management and flexible working arrangements that are the essence of LPC. Without such federation, it may be difficult to replicate LPC's small-scale and face-to-face model.

While LPC is no panacea for the many problems that face day care, the significance of its success, both in organizational and in personal terms, cannot be ignored. Perhaps the center's greatest contributions to the process of changing worklife have been indirect.

There has been cross-fertilization among human service organizations in our region, and former LPC staff members have been able to spread skills and values learned at the center. One example is a battered women's shelter established some five years ago with substantial involvement by LPC workers. While that organization is also structured as a nonprofit organization with a board of directors, the internal organization at the staff level follows principles of democratic, self-management similar to those of LPC.

A Question for Workplace Democracy Advocates

One question that LPC raises for advocates of workplace democracy is whether worker self-management can be built — and to what extent — through the nonprofit service sector. Is LPC a viable model for promoting large-scale social change?

Mondragon, the Basque cooperative network, has apparently taken another course: production cooperatives created both the democratic and economic soil from which second-level social service co-ops later grew. Starting in the service sector, as LPC has done, may leave the center unable to overcome its isolation, unable to draw upon resources generated by an allied productive sector.

A middle ground, not yet explored in the United States, would be to develop production and service cooperatives concurrently. This would have tremendous benefits for both. Production workers surely need quality day care, and day-care centers, based internally on self-management, would do better drawing support from self-managed workplaces than from organizations alien to democratic values.

In short, LPC may not by itself represent the best strategy for developing a worker-managed sector of the economy. It might nonetheless be a model for one part of such a strategy. And, in any case, as anyone who has had contact with the center will agree, it is a special place—one where parents, kids, and workers not only avoid the "danger zone" but manage to come out on top more often than not.

Notes

1. A nearby university provides subsidized labor through work-study programs. In addition, payroll and bookkeeping is handled by the university, further reducing indirect costs of employment. Typically, LPC hires five work-study students each semester as well as in the summer.

    Other sources of support are numerous, including the USDA food program, the United Way, charitable giving through the umbrella organization Friends of Durham Day Care, and direct contributions of time, money, and resources. The actual physical space that LPC occupies is in the basement of the Durham Community Church, which has rented to LPC at below-market rates since 1973.

Worker-Owned and -Operated Supermarkets in Philadelphia

Frank Lindenfeld

The Original Worker Takeovers

The Roslyn O&O and the Parkwood Manor O&O, two worker-owned and -operated Philadelphia supermarkets, stand where two A&P Company stores stood just a few years ago, before the company closed them down. Reopened in 1982 as O&Os, the two stores are now democratically managed by worker-owner committees that set store policies, hire and fire managers, and share profits among member workers on the basis of hours worked. In

FROM *Changing Work 1,* no. 1 (fall 1984): 42–46. Reprinted by permission.

place of a rigid division of labor, store workers help out wherever needed, including bagging groceries and cleanup.

Run well enough to outsell the A&Ps they replaced (Roslyn by 40 percent, Parkwood by 20 percent), the O&O's have become viable businesses. Because they do not have to support a corporate superstructure with high-priced executives—company offices, for example, are conveniently located in each store—the O&Os have lowered overhead costs, and can attract customers with prices consistently below those of their competitors. The original 25 Roslyn and 20 Parkwood worker–owners are paid about $17,000–$18,000 per year, and are more conscientious because they know that over and above their wages they will receive a share of the store's profits. Shoplifting is about one-sixth the average United States supermarket rate. They have hired an additional 13 workers at each store, and pay a nonmember store manager $23,000–$24,000 a year plus a bonus. The worker–owners are now debating how best to use their profits for expansion.

A third store, Strawberry Mansion O&O, opened in 1985. This market is the anchor tenant in a newly developed shopping center.

Yet in spite of their success so far, the O&Os were born out of economic adversity. All the workers at Roslyn and Parkwood Manor are members of the United Food and Commercial Workers Union (UFCW) Local 1357. In fact, the stores would never have existed as worker–owned and -operated businesses without the initiative and financial backing provided by the union.

In February 1982, the A&P Company (which had previously been bought by the West German conglomerate Tenglemann) announced its plans to shut down most of its Philadelphia area stores, eventually forcing nearly 2000 UFCW members out of work. It was an announcement the union had been expecting for some time. Local 1357 President Wendell Young, along with consultant Jay Guben, had already begun in midsummer 1981 to explore worker ownership as a solution to the A&P pullout. Guben had contacted the Philadelphia Association for Cooperative Enterprises (PACE) for advice. The union, Guben, and PACE staff members Sherman Kreiner and Andy Lamas joined forces in planning a buyout of the A&P stores slated for closing, to be reopened as worker cooperatives. With PACE's assistance, UFCW commissioned initial market and feasibility studies. Then, when A&P made its announcement, the UFCW Local was ready with a counter move. It made and publicized a bid for 21 of the closing stores.

At the same time, UFCW Local 1357 commissioned PACE to undertake an extensive education and training program for prospective worker–owners on how to run cooperative enterprises. More than 600 workers would attend classes and pledge $5000 each as equity toward purchasing the stores.

Two months of negotiations followed between A&P and the union. By April 1982 the company and union representatives had worked out an agreement under which the A&P would open a subsidiary, Super Fresh, to renew operations and offer employment to laid-off workers. In exchange, the union conceded 20 percent pay cuts, reductions in vacations, and reduced overtime premium pay. While Super Fresh was to have a traditional management structure, the company promised that the new stores would incorporate some degree of worker participation in decision making through a "quality of working life" program. By 1984, A&P had opened 56 Super Fresh markets in the Philadelphia metropolitan area, reemploying all of the laid-off A&P workforce.

A&P also agreed to three other concessions designed to facilitate employee ownership. It agreed that Super Fresh would contribute 1 percent of its gross annual sales to a union controlled trust, the O&O Investment Fund. Sixty-five percent of the trust monies would be distributed to workers as annual wage bonuses, with the remainder used to capitalize an employee ownership investment fund whose main purpose was to support future buyouts and startups of worker-owned enterprises (A subsequent vote of union workers changed the ratio to 90 percent bonuses and 10 percent voluntary contributions to the investment fund.) A&P further promised that should any of the Super Fresh stores close down, its employees would have an exclusive option to purchase the stores at a fair market price. Lastly, A&P agreed to sell two of the stores to employees by granting PACE an exclusive option to purchase. These stores were to be fully worker owned and operated.

Once A&P had pledged to open the Super Fresh markets, most of the 600 workers who had participated in PACE's cooperative training program opted to work at Super Fresh. Some 50 others, however, decided to go ahead with the risky and challenging business of owning their own markets. Aided by loans from the Local's Federal Credit Union, the worker – owners invested about $150,000 per store, enabling them to obtain bank financing backed by loan guarantees from the U.S. Small Business Administration. They participated in planning the reopening of Roslyn and Parkwood as worker cooperatives with technical advice from consultants Jay and Merry

Guben, and PACE's Kreiner and Lamas. Meeting three times a week for about seven months, they formed nine planning committees, including governance, union role, management selection, and worker education, among others. A steering committee comprised of one representative from each of these commitees plus three union officials was the center of planning activity until summer 1982, when newly formed boards of directors for Roslyn and Parkwood took over. Although the two stores were separately incorporated (as is the third) it was planned to join them through an umbrella association to provide common services such as bulk purchasing, insurance, advertising, and worker–manager training.

The worker education program coordinated by PACE continued until the end of 1982. Consisting of formal presentations as well as large- and small-group discussions among the prospective worker–owners, the program furnished information on the fundamentals of cooperative legal structures, supermarket business planning, and the details of cooperative management. While PACE wanted the program of education to continue longer, the other consultants felt that the new markets, once launched, should be left to operate and learn on their own, without continuing dependence on "experts." This latter view won out.

Despite its support of the cooperative and democratic principle of one worker, one vote, PACE's education program did not convince the core group of workers to abandon the capitalist stock model entirely. The O&O stores have two categories of employees: worker–owners and hired nonowner workers, almost all of whom are temporary, part-time help. These workers had to be hired in part because the stores have been doing a much larger business than anticipated. The temporary, part-time help, however, do not share in the profits and do not vote on store policies. At present, a committee of O&O workers is trying to arrive at a solution to this problem of inequality, which could be remedied either by providing nonowner workers with representation on the board of directors and other committees or by making all workers owners.

From Reactive to Proactive Strategy

PACE provided technical assistance for the creation of the third O&O market in the Strawberry Mansion section of north Philadelphia. It is also working with Spring Garden United Neighbors, a neighborhood organization composed of predominantly low- and moderate-income black and Hispanic residents, to plan for still a fourth O&O.

The Strawberry Mansion supermarket is part of a larger inner-city economic development project launched by the city of Philadelphia in conjunction with a private developer and a community development corporation. The O&O market is the major tenant in a larger shopping center, known as Strawberry Square, which will house over 20 stores and services. Financing for the shopping center came from an Urban Development Action Grant (UDAG) from the federal government and private loans. The O&O market is financed by a $1.1 million loan package based on a foundation of $5000 in equity contributions from each worker–owner ($200 cash and $4800 in loans from the UFCW credit union), plus funding from a variety of government agencies and private banks, with loans guaranteed once again by the Small Business Administration.

Expected to gross some $225,000 per week, the Strawberry Mansion O&O began with 32 full-time worker–owners, 53 part-time worker–owners, and an additional 8 part-time employees. Its workers are drawn from among a group of displaced Acme supermarket clerks, UFCW members who previously expressed interest in becoming employee–owners, and community members. PACE provided an intensive six-month education and training program for these prospective workers in 1984.

The real importance of the Strawberry Mansion O&O, however, is that it marks a transition in O&O planning from the previous phase of *reacting* to business closures to a *proactive* strategy. This means that the interaction between the labor movement, the cooperative movement, and the community will no longer be limited to waiting for the emergency situation of a plant or business shutdown to occur. Freed from the demands of immediate economic necessity, strategies for building worker cooperatives can have greater flexibility, expanded objectives, and more of a long-term perspective. For example, PACE has been working with the Nutritional Development Services of the Philadelphia Catholic Archdiocese and other religious groups to establish a revolving loan fund. This fund would facilitate the creation of several more worker-owned, democratically managed supermarkets at sites to be owned by local development corporations in low-income neighborhoods and leased back to worker cooperatives.

Achievements and Risks

Former A&P workers, under the leadership of UFCW's Young, and with technical assistance from PACE and other consultants, have made an impressive beginning in reviving closed-down stores under workers' self-management.

The workers, union officials and the consultants all feel very positive about the achievements of the O&O project. As Young put it,

> We believe that the O&O markets will serve as a workable alternative to store closings. . . . Employee owners are not as likely to leave town on a corporate whim since they are geared to serve a local market. The net result, as we see it, will be a more stable job base and more responsiveness to local market needs. We also believe that a very beneficial side effect of the O&O Supermarket opening will be to dispel the myth that the unionized workers are not productive. The workers of . . . O&O are highly motivated, and enterprising. What is *most unusual* about that is that they are not extraordinarily different from the rest of the rank and file of our union. . . . If given sufficient latitude the workers we represent can become more and more productive and responsible.

According to PACE Staff Director Andy Lamas, "The O&O experience demonstrates the enormous potential for building meaningful alliances between the cooperative movement and the labor movement. It proves the viability and durability of the cooperative form in an extremely competitive industry. And it underscores the need for intensive pre-opening *and* ongoing, post-opening worker education and training."

Yet the O&O markets have been successful in part because the workers agreed to pay themselves slightly lower wages than they were receiving from A&P, including lower overtime payments. This was possible because the O&O workers are committed to making their stores successful. Over 85 percent of the worker–owners come regularly to monthly meetings to debate store policies, while board and committee members meet once or twice a week. No one is paid extra to attend these meetings; the incentive comes from the desire to make the markets profitable enterprises. So there has been a tradeoff. In exchange for their own voluntary wage concessions, the O&O workers have helped to guarantee themselves jobs in stores they now own and control.

Where workers control their own stores, and where they stand to gain if the supermarkets prosper, accepting lower wages than the prevailing industry standard may be entirely acceptable during the startup period, since the worker–owners have the power to raise their wages when conditions become more favorable. But such a strategy of wage concessions to keep or create jobs must be looked at with caution where corporate managements continue to run the business, as is the case with the A&P/Super Fresh markets, where the great majority of UFCW members still work. For these workers, the tradeoff is less obviously in their favor.

What the Roslyn and Parkwood Manor O&O's have shown is that democratic management of supermarkets is feasible. The collective strength of O&O increased when the two markets were joined by the third store; together these stores form the potential cornerstone of an extensive network of worker-owned and democratically managed retail food markets. This network would increase the opportunity for both food workers and community people to join in cooperative work. Yet to make this a reality, a number of things must happen. The third store still has to prove itself in the competitive marketplace.

The stores will probably need to change their structure so that all store workers have a voice in market policies, eliminating the "second class" status of the temporary, part-time employees. Internal education will have to continue, involving both workers and managers. At the same time, the union itself will have to maintain its commitment to the objective of worker self-management, and the umbrella association needs to be empowered to provide needed common services. Last and perhaps most crucial, the resources of the existing O&O investment fund, as well as those of the newly formed revolving loan fund, will have to be pressed into use to finance additional units in the network. A lot rides on whether O&O can continue to survive and expand, and many people, not just in Philadelphia, will be watching the development of this emerging cooperative network with great hope and anticipation.

The Atlas Chain Company: A Union-Organized, Democratic ESOP

Robert Pankin

Can Employee Stock Ownership Plans (ESOPs) be used to provide employees real control over their companies? After having been closed by its multinational corporate owner on March 31, 1983, the Atlas Chain Company of West Pittston, Pennsylvania, reopened November 1, 1983, as an wholly employee-owned corporation. Atlas is significant to those interested in employee ownership for two reasons: (1) the early involvement of the United Automobile Workers International Union (UAW), and (2) the newly structured company's democratic organization using an ESOP process.

According to Corey Rosen of the National Center for Employee Ownership, there are over 6000 companies in the United States which have some degree of employee ownership. Most of these are ESOPs with the remainder being some form of producer cooperative. The ESOP in some cases lets a company borrow money to give stock to employees. The company gets a capital infusion while the workforce gets partial or full ownership of the company. (Chrysler, Eastern Airlines and Weirton Steel are well-known examples of ESOPs.) There are significant tax breaks for companies and banks, with both capital and interest being deductible. Most ESOPs give only minority ownership to the workers, and sometimes the stock does not carry voting rights. There are, however, some companies with majority employee ownership where line workers own and vote a majority of the stock. These are cases that most interest those who believe that the ESOP can be a tool for the humanization of the workplace.

Critics of ESOPs say that they are used as tools by management for their own purposes, not necessarily to help workers. While a company reduces its liabilities, workers may even be directly harmed in some instances by a loss of pension benefits.

FROM *Changing Work,* Spring/Summer 1985, pp. 51–56. Reprinted by permission. This article is a revised version of a paper presented to the meetings of the American Sociological Association in August 1985. This research and article have benefited greatly from the insights of Professor William F. Whyte of Cornell University. Frank Lindenfeld made many valuable suggestions, which have improved the paper. The research was partially supported by a grant from the Economic Development Administration.

In the business section of the *New York Times* on January 2, 1985, Michael Blumstein pointed out that management uses ESOPs for tax benefits, fresh capital infusion, and to fight off hostile takeovers. All these criticisms are valid for particular cases. Under the right conditions, however, ESOPs can also be used for worker benefit.

The union movement, particularly at the national or international levels, has not been very receptive to worker takeovers or employee involvement programs. From the union point of view, worker ownership can lead to reductions in wages and benefits. In difficult times, in order to maintain their jobs and future profits, workers who own their own companies may be willing to work for less. From the union perspective, this may be threatening, for a local can be perceived as undermining the national contract. The international finds itself in a dilemma: support its troubled local or or protect the national contract. Some union officials feel that Quality of Working Life or Quality Circle programs may be used, for example, to supplant contractually established grievance procedures. Workers may be placed at a serious disadvantage in management controlled programs.

In spite of such reservations, the UAW supported the worker buyout at Atlas Chain. This was a last resort strategy, however. Without the takeover, the workers' jobs would have been lost. The workers, through their local union, bought Atlas Chain using the ESOP as their major instrument.

Atlas workers gained majority control of the new Board of Directors as soon as the deal was closed. In 1986, voting in a local union meeting, they will completely control the company. There are few differences between the corporate structure of Atlas and the structure of a worker cooperative. The ESOP has been used in this case to design an organization to specifically benefit employees.

A Democratic ESOP

As a result of the buyout, Atlas is one of the most democratically structured ESOPs in the United States. The Board of Directors consists of three union officers, a professor from a local college (selected by the union), the president of the company, and two local outside businessmen. The union, which represents the majority of the workforce, therefore, has a majority on the existing board. On a one-person, one-vote basis, the union will in 1986 elect the ESOP trustee. The trustee, in turn, will be instructed to vote the stock as the union membership wishes. On this democratic basis the workers will be able to set company policy.

Stock cannot be sold publicly, and the company must buy back vested stock from a departing worker. Stock is vested on a time-in-service basis as opposed to being allocated according to amount of compensation. Higher-salaried management, therefore, cannot gain control of the company as has occurred in many other ESOPs.

Four factors led to this democratic structure. The first was the energy and desire of the employees of Atlas to organize their own company under strong union leadership. This happened in the framework of a local cooperative tradition (discussed below).

The second factor was the lessons learned from the Hyatt Clark experience, which were transferable because Craig Livingston was the attorney for the union there as well as for Local 271 at Atlas. At Hyatt it will take 10 years for the workers to gain control of the company and the Board of Directors. Workers will not be able to vote their stock until 1991. At Atlas, workers had an immediate majority on the board and will vote their stock in 1986. At Hyatt, from the worker point of view, there have been problems with management, which in 1985 almost led to a strike. At Atlas, there have been no problems of this sort.

The third factor was fortuitous. In putting together the loan package a guaranteed loan from the Small Business Adminstration was secured. The law requires that for this type of loan, the employees be able to vote their stock. This was interpreted in this case to mean that a majority of the Board of Directors had to be members of the bargaining unit.

The fourth factor was the work of the Philadelphia Association for Cooperative Enterprise (PACE). It submitted ideas for a democratically structured company, many of which reflected the lessons learned at Hyatt Clark.

Company History

The Atlas Chain and Precision Products Company was established in 1955 as a private, closely held company. Its primary product was transmission chain (this looks something like bicycle chain but comes in different sizes). In addition it manufactured conveyor belts and space program products.

Space production was crucial, because when the program was cut back, the company lost its contracts, and since that time has never shown a profit.

The company was sold by its original owners in 1967 to the Bucyrus-Erie Corporation, which could not operate the company profitably and in turn sold it to Renold Limited in 1974. During the nine years that Renold, an English multinational, owned the company, it did not operate at a profit either. Some, if not all, of the loss, may be the result of accounting procedures and financial arrangements, however. The plant was technologically updated to state of the art, and the cost was charged to the Atlas division as a loan at several points above the prime.

During the time Renold owned the company, there were labor problems. There were bitter strikes every three years when the workers' contract expired, sometimes lasting for months, and at least one of which produced violence. In August 1982 Renold announced an attempted sale or planned shutdown by March 1, 1983, later delayed to March 31. Renold tried to sell the whole operation to a single buyer, perhaps to a competitor. That was unsuccessful, but the company was prepared to sell the plant for its liquidation or scrap value.

The Buyout Process

The international union, at first, thought that Renold was looking for givebacks. The local union concluded quickly, however, that Renold was serious about closing the plant. The union had just signed one of the best contracts in its history, and the time to have used shutdown for bargaining would have been during contract talks. The union believed that at the very least the plant was marginally profitable. That, however, may not have been sufficient for the Renold management. Atlas may be a variation on the all-too-familiar theme of conglomerates closing local plants because return on investment is not large enough.

The local acted rather quickly, and by the time the international became fully aware of the shutdown plans, the local union had taken the lead in planning the worker buyout, beginning a few weeks after the announced shutdown (August 1982). The idea for employee ownership originated at an informal meeting of union members. Bill Scott, the Local 271 president, and Dominick Dente, the chair of the shop committee, had been reading the papers about the Weirton Steel buyout. Scott remembered having met James May and James Zarello, officers of the local union at Hyatt Clark Industries, at a union conference where they had spoken about their buyout.

It was decided to involve the whole membership of the local in the preliminary consideration of buying out the company, and another meeting was held where May, Zarello, and Livingston made a presentation about ESOPs in general and the Hyatt Clark case in particular.

The local membership decided to go ahead with the attempt. They took a multifaceted approach to fund raising for the feasibility study. First, each member was asked to contribute $200 to begin a "Save Our Jobs Fund." Of the approximately 150 members of the local at that time, only 4 did not contribute. In addition to the $200 contribution from union members, a successful community effort raised approximately $46,000. The success of this drive had much to do with the character of the local community. The area is subjected to frequent floods. During these times, people have become used to collectively pitching in to help neighbors. Community mechanisms for self-help may be more in place here than in other areas. The community is stable with a large base of long-time residents.

Tradition in this part of the country is strongly rooted in mining. This may be an important cultural contributor to the fund raising success. Many of the original workers hired when the plant opened had mining experience, and most of them had fathers who worked in the mines. The history of the United Mine Workers points to strong cohesion on the local level; Alvin Gouldner reported similar solidarity in his research on gypsum miners.

Another important factor is the high seniority among the workers. Most union members have 20 years or more with this company. The average worker is in his late 40s, while those who returned to work when the plant reopened are in their late 50s.

The combination of frequent crisis experience, a stable community, the mining tradition of solidarity, high seniority, and an older workforce produced a cultural setting which enhanced the success of the money raising effort.

Some of the funds for a preliminary study that was made part of the formal feasibility study came from the international UAW headquarters, which loaned the local money at low interest. An additional $18,000 came from the Pennsylvania Departments of Labor and Community Affairs.

In the beginning, the salaried employees of Atlas were not involved in the buyout process. Some of them, however, wanted to participate, and they approached the union offering to contribute their $200. They were refused by the local, which indicated that this was to be a bargaining unit project. When management people were rehired on the plant's reopening, they were required to contribute the money.[1]

Plant manager Don Hayes did not become seriously involved in the buyout effort until the end of February or early March 1983. He had an offer to stay with Renold — moving to another location — and had begun to seek other employment. Due to a conflict of interest, Hayes could not get involved on the worker side of the buyout because he was still employed by Renold until the plant closed on March 31. In addition, he represented the company in early negotiations with the workforce. After the closing, he made his final decision to stay as chief executive officer of the new company. He became completely committed to the ESOP idea.

A feasibility study done by Arthur D. Little Co. on behalf of the workers showed a positive potential for Atlas. During preliminary negotiations for the employee buy out, the union was in a controlling position. This was unlike many other employee buyouts. At Weirton Steel and Hyatt Clark, the deals were engineered by corporate lawyers, management consulting firms, and investment bankers. The results were that costs were high and the workforce had to wait a long time before gaining control of their investment. With the union "quarterbacking the deal," the workers ended up containing costs and being masters of their own fate. Control was achieved because the union decided which experts to hire to put the deal together.

Favorable to the success of the buyout negotiations was Renold's willingness to sell the plant at a low price. Some observers feel that the cost of the companies at both Weirton and Hyatt Clark was probably too much. From the workers' perspective, if they did not buy the company, the only other option for the divesting conglomerate would be to sell the plant for scrap. This was the negotiating position taken at Atlas Chain, and the amount the workers paid for the company was not much in excess of salvage value.

Help From PACE

Confidence that the feasibility study would be positive was so high that the union hired the politically influencial corporate law firm of Dechert, Price and Rhoades. At the suggestion of James May, the Philadelphia Association for Cooperative Enterprise (PACE) was also hired to do corporate structuring work. PACE helped prepare applications for crucial loans from the Pennsylvania Industrial Development Authority (PIDA) and other agencies. It prepared an ESOP plan summary for the workers and still acts as special counsel in regard to the administration of the ESOP.

The loan negotiation process was complex. In April 1983 the First Eastern Bank of Wilkes-Barre agreed to be the lead bank in the ESOP financing. In addition, First Eastern participated through the Small Business Administration and the Consumer United Group (an employee-owned insurance company) in gaining additional loans. The total loan package came to $6,680,600, with the cornerstone being the PIDA loan at 3 percent interest, the cheapest of all the loans obtained.[2]

The PIDA loan, however, did have conditions. When the plant closed, it lost major contracts with John Deere and Caterpiller. PIDA asked the new company to renegotiate these contracts before granting the loan. The PIDA staff also expressed a concern that the workers had no equity in the new enterprise. To insure a strong commitment, the workers were required to put up $1000 apiece before they could be rehired. This money became an important source of operating capital for the firm.

From the PIDA point of view, this was one of the less secure loans that it had made in two years. The authority was concerned about what changes would be made to allow Atlas to become profitable. Sources indicate that community pressure and political leverage finally tipped the balance in the loan's favor. These problems caused delays in reopening the plant, which ironically impeded negotiations with Deere and Caterpiller. This may yet jeopardize Atlas' future success.

Labor–Management Relations

The family-founded company was originally a paternalistically managed organization. When it was sold to Bucyrus-Erie, there was not much change in labor–management or shop-floor relationships. Finally, when Renold took over and Don Hayes became plant manager, management continued to be based on strong personal loyalties.

The local union is very strong. It is cohesive and well led. Until the plant closing the major concerns have been the traditional issues: economic well-being, work rules, health, and safety. While there had been strikes, these had focused on economic issues.

A "we" and "they" attitude still exists between management and labor. In the front office, which houses the salaried employees, the workers on the shop floor are referred to as "them," as distinguished from "us." The converse is true in the plant. Management is "the front office" and "they," while shop people are "workers" or "members of the bargaining unit." These distinctions point to the existence of a traditional labor–management pattern even after worker ownership.

On the other hand, the plant is now operating with just two supervisors, indistinguishable from the rest of the workers because they help with ongoing work as they are not encumbered with administrative tasks. The absence of close supervision, contrasted to the past, is related to major changes in work rules, which are now much more flexible.

As the company was getting ready to reopen, worker wages had been frozen, and the union complained that the salaries of the returning managers would be too high. They asked that they take a pay cut. Chief Executive Hayes agreed to discuss this with the salaried personnel, who turned it down. Managers were subsequently hired back at salaries that the union considered inflated.

Hayes's agreement to discuss salary cuts with other managers illustrates one change. He is now willing to take the time to negotiate on a number of traditional issues. In case the salary cut was rejected, however, he said that he had to have the right to hire the people back anyhow. This incident highlights Hayes's main point. He had been hired as chief executive and expects to make decisions. If his decision-making power is removed, he will not remain in the position.

One reason a positive management–labor relationship exists now is the time Hayes spends on the shop floor making himself accessible. He has instituted an informal consultation process and is popular with the workers. In the past, communication and information gaps existed between workers and management, and to a certain extent that gap still remains.

But moves have been made to overcome that gap with the worker-owners. The usual bimonthly meeting between management and the combined shop committee and executive board of the union for dealing with labor problems now deals with business issues. Hayes "takes over the meeting," explains, and answers questions. The workers feel that they know a lot more about what is going on. There are also weekly cost-cutting meetings between the plant superintendent and volunteers.

There are potentially serious problems. While the workforce remains in the honeymoon-euphoria stage of having started their own company, things may work well. This stage, however, inevitably ends. Whether personal trust in Don Hayes can carry the company through exceptionally hard times is problematic. There are no structures and processes in place that would help mitigate these effects.

A major element of trust in Hayes is the local union leadership. The union leaders sit on the Board of Directors, however, and could easily become identified with management. This would create conflict in the membership. In the not too distant future the local union leadership will retire, and so will Hayes. The workers who have been called back are in their 50s and 60s. In a few years most of them will retire. Atlas will face the challenge of integrating new people into a worker-owned company.

There is a built-in contradiction at Atlas. The corporate structure is democratic, but the day-to-day operations of the plant are traditional. It works because of Hayes's style of management and the exceptional cooperation he gets from the union. If either of these elements was missing, there would be massive problems.

Ownership and Control Not Synonymous

Atlas Chain raises multiple and complex issues. What lessons can be learned here? One firm conclusion that may be made is that the worker-ownership movement is growing and learning from past mistakes. The issue that this growth continues to raise, however, is that ownership and control are not synonymous. Lessons learned at Hyatt Clark and other early buyouts have been taken to heart and are being applied. If employees take over a business, they must be in control of the process. The surest way to this goal may be the Atlas method of union-hired experts with management completely left out until their expertise is needed upon reopening.

The debate over worker ownership continues. Is this a viable strategy for workers and unions? One case cannot provide answers, but the worker buyout at Atlas *has* given back jobs to up to 100 people. If control accompanies ownership of the enterprise, it seems that this is a good way to improve workers' lives.

Some observers have argued that cooperative-style enterprises on the Mondragon model are not possible in the United States. They think the Basque culture is unique, particularly its cooperative tradition. While we may not be able to duplicate Mondragon here, the Atlas case demonstrates that it will not be for lack of a cooperative tradition. The Wyoming Valley of Pennsylvania has such a tradition rooted in mining and fighting natural disasters. We may not have a national cooperative culture, yet such ways of life exist in many smaller regions. It is those traditions that we may use to build worker-owned and -controlled companies.

Notes

1. Management participates in the ESOP on a time-in-service basis.
2. Our primary information on PIDA comes from Robert Baker, formerly the Deputy Secretary for Economic Development in the Pennsylvania Department of Commerce and now with the Department of Transportation in Washington, D.C.

The Mondragon Model
of Cooperative Enterprise

Ana Gutierrez-Johnson

The Mondragon Cooperative Experience

Since the beginning of modern Western industrialization, the belief in the possibility of creating dynamic production enterprises, ruled by principles of equity and distributive justice for the workers, has remained an imperfectly fulfilled hope. Attempts have been made to create such enterprises,[1] but most were small and short-lived. This is why the thriving network of cooperative organizations centered in the Basque town of Mondragon in northern Spain has been attracting worldwide attention. This network is the first historical example of several kinds of cooperative organizations that have achieved a long-term, large-scale record of success. In particular, the producers' cooperatives, organized under principles of economic and industrial democracy, have proven to be economically successful, as well as technologically advanced.

Mondragon, with a 1984 population of about 30,000, is located in the province of Gipuzkoa, one of the four provinces of *Euskadi,* the Basque name for their own region.

Since the early 1970s, this remote industrial town has been attracting a steady flow of visitors interested in the unique model of production enterprise—and the broader model of socioeconomic development—pioneered by the cooperativists of Mondragon. Ostensibly, these cooperative organizations have solved many of the serious problems facing industrial organizations in the West. Two of the questions visitors ask most often are: "What accounts for their remarkable success?" and "Is this experience transferable elsewhere?"

This article addresses the question of success and transferability focusing only on the production enterprises. Since in the last analysis what succeeds or is transferred is an organizational pattern, the focus is on the questions of success and transferability in reference to the model of enterprise pioneered in Mondragon. In order to provide an explanation for the success of the Mondragon model, I describe the decision process through which the formal features of the first cooperative enterprise, Ulgor, were chosen.[2]

FROM *Changing Work*, 1, no. 1, (1984): 35–41. Reprinted by permission.

This is a necessary step because these features were later reproduced in all the cooperative firms, in the second-order support organizations, and in the network as a whole. Furthermore, this allows me to highlight the organizational and behavioral consequences of the choices made by the founders of Ulgor. Only then will it be possible to point out the factors that turned the Mondragon model into a fail-proof pattern for success.[3] Finally, I suggest the factors that must be taken into account when considering the transference of the model elsewhere.

The Mondragon Complex

Starting with a modest effort at creating an elementary technical school in 1943, the Basques of Mondragon have rapidly built the most comprehensive network of cooperative organizations in the world. Today this network is composed of approximately 165 organizations: 93 production enterprises, 44 educational institutions, 7 agro-industrial concerns, 14 building companies, 3 service organizations, and a network of consumers' cooperatives serving about 75,000 members*. Table 1 describes the evolution of the complex. The center of this network is Caja Laboral Popular (The Workers' Savings and Loan Mutual), a second-order credit cooperative that has provided financial support and managerial expertise for the cooperative organizations. Caja Laboral has its central office in Mondragon and 132 branches in the Basque region. The most recent addition, a branch in Madrid, is its first venture outside the Basque region. Caja Laboral is one of the 10 largest financial institutions in the Basque region, ranking 27th in Spain. Its assets are about $1 billion, using an average conversion rate of 100 Spanish pesetas to the U.S. dollar.

The producer's cooperatives form an industrial complex which not only manufactures a wide range of durable goods, intermediate goods, and capital equipment but also produces electronic and high-technology products. In 1984, these cooperatives provided jobs and lifetime employment for about 18,000 workers, about 5 percent of all employment in Euskadi, and about 15 percent of all employment in Gipuzkoa. The development of this industrial complex has been remarkable, not only during periods of industrial expansion but also during the nine-year recession that caused the demise of a large number of industrial firms in Euskadi between 1973 and 1982. By the end of 1982, about 178,000 workers were out of work in

*The consumer co-op network is itself composed of 84 supermarkets and 130 associated shops; the network employs 1200 worker members and at latest count serves 130,000 consumer members. See Christopher S. Axworthy, "Eroski at Mondragon: A Model for Canadian Consumer Co-operators" *Worker Co-ops Newsletter,* summer 1985. —Ed.

Euskadi, representing an unemployment rate of 18 percent. However, during the same period, the industrial complex of Mondragon protected its 11,000 existing jobs and created 7000 new ones. Its sales increased at an average annual rate of 25 percent, while industrial investment grew at an average annual rate of 15 percent. About 37 new cooperative enterprises were launched.

Table 1.

The Development and Distribution of the Enterprise of the Cooperative Complex of Mondragon 1957–1984, by Age of Activity

Type	1957	1967	1972	1974	1978	1980	1982	1984
Industrial	1	31	49	56	69	83	88	93
Agricultural		3	4	4	4	7	7	7
Service		1	2	6	4	5	6	3
Educational					31	40	44	44
Housing				5	14	14	14	14
Consumer coops network		1	1	1	1	1	1	1
Total	1	36	56	72	123	150	160	165

Sources: Caja Laboral Popular, *Memoria,* 1973–1982. Iñski Gorroño, Experiencia Cooperative en el Pais Vasco, 1977. T.U. (*Trabajo y Unión*), Magazine of the Cooperative Complex, 1975–1984. *ULARCO, Central Services.*

Henk Thomas and Christopher Logan[4] have analyzed comprehensively the aggregate growth performance of the industrial complex of Mondragon in sales, value added, exports, and investments. They have compared the performance of the industrial complex to the aggregate performance of the Gipuzkoan provincial economy. They have also investigated productivity and profitability, and therefore the cooperative firms' efficiency in the use of resources. Their conclusions are significant:

> During more than two decades a considerable number of cooperative factories have functioned at a level equal or superior in efficiency to that of capitalist enterprises. . . . Efficiency in terms of the use made of scarce resources has been higher in the cooperatives; their growth record of sales, exports, and employment, under both favourable and adverse economic conditions, has been superior to that of capitalist enterprises.[5]

The social performance of the industrial complex of Mondragon is also outstanding. Industrial relations have been virtually free of conflict in 28 years of functioning. Economic democracy is a reality, as all the cooperative firms are 100 percent worker owned. Industrial democracy, the participation of workers in production decisions and planning, has also been achieved through various forms of direct and indirect participation.[6] Finally, the industrial complex of Mondragon has achieved influence in Gipuzkoa and Euskadi by filling the vacuum in social policy, health care, education, employment, etc., left by the repressive government of Francisco Franco.[7] These accomplishments and the organizational behavior involved could not be attributed to chance alone. For this reason, the first step toward an explanation is the analysis of the origin of the organizational model of enterprise pioneered by the cooperativists of Mondragon.

The New Cooperativism

In 1956, five men of Mondragon, under the tutelage of Jose Maria Arizmendi, a local priest and community organizer, opened a small, community-supported worker-owned, democratically managed shop with 24 members. They had everything they needed except a legal framework. A model of worker-owned business had no legal status and was against the Spanish *zeitgeist* of the middle 1950s. The risk of arousing negative reactions from the business community and the government was high. After two years of legal ambiguity, being registered as a limited liability company but operating as a worker-owned business, they decided to avoid the risk of closure by adapting their organization to the Spanish Law of Cooperatives and registering as a producers' cooperative. This legal form was not their first choice because of the severe legal limitations placed on the growth and expansion of cooperatives. However, it was the best they could do at the time. This enterprise was named *Ulgor*, an acronym for the names of the first five founders.

Ulgor started, as most producers' cooperatives do, with borrowed resources and a modest product, a copied paraffin stove. Its assets were an organization based on worker cooperation and several key decisions that set it apart. Like other producers' cooperatives, Ulgor places a high value on labor, making it the most important factor in the production process. Ulgor did not begin with money or technology; rather, it started with people willing to contribute their work in order to achieve a goal.

Ulgor members accepted the general principles of cooperativism:[8] democratic control on the basis of one-member one-vote, capital contribution, freedom of entry and exit, the principle of "open door" access, and permanent education of the members. However, Ulgor established an identity between membership and contribution of labor, eliminating the possibility of having members who did not work in the firm. Ulgor also introduced several unorthodox *operational decisions* which modified traditional cooperative principles. These were the most important:

1. *For the acquisition of capital:* Without resources of their own, and effectively barred from capital markets, the founders of Ulgor asked for the financial backing from the people of the town of Mondragon. To protect the money received as well as to secure future financing, the founders implemented novel measures. First, they opened Caja Laboral and then they developed a concept of savings permitted by law to which no one had previously paid any attention. It was called "workers savings" and paid an interest rate of one-half percent above the one paid by credit cooperatives and savings and loan associations. Ulgor also decided to compensate its members' capital contributions for the risk involved in keeping it in the cooperative and added a variable "risk premium" to the legal interest rates. Furthermore, Caja Laboral and Ulgor took the unusual step of making annual corrections for inflation on all capital loaned for, or kept in, the cooperatives. As a result of these decisions Ulgor and Caja Laboral, in fact, offered interest rates superior to any offered to workers or common savers at the time. These measures were not forbidden by law, but through the use of ingenuity and savvy, the law was made to work on their behalf. Incentives were offered to attract capital for Ulgor and Caja Laboral.

2. *For the distribution of enterprise surplus:* A key economic decision was made by Ulgor members when they tied the annual distribution of the profits to the investment policies of the firm. Cooperative principles mandate that such profits must be distributed among the workers, after the allocations to the legal funds are made. Ulgor members respected this principle but decided not to distribute the profits in cash among the members until they retired or left the firm. Instead, each individual's share of the profits was

deposited in the account held for him or her at Ulgor, where it received the attractive interest rates described above. In real terms, this meant that Ulgor was able to capitalize 100 percent of its yearly profits. This provided a rapid mechanism for capital accumulation and supported the self-financing policy of the enterprise. The objective of this policy was to secure capital for the firm's expansion; in addition, the goal of expansion was to create job opportunities for a larger number of workers. From its very beginning, the relation between the cooperative firm and the community was established on the basis of broad reciprocity. Ulgor initiated the now established cooperative policies of providing substantial subsidies to technical and general education and making substantial contributions for improving the health and welfare of the local community. Local residents received the benefits independently of the fact of membership in the cooperatives. Funds were channeled through the Social Works Fund of the firm. The creation of this fund is mandated by cooperative legislation. However, in traditional cooperatives its function is to promote benefits for individuals, not to serve as a means of maintaining a relationship between the firm's growth and the development of the community's resources and facilities. In the long run this policy proved to be advantageous for both Ulgor and the local community.

3. *For the members' compensations:* Ulgor members decided to make their annual earnings comparable to the wages paid for similar jobs in noncooperative firms of the area. This decision set voluntary limits to their take-home pay, but it was instrumental in fostering good relations with owners and workers of noncooperative firms because it did not disrupt the wage levels of the area. The cooperative value of external solidarity had two other immediate, pragmatic consequences: it maintained the payroll level within manageable limits, and helped provide a criterion to set the minimum salaries at Ulgor. However, to balance this voluntary limit on earnings, Ulgor instituted both a minimum salary that adequately covered all the basic needs of its members and benefits in health, welfare, and retirement

that were better than average when compared to non-cooperative firms. A short-term sacrifice was balanced with a long-term advantage.

4. *To maximize equity and trust:* Another key compensation decision was made when Ulgor members voted to use a special rule of equity for the distribution of rewards in the firm. Ulgor members agreed to reward effort and responsibility differentially; however, those differentials were within an agreed-upon range. For compensation purposes, they chose a one-to-three differential between the highest- and lowest-paid jobs. This was approximately the actual spread in salaries among Ulgor members at that time. This decision introduced both a bottom and a ceiling for the compensation system. For higher-level personnel it meant a voluntary restriction on the salary levels they could reach. However, it helped to establish *bona fide* solidarity and trust within Ulgor because it dispelled any doubts regarding the personal economic ambition of those who accepted managerial and directive functions. Managers and directors gained unquestioned legitimacy, as well as the freedom to implement a vision of entrepreneurial development that the leaders of Ulgor could not have exercised in a conventional corporation or without the support of the members of the cooperative firm. It is clear that the tradeoff was between material gain and the possibility of implementing a special vision of entrepreneurial development (psychic income). Furthermore, the developmental path followed by Ulgor provided ample opportunities for challenging and satisfactory work for all those who had the ability and interest to take advantage of them. Beyond that, during periods of rapid growth, this tradeoff gave Ulgor managers a great deal of agility in the decision-making process. Managerial proposals were supported by the members, including those which introduced technological changes and administrative rationalization. The continued expansion of the industrial complex of Mondragon has allowed the maintenance of the tradeoff between material gains and psychic income for higher-level personnel. During the late 1970s and early 1980s, managerial turnover did not exceed 10 percent.

5. *For the representation of members as workers:* The
founders of Ulgor recognized that the General Assembly,
the conventional means for the democratic participation of
workers in a cooperative enterprise, was not sufficient to
ensure that all possible conflicts of interest were satisfactorily resolved. Ulgor members were particularly concerned
with the conflicts resulting from the divison of labor between managers and workers. Thus, they invented the
Social Council, an elected, permanent advisory body. The
Social Council was conceived as a means for the expression
of the collective preferences of the members, *as workers,*
regarding all terms and conditions of work. It also allowed
the workers to express their opinions on all major policy
decisions in the firm. The Social Council was created as an
arena where managerial concerns for long-range decisions
and the workers' reactions to the consequences of these
decisions on the day-to-day operations could be discussed
and negotiated.

6. *For the selection of management:* Another important decision was made when Ulgor members voted to give their
elected Board of Directors the authority to appoint
management and to be primary in judging its satisfactory
performance. This created a buffer for those cases in which
workers and managers might disagree over the management of the firm. To solve the problem created by the ap-
pointment of management within a structure in which decisions had to be made by elected representatives, Ulgor
created the Directive Council, the most important managerial decision-making body, formed by the board and
management, but in which management has voice but not
vote. Decisions made by the Directive Council were ex-
ecuted by management. The later was given full authority
to carry out its responsibilities without interference from
other bodies in the firm. At the end of the fiscal year,
management was accountable to the General Assembly of
worker–owners.

7. *For entrance of new members:* Finally, Ulgor members
decided to set the entrance fees for new members at a level
low enough to implement an "open door" principle. To

establish the annual increases in these fees, they developed
a formula based only on cost of living increases and the
relative contribution (to the wealth of the firm) made by the
workers who entered during the preceding year. If the en-
trances fees had been set in relation to the accumulated
value of the contribution of the first members, the amounts
would have been prohibitive for the common worker.

Each of these operational decisions introduced new working principles
into the traditional organizational structure of the cooperative firm. As a
result, the model of enterprise was modified in significant ways. The most
outstanding overall feature of this new model is its combination of
cooperative principles, such as "solidarity," "work," and "equity," with a
pragmatic or operational sense, which could be called "cooperative
economic reality."[9] Though this latter was not originally stated as a principle in the statutes and bylaws of Ulgor, its implicit status receives support
from the fact that, more recently, a principle called "economic rationality"
has been formally included among those from which operational decisions
are derived.[10] In any event, it is not unwarranted to suggest that it informed
such operational decisions as those to give variable returns to capital, to use
retained earnings for self-financing purposes, to choose technological rationalization and to pursue an expansive process of development.
However, since the economic rationality of the Mondragon cooperatives is
not identical to the conventional economic rationality, the term
"cooperative economic rationality" will be used in this work.

However, it is not possible to explain Ulgor's economic development as a
production unit and its expansion into Spanish and international markets as
side effects of this pragmatic organizational structure alone. *If anything,
Ulgor's formal organizational structure, as described above, explains stability
rather than growth.* Democracy and equity explain why the members did not
enter into conflict over distributional matters and why they gave their commitment to the organization's goals. Social responsiveness explains why Ulgor secured the support of the local community. External solidarity explains why
Ulgor coexisted peacefully with other industrial firms; economic rationality explains how Ulgor secured resources for its survival. However, these alone do
not explain the development of the cooperative network, the level of technological development of the firms, and the high level of administrative and organizational rationalization. This fact makes it necessary to probe further into
the possible causes of the successful development of the Mondragon network.

Obviously, the founders of Ulgor also made other decisions more closely related to the productive aspects of the enterprise. For instance, Ulgor members made the fail-proof decision of starting small, with a technology they could handle comfortably, but still seeking an expansive process. The founders of Ulgor paid an unusually high price for the industrial permit to start their operations. The reason was that this permit contained a special clause allowing the firm to produce a wide range of durable and intermediate goods, thus giving Ulgor the freedom to expand its production without having to ask for new permits each time a new product was decided upon. In seeking this expansive path, Ulgor members had necessarily to accept the risks involved, and they also had to engage in search-behavior to find ways to expand production and jobs. For instance, Ulgor sent scouts through Europe and Spain to find markets, products, and processes. Ulgor purchased more advanced European technologies and introduced them to the Basque region, acting as a technological bridge between the more advanced European countries and Spain. With more advanced technology Ulgor also introduced administrative and managerial rationalization. However, the latter were not allowed to overrun the democratic structure, which was made to coexist with the new developments.

To manage organizational and productive expansion, Ulgor members decided in favor of a fission pattern whereby, as new products were chosen, independent firms were launched to carry out the operation. These independent firms were modeled in the organizational blueprint pioneered by Ulgor. This pattern of growth can be called *"recursive"* because the same organizational features, and their goals, are reproduced in the new firms, independently of the differences in products or industries. From the point of view of expansion, this pattern preserves the organizational affinity which makes linkage formation a natural process and allows for the possibility of sharing resources jointly in order to achieve economies of scale. This recursive pattern gave unity and coherence to the Mondragon network, because it reproduced at the level of second-order organizations the same organizational principles and relations found successful at the level of first-order organizations. However, it also allowed for organizational efficacy to mobilize broadly generated resources and to undertake projects of larger dimension. The vulnerability and potential weakness of the individual firm were replaced by the strength of the network. These led to growth and development at the regional level, well beyond the individual firm.

Logically, the set of decisions leading to growth and development cannot be the same as those leading to stability. When the founders of Ulgor decided to adapt their model of enterprise to the Spanish cooperative legislation, they did so because this legislation afforded them the opportunity to establish an enterprise which gave workers rights and benefits in the production unit. However, this fact means that workers contribute their labor but also hold the ownership and the rights to management. To deal with this, the founders of Ulgor paid special attention to the general premise of traditional cooperativism of later origin,[11] one not included in the general principles of the Rochdale pioneers. This is the premise of the dual role *(doble vertiente)* assumed by the members of a cooperative: as (1) members proper, i.e., owners; and (2) beneficiaries *(usuarios)* of the services of the cooperative, i.e., workers. This is the dual role "worker-owner." The founders of Ulgor paid special attention to this principle, but defined it in terms of the kind of enterprise they had in mind.

In the traditional doctrine of cooperativism the role of members is understood as an internal role of participant in the decision making of the corporation. At Ulgor, the role of the member was defined as "protagonist of a social task."[12] Its content was given by the Spanish term *"empresario"* which conveys the compound meanings of owner–entrepreneur. The dual role means *"empresario–trabajador"* whose translation into English gives "owner–entrepreneur–worker." For the sake of simplicity I will use "entrepreneur–worker." This shift had great significance because the operational content for this general principle was coined in entrepreneurial terms. The founders of Ulgor drew their operational principles with their role as owner–entrepreneurs in mind. They also acted accordingly. They launched the operation and took measures to ensure its success as an enterprise. This explains their unorthodox additions and modifications to traditional cooperative concepts. *This entrepreneurial orientation was (and is) the factor which explains the expansion of the cooperative network and its level of technological and organizational development.*

Labor Entrepreneurship and the Cooperative Labor Enterprise

I propose to label this orientation "labor entrepreneurship" to differentiate it from conventional entrepreneurship. Labor entrepreneurship is also a behavioral posture of search for opportunities, articulation of productive resources, risk taking, and organization building. The difference in labor entrepreneurship lies in the active role assumed by the associated workers, the collective decision-making process and the labor-based vision of development. Labor entrepreneurship transformed the traditional concept of the cooperative as a private, closed, corporation into a concept of broader social enterprise. As a result of this shift, the model of cooperative implemented by Ulgor was not the traditional producers' cooperative but the "cooperative labor enterprise."

Labor entrepreneurship proved to be a powerful motivational force in the development of Ulgor first, and the complex later, because it asserted and legitimized empirically (not just ideologically) the primacy of labor in the productive process. The associated workers and their democratically elected leaders, in a context of equity and solidarity, discovered they had the power to implement a *labor-based* vision of entrepreneurship, management, and development. Under these conditions it is not difficult to explain why the leaders were willing to forego higher economic rewards, or why the workers agreed to trade off short-term benefits for longer-term ones, and to substitute social interests for individual ones. Recently, Jesus Larranaga, one of the founders of Ulgor, has evaluated the importance of the shift:

> . . . Our culture is new: it is the culture of workers who are responsible for and participate in economic entrepreneurship and management *(la gestion empresarial)*.
>
> We know that in programming our future investments we are accepting risks. This is the proper behavior for entrepreneurs.[13]

Although not explicitly stated in these terms, it is clear that the goal labor entrepreneurship made possible was (and is) the rational[14] participation of labor in the creation of wealth and in the socialization of its distribution. This rational participation involved at least the "satisfying"[15] use of productive resources, including labor.

> A cooperative enterprise . . . had to be an efficient organization which could produce at decreasing costs.[16]

However, the more effective participation of labor was achieved by the development of an organizational structure which, in the words of Don Jose Maria Arizmendi, "would not curtail individuals' efforts and commitment to the organization's goals."[17] Productive efficiency was also achieved through the use of technological innovations and through the rationalization of work processes and administration. It is clear that the members of

Ulgor accepted these forms of rationalization because they offered the path of viability within the economic order of Spain and Europe.

> . . . Step by step . . . (this experience) learned to cool impulses and to make truths relative in order to avoid the danger (of an idealism) which could have taken the *Experience* to the altar of dogmatism. . . . (emphasis original, parentheses added).[18]

The rational participation of labor in its social task also involved a definition of the means to socialize the benefits of the production process. Creation of jobs, support of education, health services, and welfare were defined as more rational means to socialize benefits than providing unlimited economic rewards to the members.

In my view, the success of the Mondragon firms and of the network was made possible by the articulation of a cooperative, value-based organizational structure, that promoted stability, with the rational, growth-oriented, behavior of labor entrepreneurship, which promoted innovation and change. These two processes blended to create a model of private enterprise open to local community goals and to the broader environments within which the firm must operate. It is a clear understanding of the nature of these environments, local, national and international, which stimulated the growth of the network and its orientation toward the use of modern and sophisticated technology and organization.

The Issue of Transferability

It would be difficult to argue that the Mondragon model of enterprise presented above is incompatible with social, economic, or political conditions in Western societies. Even its basic value principles are regarded as ideal in those societies. In my view the issue is not "*if*" it can be transferred as much as *by whom and how*. Obviously, the transference will depend on the interest and willingness of individual workers to associate according to agreed-upon tenets and to extend the benefits to a larger number of workers. But a decision to transfer the model must also take into account the main points of the preceding analysis, which include:

1. The distinction between features in the model that promote *stability* and those which lead to *growth and development*. Specifically, the central role of "labor entrepreneurship,"

which involves economic and organizational rationality, must be recognized.

2. *Labor entrepreneurship* must not be equated with traditional cooperative values nor with worker ownership or self-management. At least one of the latter is necessary for labor entrepreneurship, but alone (as we've seen) they provide only a stable democratic structure and do not foster or account for Mondragon's expansive success.

3. The importance of the *recursive* pattern of development, where the direction is from productive-unit organization (first order) to support-level organization (second order); that is, features leading to success at the productive level are selected to be reproduced by support organizations.

4. The model is not likely to emerge as a natural development of existing conditions. The Mondragon model did not emerge as a natural development of traditional cooperative values nor of Basque patterns of organization.

5. In the last analysis, as Mondragon reveals, cooperative principles must be *pragmatically* connected to *concrete operational* measures.

To conclude, I would like to point out that the model of cooperative enterprise is presented as the first step toward a larger pattern of regionwide development. However, this pattern and its features are not dealt with in this paper. I would further add that my emphasis on the organizational features of the Mondragon model of enterprise does not indicate a disregard for the role of individuals in the process. However, since what is transferable is the pattern, I have not made explicit references to the importance of the intellectual work of Don Jose Maria Arizmendi in the development of the model, or to the work of the founders of Ulgor. My point of departure has been the decision process leading to the structuring of the model, after the individuals agreed to implement it.

Notes

1. See, for instance, Jaroslav Vanek, ed., *Self-Management: Economic Liberation of Man* (Penguin Modern Economic Readings, 1975), pp. 16–26. Also, Paul Blumberg, *Industrial Democracy: The Sociology of Participation* (New York: Schocken, 1968), pp.3–4.
2. The description of this process and the data to support the conclusions are presented in Ana Gutierrez-Johnson, "Industrial Democracy in Action: The Mondragon Cooperative

Complex (Ph.D. dissertation, University Microfilms International, Ann Arbor, Michigan, 1982), Chap. 3.

3. The success rate in launching new cooperative enterprises or in transforming other models to cooperatives is nearly 100 percent. This process is supervised and aided by Caja Laboral's Entrepreneurial Division. By comparison, in the U.S. the rate of success of new business is about 2 percent.

4. Henk Thomas and Christopher Logan, *Mondragon: An Economic Analysis* (London, Boston: George Allen and Unwin, 1982).

5. Ibid., pp. 126–127.

6. Gutierrez-Johnson, "Industrial Democracy," Chap. 6.

7. Particularly policies for education, employment, health, and services to the communities.

8. The Mondragon cooperatives seem to have been influenced more by French cooperativism than the British Rochdale model. Their general principles follow those espoused by the School of Mimes. See Dionisio Aranzadi, *Cooperativismo Industrial Como Sistema* (Editorial Elexpuru Hnos,, S.A., Bilbao, 1976).

9. The concept of rationality, both economic and administrative, used here is derived from the work of James G. March and Herbert A. Simon presented in *Organizations* (New York: Wiley, 1968), Chap. 6, pp. 136-142. This concept of rationality replaces the classical concept of economic theory. Rationality for March and Simon is relative to a frame of reference, the choice of appropriate means to ends is given within a framework which results from social and psychological forces as well as others. The choice is not the optimal one because of the cognitive limits on rationality, but the one which meets or exceeds minimally satisfactory criteria. In the case of Mondragon, the framework for choice was outlived by stated values and goals. The choices were rational in the sense defined by March and Simon. Furthermore, they superceded the traditional concept of rationality in which the general context of values and social forces is left undefined.

10. Gutierrez-Johnson, "Industrial Democracy," Chap. 6, pp. 336, 339, 347.

11. See Aranzadi, *Cooperativismo Industrial,* pp. 81, 444-449.

12. Article 124, bylaws of Ulgor (1972).

13. *T.U. Magazine,* no. 260 (April 1983): 11.

14. See note 9.

15. See March and Simon, *Organizations,* pp. 140-141.

16. Don Jose Maria Arizmendi, Interview 1975, p. 22 (by Ana Gutierrez-Johnson).

17. Ibid., p. 15.

18. Jesus Larranaga, *T.U. Magazine,* no. 260 (April 1983): 10.

Mondragon: A Less Favorable Assessment

Christopher S. Axworthy

Mondragon is often talked about in hyperbolic, glowing terms. It provides the grist for so many pro-worker cooperative arguments. It is a remarkable economic success, but how does it rate as a worker co-op? A number of criteria might be looked at: Who controls the enterprise and how? What is the nature of the relationship among those involved? Is work fulfilling? In a nutshell, are the worker members in control of their workplace?

Control at Mondragon

There can be little doubt of the value of the Caja Laboral Popular (the central bank) to the development of the cooperatives at Mondragon. It has played a critical role in ensuring that good business practices are followed by individual enterprises and in ensuring low levels of defaults on loans through careful assistance in the early planning stages of any expansion of the system, and continuing managerial, financial and marketing assistance.

Traditionally, cooperatives have been seen as more or less spontaneous creations. This is far from the case at Mondragon. Here cooperatives are only established with the assistance of the Caja after a thorough enquiry into the feasibility of the venture by the Caja's Empressarial Division.

It is important to emphasize that the Caja's loans are cheap—in some circumstances they are interest-free. Consequently, the involvement of the Caja is attractive and may be absolutely critical to any new venture. The price paid for this is a considerable lack of spontaneity and independence on the part of the individual cooperatives.

So the role of the Caja reflects a very centralized managerial style. The ethos of the Caja resembles that of a stern parent. Much justification is required before any action is permitted by individual cooperatives. If the individual cooperative acts in accordance with dictates of the Caja, it will be assisted. The Caja acts as if it knows best what the individual cooperatives should do, want to do and aspire to.

FROM *Worker Co-ops Newsletter,* Fall 1985, pp. 21–22. Reprinted by permission of the author.

In addition, the Caja is not impressed by the attributes of the members who make up the individual cooperatives — they are referred to as being uneducated, happy to have a job, not very knowledgeable about the activities of their cooperative, and even of being peasants.

The relationship between the worker members and their cooperatives appears to be less than desirable. Paternalism prevails in the attitude of management toward shop-floor worker members. The managers do not appear to have a constructive relationship with shop-floor members — the relationship seems to be a formal and traditional one without camaraderie or respect. It is certainly not a warm relationship. Actually, the factories are sufficiently environmentally hazardous as to indicate a marked lack of concern for the interests of shop-floor worker members. In short, the working conditions and attitudes at Mondragon do not exude much cooperative spirit.

Anti-Trade-Union Bias

There is also evidence of a considerable anti-trade-union bias among the upper echelons at Mondragon. The social councils which exist in each factory and office are designed to fulfill the functions normally performed by trade unions and were established when trade unions were banned in Spain. These social councils are now used to support the view that unions are not necessary at Mondragon. The arguments presented replicate those made by anti-union employers.

The attitude toward expansion at Mondragon is interesting and is closely linked to the mechanism by which capital is made available to individual cooperatives. While individual cooperatives reinvest 90 percent of their earnings, the system as a whole only uses about 35 percent of its annual resources for cooperative investment. Of all the money flowing in to the Caja from the cooperatives and individual depositors at its branches, only 35 percent is made available for cooperative investments. The remaining 65 percent is invested in the private sector.

The system in fact makes little return on its cooperative investments but makes satisfactory returns on its private-sector investments. It is these investments that are used to fuel the new developments at Mondragon. Mondragon is not self-contained financially. It is a heavily subsidized system.

The growth rate is necessarily slower than it would be if all of the resources of Mondragon were ploughed back into the system. The unemployment rate in the Basque region of Spain is more than 20 percent, but in the Mondragon system only about 20 people out of a membership of 19,000 are out of work. Yet Mondragon has not sought to expand to meet the employment needs of fellow Basques, in spite of the much vaunted (but overrated) nationalistic traits of the system. It would seem that the system is more interested in consolidating its position than in expanding its benefits to its neighbors.

Conclusion

Mondragon is different, but is it a network of worker cooperatives? It is economically successful, but how does it fare from a cooperative point of view? This is an important issue because Mondragon is, and will be used as a model for worker cooperation development.

Viewed from a cooperative standpoint, Mondragon can be found lacking. Its control structure is striking for its rigidity. It is very much a case of the Caja deciding what will happen because the Caja's officials know best and will fund any developments which pass the tests they set. The system is heavily centralized and lacks spontaneity.

The organization is a conservative one that is developing slowly and cautiously and investing in the private sector in the process. It is anti-union and does not appear to value its worker members, their interests or their views. The relationship between members who are managers and those on the shop floor does not suggest a great democratization of the workplace.

A distinctive feature about Mondragon is its surplus distribution system. The earnings of a majority of worker members are equal to or even a little higher than for comparable jobs in the surrounding area. In addition, members have credited to their capital accounts their proportional share of the surplus. This deferred income is available to the members upon retirement or leaving the area. The capital accounts are adjusted for inflation on a periodic basis. Thus, worker members, through their efforts, are investing in, and benefiting from, their investment in the cooperative.

But is surplus distribution sufficient for Mondragon to be referred to as a system of worker cooperatives? There is much in the way Mondragon operates that serves to call into question its cooperative features. It is not alone among cooperative movements in this, of course.

Perhaps it is a mixture of success and longevity which explains the partial replacement of the cooperative dynamic with a more business-oriented one. This process may not be deliberate, but it seems to be widespread. If

Mondragon is to be the beacon to the cooperative system, more attention to its cooperative features is called for. It is difficult to know how much of this Mondragon is capable of, whether it has the will to bring this about and even how much of it ever existed. After all, Father Arizmendiarrieta, the guiding light behind the establishment of the Mondragon system, was very much the paternal and guiding figure the Caja is today.

13 | Strategies for Change

Americans live relatively well and enjoy political liberty, yet the system is in many respects oppressive. Most Americans are employed in hierarchical bureaucracies where subordinates have little control over the work. Domestic unemployment and poverty are endemic. Transnational corporations exploit Third World countries, and the American military intervenes against their popular revolts. We live under the shadow of thermonuclear war. An expanding arms budget wastes an increasing proportion of our tax money and at the same time necessary social services are cut back. What, then, is to be done? This is the question addressed by the two articles in this chapter.

Frank Lindenfeld contrasts four strategies for social change: the Marxist–Leninist, the social democratic, the liberal, and the anarchist. Marxist–Leninists favor violent revolution by an armed minority that will set up a government favorable to the working class. Social democrats prefer the peaceful means of building up a socialist political party that will promote reform when it is voted into office by a majority of the electorate. Liberals advocate working for reform within the system as it is, and trying to influence the major political parties from within. Anarchists favor revolutionary change but are divided as to whether or not it should be brought about by violent means. They advocate the adoption of revolutionary life styles and the building of alternative institutions to create new jobs and provide services outside the existing, exploitative system. But these measures will not be effective in leading to a social transformation unless they are accompanied by a mass political movement.

Shoshana Rihn and Marty Jezer point to the danger of believing that all that is necessary to create political change is for individuals to alter their consciousness and life style. It is not enough, they maintain, for each of us to live an exemplary life: "Our lives must also be politically relevant and contribute to revolutionary change." Living communally, growing organic food, and working in cooperatives is morally desirable but is not enough to change the system.

Alternative institutions such as workers' cooperatives and consumer cooperatives should spread, but the existing system will allow them to develop only as long as they remain small and pose no threat to the capitalist social order. Perhaps if *enough* people could find jobs in democratically organized cooperatives and collectives, the old system would collapse. ("What if they gave a war and nobody came?") The problem is that the establishment prevents people from building alternatives on any large scale because, in order to do so, they have to have access to capital. In a capitalist system, capital is monopolized by capitalists.

Thus we need *political* movements that will confront capitalism and take control of the means of production. To promote the transformation of the capitalist system into a participatory socialist one requires a mass movement with clear political goals, a movement that unites diverse factions and avoids alienating the less politicized. A key to building such a movement is consciousness raising. There needs to be a concerted educational effort to counter the ideological brainwashing by the mass media and the public schools. Such an effort would expose the exploitation of the poor, in this country and abroad, by wealthy corporations. It would expose the ways in which the ruling class exercises power despite the existence of a formally democratic electoral system, and would point out the connection between an astronomical military budget and the increasing misery of the poor. It would explain the inadequacy of individualistic solutions to collective problems. And it would persuade dissident minorities to overcome their differences and work together for structural change.

Which Way to the Revolution?

Shoshana Rihn and Marty Jezer

We are aware of a great deal of discussion and questioning and, indeed, some hot debate by people who identify themselves as radical beings, about what strategy will most likely lead to revolution. The discussion is over whether or not alternative institutions and life-style modes, and the gropings toward personal growth that often accompany such life styles, contribute to the revolutionary change that we all claim to want. . . .

A debate between the Reverend Philip Zwerling and the Reverend Douglas Wilson seems to us to typify the discussion.[1] It is Wilson's contention that the Human Potential Movement and the creation of alternative life styles *in themselves* represent a revolutionary force in American society. As two people who live the kind of lives that Wilson says will lead to meaningful change, we feel the need to state and explain our support for the political perspective articulated by Zwerling, and criticize what we believe to be the dead-end prescription for revolution that Wilson advocates.

Although we are using the Zwerling–Wilson debate as our point of reference, we feel that we are speaking to many of our friends and comrades in our own area, and hopefully to other unknown comrades elsewhere in the country, who, like ourselves, are personally grappling with the issues under discussion.

The two of us live in a relatively self-sufficient commune, pretty much outside of the consumer culture. We raise and grow our own food, cut our own wood for heat and cooking, are part of grower (farmer) and consumer (food) cooperatives, and generally try to understand ourselves within the dynamics of group process. Living with 10 other people makes this kind of self-awareness almost a prerequisite for survival.

It is very tempting for us to define our situation as inherently revolutionary, and on occasion one of us (MJ) has. . . .

The attempt to define our lives in terms of a revolutionary calling is something many of us are prone to. Wanting to change the world, we tend to judge our selves in moral and political terms. It is not sufficient to live a

FROM *WIN*, March 10, 1977. Reprinted by permission of the authors.

good, honest productive life. Our lives must also be politically relevant and contribute to revolutionary change. Thus, we often define ourselves not by the life that we actually lead, but as against the life that we think we ought to be leading. This encourages two attitudes: Either we judge ourselves too harshly for failing to live up to our ideals or we define whatever we do in terms of our ideals, applying revolutionary attributes to even the most mundane aspects of daily existence. (Growing organic food is one example of this.)

Our situation, in this, is unique. Most people have not had (or aren't aware that they've had) our options. We've made choices about careers, family, levels of affluence, etc., that are voluntary. And having made these choices, we feel compelled to justify them, to ourselves, especially, if nobody else. Certainly, for us living self-sufficiently on a communal farm as opposed to, say, building Trident submarines, working in advertising, or dealing smack, is a moral way of living. But does that make it political? Here is where we part company with Wilson and other proponents of alternative life styles as a way to revolution. He describes a number of good ways that people are living and arbitrarily (we think) assigns them a revolutionary content. Revolutionary activity is or should be at all times moral. But moral conduct is not necessarily revolutionary, or even political. Sometimes it's only moral — and personally fulfilling.

Wilson says that he respects "people who are trying new ways of eating, becoming vegetarians, making contact with their own bodies, learning what health really is, learning to do without doctors. This is part of the revolution that is already happening." Well, wealthy gourmands have always experimented with new ways of eating, and the fact that radicals are now into good food does not make their appetites any more revolutionary than those who have the money (if they live in the East) to fly in fresh organic carrots direct from California. Vegetarianism, as well, is a personal preference for right-wingers or left. Hitler didn't eat meat, and neither, for what it's worth, does one of the authors of this article. Certainly, for ecological reasons, we ought to eat less meat. But if we are going to have an organic agriculture, we are going to need (and properly utilize) massive amounts of animal manure. Besides, there are grassland areas that ought to be pastured and cannot sustain crops. So any sound agriculture is going to have to include beef, hogs, sheep, etc.

Vegetarianism is neither an indicator of moral purity nor a revolutionary way of organizing food production. Getting in touch with our bodies is only novel for people who spend their lives sitting at a desk or standing hours on end on an assembly line. Workers get in touch with their bodies playing ball or dancing. Corporate executives take saunas and have daily steam baths and massages. The way that counterculturalists get in touch with their bodies may sometimes differ. But the intent is the same and the political effect is neutral.

As for health care and doctors, we probably all believe that the American health care system needs overhauling. But learning to do without doctors does not confront the injustices of the system. Besides, doing without health care is something many people in this country have had to do simply because they cannot afford to do otherwise. Whether all of the above activities are worthwhile is beside the point. The question is whether they, in themselves, contribute to revolutionary change. We think not.

The Personal and the Political

We are not saying that politics are separate from our personal lives. The two should be integrated at all levels. Our politics should be carried into our daily lives and shape our conduct; the way that we are ought to be taken as a reflection of our politics. But if we are going to commit ourselves to revolutionary change, we are going to have to evaluate our activities in terms of a wider political perspective. It is not enough to say that we are living morally or decently or even that we are living in a way that we hope all people will live *after* the revolution. The revolution hasn't happened. And it won't happen unless we make it.

So while we favor most of the things that Wilson is enthusiastic about — from painless childbirth to organic apple pie — and pursue some of these ourselves, we do not believe that in themselves they contribute to revolutionary goals. Living communally, for instance, makes us less fragmented and alienated. It allows us to depend less on the consumer culture and more on each other. It teaches self-reliance in a collective context, and it sometimes provides us with necessary psychological support. Inasmuch as it teaches us collective responsibility and forces us to confront the destructive and selfish individualism that is part of our culture (and which we have all absorbed in varying degrees), it may even make us more effective in our political work.

Revolution by Example

What we mean by political work is evidently different from what Wilson means by the term. The strategy of alternatives that Wilson espouses (the idea of building a new society in the shell of the old) is the strategy of *revolution by example*. The idea is that if a few people perform an exemplary act (which might be civil disobedience, living collectively, organizing a food co-op, growing organic vegetables, etc.), other people will be inspired to do the same. The alternative movement will grow, reaching out to more and more people. As it grows, it will draw strength away from the old order (which in the process will become demystified), which, because it is irrelevant to freshly perceived human needs, will wither away. The A&P will give way to co-ops, GM will collapse because we will all become auto mechanics, repair our old cars and keep them running forever, and the utility companies will go broke because we'll all have homemade solar collectors or wood stoves. And, as the old order goes, a new simpler way of life, scaled to human dimension, will take its place. From the first seed of exemplary conduct a revolution will eventually grow.

This strategy has been attempted many times before and failed. This, in itself, is not sufficient reason to discard it. History is not "doomed" to repeat itself, and revolutionary movements that come to grief in one situation triumph in another. The *example* theory fails not so much because of the time or situation, but because it does not address itself to the basic contradictions of society and is inadequate in itself. (The Chinese built up alternative institutions in their liberated areas. But whereas Wilson describes alternatives as substitutes for politics, the Chinese integrated their alternative and cooperative experiments into the political struggle. To offer the idea of alternatives, as Wilson does, without a political context, is to offer a placebo for social discontent and to encourage people to abandon useful, political work.)

The Rural Alternative

Take our own experiences (one that Doug Wilson shares) of living in the country: it may seem "radical" to some who feel stuck in cities and even to some who have made the move from city to country. And it *is* "radical" in the sense that it represents a departure from the basic socioeconomic trends of the past several decades in the United States. But how can rural life in itself be considered any more inherently revolutionary than city life?

Almost certainly, a revolution in this country would include a substantial back-to-the land movement, a resurgence of agriculture and/or small-town life as a desirable option for many people. (Keeping in mind that it is the harsh economic necessities induced by capitalism that has driven so many people off the land and into the cities in the first place.) But that doesn't necessarily mean that the few people who have gone back to the land constitute a part (or a vanguard) of that movement.

We are fortunate to have bought our farm in 1968, before the price of land skyrocketed out of proportion. At the time, some of us flattered ourselves into believing that we were part of a back-to-the-land movement that had profound revolutionary implications. In fact, as more people joined us on the land we thought that we had been proven politically correct. But as these people moved back-to-the-land, the price of land began to rise. In the sense (as Wilson would have it) that our communal farm was a model that inspired others, it contributed to the difficulty that these new groups of homesteaders and communards had in buying land.

In Vermont, the failure of the rural alternative is especially striking. The flood of people who came to create a new society in the shell of the old forced land prices up even beyond the means of those who came with inherited wealth. The best agricultural land, in fact, was priced out of the range that allowed farming to be economically viable. Developers bought this land and turned it into shopping plazas and tract houses. Those of us who wanted to farm had to settle for hill farms of marginal agricultural value. (That is, we could support a self-sufficient operation, but growing food "for the people" is quite another matter.)

What we now have is a situation in which only a few of the people who came to Vermont to homestead or farm communally actually have land. Most people have had to postpone their dream, work in town, and hope to save money to buy land in the future. But inflation and the high unemployment and low wages that are endemic to rural areas eat at their savings, and most accept the fact that they will probably never own land. Gradually, the New Age organic homesteading fantasy fades. Many of the young people who moved to Vermont have become proletarianized like their working neighbors (who possibly came to Vermont years ago with similar dreams).

The point here is that communes as viable alternatives to the existing system are open only to a privileged few. And any talk about rural communes, organic gardening, eco-agriculture, feeding the people on healthy diets, etc., means talking about money, power, and control of land. Fewer and fewer people who now own land actually live on the land, much less farm it. The trend of corporate agribusiness is driving independent family farmers out of business, and this trend is inherent in capitalism; it cannot be reversed by patchwork reform. Moreover, the people who do speculate in land for profit, or mine it for short-term agricultural gain (like the agribusiness corporations) are not going to allow would-be homesteaders to squat on it out of social philanthropy.

The only way to redistribute land (as well as to redistribute the income to provide the people who live on the land with enough capital to take care of it) is by building a political movement and making an agrarian revolution. The old injunction to "raise more hell and less corn" is as meaningful today as it was during the heyday of the populist rebellion before the turn of the century.

This is a hard fact of rural life that would-be homesteaders who have turned their backs on politics continuously choose to ignore. Julius Lester, writing in a recent issue of *Liberation,* falls prey to romanticizing about the politics of organic gardening. He writes:

> I am more concerned these days about blossom end rot on my tomatoes than the rotten capitalist system. That's revolutionary in a way because every pound of food I raise (successfully) frees me that much from the tyranny of agribusiness. Everything I learn to do and make for myself makes me that much less available to exploitation by capitalism.

This is true, of course, but only as far as it goes, which isn't very far at all. Tending a garden is a long way from feeding the masses. Using compost and manure does not break the hold that the agricultural industry (or even the purveyors of organic fertilizers) has on American agriculture.

Being a political person, Lester realizes this. So he fantasizes teaching welfare recipients how to grow food in the city and of organizing a farm with poor people and old folks living on social security. Although this fantasy presupposes a political solution to the problem of food and land, Lester does not make the connection that political solutions necessitate a political process.

The fantasy of a New York skyline with cows grazing on rooftop pastures is a delightful one. But just as old tenements won't support the weight of rooftop gardens, the economic systems under which we live won't tolerate a degree of self-sufficiency that seriously cuts into its markets. The question we would ask Lester is an obvious one, but it strikes at the limitation of the rural alternative: How are you going to buy the land? Where are you going to get the money? How are you going to acquire the tractors (or work horses) chisel plows, manure spreaders, seeds, lime, and fertilizers to detoxicate and improve the soil?

Moist soil rich with humus is the best way of preventing blossom end rot on tomatoes, a condition that often occurs in hot, dry weather. A mulch helps and so does frequent watering or irrigation. But agrarian revolution leading to redistribution of land and income is the only way to change our system of agriculture and improve our dietary habits. Although growing a small organic garden may raise one's consciousness about agricultural economics and rural politics, the most productive organic garden in the world is not going to further the cause of agrarian revolution.

Feminist Carpenters

Another example that Wilson uses to describe the alternative and Human Potential Movements as a revolutionary force is the idea of women learning skills that were once the province of man. We agree with Wilson (and Zwerling) that the liberation of women is inherent to revolution. Indeed, given that this country already has a strong economic base, the battles against sexism and racism are primary parts of the process. Therefore, anything that furthers the independence of women and destroys the patterns of stereotyped sex roles ought actively to be encouraged. But let us not confuse this, which is good in itself, with necessarily contributing to a revolutionary movement.

When a woman learns carpentry and wants to make it her life's work, what can she do? First, if she has the money for land and material, she can build herself a house. Possibly, she will find work building things for her friends, helping out at barn raisings, building alternative school structures, doing interiors for a local restaurant or a women's center. She may even get paid for some of this work, although the satisfaction of doing skilled work that is socially useful will—for a while—be its own reward. Conceivably, if the number of women entering the carpentry field remains limited, she will be able to support herself doing this kind of work. But what happens when her personal solution inspires thousands to follow in her steps?

There is not enough capital in the alternative network to support many independent, politically conscious carpenters (or anyone else, for that matter). If she wants to continue her trade, she is going to have to do what most other carpenters do in order to survive. And here is where capitalism intrudes on her world, and where feminism that does not have a political perspective becomes an insufficient solution for women who want work.

If our newly trained and highly skilled carpenter joins the union (and the craft unions are notoriously a bastion of white male supremacy), or even if she hires out as an independent contractor, she may be reasonably paid, but she will find her work far less rewarding. For instance, she will have no say in the kind of structure she is building and what it is to be used for. Moreover, she will have no control over the way she and her sisters do their job. Her boss—and let's assume that it is a woman—will want to get maximum production from her carpentry crew. By this we mean that the workers will have to work as fast as possible so that she (the boss) will spend as little as possible. (If the boss is a feminist who feels sisterly toward her workers and does not demand that they work with maximum efficiency, etc., she'll very fast run out of money to pay them and capital to invest in new construction. Capitalism and feminism just do not mix.) Her work will become fragmented, repetitive, boring; she will probably not be involved in the whole of the construction. Instead, she will specialize in a particular task and will have no say in the way she performs it. She will be told what size wood to cut and where to pound every nail. The satisfaction that she felt cutting her first two by four to specification will give way to the drudgery of assembly line work.

All of this assumes that she will find work. This is no longer likely. In an expanding economy, the job market increases, and there is room at the bottom for women workers. But the era of capitalist expansion is happily coming to a close. Every country that goes socialist cuts into American economic expansion. As this process accelerates, the domestic economy suffers. Unemployment is a permanent condition. So we would have a situation of more women learning skilled trades but fewer opportunities for them to break into the job field; unless, of course, women get jobs at the expense of white males. Although there may be short-term justice in the preferential hiring of women and other minorities over white males, it is not really a solution. It merely raises the economic opportunities of one group at the expense of another.

Of course, this is how things are today; it doesn't always have to remain so. But the personal success of a few feminist carpenters in no way assures that those who follow will retrace their steps. The alternative movement (or the feminist movement) can support a few women workers, just as it now supports a few skilled "hippie" carpenters who do exquisite work but like to toke up during their breaks. But creating the opportunity for all people to do interesting, and useful work necessitates collective struggle in the political sphere. It means confronting capitalism and taking control of the means of production. Building alternatives may be a step in that direction. And a woman who becomes a skilled carpenter but doesn't have the opportunity to work in her trade is readily going to realize the political dimension of her oppression. But when Wilson cites women (or anyone) learning new skills and fulfilling a part of their previously unrecognized potential and then saying that this in itself leads to revolutionary change, he is neglecting an essential part of the revolutionary process.

Food Co-ops

Food cooperatives are another alternative institution that people with Wilson's perspective consider part of the revolutionary struggle. Food co-ops, however useful they are in making good food available to some people at decent prices, are not inherently political. We especially see this with the rise of food co-ops in middle-class and suburban neighborhoods. A bargain is, after all, a bargain, and housewives in suburbia (more than working-class families where women are more likely to hold outside jobs) have the time to do the volunteer work that keeps the co-op going.

Some food co-ops do see themselves as a tool for political organizing. They work to support local organic growers, undercut capitalist competitors (Erewhon and Celestial Seasonings no less than Kraft and General Foods), introduce new people to collective work experience, and alert people to the evils of food for profit. The goal of these cooperatives, in addition to providing an alternative to the supermarket, is to strengthen the radical movement by showing (through the experience of food shopping) the unwholesome qualities of corporate food processing and capitalist economics. This often means selling canned goods and nonorganic foods, because that is what people still think they need. It also means a program of nutritional education that requires dropping the cultural elitism and class snobbery that is so rife in the health and natural-food movement. Further, we believe, it means an end to a dependence on volunteerism, which is the privilege, again, of a small leisured elite or the commitment of a dedicated few who rapidly burn themselves out. A co-op, if it is to be a viable economic alternative, should pay its workers and give them control over their workplace.

Under the existing system, only small, economically irrelevant co-ops are likely to survive. As soon as the co-op movement expands to the point that it offers competition to the supermarkets, the food processors, and the hip health-food entrepreneurs, it is going to be wiped out. Capitalism does not invite competition from those who refuse to play by its rules.

The Problem of Cooptation

Very few alternative institutions ever get to that point. Most are coopted long before. Those agricultural cooperatives formed in the early part of this century—that were not killed by the banks and the railroads (i.e., monopoly capitalism)—are now among the largest agribusiness corporations in America. Although they were founded on cooperative principles, their operations are now very much a part of the capitalist system. Health foods and organic gardening at this point also fit comfortably into the capitalist milieu. Reactionaries and radicals are all better off eating good food. When feminists start a Women's Bank and get their capital from some of the corporations that are most intimately involved in ripping off women (Revlon and Clairol, not to mention Ma Bell and IT&T), we see how alternative movements are coopted. Capitalism is sufficiently flexible and opportunist enough to buy off opposition. A few women in high and visible positions are not beyond the capabilities of the corporate system. And the men who manage this system know that they can appease the educated white elite (who, at this point, make up the core of the alternative movement's opinion makers and activists) and steer it gently down a safe, nonrevolutionary path.

Our Political Isolation

How does a counterculture or the alternative movement become politically effective? What is our political struggle all about? For historical reasons beyond our control (McCarthyism, the cold war, etc.) and for shortcomings in our own practice (arrogance, elitism, countercultural excesses, male chauvinism, racism, etc.) a cultural gulf exists between the movement and a large proportion of the American people, including those working-class people with whom we most need to work.

Certainly, we've learned by now that countercultural styles don't necessarily denote political attitudes. The so-called greening of America represents the triumph of hip capitalism and little else. Corporate executives use Transcendental Meditation and encounter-group techniques to increase their efficiency as managers. The Human Potential Movement has more than its share of racists, sexists, and P. T. Barnum-like entrepreneurs. The swamis who have flocked to the United States (bringing with them the most archaic and oppressive patriarchal attitudes) have come knowing that the path to enlightenment is paved with gold.

To change the country we are going to have to build a movement based on political goals, not on cultural life styles. To break out of our ghetto, the left is going to have to learn from the millions of people whose lives it does not now touch and work with them for the furtherance of common goals. This is no easy task, but many on the left now recognize that this is the direction in which we have to go. The Human Potential Movement suffers from this same kind of cultural isolation. But if it is aware of it, it does not consider it a failing. It is smugly self-congratulatory as it measures personal growth. And this smugness, which again is a privilege of a small elite, works to further the gulf. Collective action and the involvement of millions of people in the workings of society are not this movement's stated goals.

We assume, because Doug Wilson is a political person, that he is aware of this. Perhaps, because he finds the prospect of building a broad-based political movement so difficult, he has opted out for the strategy of promoting individualized alternatives and revolution by example. "Most of the people in this country freak out at the word socialism," Wilson says, and this is certainly true. "A great deal of education and organizing work is necessary," he adds, and this is also true. But then Wilson gives up." "Not everyone is interested in this kind of work," he says. "If we look at the changes that have happened in the past 15 years, they are of little consequence politically, but culturally a transformation is deepening and growing." And this certainly is *not* true. Certainly, some of us have had our minds expanded. We've done important work on ourselves and even have come to like ourselves better. But the important changes have been political, and they have all gone beyond our own personal lives. We are witnessing a world turning upside down in the past 15 years. And it surprises us that Wilson doesn't realize the religious (not to mention the political) significance of this transformation: the weak are growing strong and the mighty are faltering.

We agree, however, that in the United States there is reason to look at political organizing with despair. Revolutionaries in Cuba, China, Vietnam, etc., must also have felt the same hopelessness. Yet, in the face of incredible odds, they continued to do their political work. We give up so easily!

The Danger of Individualism

An essential part of this work, as we have said, is learning to work together. Even though the Human Potential Movement is often organized into cooperative groupings (e.g., encounter groups, communal households, etc.) its emphasis on personal problems and individual solutions encourages people to become self-centered to the exclusion of the material conditions of society that shape them.

This leads to a kind of individualism that Wilson claims can be a starting point for social change. The philosophy of individualism *was* an important advance in revolutionary theory a few centuries ago when it helped to break the hold that monarchy and feudalism had on the human community. But in the context of contemporary American society, it serves only to reinforce the selfishness, competitiveness, conformity, and fear of one's neighbor, etc., that are the underpinnings of modern capitalism. In this crowded interdependent world, individualism reinforces the inability of people with common problems to work together.

Individualism is a disease of American politics. Americans are alienated from politics precisely because they have been fed a myth that they have individual rights and equal access to political power. Americans do not trust collective action because we think that strength comes from our individualism and self-reliance. It is our most popular myth: the honest sheriff (Gary Cooper), standing alone, drives the outlaws out of town. Or the clean reformer (Jimmy Stewart) cleans out the corruption in City Hall. We see it so often, ambitious liberals, each one a would-be hero on the white horse, undercutting each other for personal power, never working together to achieve common goals. This is, of course, the American way, going into battle singlehandedly, heroically to change the system. But it doesn't work; it can't work. So we get clobbered and give up. And then we tell each other that although the system may be rotten, you can't fight City Hall. But instead of abandoning this thick-headed individualism that made defeat inevitable, we turn it on ourselves and change our focus from personalized politics to personal growth. And because the Human Potential Movement encourages this process, it contributes to the individualism that is so destructive a force in political life.

Granted that Wilson in supporting alternative institutions is not defending individualism per se. But the apolitical collectivism that he defines as revolutionary often reflects individualism just the same. He cites, for instance, his conference center "where 25 people are living together in a house, for many their first experience in communal living." This, he continues, "can lead to the realization that it is possible to live together with others. This creates hope, where cynicism is pervasive. . . ." All of which is true, but a collective *experience* is not the same as a collective *solution,* and a commune that isolates itself from the larger society (as many communes do), even though it is collective in form, is not collective in substance, and is seeking a solution to the problems of society for its own exclusive membership.

A Psychological Dead-End

Personal problems are not individualized problems; they are very much rooted in the complexities of material existence. But the Human Potential Movement does not encourage its participants to look at the society that has shaped them; it does not provide people with the tools or techniques to look back upon where they come from in order to analyze the source of their discontent. Focused as it is on personal concerns, it excludes from its focus objective conditions. And inasmuch as it sees only personal solutions it leads ultimately to psychological dead-ends. In fact, it has to some extent become a part of the consumer society, with people moving from one religious or psychological discipline to another in a fruitless quest for personal happiness and fulfillment; fruitless, because most individuals cannot be fulfilled in an alienating individualized society, and humanity as a whole cannot realize its potential in a basically inhumane or anti-humane system, such as capitalism is.

We won't burden Wilson with defending such aspects of the Human Potential Movement as EST or Arica. These are attempts by shrewd entrepreneurs to exploit the loneliness and lack of community that so many Americans face in their everyday existence. For a price, some of these disciplines may work for a while and give people a taste of community. In the same way that Hostess Twinkies may appease hunger, or coffee may perk you up when you are down, EST and Arica may give you an initial psychological life. But they cannot cure the basic malaise because they do not deal with the root problems.

This is not to say that individual therapies do not have their merits. As Zwerling points out, therapy is a useful tool. Unhappy, self-hating, alienating, neurotically depressed cadres, who cannot perceive an objective situation because they have no awareness of their own subjective distortions, are not going to be effective political people. Indeed, it has been the more revolutionary societies (and the more political psychologists — Reich, for instance, and Paul Goodman in the way he used gestalt) that have been most aware of this problem and have had the most success in developing techniques to teach people to transcend their subjective hangups so that they can see reality as it is and not as they misperceive it.

There is much in common, for instance, in the way that some thera-pists use gestalt techniques. Does William Hinton's description of the way the Chinese use criticism/self-criticism differ from a good group therapy group, other than that in China the context is social more than it is per-sonal?

> To practice self and mutual criticism well one had to cultivate objectivity in several ways. First, one had to be willing to be objective about oneself. One had to be willing to seek out the kernel of truth in any criticism regardless of the manner in which it was presented. Second, one had to be objective about others; one had to evaluate others from a principled point of view with the object of helping them overcome their faults and work more effectively. One had to raise others up, not knock them down. In practice these two considerations meant that one had to pay great attention to one's own motives and methods when criticizing others, while disregarding on the main the motives and methods used by others towards oneself.
>
> Above and beyond this, one had to cultivate the courage to voice sincerely held opinions regardless of views held by others, while at the same time showing a willingness to listen to others and to change one's own opinion when honestly convinced of error. To bow with the wind, and to go along with the crowd was an irresponsible attitude that could never lead to anything but trouble for oneself, for the revolutionary movement and for China. The reverse of this, to be arrogant and unbending was just as bad.[2]

The ability to perceive the world objectively (which is the essence of criticism/self-criticism) is another way of saying that one is "centered" or "together," or that one has attained a measure of self-awareness and is mak-ing full use of her or his own powers. Learning the tools of self-analysis is important and those therapies that can do that and link it with a clearer political/social analysis are, we think, useful indeed. But a clearer vision can only become part of the revolutionary process when many people come together politically to put it into practice on the grand social scale.

To describe the Human Potential Movement as a revolutionary force is ultimately to engage in a metaphysical flight. Wilson says, "I believe we already have what we need inside ourselves, it is simply a matter of contacting that security, that awareness that we carry what we need inside ourselves and in the relationship we have with each other." And then he concludes that if only we will open ourselves up to what we have inside of ourselves, *voila* revolution!

Well, what we have inside ourselves is a lot of old baggage, the accumulated products of our own culture and socialization process and probably of previous generations as well. There is no evidence that people are either good, bad, or indifferent. We are shaped by our society and reflect our culture. We can drop out of the society, but this doesn't necessarily enable us to drop out of our culture. To change ourselves, we must change our society, and that change is never arbitrary in that "the revolution" will instantaneously make us new women and new men. It is a process that perhaps never ends, but without changing the material conditions of society the process can hardly begin.

And no matter how righteous and how decent our lives are, we cannot make a revolution, we cannot begin this process on our own. The vast majority of working Americans have neither the time nor the financial means for the Human Potential Movement or revolution by example. Furthermore, most do not see what it has to offer them. Clearly, it does not speak to their basic concerns and problems. But these are precisely the people who must be part of the struggle if we are to achieve revolutionary change. Metaphysical fantasies will not work. Wilson quotes from the song, "two and two and fifty make a million." But 2 and 2 and 50 make 54. No amount of wishful singing is going to involve the other 999,946. And without their active participation, the game is lost.

Notes

1. See *WIN,* January 13, 1977.
2. William Hinton, *Fanshen: A Documentary of Revolution in a Chinese Village* (New York: Random House, 1966), p. 395.

Routes to Social Change

Frank Lindenfeld

Can we change the basic features of the capitalist system in America, replacing it with an egalitarian, participatory-socialist society? Is structural change possible at all, as long as dissenters remain a small and very divided minority? Which strategies for change are most promising?

To contribute to the dialogue, I compare Marxist–Leninist, democratic socialist, liberal, and social anarchist approaches in this essay. These four strategies are not mutually exclusive; they overlap in a number of ways. I favor the anarchist position, though actualized changes will probably result from a *diversity* of strategies and tactics adopted by alliances of various dissenting political movements.

Social-change philosophies may be classified according to their ultimate goals (i.e., the type of future society they envisage) and the means they advocate to achieve these goals (see Table 1). Liberals accept both the nation-state and capitalism, and favor gradual reform of existing institutions through electoral politics. Social anarchists reject the capitalist system and the state. They advocate direct action instead of electoral politics, and favor nonviolent over violent revolution. The democratic socialists and the

TABLE 1

Goals and Means Advocated by Four Social-Change Philosophies

	Goals		Means		
	Capitalism	National Government	Violent Revolution	Nonviolent Revolution	Electoral Politics
Marxism–Leninsim	rejects	accepts	prefers	rejects	rejects
Democratic socialism	rejects	accepts	rejects	accepts	prefers
Liberalism	accepts	accepts	rejects	accepts	prefers
Social anarchism	rejects	rejects	accepts	prefers	rejects

From: *Social Anarchism*, 1986, no. 11. Reprinted by permission of the author.
Thanks to Len Krimerman and Kathryn M. Lindenfeld for their comments and suggestions.

orthodox followers of Marxism–Leninism would abolish capitalism, but see governments as a necessary evil. The visionaries among the Marxists and some democratic socialists anticipate a society where the state has withered away; generally, they perceive this event taking place in the far distant future. The essential difference between these two varieties of socialism is that democratic socialists think structural changes can be achieved through the electoral process, whereas Marxist–Leninists believe such changes generally will not occur without armed revolution. A closer examination of these routes to social change will yield further understanding of what may be possible in contemporary America.

Marxism–Leninism

Marxist–Leninists see government in capitalist society as the executive arm of the ruling class, helping to maintain an exploitative system. Most "orthodox" Marxists believe in the need for armed revolution to overthrow such a government. They call for a politically conscious vanguard to inspire workers to become conscious of themselves as an exploited class and to join in a revolution to replace the government with one led by the vanguard party.

Marxists (and anarchists) point out to those desiring structural transformation of the society that even where there is a democratic electoral system, such change usually cannot be achieved through parliamentary means. The ruling class uses its wealth and power to maintain its dominance. For example, it influences the outcome of elections through its control of the candidate selection process and the mass media. Participation in the electoral system can trap those who want change and cause them to become ineffective.[1] To adopt parliamentary tactics is to lend support to the legitimacy of the system; to be effective it is necessary to work outside the electoral system.

Armed force used against the ruling class is labeled illegal by them. Yet the ruling class never relinquishes its power peacefully, according to the Marxists. When a socialist government is elected, capitalists do not hesitate to employ armed force to regain their dominance. Such was the case in Chile during the 1970s when a socialist party led by Salvador Allende was voted into office. The former ruling class, assisted by the American CIA, staged a bloody coup that overthrew the Allende government and established the former rulers in power once again.

After a successful revolution, Marxists foresee a very long stage of socialism marked by government ownership of the means of production. It will be necessary for the revolutionary party to assume the position of a dictatorship to counter the efforts made by capitalists to restore their power.

Eventually, there will be a transition to a free communist society in which each produces what he or she can and is rewarded with what he or she needs. At that (future) stage, the people will have become responsible and socially conscious and will not need a state authority.

There are some objections to armed revolution used as a path to social change. As the Weathermen discovered during the late 1960s and early 1970s, bombings and other organized guerrilla actions resulted in their alienation from the very masses whose support they sought. For revolution by an armed minority to have the best chance of success, a majority of the people must have lost confidence in the authority and legitimacy of the government; they must be willing to lend support to armed rebels or at least have underlying sympathy for them. In the contemporary United States, such conditions do not exist. There is no seething, discontented working class in America ready to follow revolutionary leadership.

The political cynicism and discontent that exist in this country are symptoms of apathy and privatism rather than readiness for revolution. In the aftermath of the Vietnam war and Watergate, more Americans than ever are disenchanted with, and distrustful of, government and the major political parties. Blue-collar workers, identified by Marxists as those most likely to support a revolution, are unhappy with the erosion of their purchasing power and with the high level of unemployment. Nevertheless, many older workers are fairly conservative in outlook. Some are staunch defenders of the system because they see their jobs as dependent on the continuation of heavy military spending. Younger, better-educated workers are restless. Many choose not to vote. However, this is a far cry from being ready to take part in armed conflict to overthrow the establishment.

Another factor influencing the possibility of revolution is the attitude and organization of the police and the armed forces. Both are amply prepared to deal with violent encounters — that is their specialty. Governments effectively monopolize the means of organized violence. To bolster their power, they recruit members of the working class into the police or the National Guard. These organizations have a superiority of weapons and training. It is doubtful whether a violent revolution could succeed against the government of an advanced industrial nation such as the United States unless there was a tremendous domestic crisis and at the same time the armed forces and police were divided, disorganized, or demoralized, with some of their members actually supporting the revolutionaries. International crisis and continuing cold war strengthen nationalist sentiment and enable the ruling class successfully to label attempted revolution as treason.

A further strong argument against armed struggle is that the means we adopt shape the ends we seek. Violence breeds violence. Armed conflict is inevitably brutalizing to those who take part in it; the use of violence to bring about revolution can result in a new society more brutal than the one it replaced. Stalin's dictatorship, for example, surpassed that of the Russian czars in its disregard for life and human rights. Most successful revolutions have found it necessary to consolidate their gains by wholesale terror and the slaughter of "class enemies" and counterrevolutionaries. This happened in Russia after 1917 and in China after the 1949 revolution, although such excesses have been avoided by Cuba and Nicaragua.

Today, the strategy of violent revolution seems to me more relevant to developing countries than to highly industrialized nations such as the United States. All the social revolutions of the twentieth century have taken place in societies that were predominantly agricultural and preindustrial. The odds in favor of armed revolt succeeding seem higher in the less developed nations because their central governments are weaker and their ruling classes more openly vicious. Revolutionaries generally have more widespread support in these countries. The Sandinista revolution in Nicaragua, for example, was favored by a great majority of the people.

Regardless of the setting, a successful revolution needs majority support. Where such support already exists, however, many democratic socialists (and many Western European Marxists) argue that change could be accomplished peacefully through the electoral process.

Democratic Socialism

The major reformist political parties in the United States and Western Europe have advocated some form of democratic socialism. Historically, Social Democratic parties developed as revisionist offshoots of Marxist parties. Democratic socialists agree with the Marxist indictment of the capitalist system but advocate using the electoral process to promote the peaceful victory of a Socialist party; once in office, such a party would significantly increase public ownership and control of the means of production. In some European countries, strong Social Democratic parties have been successful in winning parliamentary majorities or pluralities and have instituted a number of reforms. They have expanded the welfare state and eroded the power of local capitalists by nationalizing banks and some of the largest industries.

On issues of war and foreign policy, the democratic socialists have been disappointing. Most of the Social Democratic parties supported their governments during World War I, with the honorable exception of the American Socialist party under the leadership of Eugene Debs. (Socialists such as Debs believed that the workers of the world should unite and refuse to take part in war. The mass slaughter of soldiers of one country by those of another country was senseless, since they came from the same working class.) Social Democratic parties in power have become almost indistinguishable in their foreign and defense policies from the pro-capitalist governments they opposed. Post–World War II democratic socialist governments in Western Europe supported cold-war programs. France, for example, which has had a socialist government for several years, continues to maintain a nuclear weapons arsenal and to test atomic bombs in the Pacific.

Assuming third parties are an appropriate path to social change, could they make a difference in the United States? There have been strong third parties in this country, such as the American Socialist Party during the early part of the twentieth century. The Socialists created considerable ferment and attracted a sizable minority vote, despite the eventual destruction of the party by the prowar and antiradical hysteria fomented by the establishment. In the present political climate, a dynamic multiissue party *could* grow in size and influence until it had the allegiance of an electoral majority by appealing to those disenchanted with both major parties. The fledgling local Green Parties of the 1980s, for example, could coalesce to form a national political party. The platform of such a party might include a call for jobs or income for all within a mixed capitalist/democratic socialist economy; equal pay for equal work; drastic cutbacks in nuclear weapons and other military spending; the development of worker- and community-controlled cooperatives; conservation of nonrenewable resources and the maximum use of alternative energy sources; and the integration of production and consumption in self-reliant towns and regions. Such a party would appeal to the poor and the unemployed, as well as to people from all walks of life, including some intellectuals, racial and ethnic minorities, and women.

In an election, however, many factors block a successful third-party campaign. The established Republican and Democratic parties monopolize the media. The high cost of mass media access prohibits a third party from reaching millions of voters available to their opponents. American third parties also face the dilemma of democratic socialism: Either they maintain a radical position and fail to attract many votes (as with the Peace and Freedom and the Citizens' parties) or, like many European socialist parties, they abandon their principles and become moderates in the hope of capturing more votes. In spite of such discouraging circumstances, the very presence of an alternative on the ballot challenges the hegemony of the well-established parties and opens the possibility of presenting radical ideas to the public through election campaigns. If enough Americans become disenchanted with the two major political parties, and if a third party manages to stay clear of factionalism and the use of Marxist rhetoric, such a party could become influential. Even if it never gained enough support to control Congress or the Presidency, the mere presence of a party that attracted 10 or 20 percent of the voters could help liberalize the Democratic party into supporting broad economic reform and turning away from cold-war policies.

In contrast with the democratic socialists, who see a third party as the best means to achieve change, American liberals have generally tried to exercize their influence within the major parties, especially the Democratic party.

Liberalism

Liberals maintain that the best way to promote change is to achieve social reforms here and now, through an evolutionary strategy, rather than to work for a revolution that may never come or a third party that may never win an election. Most social problems, liberals believe, can be solved administratively through government action. While radicals (i.e., anarchists and many Marxists) see the system as corrupt, liberals view it as basically sound, though it may need to be cured of imperfections by liberals working within established channels. Radicals seek to abolish militarism, liberals to institute better control of the military by civilians. Some radicals press for alternative, nonformal education or a deschooled society; liberals push for higher professional standards, more teachers and administrators, and larger budgets. Radicals want to replace hierarchical workplaces with participatory, self-governing organizations based on workers' control, where technical and professional knowledge would be widely shared; liberals favor job enlargement and better communication between employees and their bosses. Radicals want to eliminate economic inequality and abolish the class system; liberals sponsor wars on poverty where two-thirds of the funds are spent on administration.[2]

Liberal strategies *have* resulted in the implementation of many concrete social reforms, such as the eight hour workday, social security, Medicare, and minimum-wage laws. Also, the efforts of liberals (and radicals) to influence the Democratic party have occasionally resulted in more enlightened foreign policies. For the most part, however, even under such liberal Presidents as John F. Kennedy, America has supported the exploitation of underdeveloped countries by transnational corporations and intervened militarily against Third World liberation movements (Chomsky, 1985). By reducing discontent and promoting solidarity at home, liberal reforms may provide even greater freedom for the ruling classes to engage in imperialism abroad. Nevertheless, I think radicals should join in coalitions to support liberal reforms — as being better than no reforms at all — while working to raise people's consciousness about the limitations of such reforms and the need for a structural change in the entire system.

Having briefly discussed Marxism–Leninism, democratic socialism, and liberalism as alternative strategies for change, I now turn to social anarchism as yet another possible route.

Social Anarchism

Anarchists seek to build a democratic society free of both capitalist power concentration and state coercion. Some anarchists agree with Marxists that violent revolution is the best means to accomplish this. Others believe that the new society can be built within the spaces of the old, as cracks in the system are filled by self-managed communities and democratically organized cooperatives whose roots will eventually spread to the entire society.

The anarchist strategy for achieving social change includes at least three different levels: (1) *personal*, living the revolution in daily life; (2) *social,* developing a network of producers' cooperatives and other alternative organizations, and (3) *political,* continuing the struggle for social change by direct action. These three arenas are not separate or mutually exclusive, but reinforce one another. Moreover, *such a strategy for change is not solely an anarchist one.* It is also favored by supporters of other philosophies. Many liberals, democratic socialists, and Marxists, for example, support the principle of workers' control and the development of workers' cooperatives. What distinguishes anarchists is their avoidance of electoral politics and their insistence that what is needed is the abolition of centralized state power, not merely a change of government leaders or policies.

Living the Revolution

Even within the confines of the existing society, each of us can begin to follow our political principles in our everyday lives. This may include consuming less, moving away from individual households and into communes, sharing our incomes and resources with others, joining or helping to organize producers' cooperatives, shopping in consumer co-ops, and so on. If enough consumers found alternatives to buying new cars, television sets, and other major durable goods, the strategy might weaken the capitalist economy, rendering it more vulnerable to political change.[3] Communal households free their members for alternative uses of their time, reducing the need to work within the system to earn money. Communal living may also help liberate participants from traditional sex roles (though many men still carry with them into communal situations the sexist attitudes previously learned). Living communally may provide for some a greater freedom of choice in vocation, enabling them to undertake meaningful work without having to worry about how much they will be paid because they feel secure as part of a group based on sharing and mutual aid.

Changing our lifestyles is an important first step, but in itself it is not enough to usher in a new society. The anarchist strategy seeks also to build up a network of alternative organizations based on participatory democracy and to carry on continued direct political action against the existing social order.

Developing a Cooperative Sector

Anarchists seek to actualize the good society by creating democratically controlled workers' cooperatives and other participatory organizations. The goal, as seen by some anarchists, is to develop a growing cooperative sector of the economy alongside, and in partial opposition to, the existing capitalist- and state-controlled organizations. This cooperative sector would consist of a network of producers' cooperatives, community development credit unions, educational and technical assistance groups, and a whole array of organizations such as food co-ops, free schools, listener-supported radio and television stations, and communal farms.

A model for the development of such a network exists in the Basque area of Spain, where a network of a few hundred production organizations, educational institutions, service organizations and consumer co-ops provides jobs for 20,000 persons. These co-ops grew out of the work of a Catholic priest, Jose Arizmendi, who founded a technical school in that area during the 1950s. Five of the first graduates banded together to form the initial cooperative, Ulgor, which produces consumer durables such as refrigerators. Inspired by the success of Ulgor, other cooperatives were formed. A workers' bank, the Caja Laboral Popular, with about 200,000 members, provides technical and financial support for the cooperatives. There are also several associated educational organizations and retail cooperatives (Gutierrez-Johnson in Chapter 11). Extensive networks of producers' co-ops and supporting organizations could eventually grow in the United States out of beginnings that already exist. On the West Coast, about a dozen plywood factories are collectively owned and democratically managed by their workers. In the Philadelphia area, there are now three worker-owned O&O supermarkets, whose birth was assisted by the Philadelphia Association for Cooperative Enterprise (PACE), a technical support group. PACE has begun to develop a loan fund to help provide financing for additional O&O markets.

Anarchists stress the need for mutual support among alternative organizations so that those organizations that find themselves in trouble have someplace to turn for help. The isolation of individual co-ops prevents them from being as effective as they might be, and makes them more economically and politically vulnerable; there is a need to establish better communication among alternative groups to enable them to cope with state repression, which may grow as the alternatives gain in popularity. Also, retail collectives can begin to obtain what they need from alternative producers instead of from the establishment. Cooperatives can trade with one another for necessary goods and services. Best of all, they can create an expanding pool of meaningful jobs.

Promoting alternative organizations constitutes a strategy of replacement of the present political–economic framework by a decentralized, self-governed one. This can happen through the gradual withdrawal of people's energies from the old institutions and a redirection into the new. As the alternatives gain momentum, a parallel system may emerge that eventually can supplant the existing one in a bloodless revolution.

In contrast with this optimistic view, it has been argued that the 1960s and 1970s saw the development of many alternative organizations, yet the American system was not altered significantly (Moberg, 1979). In part, this was because such organizations did not involve more than a small fraction of the population. Further, only recently has there been a focus on cooperative *production* as contrasted with consumption. The alternative organizations with the most members, such as credit unions and food cooperatives, have generally remained apolitical.[4] This is also true of many existing workers' cooperatives, however, whose members do not see themselves as part of a wider movement. To push America in the direction of participatory socialism, such organizations need to be joined to a vital political movement. Without such a political link, cooperatives may remain ineffective islands of progress, incapable of promoting change in the wider society.

To have a significant social impact, needed are not just *alternative* organizations but *oppositional* ones. Chris Gunn (1984:207) explains the difference:

> Alternative organizations are those that have found a different way to live (produce) and want to be left alone with it. Oppositional organizations, . . . have found a different way to live and want to change society in its light. Alternative organizations . . . do not necessarily represent an attempt to confront established powers and relationships with a desire for social change. Oppositional organizations do that.

Alternative organizations may all too easily become coopted into the existing system. As David Chidakel (1975) points out, members of cooperatives may become so involved in trying to make their businesses work that the challenge of beating the capitalists at their own game may result in a victory for the system, because one cannot "play" at business in the context of a capitalist economy without taking on a capitalist mentality. Paula Giese (1982) makes a similar point in writing about food cooperatives. Often the larger and older food co-ops come to resemble their capitalist competitors, the chain supermarkets, in that they do not engage in price competition, they may underpay their employees, and they even peddle "junk, poisons, and gadgety trash" if that will result in higher sales volume. Counterinstitutions, George Lakey (1973) reminds us, become revolutionary only if they carry a revolutionary ideology, contribute to building revolutionary organizations, and take place in the context of open (nonviolent) revolutionary struggle. The movement for social change will succeed to the extent that members of worker-owned firms, food co-ops, and similar groups recognize that in addition to building economic and social alternatives, they are engaged in an oppositional political fight to build a better society.

Continuing the Struggle

A third aspect of the anarchist strategy (shared by the Marxists and democratic socialists) is to carry on a continuing political battle for the structural transformation of the economic and political order. One method for doing this is the formation of small groups to carry on the struggle, largely outside the framework of the existing electoral and judicial systems. Because it will not be possible for a government to destroy such a movement merely by arresting national leaders, the strength of the opposition will be increased by a network of autonomous local groups.

Since anarchists and other opposition groups are a tiny minority, to become effective in bringing about change they will have to build "united front" coalitions and join in common protests and demonstrations. The opposition movement must not only unite people around the demand for reform but also must raise political consciousness through popular education. Given the domination of American mass media by corporate interests, such educational efforts will not be easy. There will be a need for an alternative press, radio, and television; continuing public forums; schools for community organizers; and classes and study groups about participatory socialism within as well as outside existing educational institutions.

The heart of the opposition movement will continue to be direct action, which can be effective in promoting reforms, especially when the protests threaten to disrupt "normal" activities. This can be seen from the success of the movement against the Vietnam war and the civil rights movement. Protesters engaged in such disruptive tactics as sit-ins to bring racist businesses to a standstill, the destruction of files to prevent draft boards from conscripting youths, and blockades to prevent the shipment of weapons.[5] For effective change, there needs to be not only national action but also community organizing at the grassroots level—directing unions toward the goal of workers' control, organizing neighborhoods to demand local control of schools and police, demonstrating against nuclear power plants and weapons installations, and so on.

Another successful tactic is to organize mass resistance to those features of the state system that rely on individual compliance for their effectiveness. Any social system can withstand only so much deviance before the mechanisms of social control break down. If 1 percent of the population doesn't pay taxes, register for the draft, or send their children to public schools, a government can successfully prosecute them. But if as many as 10 or 15 percent of the people refuse to go along, it becomes extremely difficult to maintain the income tax, conscription, or compulsory school systems.

Some would argue that anarchists must remain pure, boycotting all elections and refusing to have anything to do with the courts. Others reason that reform is the enemy of revolution and that by ameliorating social conditions, through lawsuits or legislation, we postpone overall change. I disagree. The existing legal system can be used to promote reform and help raise political consciousness, as with lawsuits against job discrimination or the defense of radicals against state repression. A drawback of participation in the courts is that, like voting in elections, it reinforces belief in the legitimacy of the system. For this reason, it is desirable to argue legal cases from the political standpoint rather than merely to score enough technical points to win a case. The legal approach is suitable for piecemeal reform only. Lawsuits can reduce racist and sexist treatment of employees and can sometimes provide the poor with a greater share of public funds, but they will not abolish capitalism.

More controversial is the issue of anarchists taking part in electoral politics. Most avoid such involvement as antithetical to their beliefs. In some situations, however, they may support radical candidates or slates as part of a broader political movement. This is most attractive when a large proportion of the people are already predisposed to change, such as in some university towns and inner-city areas. It may be possible to win citywide or countywide offices, as has happened in Berkeley, California, and Burlington, Vermont. Electoral victories could lead to restructuring education, law enforcement, and the distribution of economic benefits at the local level. Most anarchists, however, would be skeptical about whether electoral politics can bring us closer to the ideal society. Radical political parties may succeed in the election of a token radical as one member in five on a City Council or Board of Education, or as two or three out of hundreds of representatives in a state legislature, without leading to the implementation of any reform policies. Also, the focus of campaign management seems usually to shift away from community organizing and toward mass media promotion of the candidate and other tactics designed to win elections. Further, even if radicals win a local election, they must still deal with the state and federal government and with the economy outside the local area.[6] The victory of a radical slate might well decrease funds returned to the locality by state and federal governments. This is a serious drawback for those concerned with how the poor might take control of their own communities. Still, local elections may provide radicals with a forum for their views, and elections can be used to organize people around the issues and problems of their own localities.

Conclusion

Those who favor a structural transformation of America cannot afford to squander their energies on internecine squabbles. Instead of criticizing competing philosophies of change, they would do better to join with others to bring about those changes. Within a broader movement to change the capitalist system, there should be room for many styles and many approaches. Because anarchists and socialists of all persuasions are a small minority, they should work with liberals and others in coalitions for the common goal of building a participatory socialist society, abandoning the factionalism and divisiveness that impede their effectiveness.

There is not necessarily any one *best* strategy for transforming the existing capitalist system. Those concerned to bring about changes may favor one or another of the approaches discussed above. The main thing is to build a political movement capable of attracting mass support — otherwise, there will be only a handful of radicals debating each other.

As part of such a movement there is a need for continuing consciousness raising and educational work that emphasize how issues are related; war, racism, sexism, poverty, and unemployment are not separate problems but manifestations of the same underlying system. When enough political and educational groundwork has been done, when enough people lose confidence in the established institutions that they question the basic assumptions of the existing social order, a majority may participate in a successful nonviolent revolution. This almost occurred in France during the spring of 1968 and in "socialist" Poland during the more recent conflict between the Solidarity movement and the Polish government. Similar events could happen in other countries, even in the United States, that might lead to the replacement of both capitalism and the nation-state. Such a nonviolent revolution cannot happen overnight. It will be the cumulative result of individuals changing their lives and life styles, building oppositional organizations and a cooperative economic sector, and engaging in continuing political struggle.

Notes

1. Marxists have espoused contradictory positions on this issue of taking part in electoral politics. In 1872, Marx himself referred to the possibility of attaining socialism by peaceful means in the United States and England (see Paul Sweezy, "Marxism Socialism" in ch. 10 above). Whether or not this is the "correct" Marxist position, it then becomes a variant of the democratic socialist theory described below. This is actually the "line" taken by most of the contemporary Western European Communist parties.
2. For a good critique of liberalism, see Wolff, 1968.
3. We must not underestimate the strength and flexibility of the system, which may withstand and even coopt a considerable assault by a minority determined to live an alternative

life style. Corporate marketing departments are busy mapping strategies for capturing dollars from New Age consumers. Moreover, if the gap between production and consumption grows too large, as it tends to do with the replacement of workers by automated machines in capitalist societies, the establishment can still take corrective action to stabilize the system. Thus there is always the possibility of further increases in military spending justified by our continuing support of small wars in the Third World and by the need to maintain an edge in the ever-escalating arms race with the Soviet Union.

4. Most credit unions are participatory in theory but not in practice. With few exceptions, they focus on loans to individual consumers rather than loans to producers' associations.

5. One unresolved issue among activists is the use of limited violence (as opposed to armed revolution) to bring about change. By limited violence I mean burning buildings that are symbolic of oppression—such as banks, ROTC buildings, war research or production centers—destruction of draft board files, and sabotage of military installations or equipment. Small numbers and high mobility enable protesters to carry out programs of destruction that either delegitimize previously "sacred" institutions or actually impede the effective functioning of the system. As far as I know, even those who approve of the destruction of property as a tactic draw the line when it comes to harming people. In this matter, they clearly differ from governments. On the negative side, small symbolic acts of violence may unleash a large repressive action by the state, furnishing a ready-made excuse for the suspension of civil liberties.

6. This is one of the reasons the socialist CCF was not more successful, even after it won elections in the Canadian province of Saskatchewan. See Lipset, 1968.

References

Chidakel, David. "'Small is Beautiful' as a book and as a bum steer." *Spark* 5, (1975), no. 1.
Chomsky, Noam. "Intervention in Vietnam and Central America: Parallels and differences." *Monthly Review,* September 1985.
Giese, Paula. "How the old co-ops went wrong." In Frank Lindenfeld and Joyce Rothschild-Whitt. eds., *Workplace Democracy and Social Change.* (Boston: Porter Sargent, 1982).
Gunn, Christopher E. *Workers Self Management in the United States* (Ithaca, N.Y.: Cornell Univ. Press, 1984).
Gutierrez-Johnson, Ana. "The Mondragon cooperative model." *Changing Work,* (1984) fall. Reprinted in Chapter 11.
Lakey, George. *Strategy for a Living Revolution.* (San Francisco: W. H. Freeman, 1973).
Lipset, Seymour. *Agrarian Socialism.* (New York: Anchor Books, 1968).
Moberg, David. "Experimenting with the future: Alternative institutions and American socialism." In John Case and Rosemary Taylor, eds., *Co-ops, Communes and Collectives: Experiments in Social Change in the 1960s and 1970s.* (New York: Pantheon Books, 1979).
Wolff, Robert. *The Poverty of Liberalism.* (Boston: Beacon Press, 1968).

Index

A & P, 334, 339
Abernathy, Ralph, 199
aggressiveness, 178, 179
agriculture, 94-5, 98, 100, 307, 314, 371, 375-6
AID, 237
alienation, 18, 21, 35n, 54, 149, 158-162
Allende, Salvador, 236, 286
alternative institutions, 368, 370-384, 393
alternative sources of energy, 99-100, 305-6
Amalgamated Clothing Workers Union, 200
American Federation of State, County & Municipal Employees, 199
anarchist thought, 96-7, 103, 261-3, 274, 282, 290-302, 368, 385, 391-7
anomy, 18, 21, 29, 35n
Arizmendi, Jose Maria, 352, 360, 362, 367, 392
assimilation, 28
Astin, Alexander, 68-9
Atlas Chain Co., 323, 340-348
automation, 151-153, 165, 169, 191
automobile transport, 107-8
Axworthy, Christopher, 324

balance of trade, 255
Baltzell, E. Digby, 223, 227
Baron, Harold, 200
Bell, Daniel, 158-9, 227
Berg, Ivar, 54
bicycles, 106, 111-116
Binet, Alfred, 76
biocenosis, 98
bioregions, 305-309
Birch, David, 154
Birmingham, Stephen, 214
black elite, 194, 214-5
black nationalism, 195-6
black power, 195, 198-9
blacks, class divisions among, 194, 197
    imprisonment of, 134, 195
    poverty among, 194, 205, 207-8
    underclass, 212-216
    unemployment of, 152
    unionization of, 201
    working class, 200-205

blaming the victim, 4, 36-47
Blauner, Robert, 156, 160
Block, Fred, 255
Blumstein, Michael, 341
Bookchin, Murray, 86, 87
Borsodi, Ralph, 312
Bourne, Randolph, 118
Bowles, Samuel, 50
Broom, Leonard, 31
Brown, Norman O., 140, 141
Brown, Scott, 168, 322
Buber, Martin, 146
Bucyrus Erie Corp., 342, 346
Business Council, 230

Cabral, Amilcar, 198
Cail, Kris, 226
Caja Laboral Popular, 323, 350, 353, 364-7, 392
candidate selection process, 225
capitalism, 3, 65, 128, 131, 149, 153, 165, 168, 195, 239-246, 265-6, 270, 292, 298, 305, 377-9, 385-6
Carmichael, Stokeley, 196
Carter administration, 152
Castro, Fidel, 236
Catholic Worker movement, 145
Changing Work, 326
Chase, Stuart, 319
Chidakel, David, 394
Chiet, Earl, 231
child care, 324-333
Chomsky, Noam, 391
Chrysler Corp., 340
Churchill, Winston, 272
CIA, 219, 236, 246-7, 386
Citizens' Party, 389
civil rights movement, 198-9
class conflict, 122, 204, 223, 240, 242, 251, 253
class consciousness, 215, 229-30
coalitions, political, 395, 397
cognitive achievement, 67-74
cold war, 387, 390
collaborator state, 248-9
collectives, 322-3, 325, 378

399